For online information and ordering of this and other b
www.codenameone.com.

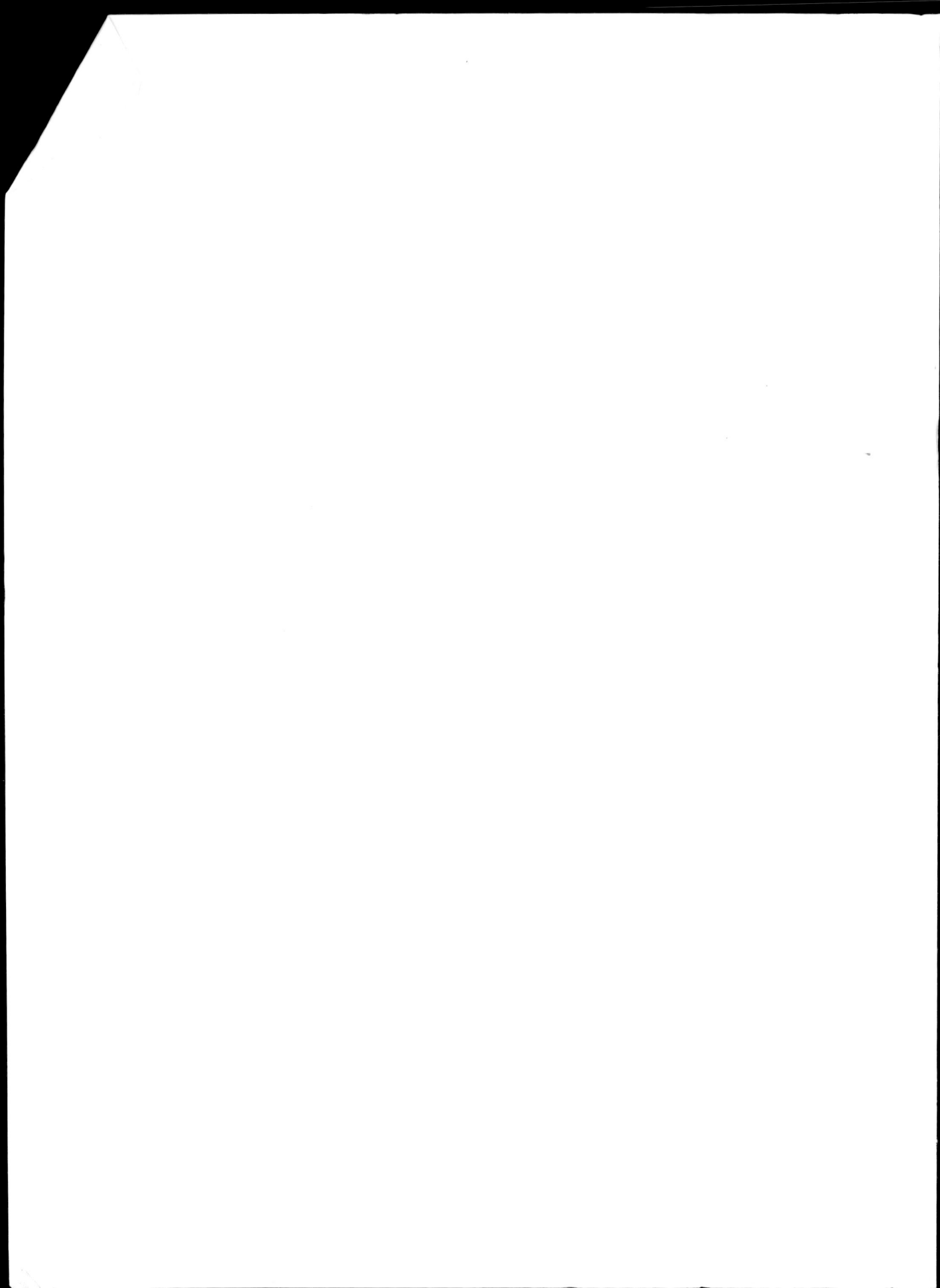

Create an Uber Clone in 7 Days

BUILD A REAL WORLD FULL STACK MOBILE APP IN JAVA

Shai Almog
Codename One Academy

Contents

3 Day 4: Search Route and Hailing

9 Day 4: Search Route and Hailing – Night Hack

10 Day 5: Driver App and Push

11 Day 6: Billing and Social Activation

12 Day 7: Transitions and Refinement

13 Summary and Moving Forward

A Appendix A: Setup Codename One

B Appendix B: Setup Spring Boot and MySQL

Preface *

Last year we launched the Codename One Academy. As part of that offering we surveyed the Codename One community and asked them: *"what would you like to learn?"*.

The response was was overwhelmingly: *"How to build an app like Uber!"*.

At first I thought about creating something in the style of Uber but I eventually settled on building something that looks really close to the native app. Almost a clone.

My motivation for going for a clone instead of coming up with a completely new design was driven by this line of thinking:

- I wanted the design to look professional and you can't go wrong with a design from a top tier vendor

- People can learn a lot by understanding the decisions Uber made—I know I did

- If I would have built something different I might have given myself "discounts" that don't exist in the real world

I used the word clone to indicate the similarity but not to indicate a carbon copy. Uber is a huge and nuanced app and I had only one week to write all the relevant applicable code.

My goal was to do the "hard stuff" and gloss over some of the deeper details. The goal is to teach with a strong focus on the mobile side. I wanted to create a book that would show you how to build a fully functional MVP (Minimum Viable Product) within a week. I wanted to illustrate the shortcuts that make sense and those that don't. This is a powerful approach whether you are building a startup or working within a large corporation.

I think developers can't deliver truly innovative ideas if we are constantly doing the same app over and over. By making this process simpler I hope that developers will adopt innovative ideas faster rather than re-do the same apps all over again.

Audience

My bookshelf is overflowing with programming books. Most of them revolve around teaching a specific technology (e.g. Java). A few discuss architecture or other big concepts. None of them teach how to build the whole thing.

these books demonstrate through small localized samples. The results don't look like a professional production app. They skip details like servers and business logic or client UI nuances. I didn't want to write that book. This book tries to address the whole thing, the full stack. Even if you don't want to become a full-stack developer, understanding the whole picture is often helpful.

Prerequisites

If you think you have basic understanding of the following you should be able to follow this book:

- Java – a basic/intermediate Java level should be enough. You will need familiarity with one of the top 3 Java IDE's (NetBeans, IntelliJ/IDEA or Eclipse)
- Maven – basic understanding we won't do anything too fancy
- REST/JSON – we will create JSON based web services with HTTP GET/POST methods. This is explained in the book but I don't explain HTTP GET/POST or JSON

> ❶ This book is "code heavy" due to its nature, if you have a difficulty reading listings this book might be difficult to follow

What you don't need to Know

While it goes without saying that we don't need to know everything. I wanted to clarify some specific details you don't need to know:

- Codename One - the book teaches the parts of Codename One that are applicable to the book
- Spring Boot - we'll discuss the parts of Spring Boot that matter. This isn't a book about Spring Boot so I won't get too deep into that but you should be able to work with it after reading the book
- SQL/MySQL/JPA - MySQL is used for storage in the book and we abstract it via JPA. While you will need to install MySQL you won't need to know SQL or how to work with it as we'll use JPA. I will cover JPA at a high level within the book while discussing the elements of interest

Get this Book for FREE!

This book contains the Uber clone part of the online course "Build Real World Full Stack Mobile Apps in Java" available here: codenameone.teachable.com/p/build-real-world-full-stack-mobile-apps-in-java

That course is **much** bigger and constantly growing. Currently it covers the process of creating a Facebook Clone, a restaurant menu application and will cover more apps in the near future (e.g. a WhatsApp Clone). The Uber clone portion of the course is over 5 hours of videos and presentations.

The total amount of materials in the course contains more than 15 hours of materials that grow on a monthly basis!

The course will also include the full book as part of the Uber clone module once exclusivity expires. If you bought this book you can use the coupon code `FreeBook60` to get a 10% discount on the price of the course.

❗ This offer is limited and will expire on October 31st 2018!

How to Read this Book?

Most tech books allow you to skip ahead or just browse through the index to find what you are looking for.

That might not work as effectively with this book. This book describes a **real world app** and as such you might find it difficult to skip ahead. By its nature **the book is "code heavy"**.
That's unavoidable due to the basic premise of the book.

Some materials that are more general purpose were placed in appendices to make them more accessible.
The first few chapters prepare you for the journey ahead. The rest of the book is divided into seven days and three night-hacks. This division matches my experience in prototyping and building similar projects over the years.

You can skip the first chapters if you are familiar with the materials within, however I suggest paying special attention to the styling portion. In the styling section I explain the style syntax I used through the entire book.

I divided the days so each day fills in a different piece of the puzzle:

- After day one you can run a mockup of the client side UI. You can even run it on the device and it will all work. I find that having something you can "touch" is a huge motivator so I always start with the UI

- After day two the backend server will work and run

- After day three the server and the client will work with each other and you will be able to connect from the client to the server

- After day four you will be able to search for a location and see a route

- After day five hailing will work and you'll have the second app for the driver side

- After day six billing will be plugged in and you'll be able to login with Facebook or Google

- After day seven settings will work, transitions and animations would be more refined

Software Prerequisites

You will need JDK 8 (Java 8) to run the current code in the book. Notice that at this time Codename One doesn't support JDK 9 but this will probably change before 2019.

You will need a Java IDE: NetBeans, IntelliJ/IDEA or Eclipse. With the Codename One plugin installed from the Codename One website. Check out Appendix A for more details on setting up Codename One.

Getting Help

This book is dense with information and listings. It also mixes concepts from several tiers into one relatively short book. It's easy to miss a detail and it's probable I missed details when writing this book.

I'm always here to answer your questions, just ask a question in the Codename One discussion forum: www.codenameone.com/discussion-forum.html

Or on StackOverflow with the codenameone tag: stackoverflow.com/tags/codenameone

> I prefer StackOverflow but their moderators can be unwelcoming for some question types

Using the Code

The code for the hello world and TODO app built in the first two chapters is available for download here: www.codenameone.com/files/HelloWorldAndTodo.zip

The code for the Uber clone application build throughout the book is available to download here: https://www.codenameone.com/files/uber-book/UberClone.zip

You may use the code from this book freely for any purpose with no restrictions or attribution. You can provide attribution if you wish to do so (and it would be appreciated).

Since it's code and there is no way to verify it I can't require that you purchase the book (or the online course) to use the code. Doing so would require restrictions that would potentially impact people who bought the book and I don't want to do that. So please consider this a moral imperative, if you make use of the source please buy the book or the course.

Important Notice About Cloning and Copyrights

Uber ™ is a trademark of Uber Technologies Inc.

This work is intended strictly for educational purposes. We don't condone the misuse of Uber's intellectual property!

The goal of this book is to teach via familiarity. Since the Uber application is well designed and familiar we chose it as our target but the book isn't meant as a "copy Uber" cookbook.

Many applications are built around ideas similar to Uber and utilize designs inspired by Uber. It's our assumption that you can learn a lot by understanding how to build something "like" Uber.

In this case we make use of Uber copyrighted work under "fair use" for teaching purposes. Shipping an application with the exact designs/logos or any similar markings goes against copyright law and might get you in trouble. That is why the demos in this book aren't available on the appstores. They would be illegal to ship.

This book is intended as a homage to Uber and their bold UI choices. As I wrote this book I developed a deep sense of respect to the nuanced work of the team that built the Uber app and I hope this is conveyed within the book.

Thanks and Acknowledgments

This work wouldn't have been possible without the immense help I got from **Chen Fishbein** and **Steve Hannah**. Both of whom supported the process of the books development throughout. Steve practically edited the book and deserves co-author credit!
This book literally wouldn't exist without both of them!

I'd also like to thank the reviewers whose feedback improved this book immensely, I would thank you each personally by name but since early reviews were anonymized I don't have access to your names!

Thank you for taking the time to read the earlier rough drafts and provide valuable feedback that undoubtedly improved this book immensely.

I do have a few names for late stage reviewers who sent feedback and words of encouragement. Special thanks goes out to: Francesco Galgani, Rémi Tournier and Steve Nganga.

Hello World

This chapter covers:

- What is Codename One?

- Creating a hello world application

- Signing a mobile application and building the native app

- Core concepts of mobile development, why mobile is different

I didn't teach my kids swimming by throwing them in the pool (that's my story and I'm sticking to it). But I think it's a wonderful way to teach a new technology so we'll start with a trivial hello world to understand the basics. I tried to write a fluent book that doesn't burden the reader with every detail but this is a tight rope to walk. I've listed further resources in the end of the chapter if you need further information.

What's Codename One?

Codename One is a Write Once Run Anywhere mobile development platform for Java/Kotlin developers. It integrates with IntelliJ/IDEA, Eclipse or NetBeans to provide seamless native mobile development.

The things that make it stand out from other tools in this field are:

- Write Once Run Anywhere support with no special hardware requirements and 100% code reuse

- Compiles Java/Kotlin into native code for iOS, UWP (Universal Windows Platform), Android and even JavaScript/PWA

- Open Source and Free with commercial backing/support

- Easy to use with 100% portable Drag and Drop GUI builder

- Full access to underlying native OS capabilities using the native OS programming language (e.g. Objective-C) without compromising portability

- Provides full control over every pixel on the screen

- Lets you use native widgets (views) and mix them with Codename One components within the same hierarchy (heavyweight/lightweight mixing)

- Supports seamless Continuous Integration out of the box

Codename One can trace its roots to the open source LWUIT project started at Sun Microsystem in 2007 by Chen Fishbein (co-founder of Codename One). It's a huge project that's been under constant development for over a decade!

As such I'll only scratch the surface of the possibilities within this book.

1.1

Build Cloud

One of the things that make Codename One stand out is the build cloud approach to mobile development. iOS native development requires a Mac with xcode. Windows native development requires a Windows machine. To make matters worse, Apple, Google and Microsoft make changes to their tools on a regular basis...

This makes it hard to keep up.

When we develop an app in Codename One we use the builtin simulator when running and debugging. When we want to build a native app we can use the build cloud where Macs create the native iOS apps and Windows machines create the native Windows apps. This works seamlessly and makes Codename One apps native as they are literally compiled by the native platform. E.g. for iOS builds the build cloud uses Macs running xcode (the native Apple tool) to build the app.

❗ Codename One doesn't send source code to the build cloud, only compiled bytecode!

Notice that Codename One also provides an option to build offline which means corporations that have policies forbidding such cloud architectures can still use Codename One with some additional overhead/complexity of setting up the native build tools. Since Codename One is open source some developers use the source code to compile applications offline but that's outside the scope of this book.

For a more thorough explanation of the underlying architecture and principals of Codename One check out Appendix F (page 415).

1.2

Getting Started

The following instructions assume you installed the Codename One plugin into your IDE. If you didn't do that you can check out the install instructions in Appendix A (page 389).

Before we get to the code there are few important things we need to go over with the new project wizard.

We need to create a new project. We need to pick a project name and I'll leave that up to you although it's hard to go wrong with HelloWorld . The following four values are important:

- **App Name** - This is the name of the app and the main class, it's important to get this right as it's hard to change this value later

- **Package Name** - It's **crucial** you get this value right. Besides the difficulty of changing this after the fact, once an app is submitted to iTunes/Google Play with a specific package name this can't be changed! See the sidebar Picking a Package Name

- **Theme** - There are various types of builtin themes in Codename One, for simplicity I pick Native as it's a clean slate starting point

- **Template** - There are several builtin app templates that demonstrate various features, for simplicity I always pick Bare Bones which includes the bare minimum

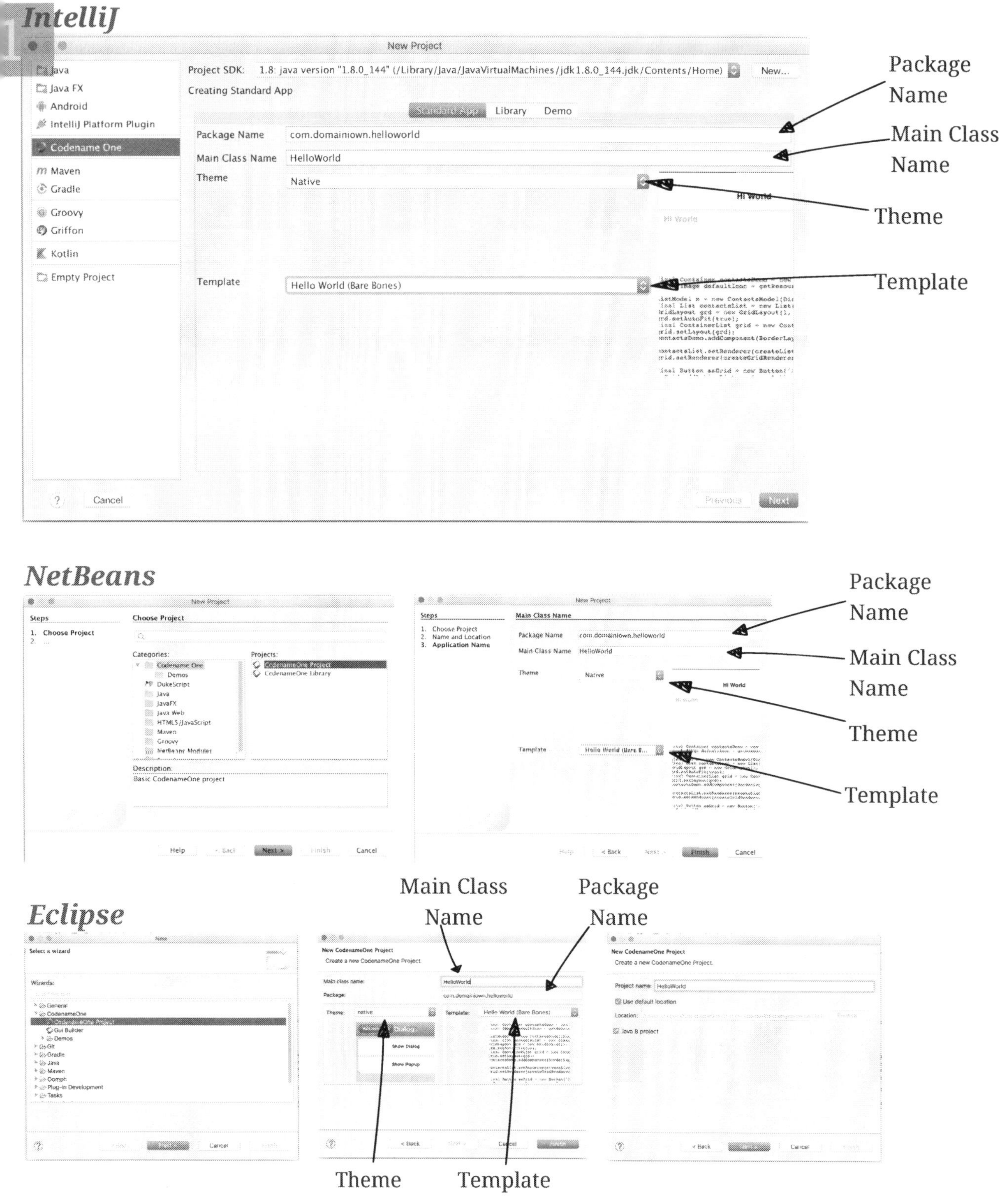

IntelliJ

NetBeans

Eclipse

Figure 1.1. The New App Wizard

Picking a Package Name

Apple, Google and Microsoft identify applications based on their package names. If you use a domain that you don't own it's possible that someone else will use that domain and collide with you. In fact some developers left the default com.mycompany domain in place all the way into production in some cases.

This can cause difficulties when submitting to Apple, Google or Microsoft. Submitting to one of them is no guarantee of success when submitting to another.

To come up with the right package name use a reverse domain notation. So if my website is goodstuff.co.uk my package name should start with uk.co.goodstuff . I highly recommend the following guidelines for package names:

- **Lower Case** – some OS's are case sensitive and handling a mistake in case is painful. The Java convention is lower case and I would recommend sticking to that although it isn't a requirement

- **Avoid Dash and Underscore** – You can't use a dash character (-) for a package name in Java. Underscore (_) doesn't work for iOS. If you want more than one word just use a deeper package e.g.: com.mydomain.deeper.meaningful.name

- **Obey Java Rules** – A package name can't start with a number so you can't use com.mydomain.1sler. You should avoid using Java keywords like this, if etc.

- **Avoid Top Level** – instead of using uk.co.goodstuff use uk.co.goodstuff.myapp. That would allow you to have more than one app on a domain

Running

We can run the HelloWorld application by pressing the Play or Run button in the IDE for NetBeans or IntelliJ. In Eclipse we first need to select the simulator .launch file and then press run. When we do that the Codename One simulator launches. You can use the menu of the simulator to control and inspect details related to the device. You can rotate it, determine it's location in the world, monitor networking calls etc.

With the Skins menu you can download device skins to see how your app will look on different devices.

> Some skins are bigger than the screen size, uncheck the Scrollable flag in the Simulator menu to handle them more effectively

ebug works just like Run by pressing the IDE's debug button. It allows us to launch the simulator in *cbug* mode where we can set breakpoints, inspect variables etc.

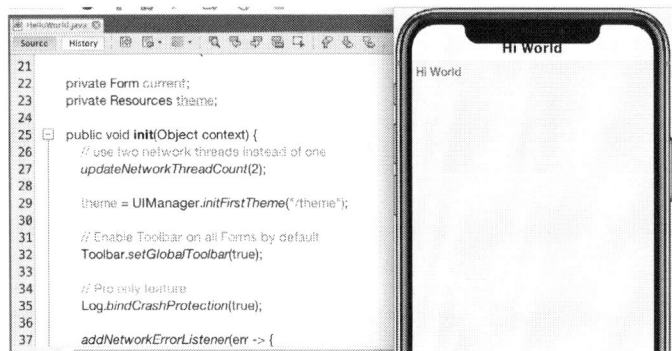

Figure 1. 2. HelloWorld Running on the Simulator with an iPhone X Skin

Simulator vs. Emulator

Codename One ships with a simulator similarly to the iOS toolchain which also has a simulator. Android ships with an emulator. Emulators go the extra mile. They create a virtual machine that's compatible with the device CPU and then boot the full mobile OS within that environment. This provides an accurate runtime environment but is **painfully slow**.

Simulators rely on the fact that OS's are similar and so they leave the low level details in place and just map the API behavior. Since Codename One relies on Java it can start simulating on top of the virtual machine on the desktop. That provides several advantages including fast development cycles and full support for all the development tools/debuggers you can use on the desktop.

Emulators make sense for developers who want to build OS level services e.g. screensavers or low level services. Standard applications are better served by simulators.

The Source Code

After clicking finish in the new project wizard we have a HelloWorld project with a few default settings. I'll break the class down to small pieces and explain each piece starting with the enclosing class:

Listing 1. 1. HelloWorld Class

```
public class HelloWorld {
    private Form current;

    private Resources theme;

    // ... class methods ...
}
```

This is the main class, it's the entry point to the app, notice it doesn't have a main method but rather callback which we will discuss soon

Forms are the "top level" UI element in Codename One. Only one Form is shown at a time and everything you see on the screen is a child of that Form

Every app has a theme, it determines how everything within the application looks e.g. colors, fonts etc.

Next let's discuss the first lifecycle method init(Object). I discuss the lifecycle in depth in the Application Lifecycle Sidebar (page 16).

Listing 1. 2. HelloWorld init(Object)

```
public void init (Object context) {
    updateNetworkThreadCount(2);

    theme=UIManager. initFirstTheme("/theme");

    Toolbar.setGlobalToolbar(true);

    Log.bindCrashProtection(true);

    addNetworkErrorLIstener ( err -> {

        err.consume();
        if(err.getError() != null){
            Log. e( err. getError ());
        }

        Log.sendLogAsync();


        Dialog . show( "Connection Error",
            "There was a networking error in the connection to " +
            err . getConnectionRequest().getUrl (), "OK" , null);
    });
}
```

init is the first of the four lifecycle methods. It's responsible for initialization of variables and values

By default Codename One has one thread that performs all the networking, we set the default to two which gives better performance

The theme determines the appearance of the application. We'll discuss this in the next chapter

This enables the Toolbar API by default, it allows finer control over the title bar area

Crash protection automatically sends device crash logs through the cloud

In case of a network error the code in this block would run, you can customize it to handle networking errors effectively. consume() swallows the event so it doesn't trigger other alerts, it generally means "we got this"

Not all errors include an exception, if we have an exception we can log it with this code

This will email the log from the device to you if you have a pro subscription

This shows an error dialog to the user, in production you might want to remove that code

it(Object) works as a constructor to some degree. We recommend avoiding the constructor for the main class and placing logic in the init method instead. This isn't crucial but we recommend it since the constructor might happen too early in the application lifecycle.

n a cold start init(Object) is invoked followed by the start() method. However, start() can be nvoked more than once if an app is minimized and restored, see the sidebar Application Lifecycle page 16):

Listing 1. 3. HelloWorld start()

```
public void start () {
    if (current != null) {
```
If the app was minimized we usually don't want to do much, just show the last Form of the application

```
        current.show();
        return;
```
current is a Form which is the top most visual element. We can only have one Form showing and we enforce that by using the show() method

```
    }

    Form hi  = new Form("Hi World", BoxLayout.y());
```
We create a new simple Form instance. It has the title "Hello World" and arranges elements vertically (on the Y axis)

```
    hi . add(new Label ( "Hi World"));

    hi.show();
}
```
We add another Label below the title, see figure 1.3 (page 15). I discuss component hierarchy later in section 2.2 (page 37)

The show() method places the Form on the screen. Only one Form can be shown at a time

Figure 1. 3. Title and Label in the UI

There are some complex ideas within this short snippet which I'll address later in this chapter when talking about layout. The gist of it is that we create and show a Form. Form is the top level UI element, it takes over the whole screen. We can add UI elements to that Form object, in this case the Label. We use the BoxLayout to arrange the elements within the Form from top to the bottom vertically.

Application Lifecycle

A few years ago Romain Guy (a senior Google Android engineer) was on stage at the Google IO conference. He asked for a show of hands of people who understand the Activity lifecycle (Activity is similar to a Codename One main class). He then proceeded to jokingly call the audience members who lifted their hands "liars" claiming that after all his years in Google he still doesn't understand it…

Lifecycle seems simple on the surface but hides a lot of nuance. Android's lifecycle is ridiculously complex. Codename One tries to simplify this and also make it portable. Sometimes complexity leaks out and the nuances can be difficult to deal with.

Simply explained an application has three states:

- *Foreground* – it's running and in the foreground which means the user can physically interact with the app
- *Suspended* – the app isn't in the foreground, it's either paused or has a background process running
- *Not Running* – the app was never launched, was killed or crashed

The lifecycle is the process of transitioning between these 3 states and the callbacks invoked when such a transition occurs. The first time we launch the app we start from a "Cold Start" (Not Running State) but on subsequent launches the app is usually started from the "Warm Start" (Suspended State).

Foreground

The app is running
in the foreground

Warm Start

Suspended

The app is
minimized and
possibly running
in the background

start()

Cold Start

init()

stop()

Minimize

Not Running

User killed the app
or didn't run it

App Exit

destroy()

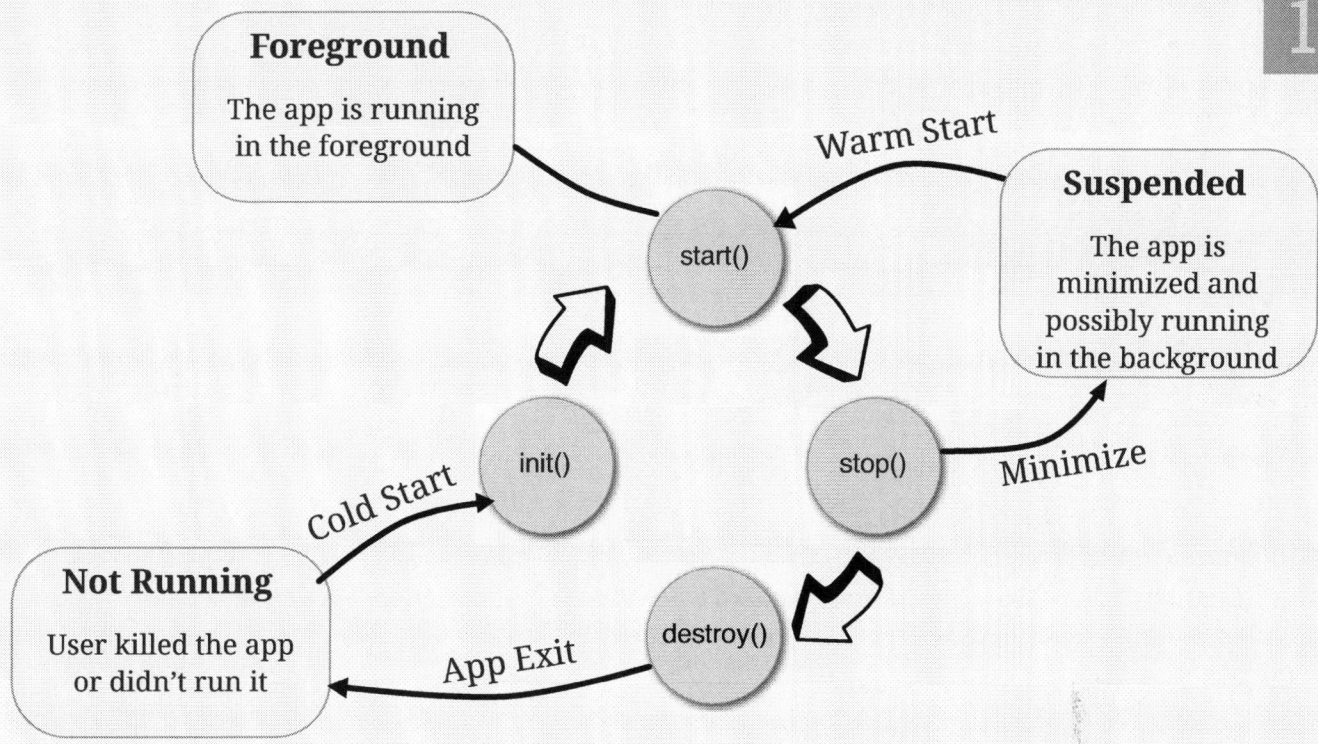

Figure 1. 4. Codename One Application Lifecycle

Codename One has four standard callback methods in the lifecycle API:

- init(Object) – is invoked when the app is first launched from a *Not Running* state

- start() – is invoked for two separate cases. After start() is finished the app transitions to the *Foreground* state.

  - Following init(Object) in case of a cold start. Cold start refers to starting the app from a *Not Running* state.

  - When the app is restored from *Suspended* state. In this case init(Object) isn't invoked

- stop() – is invoked when the app is minimized e.g. when switching to a different app. After stop() is finished the app transitions to the *Suspended* state.

- destroy() – is invoked when the app is destroyed e.g. killed by a user in the task manager. After destroy() is finished the app is no longer running hence it's in the *Not Running* state.

  ❗ destroy() is optional there is no guarantee that it would be invoked. It should be used only as a last resort

Now that we have a general sense of the lifecycle lets look at the last two lifecycle methods:

```
public  void  stop()  {
    current  = getCurrentForm();
    if (current  instanceof  Dialog) {
        ((Dialog) current). dispose ();
        current  = getCurrentForm();
    }
}
```

stop() is invoked when the app is minimized or a different app is opened

As the app is stopped we save the current Form so we can restore it back in start() if the app is restored

Dialog is a bit of a special case restoring a Dialog might block the proper flow of application execution so we dispose them and then get the parent Form

```
public  void  destroy ()  {
}
```

destroy() is a very special case. Under normal circumstances you shouldn't write code in destroy(). stop() should work for most cases

That's it. Hopefully you have a general sense of the code. It's time to run on the device.

.2.2

Run on Device

Now that we have a HelloWorld and a basic understanding of the lifecycle lets discuss building apps for devices. I'll only discuss Android and iOS for simplicity.

> While Codename One supports Windows and a few other platforms the focus of this book is on Android/iOS to keep things manageable. Windows is a more significant player in the tablet market which isn't as applicable for this app

Signing

All of the modern mobile platforms require signed applications but they all take radically different approaches when implementing it.

Signing is a process that marks your final application for the device with a special value. This value (signature) is a value that only you can generate based on the content of the application and your certificate. Effectively it guarantees the app came from you. This blocks a 3rd party from signing their apps and posing as you to the appstore or to the user. It's a crucial security layer.

A certificate is the tool we use for signing. Think of it as a mathematical rubber stamp that generates a different value each time. Unlike a rubber stamp a signature can't be forged!

Android uses a self signed certificate approach. You can just generate a certificate by describing who you are and picking a password!

Anyone can do that. However, once a certificate is generated it can't be replaced...

If you lose an Android certificate it can't be restored and you won't be able to update your app!

If this wasn't the case someone else could potentially push an "upgrade" to your app. Once an app is submitted with a certificate to Google Play this app can't be updated with any other certificate.

With that in mind generating an Android certificate is trivial.

The following chart illustrates a process that's identical on all IDE's

Your certificate will generate into the file Keychain.ks ***in your home directory***
Make sure to back that up and the password as losing these can have dire consequences

Right click the project and select "Codename One Settings"

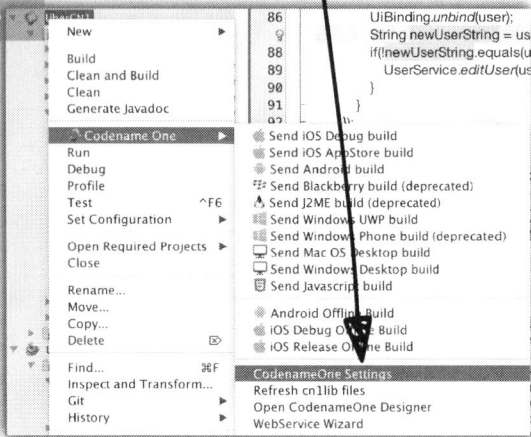

Click "Android Cetificate Generator"

Don't forget the password

Certificate Generator

Password	Password
Alias	Alias
Full Name	Full Name
Organizational Unit	Organizational Unit
Company	Company
City	City
State	State
2 Letter Country Code	2 Letter Country Code
SHA 512 (won't work on older devices)	
OK	Cancel

Alias is a simple ID for the certificate e.g. codenameone

The other details will be visible to the users of the app when they inspect your apps signature

Checking this will decrease the likelyhood of anyone forging this certificate in the forseeable future. Notice that the current likelyhood is **very** low. The new 512bit certificates only work on Android 4.1 or newer

Press OK when you are done

Figure 1. 5. Process of Certificate Generation for Android

Should I Use a Different Certificate for Each App?

In theory yes. In practice it's a pain... Keeping multiple certificates and managing them is a pain so we often just use one.

The drawback of this approach occurs when you are building an app for someone else or want to sell the app. Giving away your certificate is akin to giving away your house keys. So it makes sense to have separate certificates for each app.

Code signing for iOS relies on Apple as the certificate authority. This is something that doesn't exist on Android. iOS also requires provisioning as part of the certificate process and completely separates the process for development/release.

But first let's start with the good news:

- Losing an iOS certificate is no big deal - in fact we revoke them often with no impact on shipping apps

- Codename One has a wizard that hides most of the pain related to iOS signing

In iOS Apple issues the certificates for your applications. That way the certificate is trusted by Apple and is assigned to your Apple iOS developer account. There is one important caveat: You need an iOS Developer Account and Apple charges a 99USD Annual fee for that.

The 99USD price and requirement have been around since the introduction of the iOS developer program for roughly 10 years at the time of this writing. It might change at some point though

Apple also requires a "provisioning profile" which is a special file bound to your certificate and app. This file describes some details about the app to the iOS installation process. One of the details it includes during development is the list of permitted devices.

Development

Development Provisioning Profile

Development Certificate

Development binary can only be installed on list of devices mentioned in the provisioning profile

Appstore

Distribution Provisioning Profile

Distribution Certificate

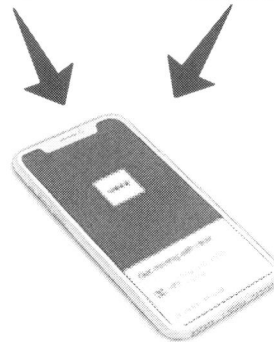

Distribution binary can be uploaded to itunes but can't be installed on the device

Itunes connect should be used to upload binary

Figure 1. 6. The Four Files Required for iOS Signing and Provisioning

We need 4 files for signing. Two certificates and two provisioning profiles:

1. Production - The production certificate/provisioning pair is used for builds that are uploaded to iTunes

2. Development - The development certificate/provisioning is used to install on your development devices

The certificate wizard automatically creates these 4 files and configures them for you.

1 In Codename One Settings click iOS Certificate Wizard

2 These are the Apple iOS developer program email and password pair. Not the Codename One password!

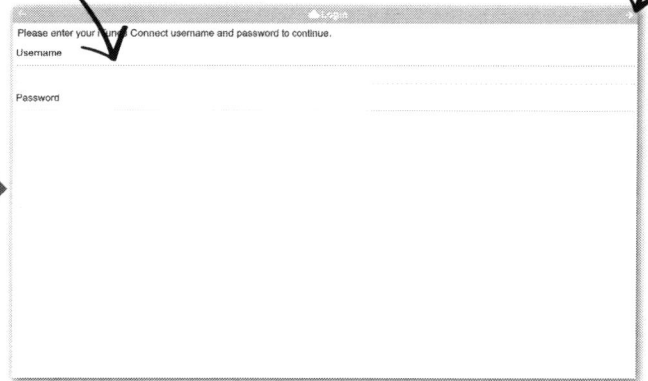

Next to proceed

Figure 1. 7. Using the iOS Certificate Wizard Steps 1 and 2

3 Here we have the list of devices that you can add to the provisioning profile. You can install

You can add devices using this menu option

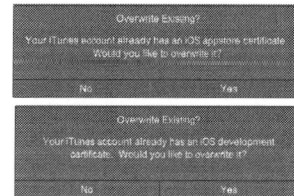

4 If you have an existing certificate you will be offered to revoke it

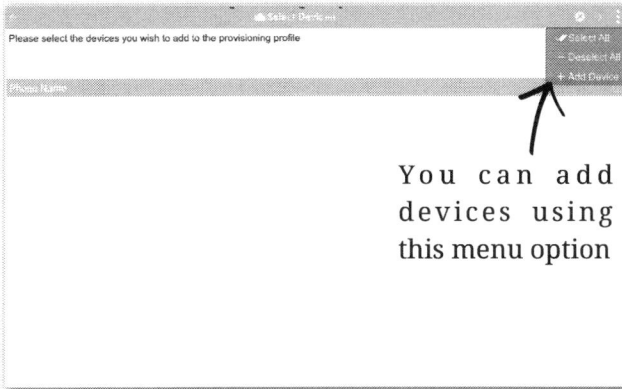

If your existing certificate is fine, you shouldn't revoke just share the single P12 file between projects

Figure 1. 8. Using the iOS Certificate Wizard Steps 3 and 4

You are shown the details of the files that should be generates

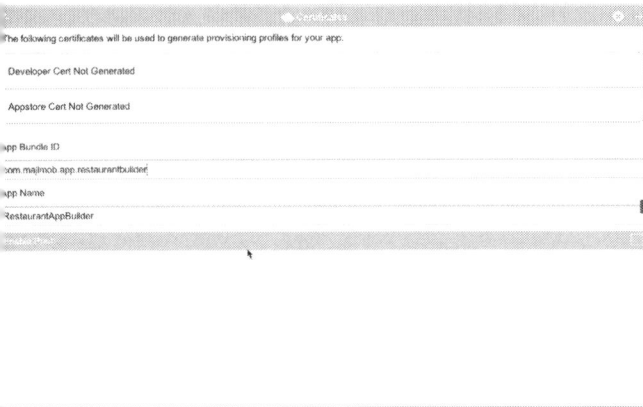

The final form shows a summary of what was performed by the wizard

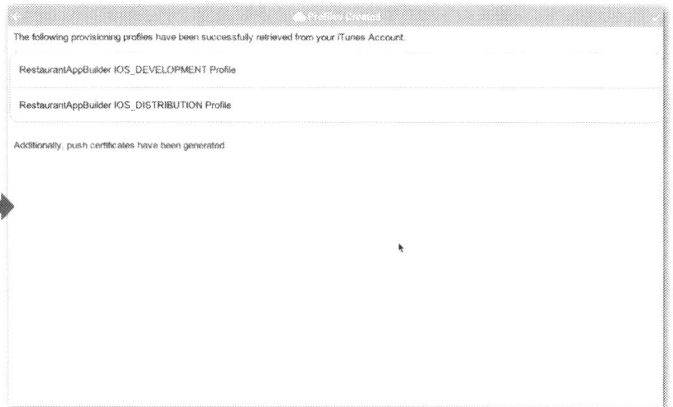

The following certificates will be used to generate provisioning profiles for your app.

Developer Cert Not Generated

Appstore Cert Not Generated

app Bundle ID

com.majmob.app.restaurantbuilder

app Name

RestaurantAppBuilder

The following provisioning profiles have been successfully retrieved from your iTunes Account.

RestaurantAppBuilder IOS_DEVELOPMENT Profile

RestaurantAppBuilder IOS_DISTRIBUTION Profile

Additionally, push certificates have been generated

Figure 1. 9. Using the iOS Certificate Wizard Steps 5 and 6

If you have more than one project you should use the same iOS P12 certificate files in all the projects and just regenerate the provisioning. In this situation the certificate wizard asks you if you want to revoke the existing certificate which you shouldn't revoke in such a case. You can update the provisioning profile in Apple's iOS developer website.

One important aspect of provisioning on iOS is the device list in the provisioning step. Apple only allows you to install the app on 100 devices during development. This blocks developers from skipping the appstore altogether. It's important you list the correct UDID for the device in the list otherwise install will fail.

There are several apps and tools that offer the UDID of the device, they aren't necessarily reliable and might give a fake number!

1 To get the UDID connect your iDevice to your computer and launch iTunes. Then click on the device icon

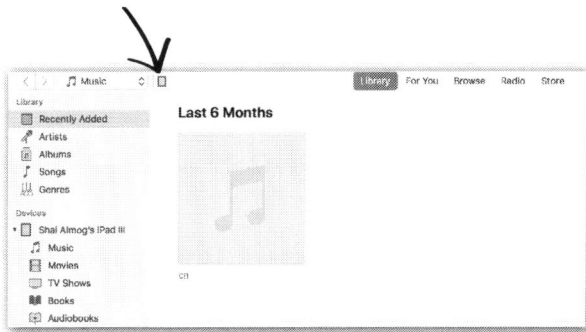

2 Click the serial number of the device

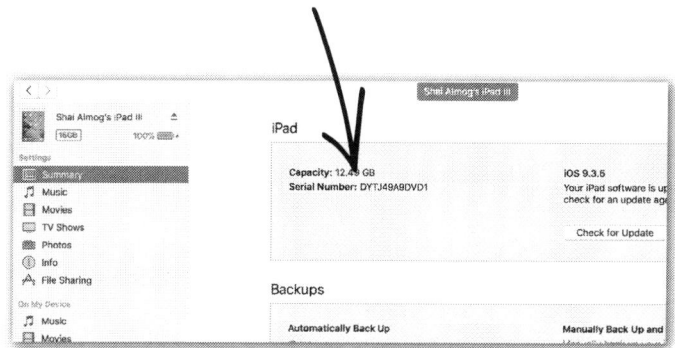

3 The serial number turns to the UDID. Notice that this is in the same UI view. The serial number updates to the UDID when you click on it

Figure 1. 10. Get the UDID of a Device

You can right click the UDID and select copy to copy it

The simplest and most reliable process for getting a UDID is via itunes. I've used other approaches in the past that worked but this approach is guaranteed.

Ad hoc provisioning allows 1000 beta testers for your application but it's a more complex process that I won't discuss here

Build and Install

Before we continue with the build we should sign up at www.codenameone.com/build-server.html where you can soon follow the progress of your builds. I discuss this further in section 1.3 (page 26). You need a Codename One account in order to build for the device.

Now that we have certificates the process of device builds is literally a right click away for both OS's. We can right click the project and select Codename One → Send iOS Debug Build or Codename One → Send Android Build.

1 ℹ️ The first time you send a build you will be prompted for the email and password you provided when signing up for Codename One

Once you send a build you should see the results in the build server page:

Successful builds are green

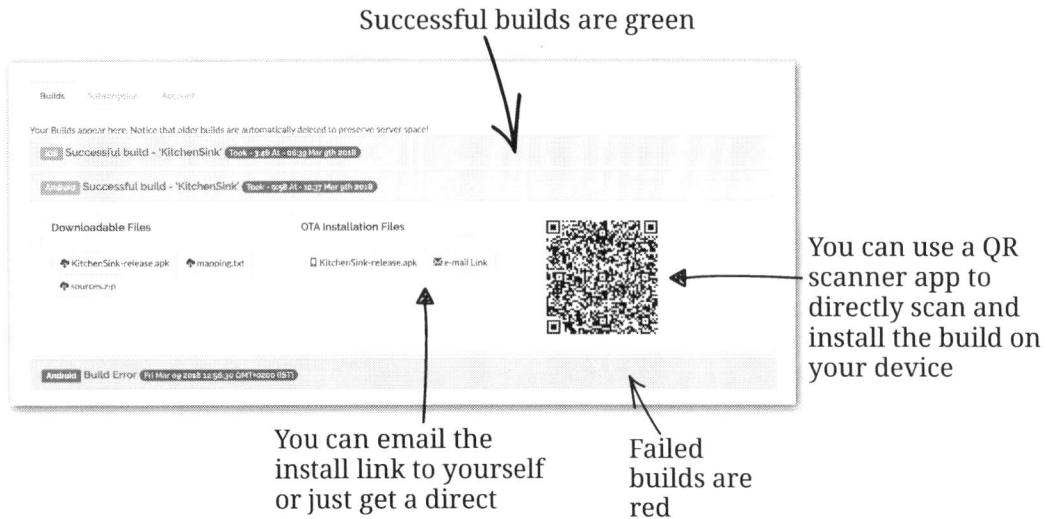

You can use a QR scanner app to directly scan and install the build on your device

You can email the install link to yourself or just get a direct

Failed builds are red

Figure 1. 11. Build Results

💡 On iOS make sure you use Safari when installing, as 3rd party browsers might have issues

Once you go through those steps you should have the HelloWorld app running on your device. This process is non-trivial when starting so if you run into difficulties don't despair and seek help at codenameone.com. Once you go through signing and installation, it becomes easier.

1.3

How Does it Work?

Let's step back a bit from the HelloWorld app and explain what we just did.

As a developer, your view of Codename One is relatively simple:

- You develop your app in Java and the Codename One API

- You debug the app with the Codename One device Simulator

- When you need a native app you can right click the project and select Send Build for iOS (or Android, Windows etc.)

That's it. There is quite a lot more to it but the basic premise is pretty close.

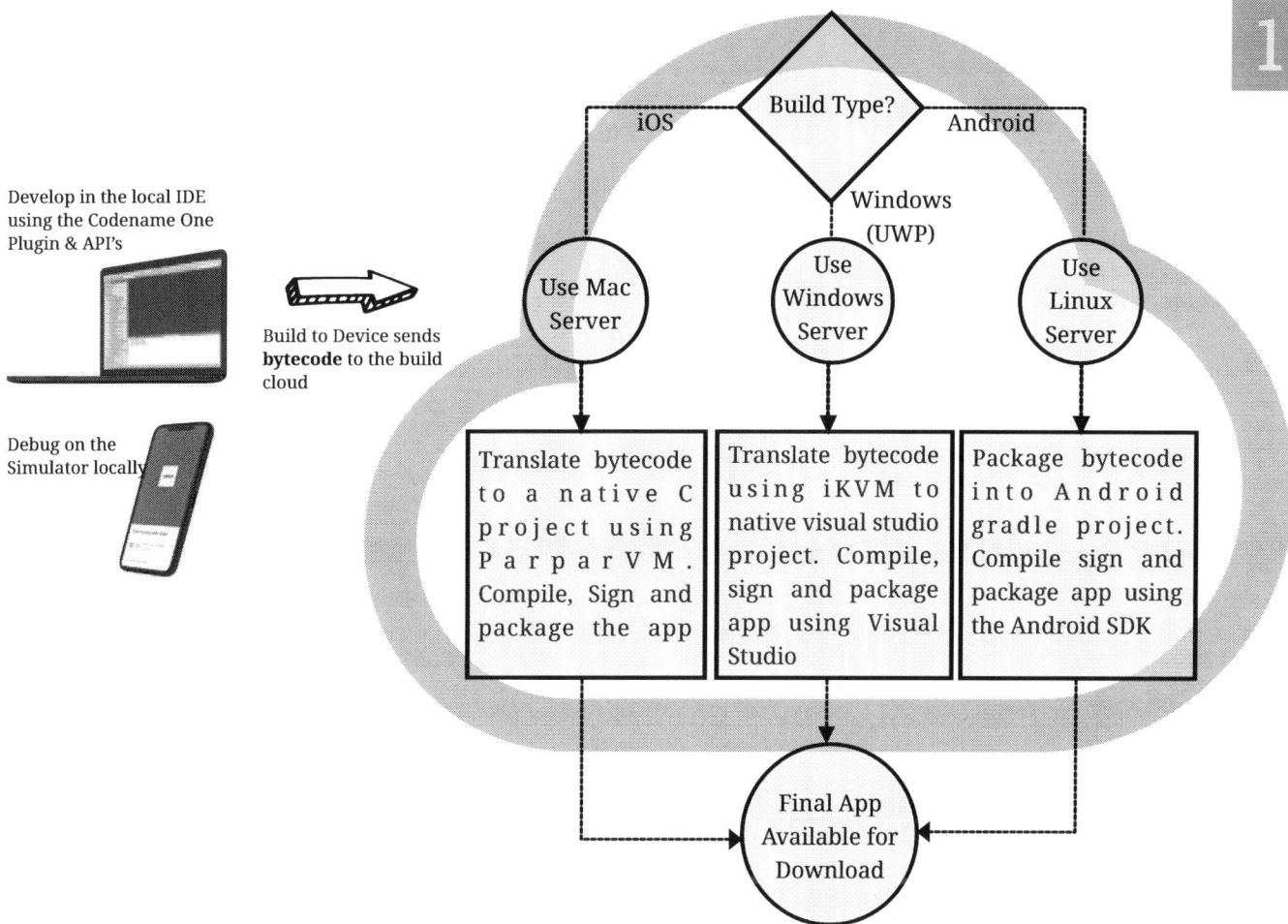

Figure 1. 12. What Happens in the Build Servers in Broad Strokes

This should give a general sense of the process under the hood. For a more thorough explanation check out Appendix F (page 415).

Mobile is Different

Before we proceed I'd like to explain some universal core concepts of mobile programming that might not be intuitive. These are universal concepts that apply to mobile programming regardless of the tools you are using.

Density (DPI/PPI)

Density is also known as DPI (Dots Per Inch) or PPI (pixels or points per inch). Density is confusing, unintuitive and might collide with common sense. E.g. an iPhone 7 plus has a resolution of 1080x1920 pixels and a PPI of 401 for a 5 inch screen. On the other hand an iPad 4 has 1536x2048 pixels with a PPI of 264 on a 9.7 inch screen... Smaller devices can have higher resolutions!

s the following figure shows, if a Pixel 2 XL had pixels the size of an iPad it would have been twice .e size of that iPad. While in reality it's nearly half the height of the iPad!

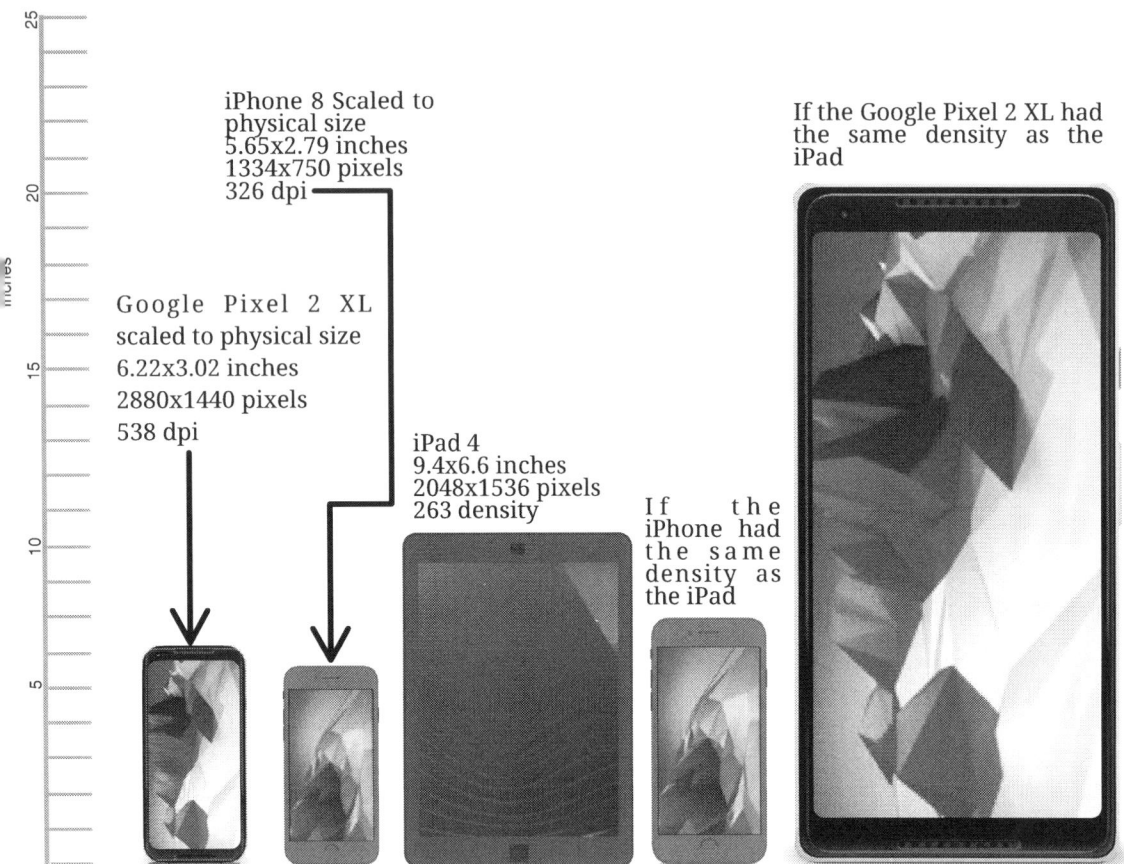

Figure 1. 13. Device Density vs. Resolution

Differences in density can be extreme. A second generation iPad has 132 PPI, where modern phones have PPI that crosses the 600 mark. Low resolution images on high PPI devices will look either small or pixelated. High resolution images on low PPI devices will look huge, overscaled (artifacts) and will consume too much memory.

iPad 4 Sized to Scale

Google Pixel 2 XL
Sized to Scale

iPhone 8 Sized to Scale

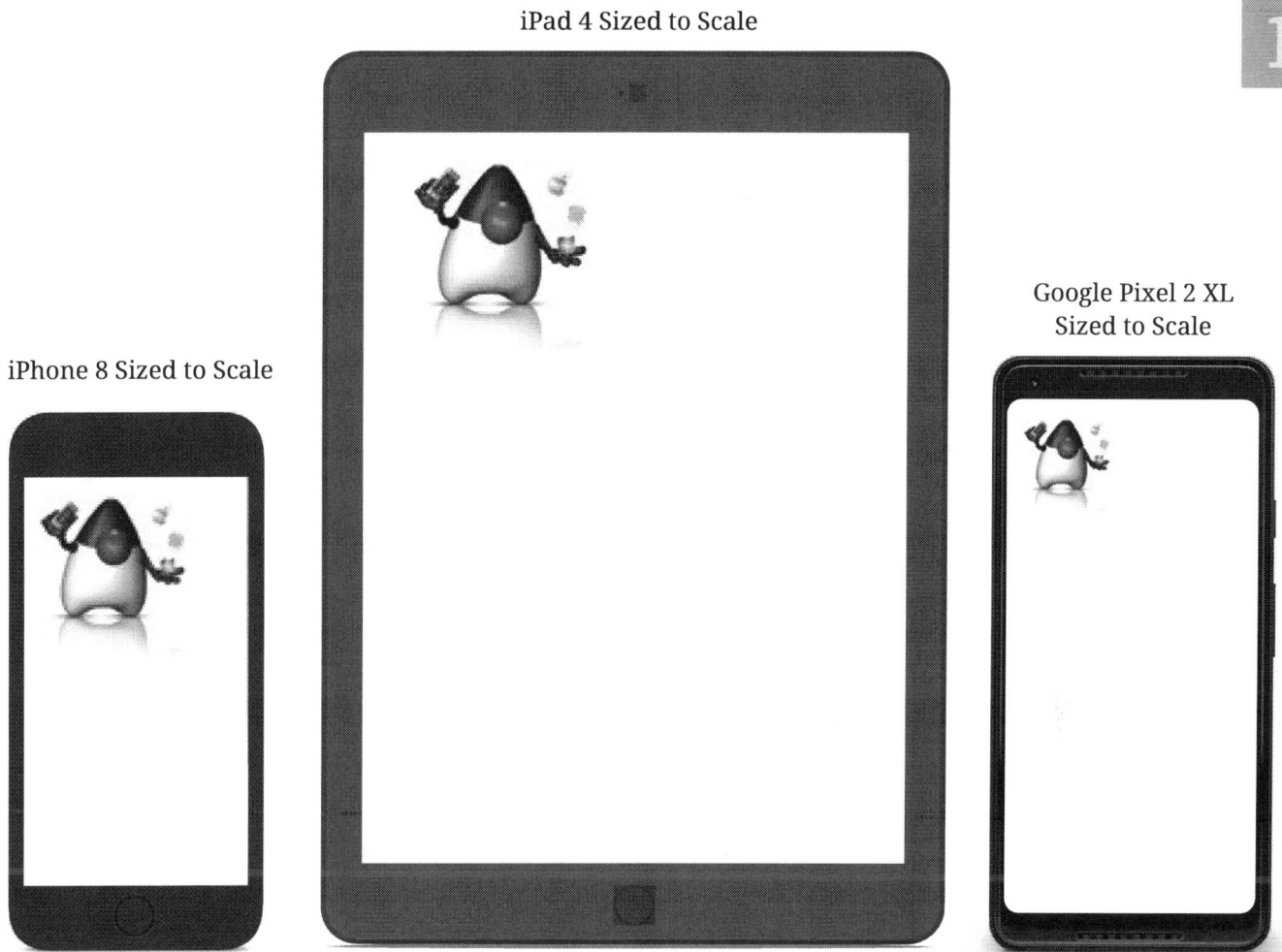

Figure 1. 14. How the Same Image Looks in Different Devices

The exact same image will look different on each device, sometimes to a comical effect. One of the solutions for this problem is multi-images. All OS's support the ability to define different images for various densities. I will discuss multi-images in Chapter 2.

This also highlights the need for working with measurements other than pixels. Codename One supports millimeters (or dips) as a unit of measurement. This is highly convenient and is a better representation of size when dealing with mobile devices.

But there is a bigger conceptual issue involved. We need to build a UI that adapts to the wide differences in form factors. We might have fewer pixels on an iPad but because of its physical size we would expect the app to cram more information into that space so the app won't feel like a blown up phone application. There are multiple strategies to address that but one of the first steps is in the layout managers.

I'll discuss the layout managers in depth in Chapter 2 but the core concept is that they decide where a element is placed based on generic logic. That way the user interface can adapt automatically to the huge variance in display size and density.

Touch Interface

The fact that mobile devices use a touch interface today isn't news… But the implications of that aren't immediately obvious to some developers.

UI elements need to be finger sized and heavily spaced. Otherwise we risk the "fat finger" effect. That means spacing should be in millimeters and not in pixels due to device density.

Scrolling poses another challenge in touch based interfaces. In desktop applications it's very common to nest scrollable items. However, in touch interfaces the scrolling gesture doesn't allow such nuance. Furthermore, scrolling on both the horizontal and vertical axis (side scrolling) can be very inconvenient in touch based interfaces.

Device Fragmentation

Some developers single out this wide range of resolutions and densities as "device fragmentation". While it does contribute to development complexity for the most part it isn't a difficult problem to overcome.

Densities aren't the cause of device fragmentation. Device fragmentation is caused by multiple OS versions with different behaviors. This is very obvious on Android and for the most part relates to the slow rollout of Android vendor versions compared to Googles rollout. E.g. 7 months after the Android 8 (Oreo) release in 2018 it was still available on 1.1% of the devices. The damning statistic is that 12% of the devices in mid 2018 run Android 4.4 Kitkat released in 2013!

This makes QA difficult as the disparity between these versions is pretty big. These numbers will be out of date by the time you read this but the core problem remains. It's hard to get all device manufacturers on the same page so this problem will probably remain in the foreseeable future despite everything.

3.2

Performance

Besides the obvious need for performance and smooth animation within a mobile app there are a couple of performance related issues that might not be intuitive to new developers: size and power.

App Size

Apps are installed and managed via stores. This poses some restrictions about what an app can do. But it also creates a huge opportunity. Stores manage automatic update and to some degree the marketing/monetization of the app.

A good mobile app is updated once a month and sometimes even once a week. Since the app downloads automatically from the store this can be a huge benefit:

- Existing users are reminded of the app and get new features instantly

- New users notice the app featured on a "what's new" list

If an app is big it might not update over a cellular network connection. Google and Apple have restrictions on automatic updates over cellular networks to preserve battery life and data plans. A large app might negatively impact users perception of the app and trigger uninstalls e.g. when a phone is low on available space.

Power Drain

Desktop developers rarely think about power usage within their apps. In mobile development this is a crucial concept. Modern device OS's have tools that highlight misbehaving applications and this can lead to bad reviews.

Code that loops forever while waiting for input will block the CPU from sleeping and slowly drain the battery.

Worse. Mobile OS's kill applications that drain the battery. If the app is draining the battery and is minimized (e.g. during an incoming call) the app could be killed. This will impact app performance and usability.

Sandbox and Permissions

Apps installed on the device are "sandboxed" to a specific area so they won't harm the device or its functionality. The filesystem of mobile applications is restricted so one application can't access the files of another application. Things that most developers take for granted on the desktop such as a "file picker" or accessing the image folder don't work on devices!

This means that when your application works on a file it belongs only to your application. In order to share the file with a different application you need to ask the operating system to do that for you.

Furthermore, some features require a "permission" prompt and in some cases require special flags in system files. Apps need to request permission to use sensitive capabilities e.g. Camera, Contacts etc. Historically Android developers just declared required permissions for an app and the user was prompted with permissions during install. Android 6 adopted the approach used by iOS of prompting the user for permission when accessing a feature.

This means that in runtime a user might revoke a permission. A good example in the case of an Uber app is the location permission. If a user revokes that permission the app might lose its location.

Ubers Permission Controversy

While working on this book I was surprised that the Uber app didn't include some common functionality in Android applications (namely SMS intercept). As I researched this it seems that in the past the Uber app used to have a **huge** set of permissions. This raised privacy concerns among power users and produced backlash of users calling for a ban.

It seems that Uber decided to take permissions seriously. They don't ask for permissions even if it comes at the expense of reduced functionality. I think that decision was made prior to Android 6 which gives end users more control over permissions and Uber should probably revisit this policy.

I think this is an important thing to keep in mind when thinking about permissions. It might be advantageous to avoid a feature if it has problematic permissions.

.4

Summary

In this chapter, we learned:

- How we can correctly define package names so vendors such as Apple and Google identify/update our app correctly

- How we should use the mobile application lifecycle to handle app state changes

- How various mobile device screen sizes impact your UI, and how to work around that to make your app work across PPI limitations

- How to understand the mobile development landscape and differentiate between it and desktop programming

- How to sign/provision a mobile app so we can build and run on a mobile device

I barely scratched the surface of Codename One in this chapter... It's a huge framework. I will go into more details in the next chapter.

Further Reading

Codename One has over a decade's worth of code and knowledge. I made an effort to make this book "all inclusive", but there are still limits to this medium. New platforms and tools are always a challenge, that's why we try to help with any question. So please engage with the online community if something doesn't work...

- Codename One Developer Guide – www.codenameone.com/manual/

- JavaDocs – www.codenameone.com/javadoc/

- Technical Support – stackoverflow.com/tags/codenameone or www.codenameone.com/discussion-forum.html

- Short Video Tutorials – www.codenameone.com/how-do-i.html

- Online course – codenameone.teachable.com/

Core Concepts 2

Now that we have a general sense of how a hello world works and some broad stroke overview of mobile development, lets see how this all fits into the concepts of Codename One. We'll accomplish that by building a small Todo list app. While we do that I'll try to explain how everything works together in the grand scheme of things...

I'll try to keep this short so we will have all the tools we need to build the Uber app client by the end of the chapter.

The Todo App 2.1

This is what we should end up with before this chapter is finished:

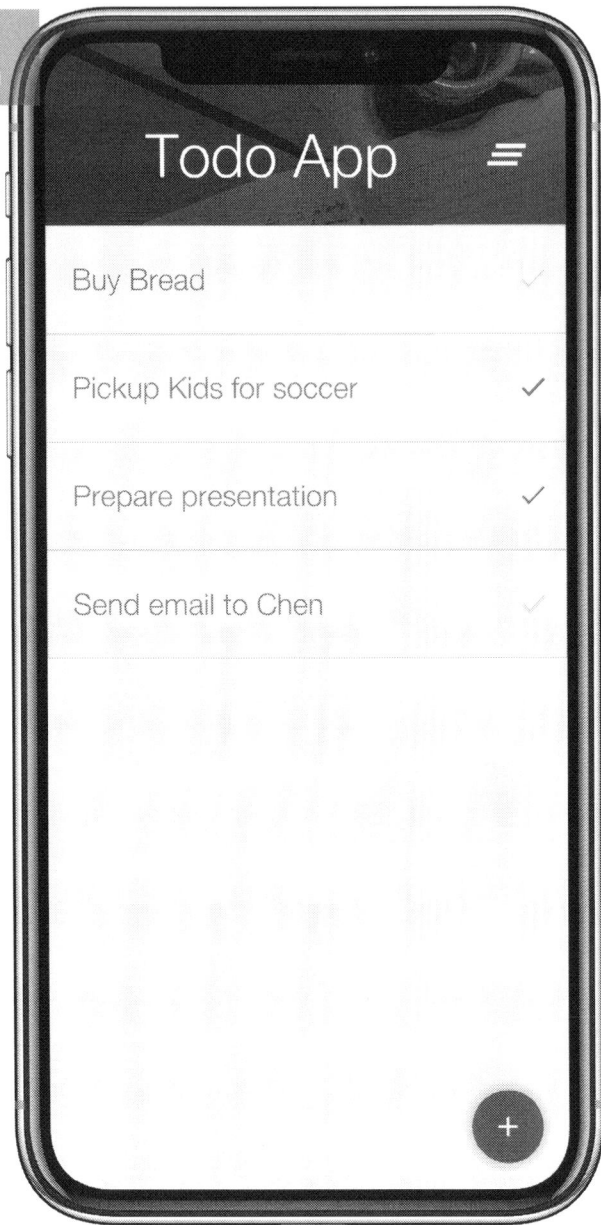

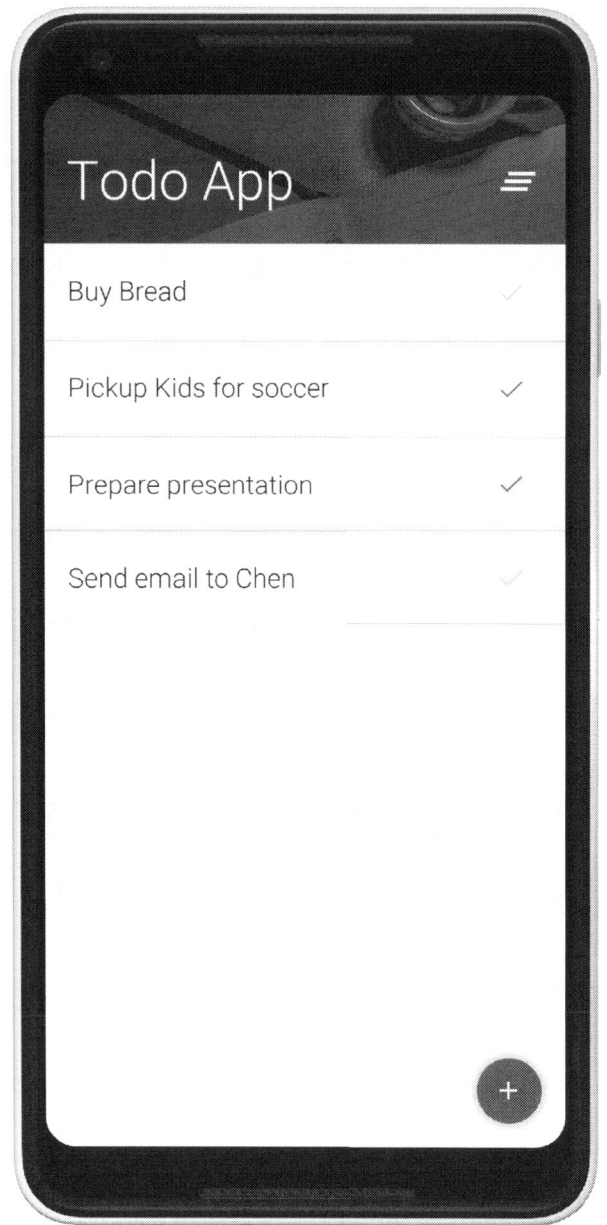

Figure 2. 1. Final Result of the Todo App

I chose to create a similar UI in this case but still respected some platform conventions e.g. notice the title is aligned differently on Android and iOS. This is intentional. I'll discuss this more in the theming section.

I'll start by creating a new project just like the hello world project before but I'll name it "TodoApp".

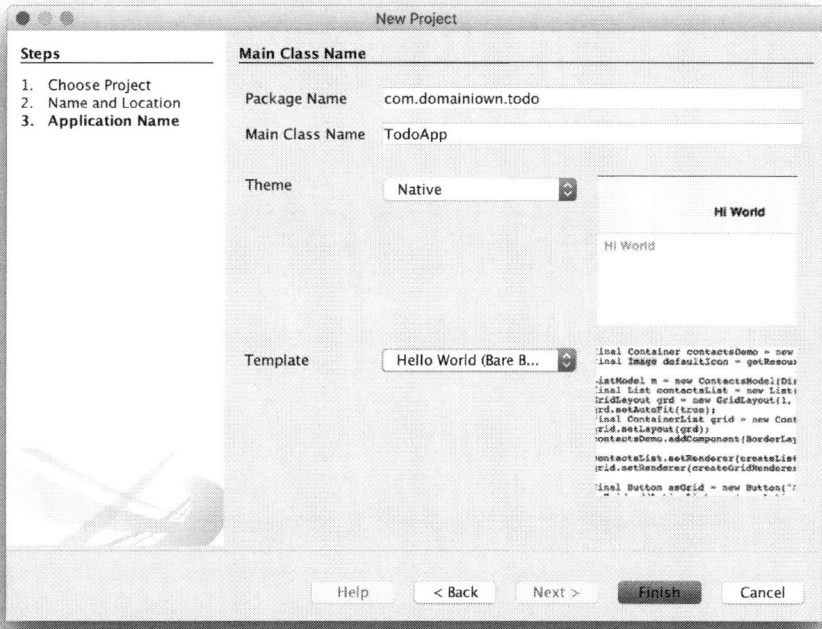

Figure 2. 2. The new Project Wizard for the TodoApp

We'll start by going over the hierarchy of the application.

Layouts and Hierarchy

Every button, label or element you see on the screen in a Codename One application is a Component. This is a highly simplified version of this class hierarchy:

Component is the base class for all the UI elements in Codename One

Container is a Component that can hold within it other components. Since a Container is a Component itself it can hold other Containers within. This allows elaborate hierarchies

SpanLabel isn't important but I included it here to show that some components derive from Container instead of Component. This lets us build elaborate components by assembling simpler components together in a Container

Component

Container

Label

TextArea

SpanLabel

Form

Button

TextField

Form is a Container that can be "shown" it's the root of the Container hierarchy all applications must have a Form. It's where the UI is placed

Button and quite a few other classes derive from Label this allows them to provide common functionality such as icons, alignment etc.

TextField derives from TextArea both allow user input using a virtual keyboard (or physical keyboard)

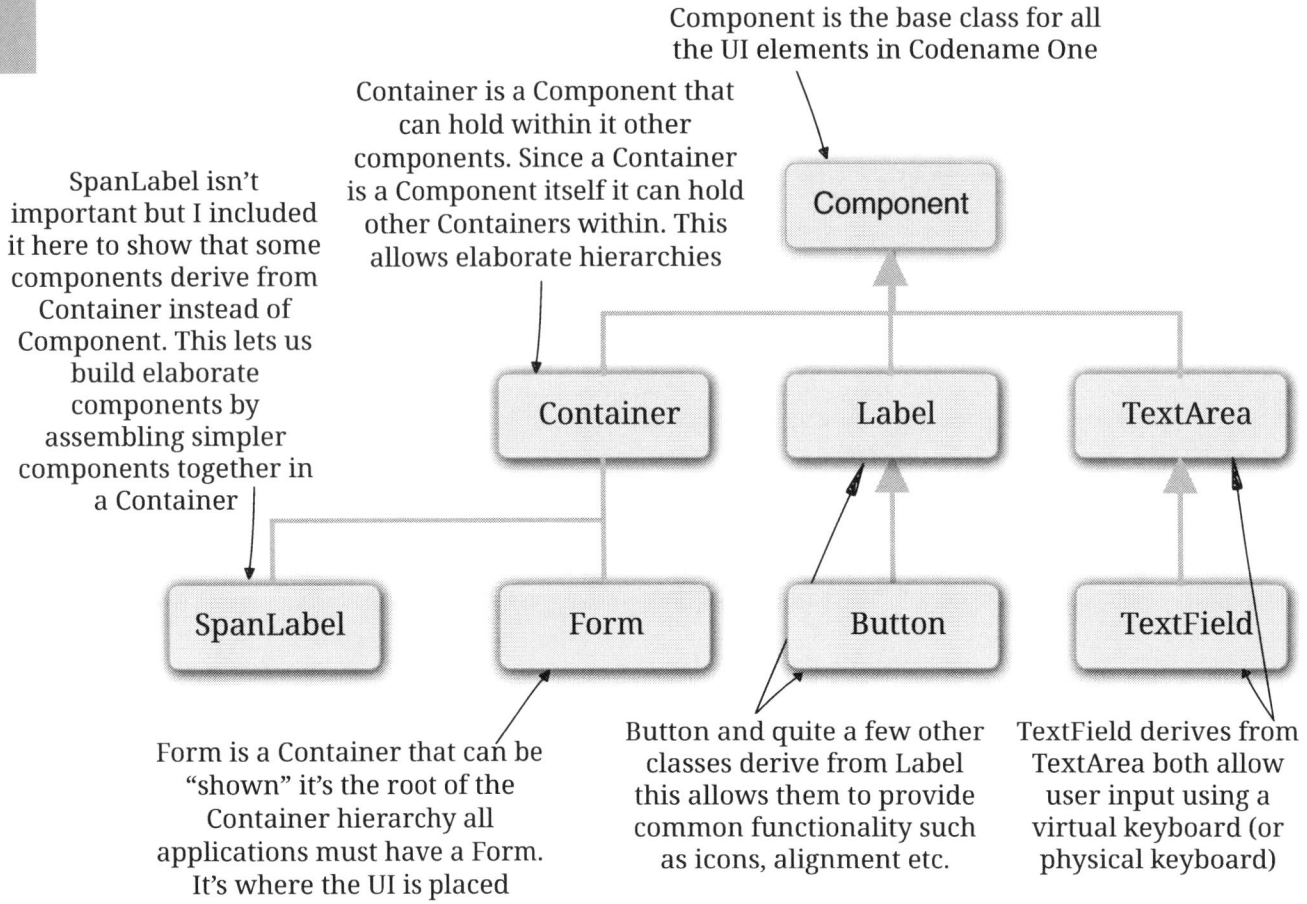

Figure 2. 3. The Core Component Class Hierarchy

A Codename One application is effectively a series of forms, only one Form can be shown at a time. The Form includes everything we see on the screen. Under the hood the Form is comprised of a few separate pieces:

- Content Pane - this is literally the body of the Form. When we add a Component into the Form it goes into the content pane. Notice that Content Pane is scrollable by default on the Y axis!

- Title Area - we can't add directly into this area. The title area is managed by the Toolbar class. Toolbar is a special component that resides in the top portion of the form and abstracts the title design. The title area is broken down into two parts:

  ○ Title of the Form and its commands (the buttons on the right/left of the title)

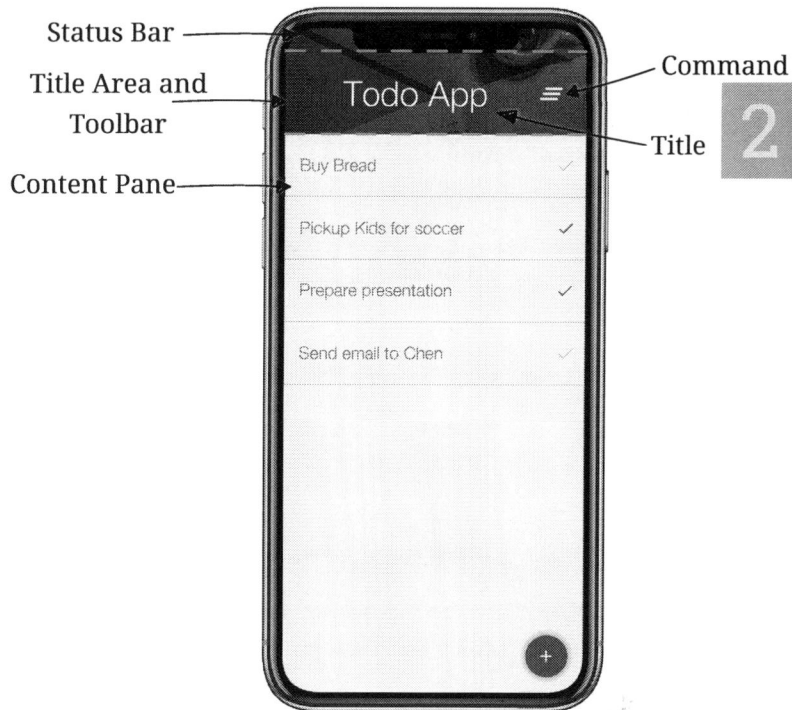

Figure 2. 4. Structure of a Form

  ○ Status Bar - on iOS the area on the top includes a special space so the notch, battery, clock etc. can fit. Without this the battery indicator/clock or notch would be on top of the title

Now that we understand this let's look at the new project we created and open the Java file TodoApp.java. In it we should see the lines that setup the UI in the start() method:

Listing 2. 1. The Default Form of TodoApp

```
Form hi = new Form("Hi World", BoxLayout.y());
hi.add(new Label("Hi World"));      ← This is the same code we had in the
hi.show();                            hello world app...
```

I'll circle back to the layout code soon. Right now I want to create a new Form for the todo app.

We can start with something like this:

Listing 2. 2. The Default Form of TodoApp

```
Form todoApp = new Form("Todo App",  BoxLayout.y ());
todoApp show();
```

I changed the title/name and removed the hi world label

think it would make more sense to separate the code to a different class. For convenience I will derive the Form class. This is a common practice in UI frameworks although it isn't a requirement, e.g. in the hello world app we just used the Form without inheriting it. First I'll need to allocate and show the new class in the TodoApp class:

Listing 2. 3. TodoApp: Create and Show the new Form

Figure 2. 5. The Initial Step - Not much to see here...

```
new TodoForm(). show();
```

Notice I don't need to save the instance of the TodoForm, I just show it immediately. I can create a Form field but there is no need for that since the Form is shown immediately.

Then I can implement the barebones `TodoForm` class. This obviously needs to reside in a new TodoForm.java file as required for public Java classes:

Listing 2. 4. TodoForm Create and Show the new Form

```
public class TodoForm extends Form {
    public TodoForm() {
        super("Todo App", BoxLayout. y());
    }
}
```

This code is equivalent to the one we had before specifically new Form("Todo App", BoxLayout.y());

I separated the code to a separate class for convenience so I can encapsulate specific functionality. Specifically API's such as adding items, the floating action button etc.

The second step is adding entries into the todo list. For that I'll use the FloatingActionButton (AKA FAB), this is a staple of Google's material design.

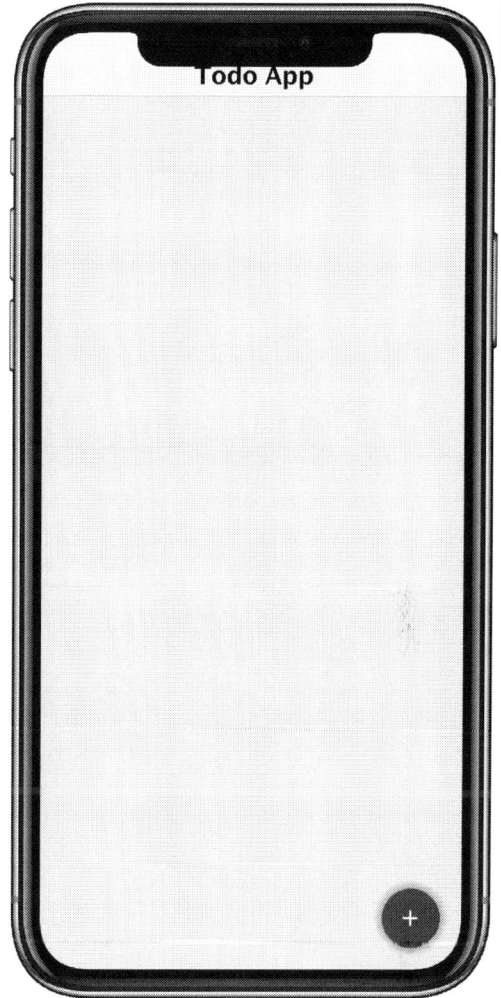

Figure 2. 6. Step 2 - The Floating Action Button That Adds Entries

Material design is Google's all encompassing UI design paradigm. It specifies how all UI elements should look/behave. It's the UI standard on Android. The Uber app uses its principles on iOS and on Android

Before I add this I'll add a stub method so the FloatingActionButton can trigger an event:

Listing 2. 5. TodoForm.addNewItem() Stub

```
private   void  addNewItem() {}
```

We'll fill this method soon...

Now I can add this to the TodoForm constructor using the code:

Listing 2. 6. TodoForm Constructor Floating Action Button

```
FloatingActionButton fab  = FloatingActionButton.
       createFAB ( FontImage. MATERIAL_ADD);

fab.bindFabToContainer(this);

fab.addActionListener(e -> addNewItem());
```

FloatingActionButton creates the round floating button, it accepts a FontImage constant which I'll cover soon

We usually add items to containers but a FAB floats on top, this method handles the "floating" aspect. this means the current Form instance.

When the FAB is clicked we invoke the addNewItem() method, I'll discuss event handling soon

FontImage and Material Icons

Material design defines several standard icons that you can find here: material.io/icons/

These icons are integrated into Codename One via an icon font. That effectively means they take up very little RAM and can adapt in terms of size/color without a problem. They are used extensively in the code because they are so convenient and powerful.

The next step would be implementing the addNewItem method that we added before.

Listing 2. 7. TodoForm.addNewItem()

We create a new object instance for each item, we'll discuss that soon

```
private void addNewItem() {
    TodoItem td = new TodoItem("", false);

    add(td);

    revalidate();

    td.edit();

}
```

We invoke Form's add method to add the item to the UI

When a Form is showing and we make a change to it we need to let the Form know we finished making changes by invoking revalidate()

We launch the device virtual keyboard so the user can start typing the text into the new item immediately

Figure 2. 7. Step 3 - Add a New Item

You won't see the virtual keyboard on the simulator since you would use your desktop's keyboard but, when running on the device, the keyboard would pop up instantly and let you type.

The most confusing aspect in the code would be the revalidate() call. Why do we need it and why doesn't Codename One revalidate every time we add an item?

revalidate() is an expensive operation. If Codename One did it every time the UI changed it would be very slow. In fact platforms such as web do it all the time (reflow) and that's considered one of the major performance penalties inherent in web development. The revalidate operation is expensive since it needs to recursively loop through all components, if one of them changes its size we need to rerun this recursive loop over again. There are shortcuts to make it faster but it's still an inherently slow process.

We can clarify this with an example. Lets say we have this code:

Listing 2. 8. Why Revalidate Matters

```
add(componentX);
// possibly some processing
add(componentY);
```

With automatic revalidate (reflow) we'd have to run revalidate twice which would make things slow.

Another benefit of revalidate()   is layout animations. We can change the UI and instead of revalidate we can ask Codename One to animate the UI into place e.g.:

Listing 2. 9. Layout Animation

```
add(componentX);
animateLayout(150);
```

This will move componentX into it's place in the layout within 150 milliseconds. It's equivalent to revalidate in effect but does that logic with "style". I'll discuss layout animations again later in this chapter.

Before that lets look at the TodoItem class:

Listing 2. 10. The TodoItem class

```java
public class TodoItem extends Container {
    private TextField nameText;
    private CheckBox done = new CheckBox();
    public TodoItem(String name, boolean checked) {
        super( new BorderLayout ());
        nameText = new TextField (name);
        nameText.setUIID( "Label" );
        add(CENTER, nameText);
        add(EAST, done);
        done.setSelected(checked);
    }
    public void edit () {
        nameText.startEditingAsync();
    }
    public boolean isChecked() {
        return done.isSelected ();
    }
    public String getText() {
        return nameText.getText();
    }
}
```

Inheriting Container makes it easy to detect if a TodoItem is checked

TextField accepts user text input with the virtual keyboard

CheckBox can be toggled between selected and unselected states

With BorderLayout we can position a component in one of 5 places: CENTER, EAST, WEST, NORTH and SOUTH

We don't want the text field to look like a text field, we want it to look like a label which we can do by setting the UIID We'll discuss this in the styling section soon

We place the text field in the center of the layout area and the check box to the right (EAST)

We'll need the last two methods when we'll save the data to to device storage (flash)

This launches the text editing, on the device and opens the virtual keyboard

The BorderLayout constants and other constants are defined in the com.codename1.ui.CN class which we import statically into every Java source file with the code import static com.codename1.ui.CN.*; I assume in the code that this static import exists in all client side files!

This brings me to the discussion of layout managers. We've used two so far: BoxLayout and BorderLayout Let's dig deeper.

ayout Managers

layout manager is an algorithm that decides the size and location of the components within a ontainer. Every Container has a layout manager associated with it. The default layout manager is lowLayout.

o understand layouts we need to understand a basic concept about Component. Each component has "preferred size". This is the size in which a component "wants" to appear. E.g. for a Label the referred size will be the exact size that fits the label text, icon and padding of the component.

layout manager places a component based on its own logic and the preferred size (sometimes eferred to as "natural size"). A FlowLayout will just traverse the components based on the order they vere added and size/place them one after the other. When it reaches the end of the row it will go to he new row.

> *Use* **FlowLayout** *Only for Simple Things*
>
> FlowLayout is great for simple things but has issues when components change their sizes dynamically (like a text field). In those cases it can make bad decisions about line breaks and take up too much space

Flow Layout sizes components based on their preferred size and arranges them from left to right. When we reach the end of the line it breaks a line

Flow layout has several modes including a center mode that center aligns elements. It can align elements to the right and align vertically as well

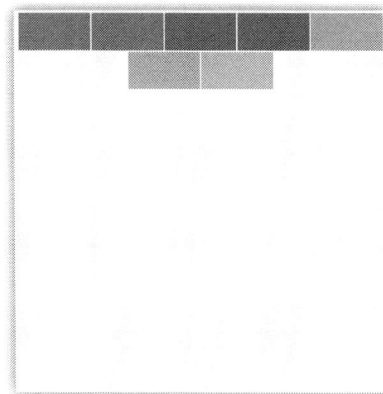

Figure 2. 8. Layout Manager Primer Part I

Border Layout can position elements in the NORTH, SOUTH, EAST, WEST and CENTER. Components take their preferred size on the opposing axis. Center takes up the available space by default

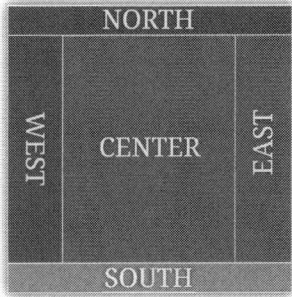

Border Layout has several modes including absolute center mode where the center component takes up only its preferred size

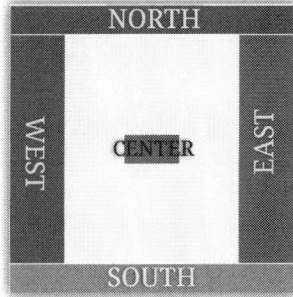

BoxLayout Y arranges components vertically, giving them the available width and their preferred height

BoxLayout X arranges components horizontally, giving them the available height and their preferred width

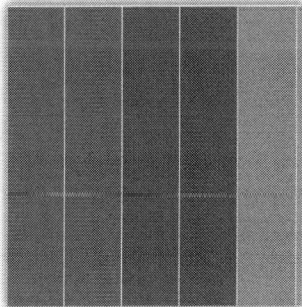

GridLayout arranges components in a grid and gives every element the same size to match the preferred size of the largest elements

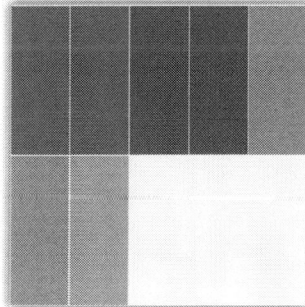

LayeredLayout places components one on top of the other. They have some spacing here so you can see the layers below

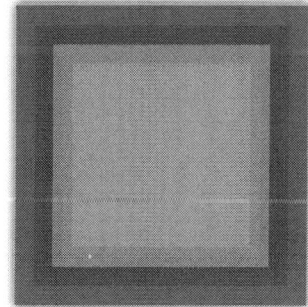

Figure 2. 9. Layout Manager Primer Part II

ℹ There are a few other interesting layouts in Codename One such as TableLayout, GridBagLayout, MigLayout etc. but I don't use them in the book

Scrolling doesn't work well for all types of layouts as the positioning algorithm within the layout might break. Scrolling on the Y axis works great for BoxLayout Y which is why I picked it for the TodoForm:

Table 2. 1. Scrolling in Layout Managers

Layout	Scrollable
Flow Layout	Possible on Y axis only
Border Layout	Scrolling is blocked
Box Layout Y	Scrollable only on the Y axis

Layout	Scrollable
Box Layout X	Scrollable only on the X axis
Grid Layout	Scrollable
LayeredLayout	Not scrollable (usually)

Nesting Scrollable Containers

Only one element can be scrollable within the hierarchy, otherwise if you drag your finger over the Form Codename One won't know which element you are trying to scroll. By default form's content pane is scrollable on the Y axis unless you explicitly disable it (setting the layout to BorderLayout implicitly disables scrolling).

It's important to notice that it's OK to have non-scrollable layouts, e.g. BorderLayout, as items within a scrollable container type. E.g. in the TodoApp we added TodoItem which uses BorderLayout into a scrollable BoxLayout Form.

Layouts can be divided into two distinct groups:

* Constraint Based - BorderLayout (and a few others I won't discuss in this book such as GridBagLayout, MigLayout and TableLayout)
* Regular - All of the other layout managers

When we add a Component to a Container with a regular layout we do so with a simple add method:

Listing 2. 11. Adding to a Regular Container

```
cnt. add(new Label ( "Just Added" ));
```

This works great for regular layouts but might not for constraint based layouts. A constraint based layout accepts another argument. E.g. BorderLayout needs a location for the Component:

Listing 2. 12. Adding to a Regular Container

```
cnt. add(NORTH,new Label ( "Just Added"));
```

This line assumes you have an import static com.codename1.ui.CN.*; in the top of the file. In BorderLayout (which is a constraint based layout) placing an item in the NORTH places it in the top of the Container.

Terse Syntax

Almost every layout allows us to add a component using several variants of the add method:

Listing 2. 13. Versions of add

```
Container  cnt  = new Container( BoxLayout. y());
cnt. add(new Label ( "Just Added" ));          ←  Regular add
cnt. addAll ( new Label ( "Adding Multiple" ),  ←  addAll accepts several components
     new Label ( "Second One"));                   and adds them in a batch

cnt. add(new Label ( "Chaining" )).             add returns the parent Container
     add(new Label ( "Value" ));   ←            instance so we can chain calls like that
```

In the race to make code "tighter" we can make this even shorter. Almost all layout managers have their own custom terse syntax style e.g.:

Listing 2. 14. Terse Syntax

```
Container  boxY = BoxLayout. encloseY ( cmp1, cmp2);
Container  boxX = BoxLayout. encloseX ( cmp3, cmp4);
Container  flowCenter  = FlowLayout.
     encloseCenter ( cmp5, cmp6);
                                        Most layouts have a version of enclose
                                        to encapsulate components within
```

FlowLayout has variants that support
aligning the components on various axis

To sum this up, we can use layout managers and nesting to create elaborate UI's that implicitly adapt to different screen sizes and device orientation.

Styles

2.2.2

The next stage in the evolution of the application is making it look good. To understand what that means I need to introduce you to 3 important terms in Codename One: Theme, Style and UIID.

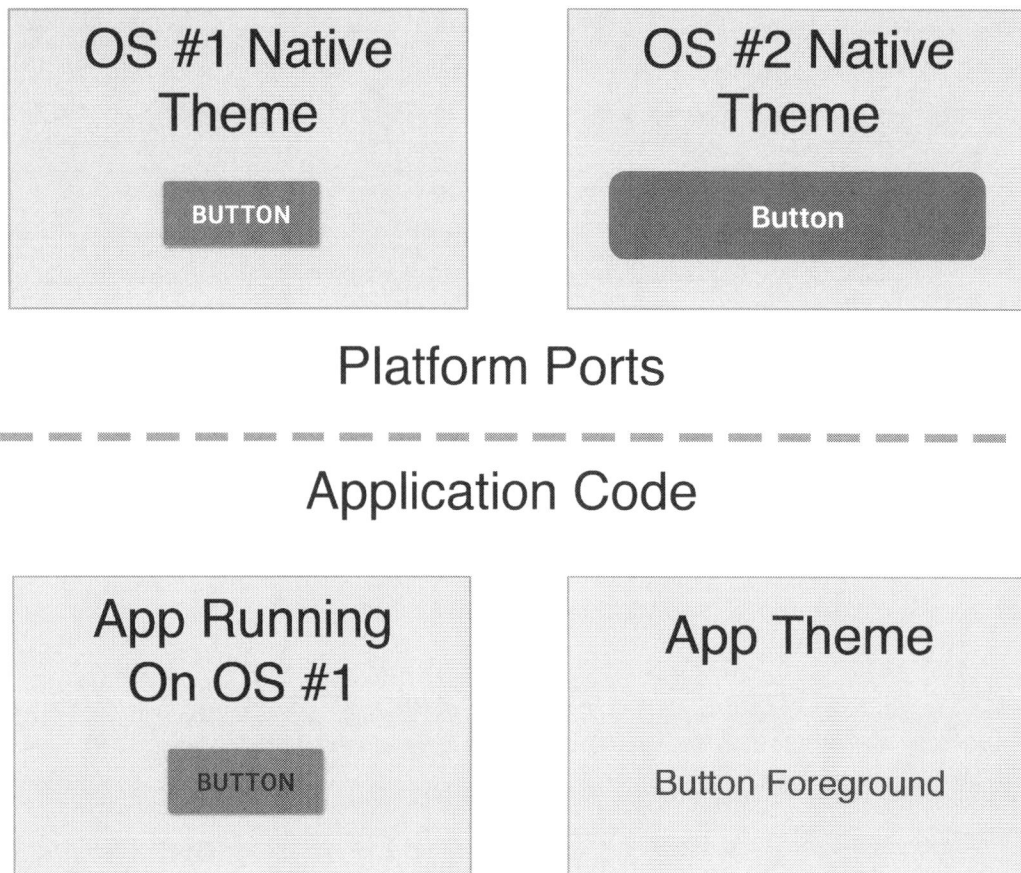

Figure 2. 10. Themes as Layers

Themes are very similar conceptually to CSS, in fact they can be created with CSS syntax as explained in Appendix C (page 399). The various Codename One ports ship with a native theme representing the appearance of the native OS UI elements. Every Codename One application has its own theme that derives the native theme and overrides behavior within it.

If the native theme has a button defined, we can override properties of that button in our theme. This allows us to customize the look while retaining some native appearances. This works by merging the theme to one big theme where our application theme overrides the definitions of the native theme. This is pretty similar to the cascading aspect of CSS if you are familiar with that.

Themes consist of a set of UIID definitions. Every component in Codename One has a UIID associated with it. UIID stands for User Interface Identifier. This UIID connects the theme to a specific component. You may recall we wrote this code before:

Listing 2. 15. setUIID on TextField

```
nameText.setUIID ( "Label" );   ◁───┤ This is a text field component that will look like a Label
```

Effectively we told the text field that it should use the UIID of Label when it's drawing itself. That way the text field looks like a Label. It's very common to do tricks like that in Codename One. E.g. button.setUIID("Label") which would make a button appear like a label and allow us to track clicks on a "Label".

The UIID's translate the theme elements into a set of Style objects. These Style objects get their initial values from the theme but can be further manipulated after the fact. So if I want to make the text field's foreground color red I could use this code:

Listing 2. 16. setUIID on TextField

```
nameText.getAllStyles().setFgColor(0xff0000);
```

The color is in hexadecimal RRGGBB format so 0xff00 would be green and 0xff0000 would be red.

getAllStyles() returns a Style object but why do we need "all" styles?

Each component can have one of 4 states and each state has a Style object. This means we can have 4 style objects per Component:

- **Unselected** - used when a component isn't touched and doesn't have focus. You can get that object with getUnselectedStyle() .

- **Selected** - used when a component is touched or if focus is drawn for non-touch devices. You can get that object with getSelectedStyle()

- **Pressed** - used when a component is pressed. Notice it's only applicable to buttons and button subclasses usually. You can get that object with getPressedStyle().

- **Disabled** - used when a component is disabled. You can get that object with getDisabledStyle().

The getAllStyles() method returns a special case Style object that lets you set the values of all 4 styles from one class so the code before would be equivalent to invoking all 4 setFgColor methods. However, getAllStyles() only works for setting properties not for getting them!

> Don't use getStyle() for manipulation. getStyle() returns the current Style object which means it will behave inconsistently. The paint method uses getStyle() as it draws the current state of the Component but other code should avoid that method. Use the specific methods instead: getUnselectedStyle(), getSelectedStyle(), getPressedStyle(), getDisabledStyle() and getAllStyles()

As you can see, it's a bit of a hassle to change styles from code which is why the theme is so appealing.

Designer Tool

As I mentioned before, we can customize the theme using a CSS like syntax which I discuss in Appendix C (page 399). Here I'll explain the usage of Codename One Designer and the simulator theming tools to customize the look of components.

The theme is stored in the theme.res file in the src root of the project. We load the theme file using this line of code in the init(Object) method in the main class of the application:

Listing 2. 17. Theme Loading Code

```
theme = UIManager. initFirstTheme( "/theme");
```

This code is shorthand for resource file loading and for the installation of theme. You could technically have more than one theme in a resource file at which point you could use initNamedTheme() instead. The resource file is a special file format that includes inside it several features:

- Themes
- Images
- Localization Bundles
- Data files

It also includes some legacy features such as the old GUI builder.

> **ℹ** I'm mentioning these for reference only I don't discuss the new/old GUI builders in this book

We can open the designer tool by double clicking the res file. The UI can be a bit overwhelming at first so I'll try to walk slowly through the steps.

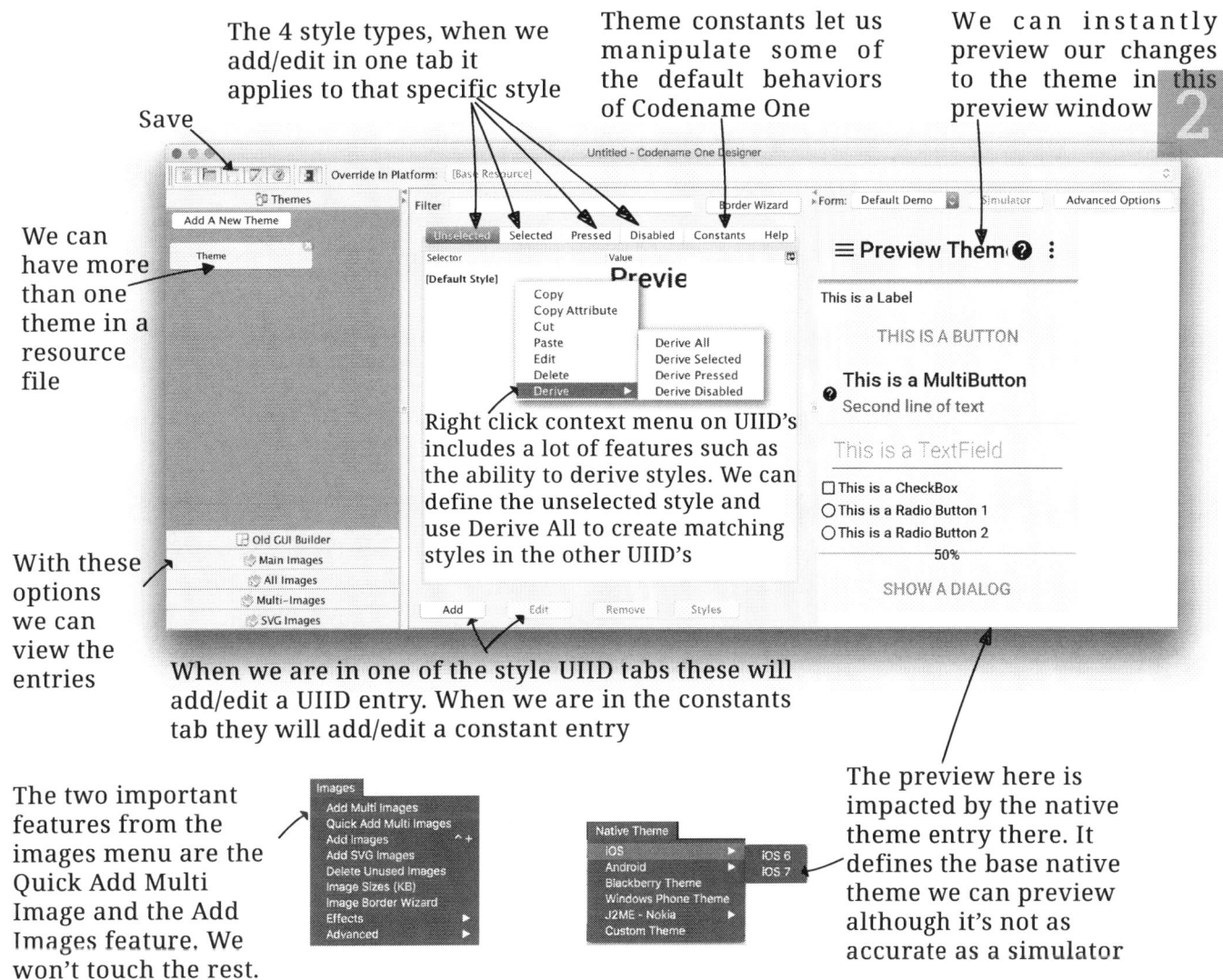

The 4 style types, when we add/edit in one tab it applies to that specific style

Save

Theme constants let us manipulate some of the default behaviors of Codename One

We can instantly preview our changes to the theme in this preview window

We can have more than one theme in a resource file

Right click context menu on UIID's includes a lot of features such as the ability to derive styles. We can define the unselected style and use Derive All to create matching styles in the other UIID's

With these options we can view the entries

When we are in one of the style UIID tabs these will add/edit a UIID entry. When we are in the constants tab they will add/edit a constant entry

The two important features from the images menu are the Quick Add Multi Image and the Add Images feature. We won't touch the rest.

The preview here is impacted by the native theme entry there. It defines the base native theme we can preview although it's not as accurate as a simulator

Figure 2. 11. Codename One Designer Feature Map

Lets start with something simple, like the title design of the app. For this we will need the todo-title.jpg file or equivalent. In my case the file is an 800x356 image but any reasonably sized image with the right colors will do.

Figure 2. 12. todo-title.jpg

The first step is to add the image. In the designer tool we go to the Images → Add Image menu. Pick your image in the file chooser.

Make sure to pick a JPEG or PNG image. It shouldn't be **huge**, 1024px wide would be plenty for this. Notice that if you pick a different format (e.g. Jpeg2000, tiff, svg, gif etc.) it might not work. Some images, specifically those from cell phone cameras, include orientation information and that would be ignored. If your image is flipped, make sure to edit it first

1 Select the Images menu and click Add Images

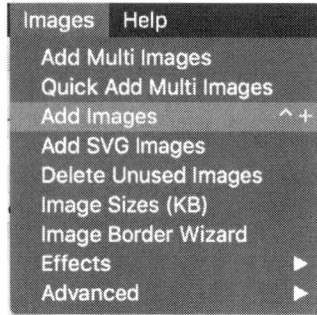

2 Pick the image in the file picker dialog box

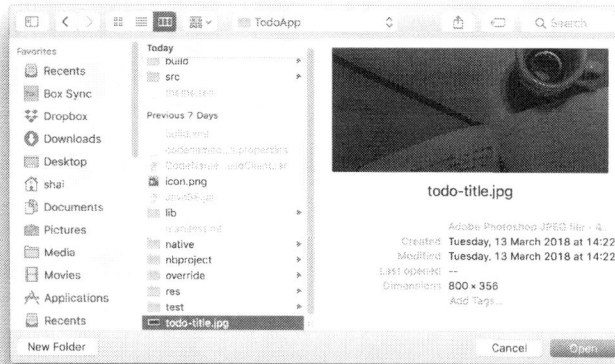

3 You should be able to see the image in the Main Images section

Figure 2. 13. Add a New Image

Multi Images

As I mentioned before, images look radically different on devices with different densities. A common solution is to bundle multiple versions of the image; One for each DPI. Codename One takes that same approach and also simplifies it with multi-images.

A Multi Image is a concept that exists only within the resource file. When we read a Multi Image from the file, it's indistinguishable from a regular image. During the resource file loading process only the image closest to the current DPI is loaded and the rest of the images are skipped.

This begs the question: why not use a regular image and just scale it?

- Scaling images on the device produces some artifacts in scaling as the high quality scaling algorithms are very slow

- To scale we'd want the largest possible image as scaling down is superior to scaling up, this would be memory intensive

Still there is an obvious tradeoff of application size when working with Multi Images so use this feature with care.

Codename One supports the following densities for multi-images:

Table 2. 2. Densities

Constant	Density	Example Device
DENSITY_VERY_LOW	~ 88 ppi	
DENSITY_LOW	~ 120 ppi	Android ldpi devices
DENSITY_MEDIUM	~ 160 ppi	iPhone 3GS, iPad, Android mdpi devices
DENSITY_HIGH	~ 240 ppi	Android hdpi devices
DENSITY_VERY_HIGH	~ 320 ppi	iPhone 4, iPad Air 2, Android xhdpi devices
DENSITY_HD	~ 540 ppi	iPhone 6+, Android xxhdpi devices
DENSITY_560	~ 750 ppi	Android xxxhdpi devices
DENSITY_2HD	~ 1000 ppi	
DENSITY_4K	~ 1250ppi	

To add a Multi Image we usually create the resource for a high DPI device we then use the menu option Images → Quick Add Multi Image to pick said image and select its DPI from the list of DPI's. E.g. we can ask our designer for a resource designed for the Pixel 2 XL which is a DENSITY_HD device. Then use the Quick Add Multi Image menu and select DENSITY_HD in the following prompt.

The system automatically generates all the other DPI's by scaling down from the DENSITY_HD image and scaling up to the higher DPI's. You can then select the Multi Image entry in the designer and customize individual images within if necessary.

Since scaling is done on the desktop it uses the high quality scale algorithm. Notice you can manually customize individual resolutions of the Multi Image as well.

Now we can go back to the theme view in the designer tool and press the Add button in the Unselected tab.

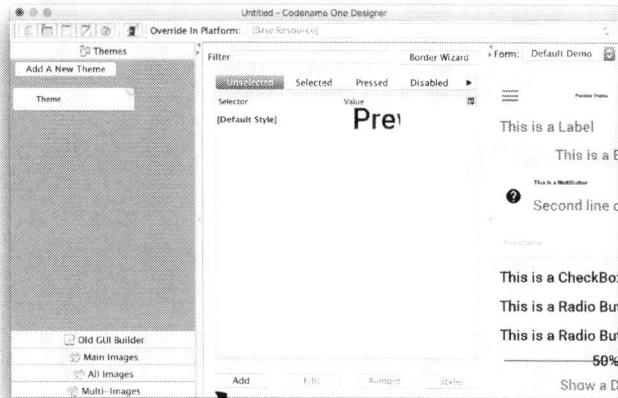

Add Theme Entry

Figure 2. 14. The Add Button

After pressing that button we should see something that looks like this:

To set the background image of the Toolbar we need to uncheck "Derive"

We are adding an entry in the Unselected

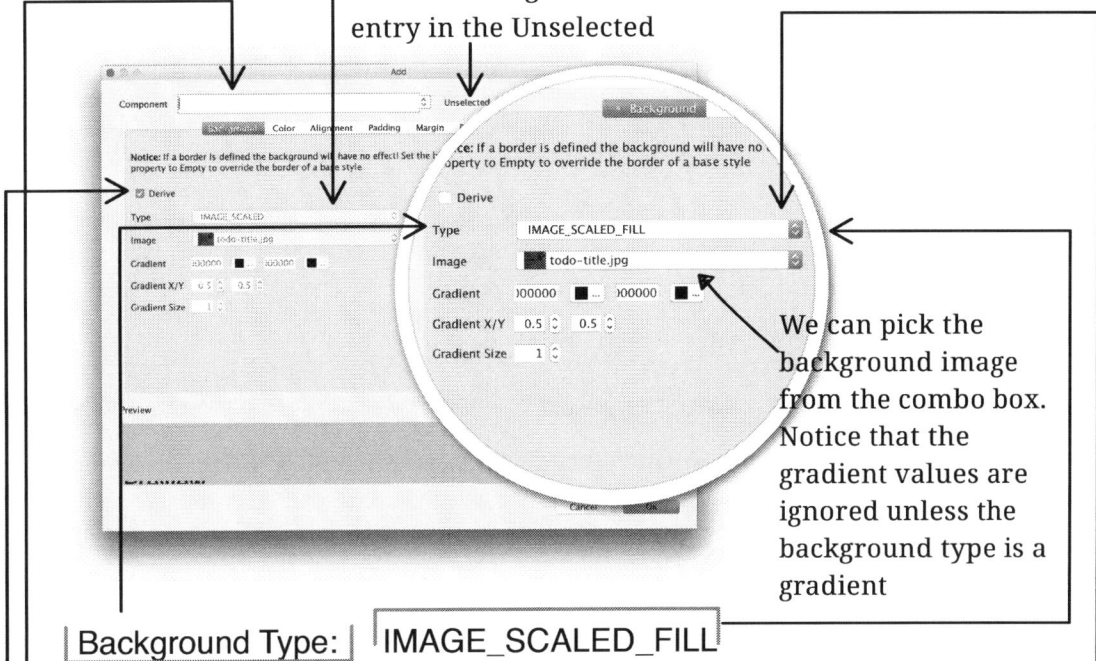

We can pick the background image from the combo box. Notice that the gradient values are ignored unless the background type is a gradient

Background Type: IMAGE_SCALED_FILL

The UIID we are adding or editing. You can type in any arbitrary name when adding. You can also pick from pre-existing options in the combo box. Right now we can type Toolbar here

When Derive is checked we derive this specific attribute from the native theme

There are many background type options. Here I pick IMAGE_SCALED_FILL which will scale the image to take up all the available space and keep aspect ratio

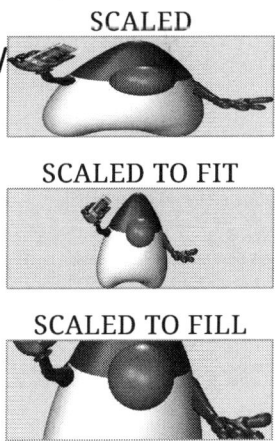

SCALED

SCALED TO FIT

SCALED TO FILL

Figure 2. 15. Add the Theme Entry for the Toolbar

💡 Don't forget to press the save button in the designer after making changes

There are several other options in the add theme entry dialog. Lets go over them and review what we should do for each tab in this UI:

The foreground color of the component e.g. the text color of a label in this case we don't need the foreground as we'll style it in the "Title" UIID

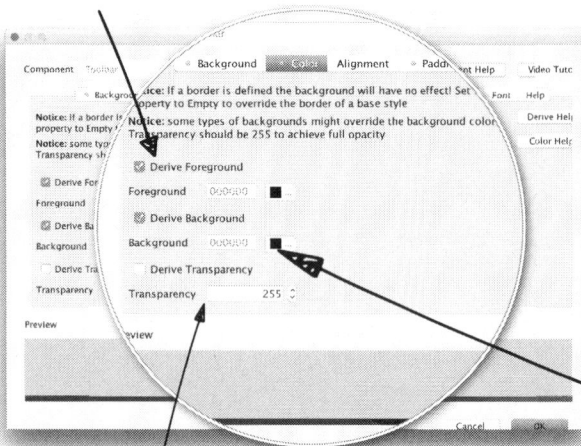

Alignment can be left/right or center. This isn't applicable to all components and will only work for components deriving from Label or TextArea.

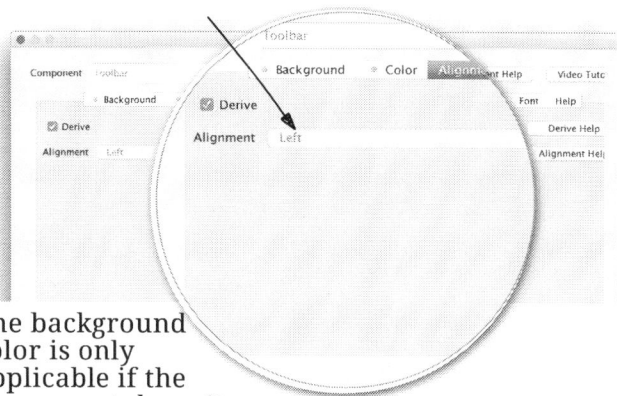

The background color is only applicable if the component doesn't have a border and doesn't have a background type

Transparency of 255 indicates completely opaque and 0 indicates complete transparency. It's best to define it to 255 as the image we show is opaque

Padding is the extra space the component takes beyond its "natural size". It can be expressed in millimeters, pixels or percentage of the screen size. We almost always use millimeters for padding. Notice that in the screenshot below I ignore the right margin as the title on Android is aligned to the left

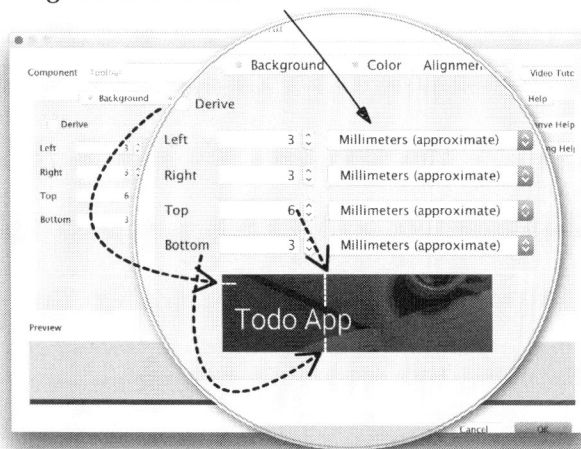

Margin is the space between this component and the other components next to it. We often set it to 0 when we want to take up available space

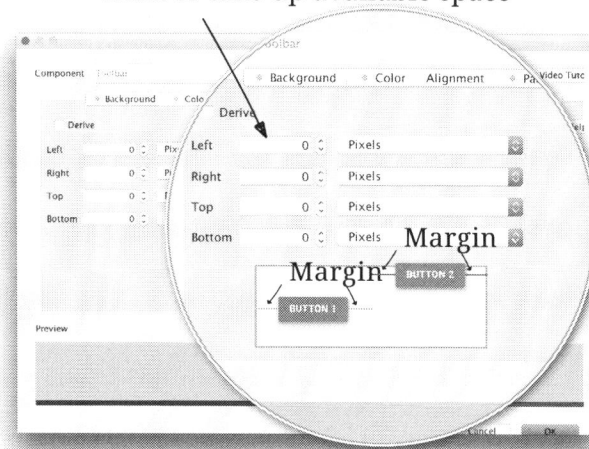

Figure 2. 16. The Rest of the Add Theme Entry Dialog - Part I

When a border is defined it overrides the background and color. That's why it's important to define it as "Empty" sometimes. The Toolbar has a shadow border defined on Android. We want to disable that so our background image will show. We can edit the border with the "..." button and we can create a 9-piece border using the "Image Border Wizard"

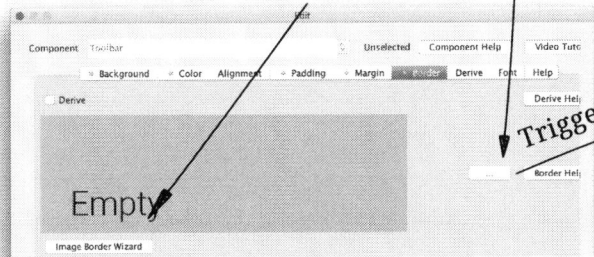

This is a round border we use in the FloatingActionButton

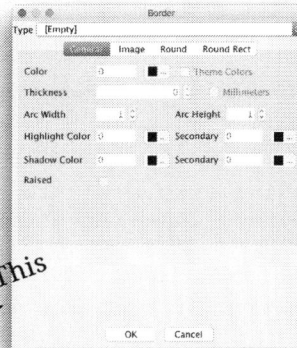

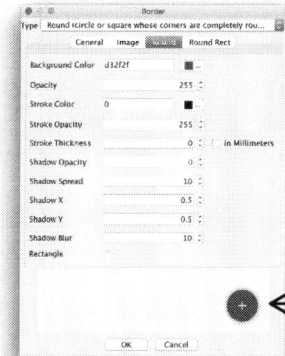

Derive inherits the styling of the given UIID you can type the UIID on the left and select the right state on the right

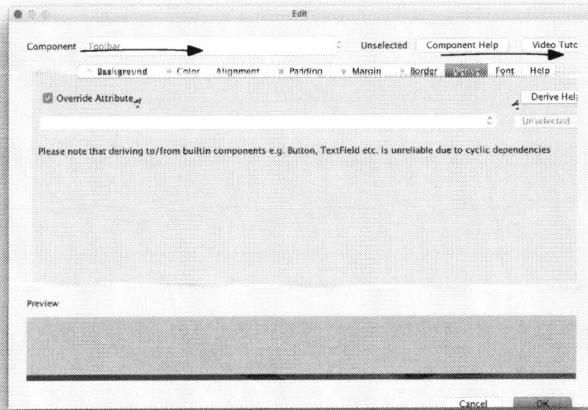

There are multiple simple border types in the border editing dialog but the ones we use most of all are the Round, RoundRect, Line, Underline and Image (AKA 9-piece)

When we select the Round Border we can create either a circle or a pill shape (by activating the rectangle flag)

The Font UI is somewhat confusing due to a heavy dose of legacy features. For modern applications it makes sense to pick a native true type font from the combo box here and size it in millimeters

Toolbar doesn't need a font since it doesn't have text so I chose to show the font styling for Title because fonts are important

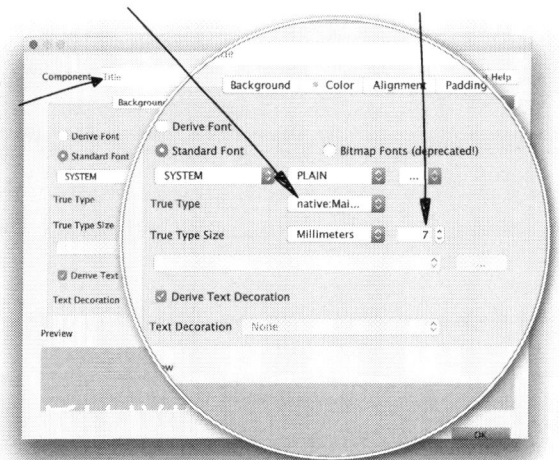

Figure 2. 17. The Rest of the Add Theme Entry Dialog - Part II

Let's pause for a moment. We can't go through the entire book and post images like this for every UIID we run into... It would turn into a picture book!

Furthermore, you might prefer to work with CSS instead of using the designer tool. So we need a more concise way to express the settings in the designer tool. In this case I can write the settings for the Toolbar UIID like this:

Listing 2. 18. Toolbar Styling

```
Background Type: IMAGE_SCALED_FILL
Transparency: 255
Padding Left: 3mm ←                    ─┤Notice I enumerate the padding for each side
Padding Right: 3mm
Padding Top: 6mm
Padding Bottom: 3mm ←
Margin: 0px ←                          ─┤Since the margin is identical on all
Border: Empty                            │sides I only list it as margin
```

ignore everything that I didn't derive. This is far more concise and in some regards much simpler than the images!

If you are still in doubt, you can use the project sources and open the file using the designer tool to review the settings in the resource file.

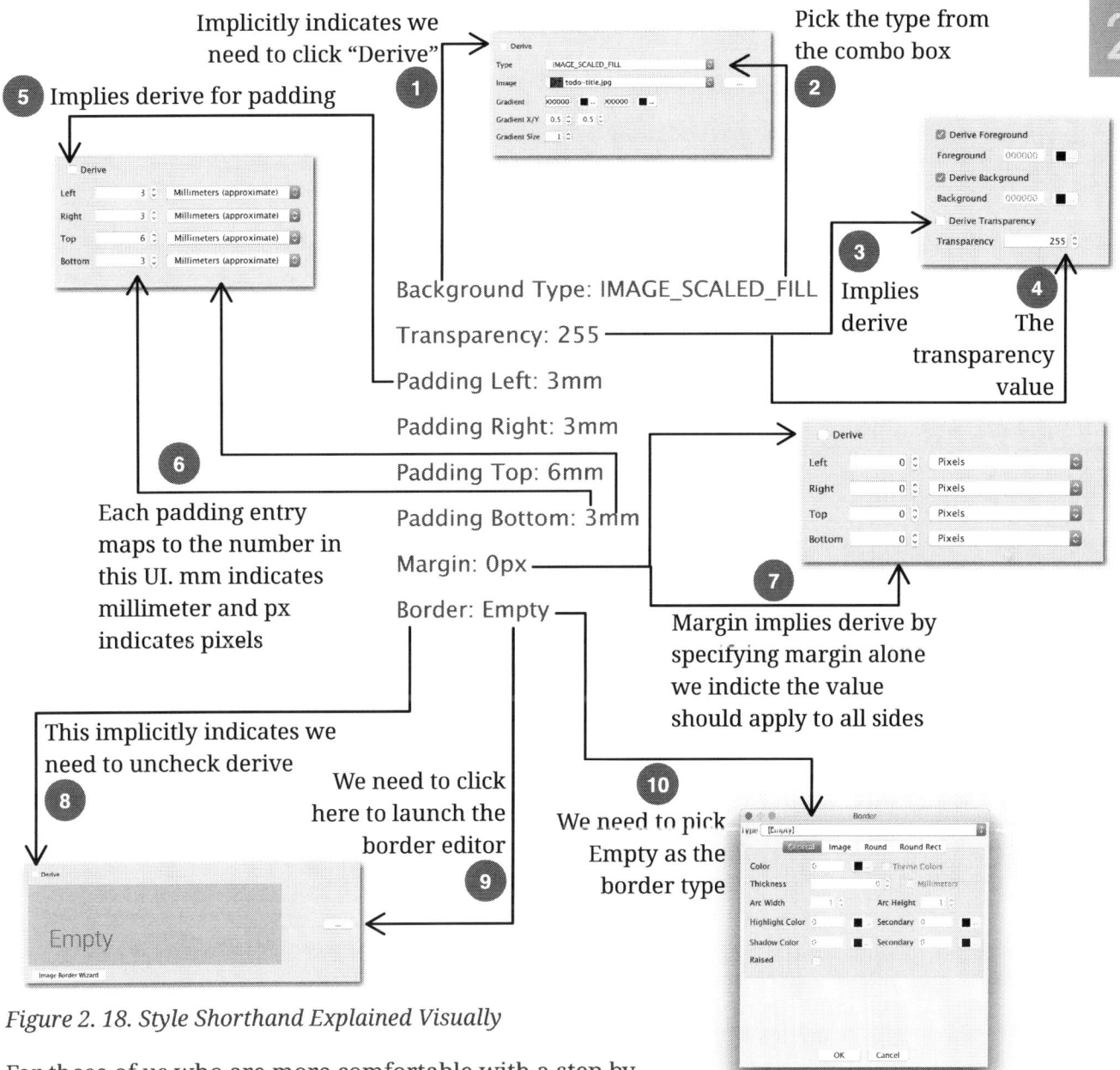

Figure 2. 18. Style Shorthand Explained Visually

For those of us who are more comfortable with a step by step guide this is the exact process to produce this style:

- Double click the theme.res file in the src directory to open the designer tool

- Click Theme on the left hand side

- Click the Add button on the bottom of the screen. You should see the Add dialog box with the Background tab selected

Background Type: IMAGE_SCALED_FILL

- Uncheck the Derive check box
- Pick IMAGE_SCALED_FILL in the Type combo box. This assumes you already added a single image to the theme, it should be selected already in the Image combo box

Transparency: 255

- Switch to the Color tab
- Uncheck the Derive Transparency checkbox
- Type into the Transparency spinner 255

Padding Left: 3mm
Padding Right: 3mm
Padding Top: 6mm
Padding Bottom: 3mm

- Switch to the Padding tab
- Uncheck the Derive checkbox
- Fill into the spinners the values 3, 3, 6 and 3 in this order
- In all the combo boxes pick Millimeters (approximate)

Margin: 0px

- Switch to the Margin tab
- Uncheck the Derive checkbox
- Fill into all the spinners the value 0

Border: Empty

- Switch to the Border tab
- Uncheck the Derive checkbox
- Click the ... button on the right hand side. This should open a Border dialog
- Pick Empty in the Type combo box
- Click OK to accept the dialog

- Click OK to add the new entry

- Select File → Save to save your changes

Picking the Right Font

Before we proceed I'd like to take a moment to discuss fonts. Codename One lets you place a TTF font file in the project and work with that. If I was aiming for 100% pixel perfect UI I might have done that but for most cases the native OS font is the best option.

Codename One has several builtin "native:" font families that map to the OS native font for the various platform e.g. on iOS 9+ this will map to the San Francisco font and in older OS's to Helvetica Neue. On Android this will use Roboto and so forth. There are multiple types of "native" font options ranging in weight and style but I mostly use the "light" version (named native:MainLight in the designer tool) which closely resembles the Uber font.

Discovering UIID's and Edit In Place

You know that the Toolbar is the UIID for the title area because I told you so. But how would you have discovered that on your own?

For that we need the Component Inspector tool which you can launch from the simulator's Simulate → Component Inspector menu option.

Once launched, you should see the inspector UI and you can gain insight into the layout/theme of the running application.

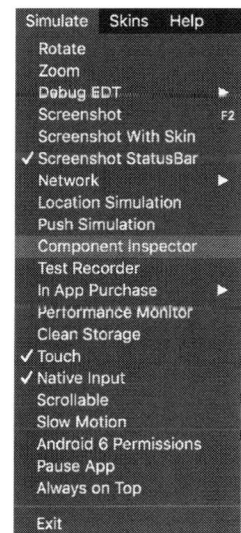

Figure 2. 19. Launching the Component Inspector

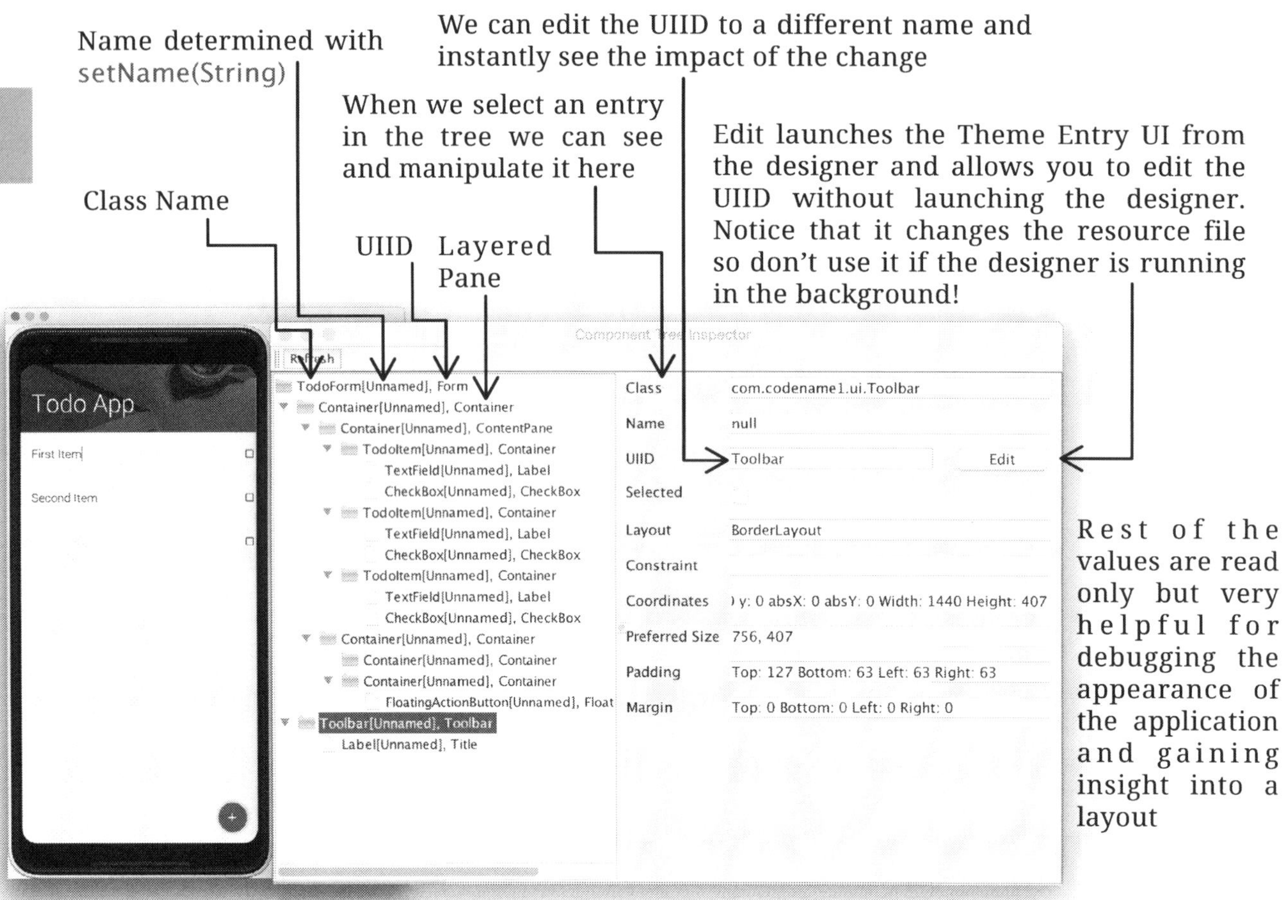

Name determined with
setName(String)

We can edit the UIID to a different name and instantly see the impact of the change

Class Name

When we select an entry in the tree we can see and manipulate it here

Edit launches the Theme Entry UI from the designer and allows you to edit the UIID without launching the designer. Notice that it changes the resource file so don't use it if the designer is running in the background!

UIID   Layered Pane

Rest of the values are read only but very helpful for debugging the appearance of the application and gaining insight into a layout

Figure 2. 20. The Component Inspector Tool

Now that we have a grasp of the tools and we understand how to theme the UI, let's go over the other elements. First we have the Title which I already mentioned before. The Toolbar UIID contains the background image but the Title UIID contains the text of the title.

The Title UIID is **much** simpler:

Listing 2. 19. Title Styling

Foreground Color: 0xffffff ← White text for the title, notice you can just type the hex value into the foreground color field in the designer

Transparency: 0 ← Transparent background means we don't need a background color

Font: native:MainLight 7mm ← That's a relatively thin large font, standard fonts are usually between 2.5mm to 3mm

Once this is done the Todo title is very close to the final result. You can see what we have so far here on the right.

Todo App

Figure 2. 21. Title on Android Hence the Left Alignment

ℹ️ Notice that the title in iOS would be center aligned because the alignment attribute is derived from the native OS theme

The title looks almost done. Let's move to the design of the body, I'll split the design of the body into two steps to simplify it.

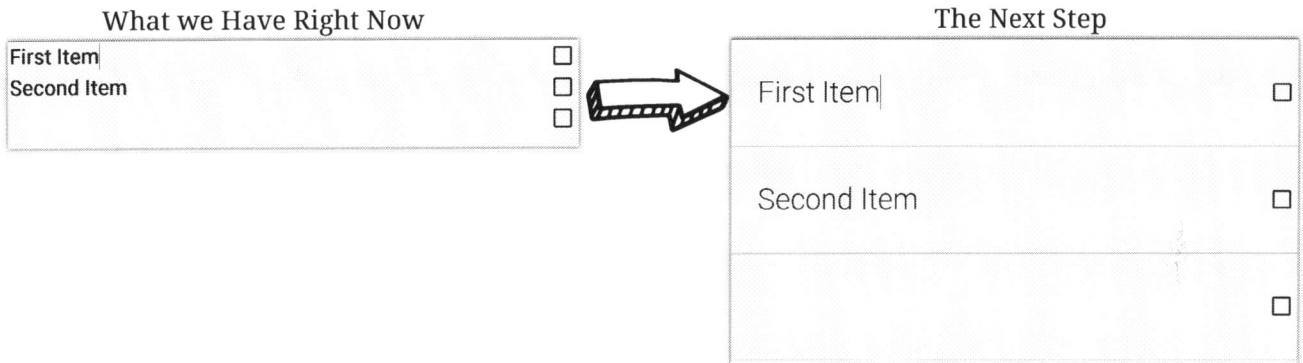

What we Have Right Now | The Next Step

First Item
Second Item

First Item

Second Item

Figure 2. 22. What we have now and the Next Step

Let's start with the obvious. The image on the left is compact and demonstrates clearly the importance of good padding/font choices!

As you recall we styled the text fields with the Label UIID. We can fix the padding and font by using the following style on Label:

Listing 2. 20. Label Styling

```
Padding Left: 3mm
Padding Right: 3mm
Padding Top: 4mm
Padding Bottom: 4mm
Font: native:MainLight 3.5mm
```

💡 Use Derive All in the designer tool to apply this style to the other style modes. When I don't say otherwise do it by default on every Component UIID that can be selected/edited

All this work brought us close to our final destination. The next part of the change would be the lines between the entries. Our gut reaction might be to define an underline for Label. That would work but since the Label doesn't reach the edge of the Form we would have a gap.

So what we really want is to underline the whole TodoItem entry. We can do

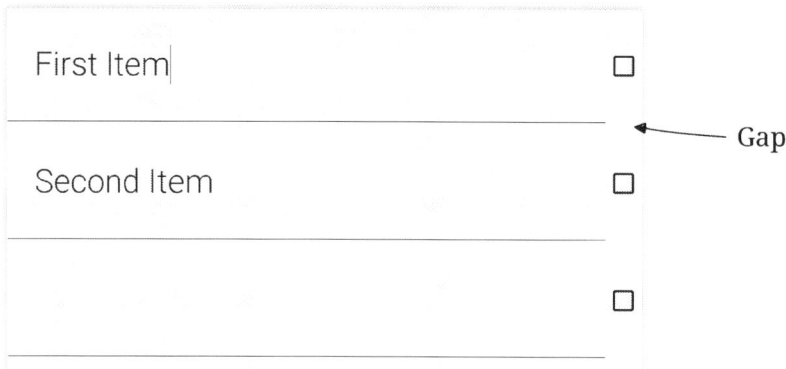

Figure 2. 23. Why Underline on Label isn't what we Want

that in code using this code in the TodoItem constructor:

Listing 2. 21. Underline the TodoItem Using Java Code

Changes made to this object will automatically apply to all 4 style objects

```
Style  s = getAllStyles();
s. setPaddingUnit ( Style . UNIT_TYPE_PIXELS);
s. setPadding( 0,  2,  0,  0);
s. setBorder(Border. createLineBorder ( 2,  0xcccccc));
```

We want to define padding in pixels so we can draw a 2 pixel border

Padding is defined as top/bottom/left/right order. We leave a two pixel padding for the border

We draw a gray underline 2 pixel border

> **ℹ** We don't need this code if we use the styling approach through setUIID()

Currently a TodoItem has the Container UIID. When we set the Style object value we change it on an individual object instance. So these changes don't impact other Container instances.

> **🔥** Customizing the Container UIID in the theme is a bad idea. A lot of things rely on the Container UIID and if you change it the impact could be wide

Still I'd rather do things in the theme normally and we can, we just need to change the UIID of the TodoItem class like this:

Listing 2. 22. Underline the TodoItem Using the Theme

```
setUIID ( "Task" );
```

Then I can define the style in the designer tool as such:

Listing 2. 23. Task Styling

```
Padding Left: 0px
Padding Right: 0px
Padding Top: 0px
Padding Bottom: 2px
Border: Underline 0xcccccc 2px
```

And this brings us almost to the last stage of the design changes. We have two more items we'd need to add/change to reach the final design.

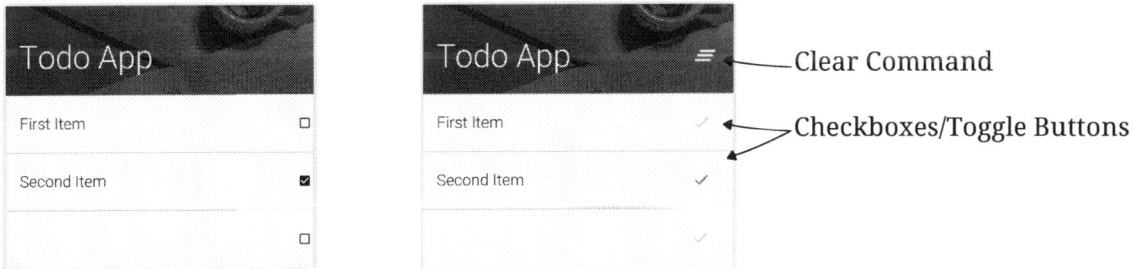

Clear Command

Checkboxes/Toggle Buttons

Figure 2. 24. Final UI Changes for the Todo App

These two final changes to the UI combine code and theming. Lets start with the checkboxes. I used the CheckBox class to represent those. I could customize the image of the CheckBox using the theme, but that isn't very flexible. Instead I chose to add these lines to the TodoItem constructor:

Listing 2. 24. CheckBox to Toggle Button in the TodoItem Constructor

```
done.setToggle (true);
FontImage.setMaterialIcon(done,
    FontImage .MATERIAL_CHECK, 4);
```

CheckBox can look like a toggle button and effectively hide the default check mark

We set the icon for the checkmark manually from the material icons

Both CheckBox and RadioButton can act as if they are a button and hide the checkmark symbol. This allows a lot of flexibility. However, this also means we need to customize the styling. Once we enable the toggle mode of a Checkbox its UIID changes from CheckBox to ToggleButton.

To make this look like the desired image we need to do the following:

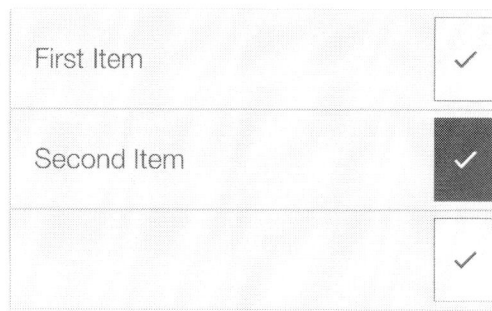

Figure 2. 25. The Current Result Looks Like This

Listing 2. 25. ToggleButton Styling

Foreground Color: 0xcfcfcf
Transparency: 0 ←
Border: Empty ←

We don't want a background color as we'll use the background of the parent

The border drawn around the button by default should be disabled explicitly

We also need to override the selected and pressed states of the ToggleButton class:

Listing 2. 26. ToggleButton Selected and Pressed Styling

Foreground Color: 0x6868FD ←
Border: Empty ←
Derive: ToggleButton Unselected

We set the foreground when a button is pressed which will make it purple

We define an empty border as the toggle button has a border too

We derive other settings from the unselected version of the component

This makes the toggle checkboxes act like the ones in the finished version and the only thing that remains is the clear command.

The commands fit into the toolbar and are added using syntax such as this:

Listing 2. 27. TodoForm Constructor Adding the Clear Command

```
getToolbar().addMaterialCommandToRightBar("" ,
    FontImage.MATERIAL_CLEAR_ALL, e -> clearAll());
```

Adds a command with a material icon

We pick the icon as clear all and invoke the clearAll method when it's clicked

I'll get to clearAll() soon but I want to finish the styling first.

There are many ways to add commands and they don't have to use the material icons. It's just convenient.

iOS	Android

Figure 2. 26. Title Command Before Styling

If you look at the UI before we apply the style you will notice the command image is also much smaller. The FontImage class uses the size of the existing font in the style to define the size of the icon. So if we increase the size of the font in the TitleCommand UIID it should apply to the icon too.

Listing 2. 28. TitleCommand Styling

```
Foreground Color: 0xffffff
Transparency: 0
Font: native:MainLight 5mm
```

The title was styled as 7mm so this is reasonably smaller

With this, the application should now look like it does in figure 2.1 (page 36) and the UI design aspect is complete!

But before we move on to event handling let's cover the clearAll method. In order to do that I'll also need to stub save and load methods which I'll implement later in the persistence section:

```
private void clearAll() {  ←───────────── Clear all removes all of the checked Todo items
    int  cc = getContentPane().getComponentCount();
    for ( int  i  = cc - 1 ;  i  >= 0 ;  i --) { ←
        TodoItem t  = (TodoItem) getContentPane().getComponentAt ( i );
        if ( t . isChecked() )  {
            t . remove();
        }
    }
    save();
    getContentPane().animateLayout(300);
}
private  void  load()  {}
private  void  save()  {}
```

We're looping backwards from the end. That means that if we remove a component the offset still won't change

If an item is checked we remove it from its parent (the content pane)

This is a type of revalidate() that animates. After the components are removed the remaining components will slide into place for 300ms

We'll implement these later in the chapter, for now a stub will do

And with this, clear will work as well by clearing the checked items from our todo list.

Event Handling

Now that we have the UI working lets dig deeper into the functionality and events. I've used events before in the code but skimmed over them e.g. this is code we had for handling the click event on the FloatingActionButton:

Listing 2. 30. TodoForm Constructor The FloatingActionButton Event

```
fab.addActionListener (e  -> addNewItem());
```

If you are new to Java or haven't used it in a while this code might look weird. It's a lambda expression which was added to Java 8. The equivalent code in Java 5 would be:

Listing 2. 31. The FloatingActionButton Event Without Lambda

```
fab.addActionListener(new ActionListener() {
    public void actionPerformed(ActionEvent e) {
        addNewItem();
    }
});
```

Action listener is an interface from com.codename1.ui.events

This is the same addNewItem call we had in the lambda, the rest is boilerplate

2

You will notice that the lambda expression strips away a lot of the "dead weight code". If we have more than one line of code to write we can still use a lambda expression with curly brackets as such:

Listing 2. 32. The FloatingActionButton Event Lambda with Brackets

```
fab. addActionListener (e -> {
    addNewItem();
});
```

Notice we also had to add a semicolon

Observers and Event Types

The approach of adding a listener is called the observer pattern and it's common for most modern UI frameworks/OS's. We can register an interest in receiving an event and deregister that interest when we no longer need the event (e.g. removeActionListener).

💡 We usually don't need to remove a listener to "cleanup". The garbage collector will remove both the component and the listener together when we are done with both

ActionListener is the workhorse of events in Codename One but there are also some other similar event types such as DataChangedListener which is used to monitor changes to the TextField as you type etc.

We can demonstrate event handling in our app by adding the infrastructure for persistence support. You might notice that the UI of the app doesn't include a save button. Mobile apps usually save automatically. This makes sense... You might work on something, get a phone call and forget about it. Saving implicitly makes a lot of sense for a mobile device.

mentioned the save() method before. I'd like to create event handlers that invoke it whenever data changes. To do this I'll need to first change some things in TodoForm:

Listing 2. 33. Event Changes to TodoForm

```java
public class TodoForm extends Form {
    private ActionListener saver;
    public TodoForm() {
        // most of the constructor didn't change          We will add a load() method soon
        load();  ←————————————————————————              similar to the save() method
    }
    private ActionListener getAutoSave() {
        if (saver == null) {  ←————————————             saver is an ActionListener
            saver = (e) -> save();                       that invokes save()
        }
        return saver;
    }
    private void addNewItem() {
        TodoItem td = new TodoItem("", false,
            getAutoSave());  ←————————————              saver is passed to the TodoItem where
        // rest of the method didn't change             it receives change notifications
    }
    // rest of the class didn't change
}
```

This implies changes to the TodoItem:

Listing 2. 34. Event Changes in the TodoItem

```java
public class TodoItem extends Container {
    public TodoItem(String name, boolean checked, ActionListener onChange) {
        // most of the constructor didn't change
        nameText.addActionListener(onChange);  ←——┐ We use the action listener and bind
        done.addActionListener(onChange);          it directly to the saver call
    }
    // rest of the class didn't change
}
```

This code invokes save on any UI change without an explicit action from the user.

Event Dispatch Thread

Codename One is single threaded. All events and almost all method calls occur on a single thread called the Event Dispatch Thread (EDT). By using just one thread Codename One can avoid complex synchronization code and focus on simple functionality that assumes only one thread.

> You can assume that all code will occur on a single thread and avoid complex synchronization logic within your own code

Every call you receive from Codename One will occur on the EDT. E.g. every event, calls to paint(), lifecycle calls (start() etc.) always occurs on the EDT.

This is pretty powerful, however it means that as long as your code is processing nothing else can happen in Codename One!

> If your code takes too long to execute then no painting or event processing will occur during that time, so a call to Thread.sleep() will actually stop everything!
> This is commonly known as "blocking the EDT" and would grind your performance to a halt

When you need to run a CPU intensive task you should spawn a Thread and do the work there. Codename One's networking code automatically spawns its own network thread and performs all networking on separate threads. However, this also poses a problem...

Codename One assumes all modifications to the UI are performed on the EDT but if we spawned a separate thread (or did networking). How do we force our modifications back into the EDT?

For that purpose we have two methods:

- callSerially(Runnable) – a thread can invoke callSerially to execute the given Runnable object on the EDT
- callSeriallyAndWait(Runnable) – identical to callSerially but it returns when the Runnable finished its execution

Listing 2. 35. callSerially Sample

```
myButton addActionListener(e -> {
    new Thread() {                          We are on the EDT in the event
        public void run() {                 callback, we launch a new thread
            runIntenseComputation();        This is a CPU intensive method that
            callSerially(() -> updateTheUI());   doesn't change the UI
        }
    }.start();
});
                     updateTheUI will run on the EDT as
                     it's invoked from a callSerially
```

This allows us to use a thread for a CPU intensive task and get back into the UI when we are done.

> 🛈 Codename One supports a more elaborate tool called invokeAndBlock which spawns a thread while "legally" blocking the EDT

2.2.4
IO and Storage

There are 3 standard storage locations in Codename One:

- **Storage** - This is an OS specific storage location that's closely coupled to the app. It's normally very portable and also simple, things such as directories or paths aren't supported

- **FileSystemStorage** - This is often confused with storage because in some OS's there is an overlap. This is the native OS File System. It provides more capabilities such as directories. The downside is complexity and potential compatibility issues due to device differences. This system always expects a full file path

- **SQLite** - The standard SQL database built into iOS, Android and Windows devices

I'll only focus on Storage right now as we won't use the others in this application. Lets look at the implementation of save() and load().

Listing 2. 36. Save and Load in TodoForm

```
private void save() {
    try (DataOutputStream dos = new DataOutputStream(
            createStorageOutputStream("todo-list-of-items"))) {
        dos.writeInt(
            getContentPane().getComponentCount());
        for(Component c : getContentPane()) {
            TodoItem i = (TodoItem)c;
            dos.writeBoolean(i.isChecked());
            dos.writeUTF(i.getText());
        }
    } catch(IOException err) {
        Log.e(err);
        ToastBar.showErrorMessage("Error saving todo list!");
    }
}
private void load() {
    if(existsInStorage("todo-list-of-items")) {
        try(DataInputStream dis = new DataInputStream(
                createStorageInputStream("todo-list-of-items"));) {
            int size = dis.readInt();
            for(int iter = 0 ; iter < size ; iter++) {
                boolean checked = dis.readBoolean();
                TodoItem i =
                    new TodoItem(dis.readUTF(), checked, getAutoSave();
                add(i);
            }
        } catch (IOException err) {
            Log.e(err);
            ToastBar.showErrorMessage( "Error loading todo list!");
        }
    }
}
```

This opens a storage file for writing with the given name

DataOutputStream provides convenient methods like writeInt and writeUTF

We write the values of every component in binary form

Exceptions aren't likely for this case but if they happen we log them and show an error message using the ToastBar

The first time we run the input file won't exist

Notice that this is the exact inverse of the write method

The ToastBar class presents a small notification typically at the bottom of the Form. These notifications expire by default after a few seconds

could have used the JSON parser or some other tool for writing/reading the data but I chose to do something simple right now.

We can now run the Todo App and it will remember everything we add and change within the application. The Todo app is now complete!

2.3

Summary

In this chapter, we learned:

- How to manage layout and scrolling behavior so we can build complex component hierarchies
- Styling components using the designer tool and UIID's to create elaborate looks for our applications
- How to use background threads with Codename One and go back and forth to the main event dispatch thread. We can thus create more performant applications by leveraging the CPU more effectively
- How to save and load information from persistent storage so our application can retain data between executions

After this chapter you should have enough understanding of Codename One to get you through the book. I'll still take detours along the way to explain some things I didn't get to in these first two chapters but I'm anxious to dive into the Uber app as I'm sure you are!

There is still one small chapter and then we can get started...

Spring Boot Overview 3

This chapter covers:

- What is Spring Boot?
- Why use Spring Boot?
- Why MySQL?

This book focuses on mobile development so we won't discuss server code as much. However, we will need a basic server in order to implement a clone of Uber and for that we'll use Spring Boot.

If you want to learn Spring Boot I recommend picking up a more comprehensive book dedicated to it. I will barely scratch the surface of this amazing tool. But if you just want to "get by" this tutorial should be enough to understand the contents of this book. That's one of the cool things about Spring Boot, you don't need to know much in order to use it very effectively.

You can also check out the Spring Boot website which has plenty of material about Spring boot that you can browse online: projects.spring.io/spring-boot/

This chapter is very light in content and very high level. I go into more detail in Day 2 when I cover the practicality of building the server.

What's Spring Boot? 3.1

Spring Boot makes it easy to create stand-alone, production-grade Spring based Applications that you can "just run". We take an opinionated view of the Spring platform and third-party libraries so you can get started with minimum fuss. Most Spring Boot applications need very little Spring configuration.

— Spring.io description of Spring Boot

find that description a bit high level but it's very accurate. To me Spring Boot is about making server side Java simple. One of the common complaints about Java is how hard it is to "just get started". This is especially true in server side Java EE or in Spring (as opposed to Spring Boot). When you want to build a server in Java you need a lot of configuration, setup and have endless options.

That's great for some advanced users but that results in complexity across the board when compared to tools such as Ruby on Rails. In some regards Spring Boot is the answer to that, a one stop solution.

Spring Boot is a full fledged single stop solution that you can configure initially via a simple wizard. The server can be run directly like any other JAR and requires no server program or storage API's. The web server is embedded into a self contained jar together with all the API's e.g. database connectivity etc. In that sense it "feels" like creating a simple desktop application and hides a lot of the complexities you normally see with Java server development.

Why Spring Boot

There are several options for building a server but I chose to go with Spring Boot because:

- It's Java based - that means the client and server code are written in the same language, which is a huge advantage

- It's popular

- It's modern

- It's easy to use and install

- It's scalable – from a small cheap install all the way up to enterprise grade scale

- Works with all major IDE's

Having said that most of the code we do in the server is easily replicable in other technologies.

What will we Use?

We will only scratch the surface of Spring Boot. We will use the API's for database mapping (JPA/Hibernate), the websockets and webservices API's. We will make some use of dependency injection, security and other facilities but one of the nice things about Spring Boot is the fact that it's almost invisible. When it works it "just works", and simple features such as POJO/JSON mapping are seamless.

For storage we will map to MySQL which is pretty simple to work with. Initially I considered using GIS extensions for MySQL and Hibernate but after consideration decided against them as they raise the complexity level without contributing to the usability/readability of the code.

For an app like Uber, those extensions might be overkill but if you need more elaborate functionality or better scale you might want to look at those GIS options.

Why MySQL?

3

Over the past few years almost every startup has picked a no-SQL solution as the database of choice. We did the same thing because the PaaS we chose didn't have an SQL option at the time.

That was a decision we ended up regretting. Access to the underlying data for ad hoc query/reports is harder. External tools such as reporting tools aren't at the same level as the ones designed for SQL and a lot of the work we used to delegate to DBA's is now the responsibility of developers.

No-SQL databases have their place but they can trap your data in unstructured schemas that make migration hard. Moving from SQL to no-SQL is comparatively easier. Most startups don't need the level of scale no-SQL databases are capable of but do need some of the hacks that are easier in SQL.

Notice that I refer to MySQL in this text but everything works fine with MariaDB as well. In our production Linux servers we usually use MariaDB while development on the Mac is easier with MySQL which has (at this time) better Mac OS integration.

Summary

3.4

In this chapter, we learned:

- What's Spring Boot in broad strokes
- Why I picked Spring Boot for this book instead of some other technology
- Why I chose to go with MySQL instead of something more "creative"

This was short because basic Spring Boot is so damn easy. I'll teach the basics as we build the actual server during day two of our process.

Day 1: The Mockup 4

This chapter covers:

- Analysis of the Uber UI/UX, reviewing some of the design decisions made by the Uber team
- The core theme and style of the Uber application as it applies to our themes
- Creating the classes, flow and UI that handles the first app activation process

I always start apps by building a mockup of the front-end first. We are driven by visual feedback. The ability to see and interact with the app clarifies the problem space and motivates you to move forward. Back-end and business logic become easier as you can associate them with requirements from the GUI.

One of the benefits of having mockup code is that it's easy to experiment with the mockup. E.g. comment code in/out and see how it impacts everything, move UI elements around to judge impact etc.

Deconstructing Uber 4.1

As you can see, the Uber app is complex. This screenflow simplifies a lot of the nuances within the app. When we review what the app actually does, the simplicity and elegance pop out.

Before we start looking into the individual UI elements that are a part of the app, I'd like to highlight some decisions made by the Uber team.

This is the first view in the Uber app on a new install. It's implemented in the LoginForm class

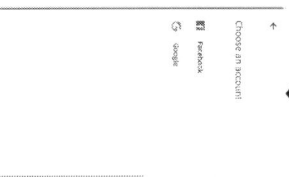

When you click the right arrow in "Enter your mobile number" button you reach this Form the EnterMobileNumberForm

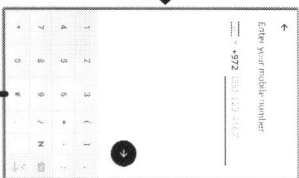

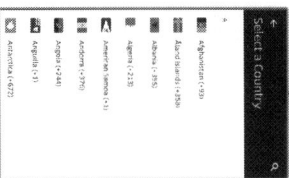

When the right arrow is pressed the 4 digit code form is shown the code is in the Form EnterSMSVerificationDigitsForm

If you already have an account you will be prompted for a password of that account after the app that account was activated, this is the EnterPasswordForm

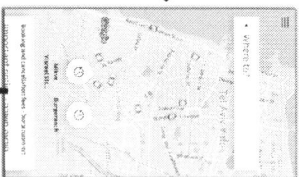

The MapForm is the first Form shown after the app was activated, which is the central part of the app MapForm

When we click "Where to?" We are presented with this search UI and see the Map. Then drag the map to navigate and hail a Taxi this is still in MapForm

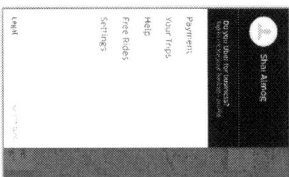

We can drag down the bottom portion of the search UI and with the ability to update the search fields

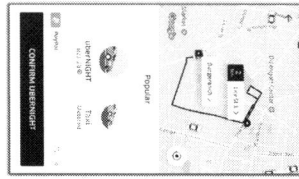

When we press search we are presented with the ability to hail a Taxi this is still in MapForm

Social login lets us login via Google or Facebook. The applicable code is in FacebookOrGoogleLoginForm

The country picker UI opens from the enter mobile number Form. It's implemented in the CountryPickerForm class

When you enter a wrong SMS verification number you are presented with this error message

When we press the menu button in the top left side of the MapForm or drag from the left side we can pull out this side menu implemented in the SettingsForm class

We can reach this Form from the Settings entry in the side menu it's implemented in the SettingsForm class

implemented in the CommonCode class

Figure 4. 1. The Screen Flow of the Uber Application

Portrait Only UI

The Uber app is locked to portrait mode. That is sometimes annoying, as landscape mode has advantages, but in an app like Uber that makes some sense.

The app was designed for phones, as it's unlikely you would hail a cab with a tablet. This effectively limits the form factors supported and makes the process of QA far easier.

It makes our work as developers far easier as well as we can lock the display to portrait and make assumptions about the way the UI looks.

iOS and Android Look Almost Identical

This is the native Uber app login form on an Android device and on an iOS device:

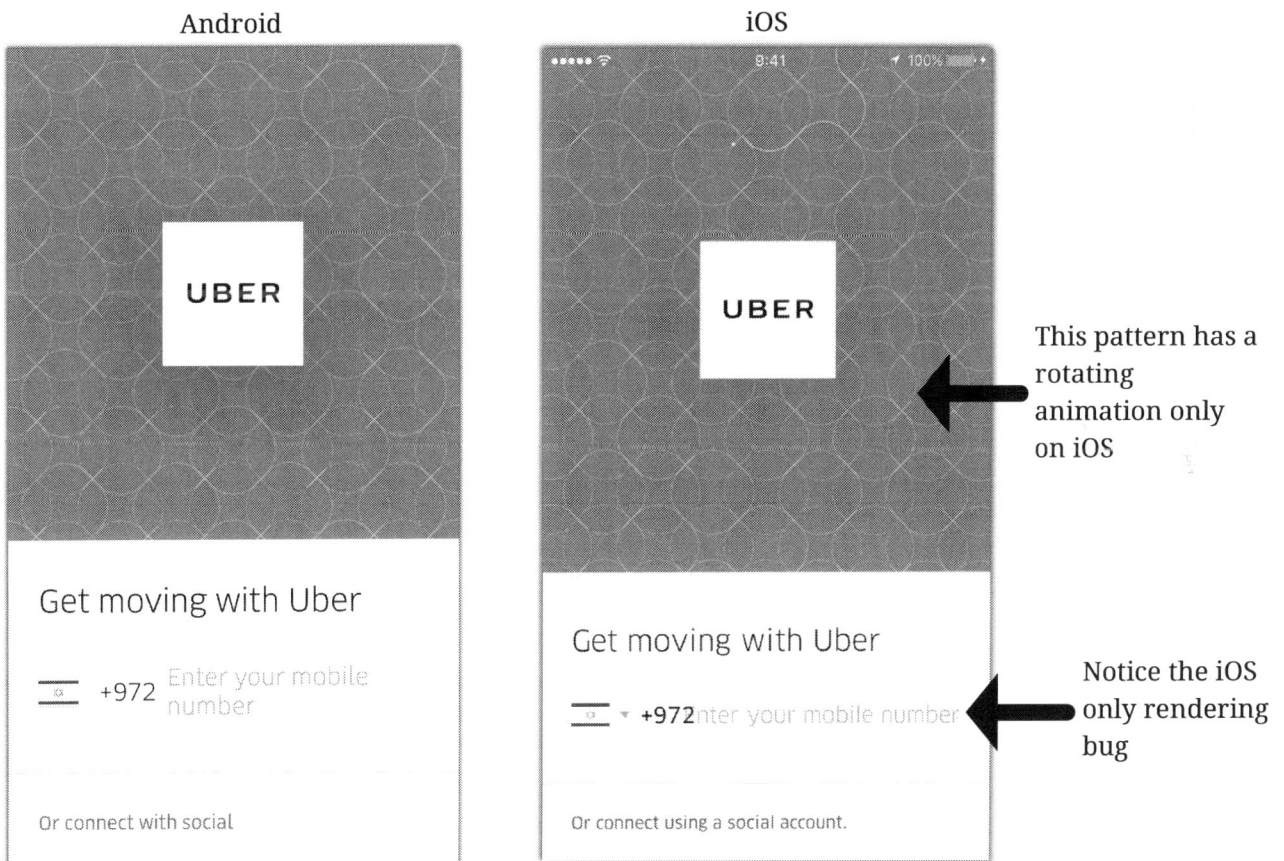

Figure 4. 2. The Native Uber Login UI in Android and iOS

Notice that the UI looks almost identical!

Notice that there is a bug in the iOS version that doesn't consider the length of the country code. This bug doesn't exist on Android.

One thing that isn't noticeable from the screenshot is that the iOS version has a cool special effect in the background pattern that doesn't exist in the Android version. Another thing that isn't obvious is subtle transition animations that differ between the platforms but we'll discuss that more in depth soon enough.

The app itself uses concepts from material design such as the back button arrow and underline style text field. These are used consistently, both in iOS and Android.

4

4.1.3

Inconsistent Titles and Simple Design

The design of the UI is mostly simple and flat, which looks great. Simple is beautiful!

However, some of the forms have black on white title bars. The map has no title bar, only a transparent title with the side menu hamburger. Some forms use a black title bar with white text

> ℹ️ "Hamburger" refers to the three horizontal lines on the top left side of many applications. This is the button that lets you open a side menu options

This isn't hard to replicate but it means that some generic code would need customization, as styles for the TitleCommand UIID and other UIID's can't be used as is.

4.2

The UI Elements

In this section we'll step through the UI forms in the application and implement simple mockups representing these elements.

Before we begin, let's setup the base project and the API's we'll need for this stage.

4.2.1

Setup

We'll start by creating a new Codename One project with a bare-bones application and native theme. I used the package name com.codename1.apps.uberclone and the main name UberClone. You can pick any arbitrary name.

In this application we need to install the cn1libs (Codename One Libraries/Extensions):

- SMSActivation - we need this for the country selection options
- Google Maps - for the map UI

We'll add more later on, but for the mockup level this should be enough. For more information about installing cn1libs check out Appendix D (page 405).

> ❗ You need to configure the keys for iOS/Android in the Google Maps cn1lib as explained in github.com/codenameone/codenameone-google-maps/ this is discussed in Appendix D (page 405)

I made three changes to the main class:

Listing 4. 1. UberClone: Changes to the Main Class

```
public  void  init(Object context) {                    The following 3 lines are generated in a
    theme = UIManager.initFirstTheme("/theme");         default barebone project, we discussed
    Toolbar.setGlobalToolbar(true);                     them in the hello world section
    Log.bindCrashProtection(true);
    Label.setDefaultGap(convertToPixels(2));            The gap between the label icon and the
    Display.getInstance().lockOrientation(true);        text is a bit small by default so we make
}                                                       it 2mm wide which is more reasonable
public  void  start() {
    if (current != null) {                              We need to lock the orientation of the UI to
        current.show();                                 portrait for consistency with the Uber app
        return;
    }
    new LoginForm().show();                             This shows the login form which we'll discuss soon
}
```

Other than that I also did the following in the Codename One Settings UI.

> 💡 You can launch Codename One Settings by right-clicking the project and selecting Codename One → Codename One Settings

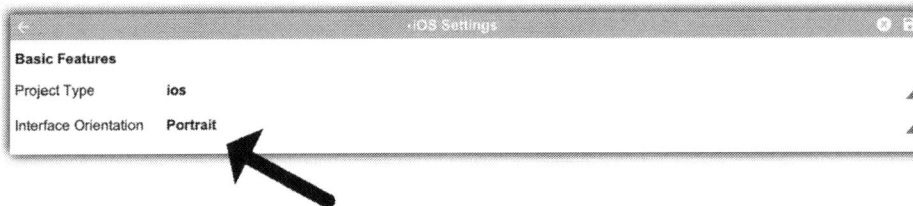

Figure 4. 3. Portrait mode for iOS

Notice that iOS requires this setting in the configuration and the lockOrientation call isn't enough for that platform.

Common Styles

Reminder: the styles that follow are written using the syntax I defined in section 2.2.2 (page 49). You would need to add them to the designer tool or write them as CSS code.

Some styles are essential to begin with so we need to add the following styles into the theme. Notice that a lot of these styles are a result of trial and error to get the UI to look like the designs. It's hard to get pixel perfect designs without trying and fidgeting with the numbers.

The process of choosing the values boiled down to trying, grabbing device screenshots. Adjusting. Rinse repeat. It sounds like a lot of work but it's not too hard as you quickly get a sense of what needs fixing.

I defined Form as white, which is really the main thing here. On Android by default they are a bit "off white". If you look at the images in the screen flow diagram (Figure 4.1 page 82) you would see that the vast majority of the UI elements are white.

Listing 4. 2. Form Styling

```
Background Color: 0xffffff
Transparency: 255
```

I defined Label as heavily padded with a light font. Black on white. This is consistent with the common usage of labels within the app. You can see this in practically every Form in the app including the LoginForm (4.2 page 83). The elements have a lot of whitespace that separates them:

Listing 4. 3. Label Styling

```
Foreground Color: 0x000000
Transparency: 0
Padding: 4mm
Margin: 0
Font: native:MainLight 3.2mm
```

I defined Toolbar as transparent without the border that exists on some platforms. Notice that this doesn't handle the inconsistent title issue (see section 4.1.3 page 84) which I will discuss later:

Listing 4. 4. Toolbar Styling

```
Transparency: 0
Border: Empty
```

I defined TitleCommand as black on transparent. This is a bit problematic with the black toolbar (see section 4.1.3 page 84) which requires a bit of a hack in code to work. The padding numbers are there to make the collapsible toolbar possible. This collapse effect features in several forms such as the countries form (covered later in section 4.2.3 page 92):

Listing 4. 5. TitleCommand Styling

```
Foreground Color: 0x000000
Transparency: 0
Padding Left: 4mm
Padding Right: 4mm
Padding Top: 3mm
Padding Bottom: 1mm
Margin: 0
Font: native:MainLight 4mm
```

The TextField in the Uber app is based on the material design simple underline text field even when running on iOS so we need the text field to have an underline border and work with black on white. You can see this in the phone number entry Form (Figure 4.10 page 107). We keep padding low and margin a bit higher so the line won't be too far from the text input and its start will align on the left with the text:

Listing 4. 6. TextField Styling

```
Foreground Color: 0x000000
Transparency: 0
Padding Left: 0
Padding Right: 0
Padding Top: 3mm
Padding Bottom: 1mm
Margin Left: 4mm
Margin Right: 4mm
Margin Top: 0
Margin Bottom: 0
Border: Underline 0x000000 2px
Font: native:MainLight 3mm
```

The selected version of the TextField UIID has the exact same values with a 4 pixel underline to highlight the selection.

The TextHint style is essential when we customize the text field so it aligns properly. The font here is a smaller regular font which looked closer to the current app look:

Listing 4. 7. TextHint Styling

```
Foreground Color: 0xa4a4ac
Transparency: 0
Padding Left: 0
Padding Right: 0
Padding Top: 3mm
Padding Bottom: 1mm
Margin Left: 4mm
Margin Right: 4mm
Margin Top: 0
Margin Bottom: 0
Font: native:MainRegular 2.8mm
```

Uber uses FloatingActionButton on iOS just like they do on Android. We can see it in all the signup stages including in the enter phone number Form (Figure 4.10 page 107). For us that's pretty cool as we have standard support for floating action buttons in Codename One. The color scheme used by Uber is white icon over a black circle:

Listing 4. 8. FloatingActionButton Styling

```
Foreground Color: 0xffffff
Background Color: 0x000000
```

Countries Button

Figure 4. 4. The Countries Button

One element that is used in two forms in the countries button. Check out the Login Form (Figure 4.2 page 83) where you can see the button with the flag and dial code. Clicking this button in the login form brings us to the phone entry form where it appears again.

Clicking the same button in the phone entry Form leads us to the Country Picker Form (Section 4.2.3 page 92).

This class is a bit large so I'll split it into two pieces:

Listing 4. 9. The country code picker button

```
public class CountryCodePicker extends Button {          The class acts as a Button which
    private   Resources flagResource;                    makes it easy to integrate into
                                                          the rest of the code
    public  CountryCodePicker()  {
        setUIID("CountryCodePicker");                     This resource file includes a
        addActionListener(e -> showPickerForm());         list of flag images
        String   code = L10NManager.getInstance().getLocale();
        if(code != null) {
            String[] countryCodes;
            if(code.length() == 2) countryCodes = COUNTRY_ISO2;
            else {
                if(code.length() != 3) return;           We try to "guess" the current country
                countryCodes = COUNTRY_ISO3;             based on the localization settings,
            }                                            L10NManager is the Codename One
            code = code.toUpperCase();                   localization API
            try {
                flagResource = Resources.open("/flags.res");
            } catch (IOException err) {                    ↑
                Log.e(err);                              The flags.res file is included in
            }                                            the SMSActivation cn1lib
```

89

We don't have all the flags for all the countries. Without
a blank icon the alignment might seem "broken"

```java
Image blankIcon = Image.createImage(100, 70, 0);
for (int iter = 0 ; iter < countryCodes.length ; iter++) {
    if (code.equals(countryCodes[iter])) {
        setText("+" + COUNTRY_CODES[iter]);
        setIcon(flagResource.getImage(COUNTRY_FLAGS[iter]));
        if (getIcon() == null) setIcon(blankIcon);
        return;
    }
}
}
}
protected void showPickerForm() {
    // ...
}
}
```

This and other constant arrays are statically
imported from the class ActivationForm

showPickerForm is useful for overriding. In
the login form clicking this button should
lead to a different Form

This leads us to the implementation of the showPickerForm method:

Listing 4. 10. CountryCodePicker showPickerForm Method Implementation

```
final   Form f = getCurrentForm();
final   Transition t = f.getTransitionOutAnimator();
f.setTransitionOutAnimator(CommonTransitions.createEmpty());
Form tf = new CountryPickerForm(this, flagResource);
tf.addShowListener(new ActionListener() {
    public void actionPerformed(ActionEvent evt) {
        f.setTransitionOutAnimator(t);
        f.removeShowListener(this);
    }
});
tf.show();
```

The cover transition collides with the default slide transition producing a weird effect

To workaround the cover transition collision we keep the original transition instance

Then we remove the out transition so the cover effect will work properly

We can't use a lambda expression here because of this line. this would have referred to CountryCodePicker instead of the ActionListener in a lambda

We then bind a show listener that restores the old transition after we are done

That's important for when the user will click to move to the next form. In that case we want to have the slide transition back in place.

I defined the UIID for CountryCodePicker as such:

Listing 4. 11. CountryCodePicker Styling

```
Foreground Color: 0x000000
Transparency: 0
Padding Left: 4mm
Padding Right: 2mm
Padding Top: 3mm
Padding Bottom: 4mm
Margin: 0
Border: Empty
Font: native:MainLight 3mm
```

CountryPickerForm

The country picker form looks like this:

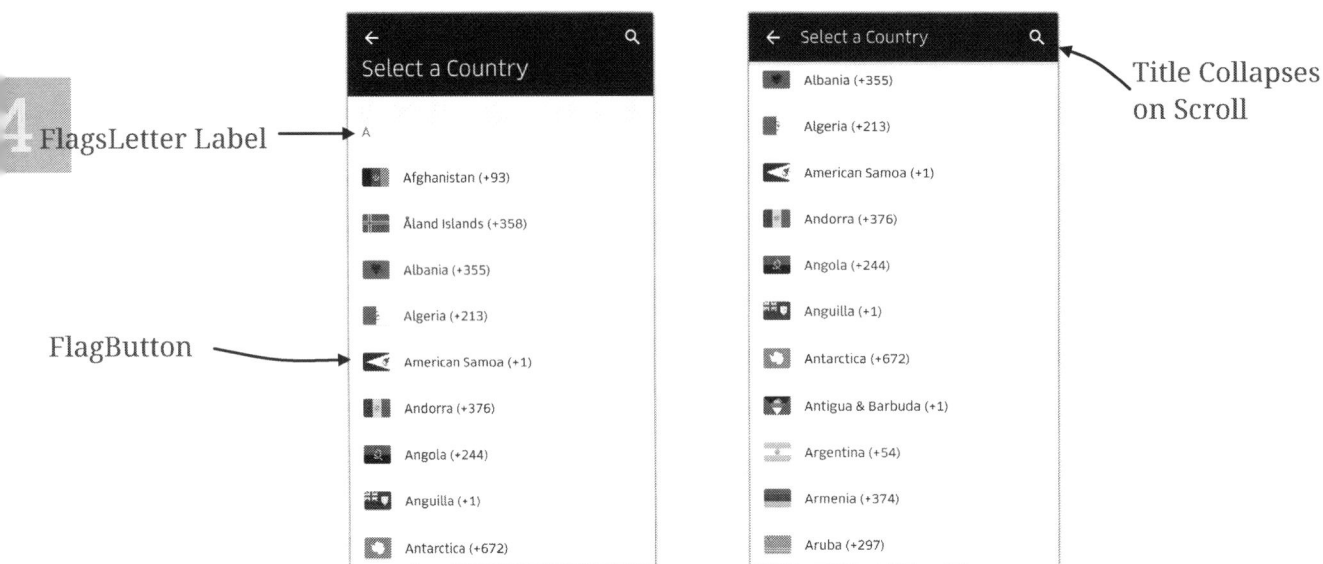

FlagsLetter Label

FlagButton

Title Collapses
on Scroll

Figure 4. 5. The Country Picker Form on an Android Device

This UI is relatively simple but it has one small nuance. The title area is black. I discussed the inconsistent title areas (see section 4.1.3 page 84) before and this is fixable but it requires some custom code.

Listing 4. 12. Country code picker form

```
public class CountryPickerForm extends Form {
    public CountryPickerForm(Button sourceButton, Resources flags) {
        super(BoxLayout.y());
        CommonCode.initBlackTitleForm(this, "Select a Country",
            val -> search(val));
        Image blankIcon = Image.createImage(100, 70, 0);
        char lastChar = (char)-1;
```

We arrange the following components vertically on the Y axis

The initBlackTitleForm method is a static method in the common utility class. We'll cover it shortly in section 4.2.3 initBlackTitleForm (page 95)

Again we don't have flags for all the countries so we need a blank space icon so the elements align

Listing 4. 12. Country code picker form

```
        for(int iter = 0 ; iter < ActivationForm.COUNTRY_CODES.length ; iter++) {
            Button b = new Button(ActivationForm.COUNTRY_NAMES[iter], "FlagButton");

            char current = b.getText().charAt(0);
            if(current != lastChar) {
                lastChar = current;
                Label l = new Label("" + lastChar, "FlagsLetter");
                add(l);
            }

            b.setIcon(flags.getImage(ActivationForm.COUNTRY_FLAGS[iter]));
            if(b.getIcon() == null)  b.setIcon(blankIcon);
            String currentCountryCode = ActivationForm.COUNTRY_CODES[iter];
            b.addActionListener(ee -> {
                sourceButton.setIcon(b.getIcon());
                sourceButton.setText("+"  + currentCountryCode);
                sourceButton.getComponentForm().showBack();
            });
            add(b);
        }
    }
    protected  void  initGlobalToolbar() {
        super. initGlobalToolbar();
        getToolbar().setUIID("BlackToolbar");
    }
    void  search(String s) {}
}
```

Here we loop over all the country codes and create a button with the FlagButton UIID for every entry

We need to implement the alphabet letter headers, every time the first character of a country changes we add a label representing the entry

When an entry is selected we update the text and icon of the CountryCodePicker Button (Listing 4.9 page 89) that launched this Form

We need to override the toolbar initialization so we can set the proper BlackToolbar UIID

This is a blank placeholder for now...

defined `FlagButton` as a black on white light font element with big padding to fit the design. It's really a label with a slightly larger font:

Listing 4. 13. FlagButton Styling

```
Font: native:MainLight 3.2mm
Derive: Label
```

defined `FlagsLetter` a gray background with similar values to `FlagButton` so they will match and align. To get the values for this I picked the colors from the screenshot (Figure 4.5 page 92):

Listing 4. 14. FlagsLetter Styling

```
Foreground Color: 0x525760
Background Color: 0xf9f9f9
Transparency: 255
Derive: Label Unselected
```

defined `BlackToolbar` as just black; not much else:

Listing 4. 15. BlackToolbar Styling

```
Background Color: 0x000000
Transparency: 255
Alignment: Left
Padding: 1mm
Margin: 0
```

initBlackTitleForm

The form with the black title requires some work which should be reusable, as a black title area is used in several places within the Uber application.

For this purpose we have the CommonCode class which stores common static code in the application. This is a non-trivial task as the logic needs to support the animated collapse of the title area as the user scrolls down, as illustrated in Figure 4.5 (page 92).

Listing 4. 16. Initializing the black toolbar and its animation

```
public static void initBlackTitleForm(Form f, String title,
        SuccessCallback<String> searchResults) {
    Form backTo = getCurrentForm();
    f.getContentPane().setScrollVisible(false);
    Button back = new Button("", "TitleCommand");
    back.addActionListener(e -> backTo.showBack());
    back.getAllStyles().setFgColor(0xffffff);



    FontImage.setMaterialIcon(back, FontImage.MATERIAL_ARROW_BACK);
    f.setBackCommand(new Command("") {
        public void actionPerformed(ActionEvent evt) {
            backTo.showBack();
        }
    });



    Container searchBack = null;
    if(searchResults != null) {
        Button search = new Button("", "TitleCommand");
        search.getAllStyles().setFgColor(0xffffff);
        FontImage.setMaterialIcon((search, FontImage.MATERIAL_SEARCH);
        search.addActionListener(e -> {});
        searchBack = BorderLayout.north(
            BorderLayout.centerEastWest(null, search, back));
    } else {
        searchBack = BorderLayout.north(
            BorderLayout.centerEastWest(null, null, back));
    }
```

The method accepts a callback for the case of a search operation, this isn't implemented yet but if it's null a search icon isn't added

We add the back command as a button which allows us to place it above the title in a custom way and animate the position

We can't use the TitleCommand UIID "as is" since it uses a black on white scheme in other forms. I could have used a different UIID here

In Android and other devices where we have a physical back button we want to associate a command with that button. You can debug the physical back key by pressing escape in the simulator

If we have a search callback we should build the layout that includes the search button otherwise we should create a layout without it

We place the title on top of the back button container using a layered layout. It doesn't seem to be on top because of the top margin pushing it below the back arrow icon

```
Label titleLabel = new Label(title, "WhiteOnBlackTitle");
titleLabel.getAllStyles().setMarginTop(back.getPreferredH());
titleLabel.getAllStyles().setMarginUnit(Style.UNIT_TYPE_PIXELS,
    Style.UNIT_TYPE_DIPS, Style.UNIT_TYPE_DIPS, Style.UNIT_TYPE_DIPS);
f.getToolbar().setTitleComponent(
    LayeredLayout.encloseIn(searchBack, titleLabel));
f.getAnimationManager().onTitleScrollAnimation(titleLabel.
    createStyleAnimation("WhiteOnBlackTitleLeftMargin", 200));
f.setTransitionInAnimator(CommonTransitions.createCover(
    CommonTransitions.SLIDE_VERTICAL, false, 300));
f.setTransitionOutAnimator(CommonTransitions.createUncover(
    CommonTransitions.SLIDE_VERTICAL, true, 300));
}
```

This one line allows the title to collapse into place next to the arrow

Cover transition is used in the back title forms on iOS, notice that cover transitions expect in and out values for cover and uncover

The reason we placed the title below the arrow with a margin is the animation. We can animate the position of the label fluidly by changing the margin value. Following that the createStyleAnimation call translates the style of the title which currently has a large top margin to one without top margin but with side margin. This means that the change in the style causes the title to move next to the back arrow see 4.2 WhiteOnBlackTitleLeftMargin Styling (page 97).

A crucial piece of the title area collapse code are the WhiteOnBlackTitle and the WhiteOnBlackTitleLeftMargin UIID's.

The WhiteOnBlackTitle style represents the version of the title as it appears on top of the black background title:

Listing 4. 17. WhiteOnBlackTitle Styling

```
Foreground Color: 0xffffff
Transparency: 0
Padding Left: 3mm
Padding Right: 3mm
Padding Top: 1mm     ←          The thing to notice here is the padding value
Padding Bottom: 3mm             which we use to move the title around
Margin: 0  ←                    The margin is also manipulated as part of this process
Font: native:MainLight 4mm
```

The WhiteOnBlackTitleLeftMargin style is a style that positions the title next to the back arrow by removing the top margin and adding left side margin. It also reduces the font size a little bit and sets the padding to a more even set:

Listing 4. 18. WhiteOnBlackTitleLeftMargin Styling

```
Padding: 3mm
Margin Left: 8mm  ←         The large margin is there to leave room for the back
Margin Right: 0            arrow as this is a LayeredLayout and the title would
Margin Top: 0             literally render on top of the arrow without it
Margin Bottom: 0
Derive: WhiteOnBlackTitle Unselected
Font: native:MainLight 3mm
```

Login

The Login Form (Figure 4.2 page 83) is relatively simple. It includes a logo, a background pattern, and some other elements such as the Country Form Picker discussed in section 4.2.3 (page 92).

We'll start by creating the basic UI. Since the LoginForm is a bit large I'll split the code into the declarative code and discuss the constructor body separately:

Listing 4. 19. LoginForm Declaration and Methods

```java
public class LoginForm extends Form {          ⟵——— As we did before we derive Form
    public LoginForm() {                        ⟵———
        super(new BorderLayout());              ⟵———         We'll dive into the constructor in the next listing
        // ... rest of the constructor code ...              The Form uses BorderLayout
    }                                                        to position its content
    @Override
    protected boolean shouldPaintStatusBar() {  ⟵———  StatusBar is a space on the top of
        return false;                                 the screen in iOS that pushes the
    }                                                 UI down, we want to hide it here
    @Override
    protected void initGlobalToolbar() {
    }
}
```

In iOS the app draws under the battery indicator (or notch) so it shouldn't include content in that area. Codename One includes builtin spacing for that (AKA StatusBar) but it sometimes gets in the way if we have a design that draws in that area.

Next let's examine the body of the constructor:

Listing 4. 20. LoginForm Constructor Body

Initially I wrote the word UBER. Without the right font it looked "weird". Using an image for a logo is generally the best approach

```
Label squareLogo = new Label("" ,
    Resources.getGlobalResources().
        getImage("uber-logo.png"),    "SquareLogo") {
    protected  Dimension calcPreferredSize() {
        Dimension size = super.calcPreferredSize();
        size.setHeight(size.getWidth());
        return  size;
    }
};
Container logo = BorderLayout.centerAbsolute(squareLogo);
logo.setUIID("LogoBackground");
add(CENTER, logo);
Label getMovingWithUber =
    new Label("Get moving with Uber",  "GetMovingWithUber");
CountryCodePicker countryCodeButton = new CountryCodePicker() {
    protected  void  showPickerForm() {
        new EnterMobileNumberForm().show();
    }
};
```

The resource file includes the logo image when we loaded it in the init(Object) method it was saved as a global resource

We want the logo to be square so height and width would be identical, I picked width as I know it's larger but I could have used Math.max()

We override the behavior of the country picker button for consistency with the native Uber app which navigates to the next Form

We place the entire tiled section and logo in the center of the form so they will take up the available space. We place the logo itself in the absolute center so it will float in the middle

This looks like a text field but acts like a button in the native app. Constraining the rows and size is important for proper layout. Notice that SpanButton has two UIID's. This UIID applies to the text of the button. The other UIID applies to the border and background

Using Container as a UIID is a common trick to make a component transparent with 0 padding/margin

```
SpanButton phoneNumber = new SpanButton("Enter your mobile number",
    "PhoneNumberHint");
phoneNumber.getTextComponent().setColumns(80);
phoneNumber.getTextComponent().setRows(2);
phoneNumber.getTextComponent().setGrowByContent(false);
phoneNumber.setUIID("Container");
phoneNumber.addActionListener(e -> new EnterMobileNumberForm().show());
Container phonePicking = BorderLayout.centerCenterEastWest(
                phoneNumber, null, countryCodeButton);
phonePicking.setUIID("Separator");
Button social = new Button("Or connect with social",
    "ConnectWithSocialButton");
social.addActionListener(e -> new FacebookOrGoogleLoginForm().show());
add(SOUTH, BoxLayout.encloseY(getMovingWithUber, phonePicking,
    social));
```

The rest of the UI is relegated to the SOUTH of the form, this would have issues in landscape mode but since the app is portrait locked this shouldn't be a problem

A common practice in the Uber app is the usage of components that seem like text input components but are really navigational components or buttons as we see with the getMovingWithUber label above. We can use a button to masquerade a text field and this actually provides some benefits. If we would have left the text field in this case the entire UI would have shifted when the virtual keyboard opened. Moving to a separate Form is a simple and elegant solution.

We use several styles to accomplish this and 2 images.

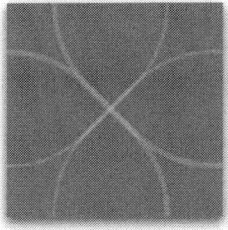

Figure 4. 6. tile.png is the image which we tile behind the logo to produce the background effect

Figure 4. 7. uber-logo.png is the image we use for the logo itself

The SquareLogo style is just a white background for the logo. Technically I could have just used a square logo image here:

Listing 4. 21. SquareLogo Styling

```
Foreground Color: 0x000000
Background Color: 0xffffff
Transparency: 255
Padding: 2mm
Margin: 0
Derive: WhiteOnBlackTitle Unselected
Font: native:MainLight 3mm
```

The LogoBackground style is used for the image tile:

Listing 4. 22. LogoBackground Styling

Background Type: IMAGE_TILE_BOTH
Image: tile.png
Transparency: 255
Margin: 0

Notice the image is tiled across the entire background on both axis

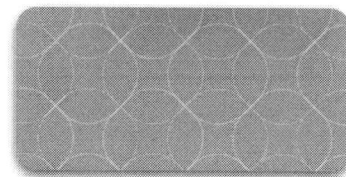

The GetMovingWithUber style covers the font for the get moving title label it also pads in just the right amount for this element:

Listing 4. 23. GetMovingWithUber Styling

Padding Left: 4mm
Padding Right: 4mm
Padding Top: 4mm
Padding Bottom: 3mm
Font: native:MainLight 4.8mm
Derive: Label

Get moving with Uber

The PhoneNumberHint shows the "hint style" text next to the country picker button. It has 0 padding on the left to keep it close to the country picker button:

Listing 4. 24. PhoneNumberHint Styling

Foreground Color: 0xa4a4ac
Transparency: 0
Padding Left: 0
Padding Right: 4mm
Padding Top: 3mm
Padding Bottom: 5mm
Margin: 0
Font: native:MainLight 3.7mm

72 Enter your mobile number

The `Separator` style is a simple container with an underline to separate the social connection button. It has a 2px padding to leave room for the underline:

Listing 4. 25. Separator Styling

```
Transparency: 0
Padding Left: 0
Padding Right: 0
Padding Top: 0
Padding Bottom: 2px
Margin: 0
Border: Underline 0xededed 2px
Font: native:MainLight 3.7mm
```

And finally the `ConnectWithSocialButton` style represents the blue text in the bottom that launches the social connect. Again it's mostly padding, font and color:

Listing 4. 26. ConnectWithSocialButton Styling

```
Foreground Color: 0x2775a4
Padding: 4mm
Derive: Label
Font: native:MainLight 3mm
```

Or connect with social

This might seem like a lot but it's mostly just playing with the styling which we can do in the visual tool. The result is pretty darn close to the original...

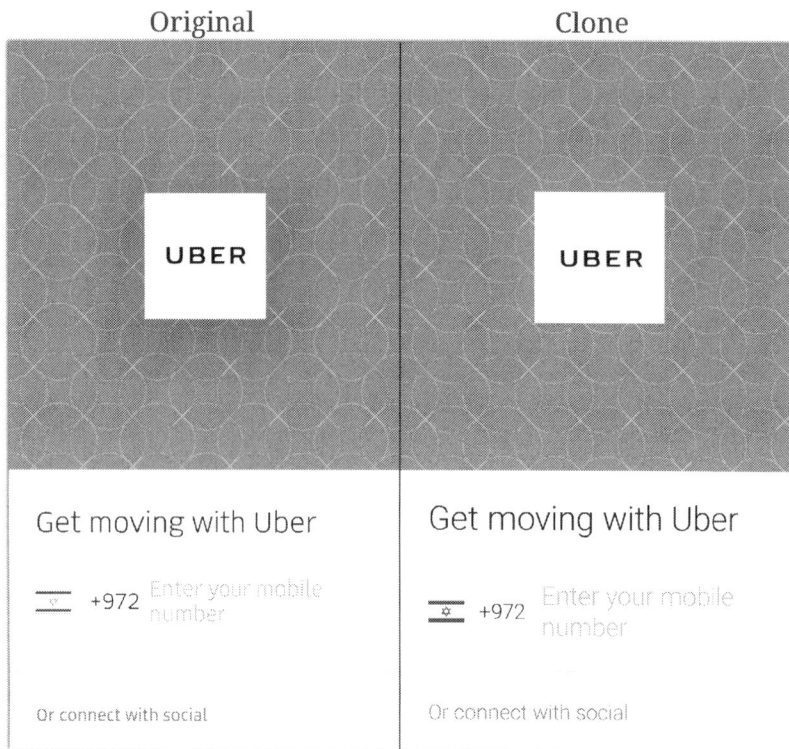

Original	Clone

Figure 4. 8. The original login form next to the new one

ℹ ***Not Pixel Perfect***
I didn't clone the fonts and didn't spend too much time on that. This was intentional for simplicities sake

There are two things that we are missing here. The first and probably more obvious: the drop shadow behind the logo.

The other isn't visible in the screenshots. The background rotates on iOS and animates. This doesn't happen on Android but is a pretty neat effect which I would like to reproduce at least partially...

I'll discuss the latter in Day 7 of the book.

Shadow
The simplest thing to do is generate a square image of the logo that already has a translucent shadow within. This is pretty trivial to anyone versed in photoshop and looks great on the device...

However, my goal is to teach programming not photoshop so I'm picking the "hard way" of solving this.

The Codename One Effects class lets us create a shadow image for the given dimensions or image. Since the logo is square we can just use the dimensions approach:

Listing 4. 27. LoginForm: Creating a shadow image

```
final Image shadow = Effects.squareShadow(squareLogo.getPreferredW(),
    squareLogo.getPreferredH(), convertToPixels(14), 0.35f);
```

This creates an image of a shadow based on the size of the logo and spreads the shadow 14 millimeters. The shadow is given 35% opacity which means it's pretty subtle.

So now we have an image of the shadow but the logo image and background are already fixed so we need something new:

Listing 4. 28. LoginForm: Placing the shadow

```
Container logo = LayeredLayout.encloseIn(
    BorderLayout.centerAbsolute(new Label(shadow, "Container")),
    BorderLayout.centerAbsolute(squareLogo)
);
```

Instead of using the logo as is we place the shadow in a layer below using the LayeredLayout and this will produce the desired effect with one HUGE caveat. It's really slow!

Shadows are CPU Intensive

We use gaussian blur to generate shadows and that's a very slow algorithm

The solution is to delay the execution of the code to a point in time where we have CPU resources available to process the shadow effect. The UI will appear and the shadow will appear a second later when it's ready.

Listing 4. 29. LoginForm: Shadow in a thread

```
Label placeholder = new Label();
Container logo = LayeredLayout.encloseIn(
        placeholder,  ←
        BorderLayout.centerAbsolute(squareLogo)
);
startThread(() -> {  ←
        final  Image shadow = Effects.squareShadow(squareLogo.getPreferredW(),
            squareLogo.getPreferredH(), convertToPixels(14), 0.35f);
        callSerially(() -> {  ←
            logo.replace(placeholder, BorderLayout.centerAbsolute(
                new Label(shadow,  "Container")),  null);
            revalidate();  ↑
        });
},  "Shadow Maker").start();
```

The placeholder is there so we can put the shadow into place when it's ready

We could have just used new Thread() which is pretty much the same

When the shadow image is ready we go back to the EDT using callSerially

replace switches out the placeholder component for the shadow

Once all of this is done the shadow "just works".

4.2.5

Social Login

The social login form is shown when you click the login with social button. It's a bare/simple form, in fact I cropped the image as the rest of it is "just white".

There isn't that much to say about the UI or the code. Both are very simple...

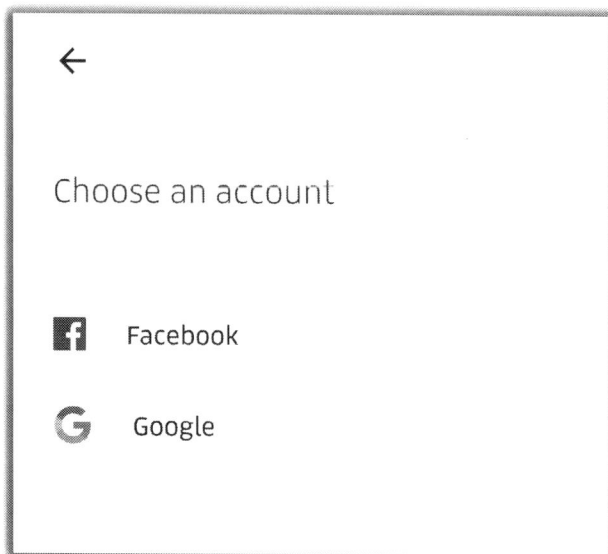

←

Choose an account

f   Facebook

G   Google

Figure 4. 9. Social login option from the main form

Listing 4. 30. Social login UI

```java
public class FacebookOrGoogleLoginForm extends Form {
    public  FacebookOrGoogleLoginForm() {
        super(BoxLayout. y());
        Form previous = getCurrentForm();
        getToolbar().setBackCommand("",
            Toolbar.BackCommandPolicy.AS_ARROW, e -> previous. showBack());
        add(new Label("Choose an account", "FlagButton"));
        Resources r = Resources.getGlobalResources();
        Button facebook = new Button("Facebook",
            r.getImage("facebook.png"), "FlagButton");
        Button google = new Button("Google",
            r.getImage("google.png"), "FlagButton");
        add(facebook).add(google);
    }
}
```

We use standard back navigation since the toolbar is pretty simple here

I grabbed the icons for Google and Facebook and added theme to the theme.res file so they will appear here

Enter Mobile Number

The enter mobile number UI looks almost identical in iOS with the Android style underline text field and next floating action button.

These elements are easily implemented in Codename One...

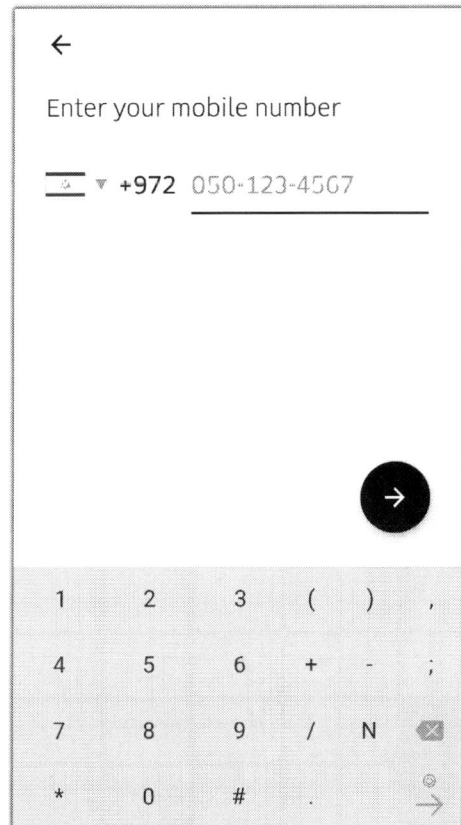

Figure 4. 10. Enter Mobile Number UI

Listing 4. 31. Mobile phone number entry

```java
public class EnterMobileNumberForm extends Form {
    public EnterMobileNumberForm() {
        super(BoxLayout.y());
        Form previous = getCurrentForm();
        getToolbar().setBackCommand("", Toolbar.BackCommandPolicy.AS_ARROW,
            e -> previous.showBack()); ←
        add(new Label("Enter your mobile number", "FlagButton"));
        CountryCodePicker countryCodeButton = new CountryCodePicker();
        TextField phoneNumber = new TextField("", "050-123-4567", 40,
            TextField.PHONENUMBER); ←
```

The PHONENUMBER constraint determines the virtual keyboard type that will appear, it doesn't limit input and doesn't validate

We use standard back navigation since the toolbar is pretty standard here

```java
        add(BorderLayout.centerEastWest(phoneNumber,
            null, countryCodeButton)); ↑
```

The phone number text field is right next to the country code button. We place it in the center of a border layout so it will take up all available space

```java
        Style ps = phoneNumber.getUnselectedStyle();
        Style cs = countryCodeButton.getUnselectedStyle();
        int pl = cs.getPaddingLeft(isRTL());
        int pr = cs.getPaddingRight(isRTL()); ←
        countryCodeButton.getAllStyles().setPaddingUnit(
            Style.UNIT_TYPE_PIXELS);
        countryCodeButton.getAllStyles().setPadding(ps.getPaddingTop(),
            ps.getPaddingBottom(), pl , pr);
```

We want the padding on the text field and button to match so they align properly

```
setEditOnShow(phoneNumber); ←
FloatingActionButton fab = FloatingActionButton.createFAB(
        FontImage.MATERIAL_ARROW_FORWARD);
fab.bindFabToContainer(this);
fab.addActionListener(e -> {
        String number = phoneNumber.getText();
        if(number.startsWith("0")) {
                number = number.substring(1);
        }
        new EnterSMSVerificationDigitsForm(
                countryCodeButton.getText() + "-" + number).show();
    });
}
```

> You can start editing a text field by invoking startEditing however with a form that isn't showing yet we need this special case

Once paddings are set they are always in pixels so we need to change the style to use pixels. I don't want to impact the left/right padding values so I extract them first and save them so I can restore them into the UI. I could technically create a separate UIID to align both but I want to do this in the code so future changes to the theme won't break alignment (see Figure 4.11 to the right)

We don't have any new UIID's we need to define for this Form so we can move ahead...

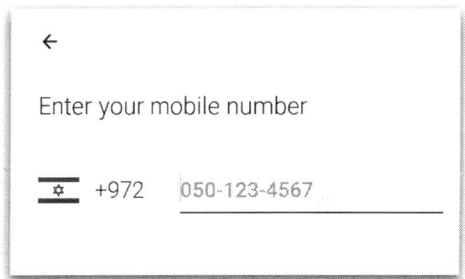

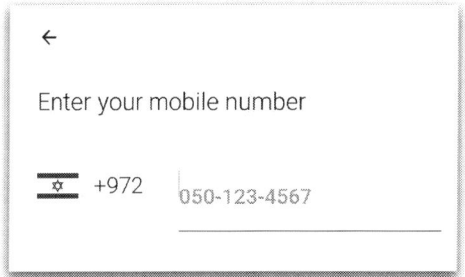

Figure 4. 11. With/without the padding code

SMS Verification

The SMS verification form accepts the four digits from the user. Currently the Android version of Uber doesn't automatically intercept the incoming SMS which is really odd. When we get to the implementation we might add it.

This form includes two variants, input and error mode. When an error occurs it follows the standard Android error look. However, since the text field is broken across 4 different fields the error spans all four entries.

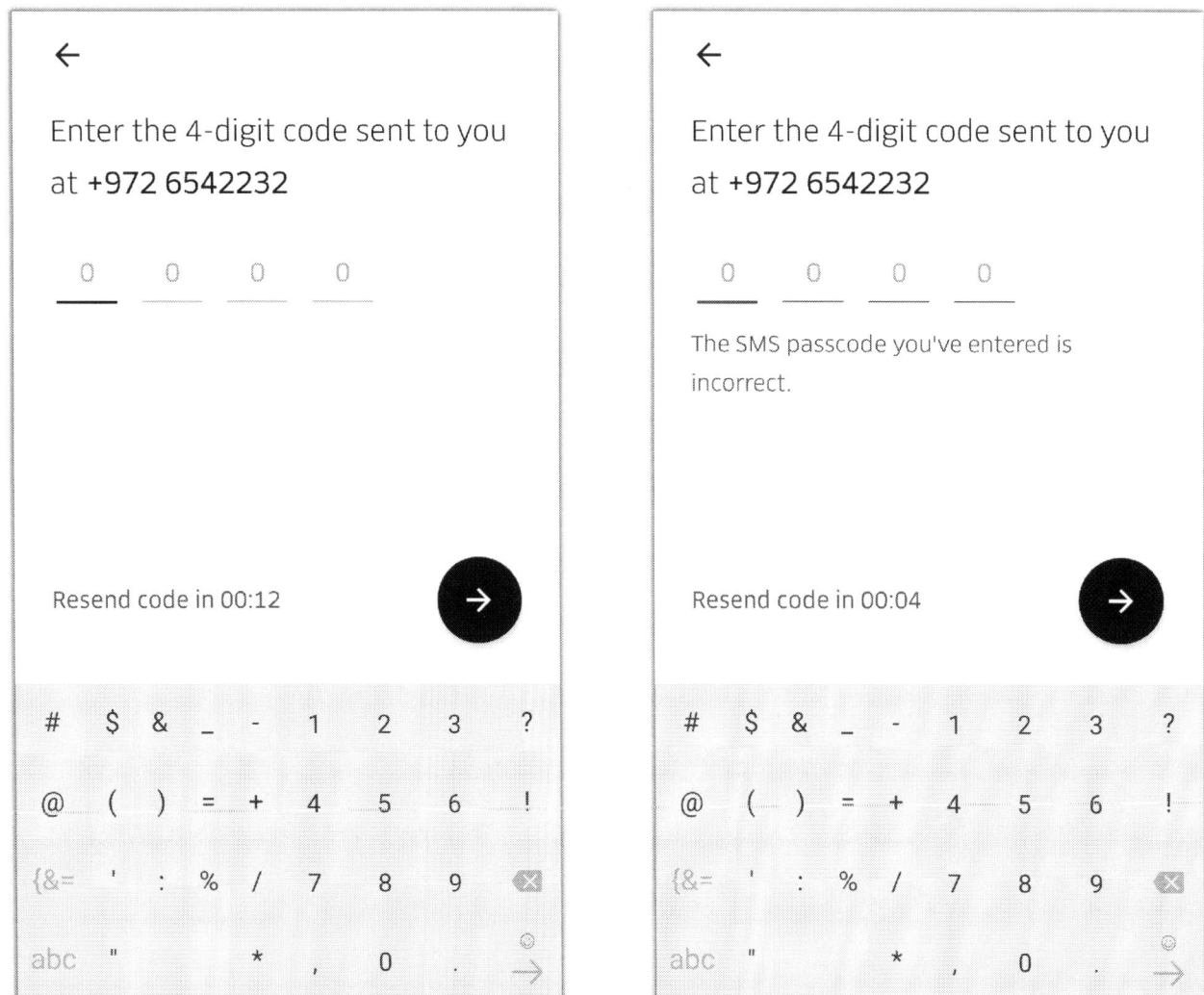

Figure 4. 12. SMS Verification Input as Four Digits and Verification Error Message

In order to implement this I broke up the input to four text fields but I wrote the code in a way that's generic enough so we can use more. Since the listing is pretty big I'll break it down to smaller pieces:

Listing 4. 32. EnterSMSVerificationDigitsForm Class

```java
public class EnterSMSVerificationDigitsForm extends Form {
    public EnterSMSVerificationDigitsForm(String phone) {
        super(new BorderLayout());
        // ... constructor code ...
    }
    // ... methods ...
}
```

The Form uses BorderLayout again and accepts the phone number for verification

The class doesn't include variables only private methods and the constructor. Lets start by reviewing the constructor body and follow up with the individual methods:

Listing 4. 33. EnterSMSVerificationDigitsForm Constructor Body

```java
Form previous = getCurrentForm();
getToolbar().setBackCommand("", Toolbar.BackCommandPolicy.AS_ARROW,
    e -> previous.showBack());
Container box = new Container(BoxLayout.y());
box.setScrollableY(true);
box.add(new SpanLabel("Enter the 4-digit code sent to you at " +
    phone, "FlagButton"));
TextField[] digits = createDigits(4);
setEditOnShow(digits[0]);
box.add(BoxLayout.encloseX(digits));
SpanLabel error = new SpanLabel(
    "The SMS passcode you've entered is incorrect", "ErrorLabel");
error.setVisible(false);
box.add(error);
```

We create an array of text fields to loop over. This allows us to easily change the code to accept any number of digits

The error label is always there we just hide it

Yes, this works and adds all the components in the array

```
add(CENTER, box); <-----------------------------------
Label resend = new Label("Resend code in 00:12", "ResendCode");
add(SOUTH, resend); <-----------------------------------
FloatingActionButton fab = FloatingActionButton.createFAB(
    FontImage.MATERIAL_ARROW_FORWARD);
fab.bindFabToContainer(this);
fab.addActionListener(e -> {
    if (!isValid(toString(digits))) {
        error.setVisible(true);
        errorFields(digits);
        repaint();
        return;
    }
    new EnterPasswordForm().show();
});
```

For now we don't animate the resend text. Notice that we use BorderLayout to position the resend label at the bottom and place the rest of the stuff in a BoxLayout in the center

The class uses multiple TextField instances to form a continuous input experience that only allows one digit per TextField.

This leads us directly to the createDigits method which creates the text fields we use for input:

Listing 4. 34. EnterSMSVerificationDigitsForm createDigits Method

```
private TextField[] createDigits(int count) {
    TextField[] response = new TextField[count]; <---
    for(int iter = 0 ; iter < count ; iter++) {
        TextField t = new TextField("", "0", 1, TextField.NUMERIC);
        t.setUIID("Digit");
        t.getHintLabel().getAllStyles().setAlignment(CENTER);
        response[iter] = t;
    }
```

The generic creation code creates the array of numeric text fields and aligns the hints to the center

```
for(int iter = 0 ; iter < count - 1 ; iter++) {
    onTypeNext(response[iter],response[iter + 1]);  ←┐
}                                                     │
                                                      │
return  response;                                     │
}
```

This logic makes sure that once we type a character the input will automatically move to the next text field

4

The text field hints are aligned to the center to make them look better for single character entry so they will match better with the text field padding.

Now that we have all of that in place we can just go over the rest of the methods in the class:

Listing 4. 35. EnterSMSVerificationDigitsForm Remaining Methods

```
private  void  errorFields(TextField... fields) {
    for(TextField f : fields) {
        f.getAllStyles().setBorder(  ←
            Border.createUnderlineBorder(2, 0xcc0000));
        f.getSelectedStyle().setBorder(
            Border.createUnderlineBorder(4, 0xcc0000));
    }
}


private  String  toString(TextField[] digits) {  ←
    StringBuilder s = new StringBuilder();
    for(TextField t : digits) {
        s.append(t.getAsInt(0));
    }
    return  s.toString();
}
```

In case of an error we just change the underline style. We could have also done this by invoking setUIID which might have been more elegant

The value we get for validation is a String so combining the individual values to a String is helpful

```java
public  boolean  isValid(String s) {
    return  s.startsWith("0");
}
private  void  onTypeNext(TextField current, TextField next) {
    current.addDataChangedListener((i, ii) -> {
        if (current.getText().length() == 1) {
            current.stopEditing();
            next.startEditingAsync();
        }
    });
}
```

For now this is implemented as a stub so we can get through the mockup

We bind a listener to each text field and if the length of the text is 1 we stop editing and move to the next text field

setUIID() is generally preferable to setting the values on the Style object directly. It maintains the separation between the "theme" and the UI itself. That allows us to re-skin the app easily and makes the code more maintainable. I still use the Style object for things that don't make sense in the theme such as localized customization. Coloring an error in red is a good example of something that can fit both in the theme and the code.

To finish this we need to add a few styles.

The Digit style is a special case of the text field specifically designed for this form. The main reason for a special style is the problematic center alignment in text field. Because of the way this works I preferred using a 1 millimeter padding on the sides to give the feel of center alignment in this case. Another important bit is the smaller margin that makes the fields stand closer to one another and the slightly smaller font.

Listing 4. 36. Digit Styling

```
Padding Left: 1mm
Padding Right: 1mm
Padding Top: 3mm
Padding Bottom: 1mm
Margin Left: 4mm
Margin Right: 0
Margin Top: 0
Margin Bottom: 0
Derive: TextField Unselected
Font: native:MainLight 2.7mm
```

The selected version of Digit has a 4 pixel tall underline black border.

> **ℹ** ***Avoiding Center alignment in text fields***
>
> Center alignment works in text area, label etc. However, it's flaky in text fields because it's really hard to get the position right when moving from lightweight to native editing

The ErrorLabel style represents the text with the error that we can see in Figure 4.12 (page 110). It's just red text:

Listing 4. 37. ErrorLabel Styling

```
Foreground Color: 0xcc0000
Background Color: 0xffffff
Padding: 3mm
Margin: 0
Font: native:MainLight 2.8mm
```

The SMS passcode you've entered is incorrect.

The ResendCode style just pads the text so it will align properly with the FloatingActionButton:

Listing 4. 38. ResendCode Styling

Padding Left: 3mm
Padding Right: 0
Padding Top: 0
Padding Bottom: 6mm
Margin: 0
Font: native:MainLight 2.7mm

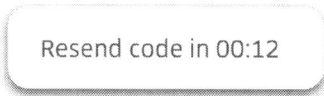

Resend code in 00:12

4.2.8

Enter Password

The enter password form is a pretty trivial step once we've been through the verification so I'll gloss over it relatively quickly.

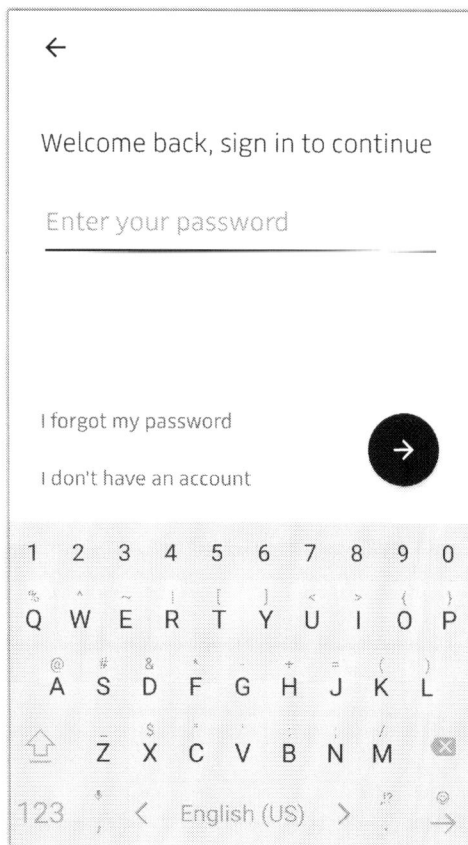

Figure 4. 13. The Enter Password Form

Listing 4. 39. The enter password UI

```java
public class EnterPasswordForm extends Form {
    public EnterPasswordForm() {
        super(new BorderLayout());
        Form previous = getCurrentForm();
        getToolbar().setBackCommand("", Toolbar.BackCommandPolicy.AS_ARROW,
            e -> previous.showBack());
        Container box = new Container(BoxLayout.y());
        box.setScrollableY(true);
        box.add(new SpanLabel("Welcome back, signin to continue",
            "FlagButton"));
        TextField password = new TextField("", "Enter your password", 80,
            TextField.PASSWORD);
        setEditOnShow(password);
        box.add(password);
        SpanLabel error = new SpanLabel("Password error", "ErrorLabel");
        error.setVisible(false);
        box.add(error);
        add(CENTER, box);
        Button forgot = new Button("I forgot my password",
            "ForgotPassword");
        Button account = new Button("I don't have an account",
            "ForgotPassword");
        add(SOUTH, BoxLayout.encloseY(forgot, account));
        FloatingActionButton fab = FloatingActionButton.createFAB(
            FontImage.MATERIAL_ARROW_FORWARD);
        fab.bindFabToContainer(this);
        fab.addActionListener(e -> {
            new MapForm().show();
        });
    }
}
```

As usual the standard back button arrow is used to navigate to the previous Form

We launch with the keyboard open on the password field

The only piece that is slightly different from the verification stage is the 2 buttons on the bottom left for forgotten password/no account

won't implement the functionality of the two buttons in the bottom left of this form as they won't teach anything new.

However the styling that these two buttons use is `ForgotPassword` which is new. It's mostly due to spacing so the text aligns against the `FloatingActionButton`.

Listing 4. 40. ForgotPassword Styling

```
Foreground Color: 0x2775a4
Transparency: 0
Padding Left: 4mm
Padding Right: 4mm
Padding Top: 0
Padding Bottom: 2.5mm
Margin: 0
Font: native:MainLight 2.5mm
```

I forgot my password

I don't have an account

With these changes the initial part of the sign-in process should be done. You can now run this in the IDE and should be able to walk through the sign-up steps of the wizard.

4.3
Summary

In this chapter, we learned:

- We can use a button to masquerade a text field and this actually provides some benefits

- Shadows are CPU Intensive so we can delay the execution of the code and perform the shadow operation later when CPU becomes available

- How to build a signup wizard for an application with SMS/Social activation UI

With this we concluded the basic mockup. We should now have a working mock that can run on the simulator/devices.

We covered a lot of ground but a lot of it is relatively simple and mechanical. But there is still a lot ahead. In the startup spirit we'll work into the night today, this isn't something we'll do every day though...

Day 1: The Mockup – Night Hack

This chapter covers:

- Basic mockup of the map form and the main app side menu
- The creation of a fully functioning mockup of the user app
- Creating an Avatar representation and masking images
- Adding a generic side menu bar/hamburger user interface

There's a lot to digest in this first day so I've split it into a night hack. Since the map is such a central part of this UI it deserves its own chapter.

The Map

The main event for the app is the map. Everything up to this point was just buildup.

The hamburger menu represents the side menu which we will discuss soon

The "Where to?" field is a button that leads to a different UI. This UI is overlaid on top of the map so it's a part of this Form

The two icons on the bottom represent historic rides which I'll hardcode

The bottom notice is something I won't implement within the app. It's possible but it's not trivial. I will implement the gradient overlay though

Figure 5. 1. The Native Uber Map UI

The UI Looks different in the simulator

Since the simulator uses the JavaScript version of Google Maps it looks different to the native device rendering we get from a device build

Before we begin with the Map we need a way to position an image of a driver car in the right place and for that we need the map layout. For now I'll just place one unmoving Taxi and we'll deal with the positioning later on.

5.1.1
Map Layout

The MapLayout is a special layout manager for positioning components at specific latitude/longitude coordinates on top of a Map. You can write your own Layout class and determine the explicit position of an object based on an abstract algorithm. In this case we used the algorithm with the native map for that logic.

In this layout manager I make some assumptions such as the assumption that the layout manager is placed exactly on top of a MapContainer within a LayeredLayout. This means that when we position a component it will be exactly above the map

The MapLayout class is a bit long so I'll break it down to smaller pieces instead of one big unreadable block.

Listing 5. 1. Map Layout Class and member definitions

```
public class MapLayout extends Layout implements
    MapListener { ←
    private static final String COORD_KEY = "$coord";
    private static final String HORIZONTAL_ALIGNMENT= "$align";
    private static final String VERTICAL_ALIGNMENT = "$valign";
    private final MapContainer map;
    private final Container actual;
    private boolean inUpdate;
    private Runnable nextUpdate;
    private int updateCounter;


    public static enum HALIGN {←
        LEFT {
            int convert(int x, int width) { return x; }
        },
        CENTER {
            int convert(int x, int width) { return x - width / 2; }
        },
        RIGHT { int convert(int x, int width) { return x - width; }
        };
        abstract int convert(int x, int width);
    }
```

The first step in implementing the layout manager is extending the layout class. Notice I also implement the MapListener interface so the layout can update positions when the map changes

These enums define alignment relatively to the given position, I use the convert method to calculate the actual X/Y coordinate in a generic way

```
public static enum VALIGN {  ←——— This is identical to HALIGN on the y axis
    TOP {
        int convert(int y, int height) { return y; }
    },
    MIDDLE {
        int convert(int y, int height) { return y + height / 2; }
    },
    BOTTOM {
        int convert(int y, int height) { return y + height; }
    };
    abstract int convert(int y, int height);
}
// rest of class body will go here...
}
```

Now that we have the enclosing class lets look at some of the boilerplate code needed to create a layout manager. Up until now we used pre-existing layout managers but you can do this yourself too.

The map layout is a constraint based layout like BorderLayout. That means you need to add a component to the map layout with a constraint, in this case a Coord object. E.g. for BorderLayout we use container.add(CENTER, myCmp) so here we would use container.add(new Coord(latitude, longitude), myCmp) as opposed to container.add(myCmp):

Listing 5. 2. Map Form Boilerplate code

```
public MapLayout(MapContainer map, Container actual) {
    this.map = map;
    this.actual = actual;
    map.addMapListener(this);  ←——— We break encapsulation to some
}                                       degree by binding the map listener
```

```java
@Override
public void addLayoutComponent(Object value, Component comp,
    Container c) {    ←
    comp.putClientProperty(COORD_KEY, (Coord)value);
}
```

Coord represents a coordinate in the map,
it includes the latitude/longitude values

The map layout is a constraint based
layout similarly to BorderLayout.
Notice I do a cast so if someone adds
a component with a different object
type as a constraint he will get a class
cast exception

```java
@Override
public boolean isConstraintTracking() {
    return true;
}
@Override
public Object getComponentConstraint(Component comp) {
    return comp.getClientProperty(COORD_KEY);
}
@Override
public boolean isOverlapSupported() {
    return true;
}
public static void setHorizontalAlignment(Component cmp, HALIGN a) {
    cmp.putClientProperty(HORIZONTAL_ALIGNMENT, a);    ←
}
public static void setVerticalAlignment(Component cmp, VALIGN a) {
    cmp.putClientProperty(VERTICAL_ALIGNMENT, a);
}
@Override
public Dimension getPreferredSize(Container parent) {
    return new Dimension(100, 100);    ←
}
```

We hint to the layout the
position we would like for the
component relatively to the
coordinate on the X and Y axis

Most layout managers should
define a preferred size but
since we will always reside on
top of a map we can rely on
its preferred size to define the
amount of space required

The breaking of encapsulation isn't an ideal coding practice but it can work for our current purpose. In the future I hope to create a more generic version of this class in the Map cn1lib. Even when we do that, this code is still useful as an explanation of how things like this work.

Up until now we did the easy stuff, lets look at the actual layout logic. The layout logic loops over the components and decides on their position. For most layout managers this is surprisingly easy but for MapLayout we need to decide the position based on the current status of the native map.

That's a problem because the native map can change and it can do so on a separate thread... If we invoke a simplistic API like getScreenCoordinate() (the version that doesn't accept arguments) our map wouldn't move and might even deadlock. getScreenCoordinate() is a blocking call and our app might get stuck waiting for a coordinate location while the map needs something from us. So we need to process the data in batches and have a smart fallback strategy:

Listing 5. 3. Map Form layoutContainer

```
@Override
public void layoutContainer(Container parent) {
    for (Component current : parent) {
        Coord crd = (Coord)current.getClientProperty(COORD_KEY);
        Point p = (Point)
            current.getClientProperty(POINT_KEY);
        if(p == null) {
            p = map.getScreenCoordinate(crd);
            current.putClientProperty(POINT_KEY, p);
        }
        HALIGN h = (HALIGN)
            current.getClientProperty(HORIZONTAL_ALIGNMENT);
        if (h == null) {
            h = HALIGN.LEFT;
        }
        VALIGN v = (VALIGN)
            current.getClientProperty(VERTICAL_ALIGNMENT);
        if(v == null) {
            v = VALIGN.TOP;
        }
```

This is the entire layout code! We get the current coordinate from the constraint and set the size/position

Coordinates are cached and fetched in batches asynchronously, this is pretty important as communicating with the native map is challenging

```
        current . setSize ( current . getPreferredSize  ());  ←
        current . setX (
            h. convert ( p. getX()   –  parentX,  current . getWidth ()));
        current . setY (
            v. convert ( p. getY()   –  parentY,  current . getHeight ()));
    }
}
```

We set X and Y based on the screen
coordinates we got from the map

Normally we shouldn't call setSize,
setX or setY but a layout manager is a
special case. Here, we give all
components their natural preferred
size which in our case makes a lot of
sense

Notice we use the alignment enum to calculate the actual position this allows us to position a car in the center position and a pin in the bottom center.

Next we need to track position update events from the map and update the layout:

Listing 5. 4. Map Form mapPositionUpdated()

```
@Override  ←
public void  mapPositionUpdated(Component source,
    int zoom, Coord center) {  ←
    Runnable r = new Runnable() {
        public void  run() {
            inUpdate = true;
            try {
                List<Coord> coords = new ArrayList<>();
                List<Component> cmps = new ArrayList<>();
                int len = actual.getComponentCount();
```

This is the event callback for map
update, every time the map is
panned or zoomed we revalidate
the parent to force re-layout

This method breaks the
separation between layout
manager and parent
component so this isn't a
best practice but for this
unique case it's necessary

enter position and a pin in the bottom center.

Next we need to track position update events from the map and update the layout:

```java
            for (Component current : actual) {
                Coord crd = (Coord)
                    current.getClientProperty(COORD_KEY);
                coords.add(crd);
                cmps.add(current);
            }
            int startingUpdateCounter = ++updateCounter;
            List<Point> points = map.getScreenCoordinates(coords);
            if (startingUpdateCounter != updateCounter ||
                len != points.size()) {
                return;
            }
            for(int i = 0 ; i < len ; i++) {
                Component current = cmps.get(i);
                Point p = points.get(i);
                current.putClientProperty(POINT_KEY, p);
            }
            actual.setShouldCalcPreferredSize(true);
            actual.revalidate();
            if(nextUpdate != null) {
                Runnable nex = nextUpdate;
                nextUpdate = null;
                callSerially(nex);
            }
        } finally    {
            inUpdate = false ;
        }
    }
};
```

We fetch the coordinates for each one of the components after the position changes. We do this in a batch which is **much** faster than doing this one by one

Another update must have run while we were waiting for the bounding box. In this case, that update would be more recent than this one

We defer updates with callSerially to prevent potential conditions where the map didn't finish updating

```
        if(inUpdate) {
            nextUpdate = r;
        } else {
            nextUpdate = null;
            callSerially(r);
        }
    }
```

Since this method calls back into the map API using the `getScreenCoordinates` method it's important the map finishes whatever it's doing first. Once this is in place we can add a `Container` layer on top of the map and position components using world coordinate system (latitude/longitude).

The MapForm

Now that this is out of the way let's jump right into the map code...

> **You need your google maps key**
>
> Before doing this you need a unique JS maps key from Google in order to run this and you need to complete the Google Maps configuration in `Codename One Settings` as explained here: github.com/codenameone/codenameone-google-maps/ it's also discussed in Appendix D (page 405)

As this is a non-trivial class I'll split the code into the class declaration and the constructor body. I'll start with the former:

Listing 5. 5. MapForm Class Declaration

```
public class MapForm extends Form {
    private static final String MAP_JS_KEY = "Alza--";
    private Image square;
    private int shadowHeight;
```

You need the JS key from Google Maps as explained here github.com/codenameone/ codenameone-google-maps/

This is the shadow on the "where to" mode of this Form we need its height so we can draw it correctly later

We use this to draw the small square next to the "Where to?" button/text field

```
private  Image dropShadow;
private  static  final  Coord telAviv =
    new Coord(32.072449, 34.778613);
public  MapForm() {
    super(new LayeredLayout());
    setScrollableY(false);
    // ... body of constructor ...
}
```

The dropShadow is drawn in the where to mode of the form we'll discuss soon, it provides a sense of depth to the UI

For the mockup we'll hardcode locations in this case I just positioned everything

LayeredLayout is used for placing components on top of the map in arbitrary fixed positions e.g. the "Where to?" button. We usually use BorderLayout which implicitly disables scrollability. LayeredLayout doesn't do that and the forms content pane is scrollable on the Y-axis by default

```
@Override
protected  void  initGlobalToolbar() {
    setToolbar(new Toolbar(true));
    CommonCode.constructSideMenu(getToolbar());
}
private  Container  createHistoryButton(
        String title) {
    FloatingActionButton history = FloatingActionButton.createFAB(
        FontImage.MATERIAL_HISTORY, "History");
    TextArea historyLabel = new TextArea(title, 3, 4);
    historyLabel.setUIID("HistoryLabel");
    historyLabel.setEditable(false);
    historyLabel.setGrowByContent(false);
    Container h = BoxLayout.encloseY(history, historyLabel);
    h.setLeadComponent(history);
    return  h;
}
}
```

We do two important things here... We use the overlay toolbar which "floats" on top of the UI. We initialize the side menu which we will discuss soon in section 5.1.4 (page 146)

This is a generic method to create the "historic rides" buttons on the bottom of the form

The history buttons are FloatingActionButton instances with custom styling

We use TextArea instead of SpanLabel because the history element should act as a single component with lead component

Lead components can take over a hierarchy of several components and handle events for all of them. In this case clicking the TextArea will act as if the FloatingActionButton was clicked and vice versa.

This should make the body of the constructor much clearer:

Listing 5. 6. MapForm Constructor Body

```
shadowHeight = convertToPixels(4);
callSeriallyOnIdle(() -> {
    int t = convertToPixels(3);
    dropShadow = Effects.squareShadow(getDisplayWidth() +
        shadowHeight * 2,  shadowHeight * 2,  shadowHeight,  0.3f);
});
setTransitionOutAnimator(
    CommonTransitions.createEmpty());
MapContainer mc = new MapContainer(MAP_JS_KEY);
mc.setShowMyLocation(true);
add(mc);
Container mapLayer = new Container();
mapLayer.setLayout(new MapLayout(mc, mapLayer));
add(mapLayer);
mc.zoom(telAviv, mc.getMaxZoom() + 1);
Resources gr = Resources.getGlobalResources();
Label car = new  Label(gr.getImage("map-vehicle-icon-uberX.png"));
car.getAllStyles().setOpacity(140);
```

Notice we opted for callSeriallyOnIdle unlike the LoginForm where the animation might have prevented idle from occurring. The shadow is used later on in the showNavigationToolbar method

The transitions in the main application are based on cover so we disable the transition as a side slide followed by cover would look funny

The map is on the lowest layer and everything is placed on top of it

We place a car on top of the map in Tel Aviv. Notice that the car is just a label... The opacity is set to 140 to match the translucent cars in the native app

This layer is on top of the map and uses the MapLayout. Here we will place the car and other landmarks we need

```
mapLayer.add(telAviv, car);
square = Image.createImage(convertToPixels(0.7f),
    convertToPixels(0.7f),  0xff000000);
Button whereTo = new Button("Where To?", square,  "WhereTo");
whereTo.setGap(convertToPixels(3));
add(BoxLayout.encloseY(whereTo));
Container h1 = createHistoryButton("Mikve Yisrael Str...");
Container h2 = createHistoryButton("Burgeranch");
ScaleImageLabel gradient = new ScaleImageLabel(
    gr.getImage("gradient-overlay.png"));
gradient.setBackgroundType(Style.BACKGROUND_IMAGE_SCALED_FILL);
add(BorderLayout.south(gradient));
add(BorderLayout.south(FlowLayout.encloseCenter (h1, h2)));
```

This is the small square we place next to the "Where to?" button. We could have used a unicode value too but it wasn't available in all the fonts

The bottom of the map has a gradient overlay that darkens the bottom. This is probably in place to make the history labels readable

Notice the "Where to?" element is just a button as it moves us to a separate UI and isn't really a TextField

That was a lot to cover but there's more... We did mention 3 new styles in the code which isn't that much, all things considered.

First we have the WhereTo style which pads and sets the element to white. Besides that it sets margin to the top to give enough room for the menu area. It uses a very subtle round rect border with a drop shadow to match the native design which has subtle round corners.

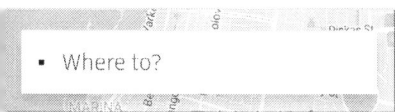

Figure 5. 2. The Where to Button

Listing 5. 7. WhereTo Styling

```
Foreground Color: 0x535861
Background Color: 0xffffff
Transparency: 0
Padding Left: 3.5mm
Padding Right: 3.5mm
Padding Top: 4mm
Padding Bottom: 4mm
Margin Left: 2mm
Margin Right: 2mm
Margin Top: 12mm
Margin Bottom: 0
Border: RoundRect 0.3mm radius, 60 shadow opacity, 4mm shadow spread, 4mm shadow blur
Font: native:MainLight 3.2mm
```

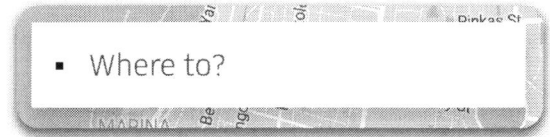

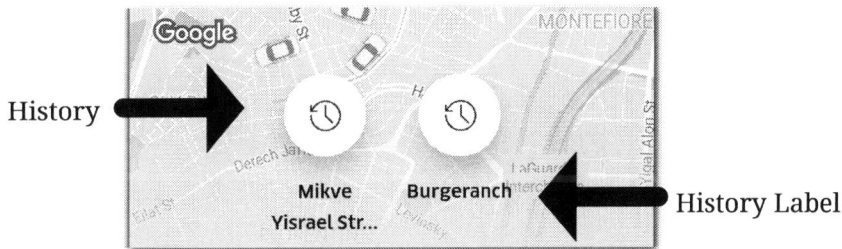

Figure 5. 3. The History Elements

Next we have the History style which is a simple specialization of the FloatingActionButton UIID to match the colors of the history entry.

Listing 5. 8. History Styling

```
Foreground Color: 0x000000
Background Color: 0xffffff
Transparency: 255
Derive: FloatingActionButton Unselected
```

And the last style we have is the HistoryLabel style which doesn't do much. It makes sure to reduce the top margin so it can be close enough to the history button itself and the font is kept small so we can fit several entries in the form:

Listing 5. 9. HistoryLabel Styling

```
Foreground Color: 0x000000
Transparency: 0
Padding Left: 2mm
Padding Right: 2mm
Padding Top: 0
Padding Bottom: 2mm
Margin: 0
Font: native:MainRegular 2.2mm
```

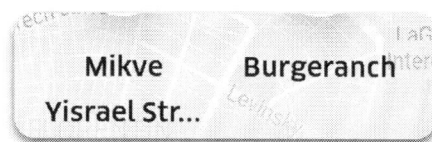

Finally there is one more subtle thing... The hamburger side menu icon has a subtle white/black effect that differs from the icon font menu. This is probably so it will be visible over dark and light areas of the map.

I've separated it into an image which I added as a multi image to the designer tool. I then set the menuImage theme constant to this image.

Theme constants are accessible in the next to last tab within the theme in the designer. You can click Add when that tab is selected and add a constant that's picked up by Codename One. There is a large list of constants within the designer tool. The menuImage theme constant allows you to replace the side menu icon.

Navigation UI

When we press the "Where to?" button we get a UI that looks a bit like a new Form but it isn't really.

If we select the "From" entry, the UI becomes something else...

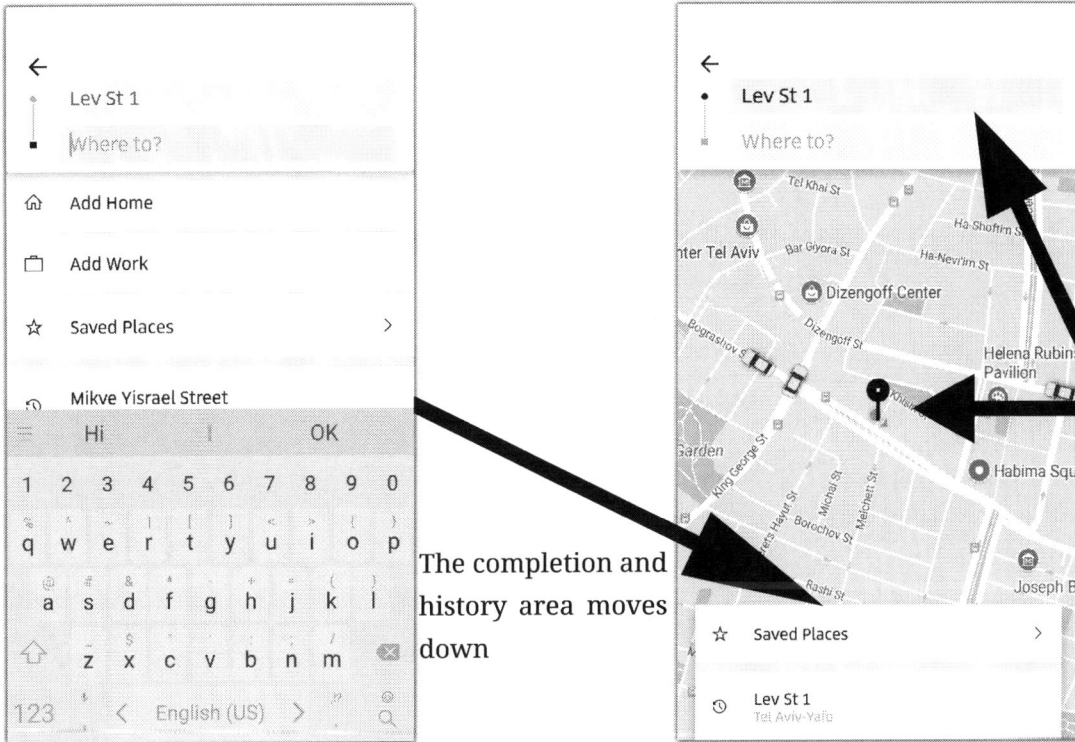

The map can be panned. Panning updates the value in the From field

The completion and history area moves down

Figure 5. 4. The two modes of the "Where to?" UI

There is another subtle behavior that I only noticed when I started playing with this UI. Notice the line and the shapes next to the fields...

When you move the focus between the fields the shapes flip to highlight the focused field.

> This is a simplification of the full UI paradigm we have in this field, I'll revisit this in the section on search

We could build something like this UI with a Dialog or InteractionDialog but I chose to go with a simple Container instances on top of the map. To do this I first had to add a listener to the "Where to?" button:

Listing 5. 10. MapForm Adding listener to the where to button

```
whereTo.addActionListener(e -> showNavigationToolbar());
```

This raises the question of what's in showNavigationToolbar:

Listing 5. 11. MapForm showNavigationToolbar

We create a new layer on top of the current layers in the form. Layers are associated with a component class which allows us to keep it unique (See Sidebar 5.1 Layers In Codename One page 139)

```
void showNavigationToolbar() {
    final Container layer = getLayeredPane(MapForm.class, true);
    Button back = new Button("", "TitleCommand");
    FontImage.setMaterialIcon(back, FontImage.MATERIAL_ARROW_BACK);
    TextField from = new TextField("", "From", 40, TextField.ANY);
    TextField to = new TextField("", "Where to?", 40, TextField.ANY);
    Image circle=Image.createImage(square.getWidth(), square.getHeight(), 0);
    Graphics g = circle.getGraphics();
    g.setColor(0xa4a4ac);
    g.setAntiAliased(true);
    g.fillArc(0, 0, circle.getWidth(), circle.getHeight(), 0, 360);
    final Label fromSelected = new Label(square);
    final Label toSelected = new Label(circle);
    from.getHintLabel().setUIID("FromToTextFieldHint");
    from.setUIID("FromToTextField");
    to.getHintLabel().setUIID("FromToTextFieldHint");
    to.setUIID("FromToTextField");
    Container navigationToolbar = BoxLayout.encloseY(back,
            BorderLayout.centerCenterEastWest(from, null, fromSelected),
            BorderLayout.centerCenterEastWest(to, null, toSelected));
    navigationToolbar.setUIID("WhereToToolbar");
```

We replicate the "look" of a title area without actually creating a title area

The square image already exists from before. We created it for the "Where to?" button. We add a new circle image that we can place next to the from/to fields

We place the text fields in a border layout next to the labels representing the circle and square. We place that in a box layout Y container and that's effectively the entire UI of the top portion

The background is painted in the paintWhereToToolbarBackground method which we'll discuss next

```
navigationToolbar.getUnselectedStyle().setBgPainter((g1, rect) ->
    paintWhereToToolbarBackground(g1, rect, fromSelected,
        circle, toSelected));
back.addActionListener(e -> {
    navigationToolbar.setY(-navigationToolbar.getHeight());
    navigationToolbar.getParent().animateUnlayout(200, 120, () -> {
            layer.removeAll();
            revalidate();
    });
});
layer.setLayout(new BorderLayout());
layer.add(NORTH, navigationToolbar);
navigationToolbar.setWidth(getDisplayWidth());
navigationToolbar.setHeight(getPreferredH());
navigationToolbar.setY(-navigationToolbar.getHeight());
layer.animateLayout(200);
}
```

5

The entire layer uses border layout, north makes sense for this as we want it to span the width but maintain preferred height in the north. We'll use the center for the rest of the UI soon

The component animates down from the top with animate layout. We pre-position it above the Form so animate layout will slide everything from the top

In the code, the method setBgPainter of Style applies a background painter to the style. Each component in Codename One has a background which we normally define with a Style. The Style is constructed from the UIID we define in the theme.

We can derive the component and override the paint method to draw it ourselves but that's hard to do as there are a lot of nuances involved. This is where the background painter (AKA bg painter) comes in. Instead of using the Style/UIID to draw the background we can use custom drawing code that renders the background. This is accomplished via the Painter interface that we can pass in the setBgPainter call. We can thus customize the way components are drawn without deriving them, and still keep the code generic.

The next step in the "Where to?" UI is the paintWhereToToolbarBackground. It renders the background and drop shadow:

Listing 5. 12. paintWhereToToolbarBackground

The background painter lets us control the shadow from the top area and draw the line between the circle/square images

```
private void paintWhereToToolbarBackground(Graphics g1, Rectangle rect,
    final Label fromSelected, Image circle, final Label toSelected) {  ←
    g1.setAlpha(255);
    g1.setColor(0xffffff);  ←
```

The fact that we have a background painter makes some of the aspects of the UIID less significant (e.g. background color) but we still need it for padding, margin etc.

```
    if(dropShadow != null) {  ←
        g1.drawImage(dropShadow, rect.getX() - shadowHeight,
            rect.getY() + rect.getHeight() -
            dropShadow.getHeight() / 4 * 3);  ←
        g1.fillRect(rect.getX(), rect.getY(), rect.getWidth(),
            rect.getY() + rect.getHeight() - shadowHeight);
    } else g1.fillRect(rect.getX(), rect.getY(),
                rect.getWidth(), rect.getHeight());
    g1.setColor(0xa4a4ac);
    g1.setAntiAliased(true);
    int x = fromSelected.getAbsoluteX() +
        fromSelected.getWidth() / 2 - 1;
    int y = fromSelected.getAbsoluteY() + fromSelected.getHeight() /
        2 + circle.getHeight() / 2;  ←
    g1.fillRect(x, y, 2, toSelected.getAbsoluteY() - y +
        toSelected.getHeight() / 2 - circle.getHeight() / 2);
}
```

The shadow image is created asynchronously by the callSeriallyOnIdle code in the constructor so it might not be ready when this is drawn

We fill the rectangle on top of the drop shadow covering half of it. This makes it feel like a directional shadow

I used fill rect instead of draw line to make a 2 pixel wide line, I could have used draw line with stroke but this is simpler and probably faster

The background painter provides a lot of fine grained control over component rendering. We can literally draw anything as the background of any component without changing the code of that component...

This works nicely for the top area and requires a few additional UIID's, specifically: WhereToToolbar, FromToTextField and FromToTextFieldHint.

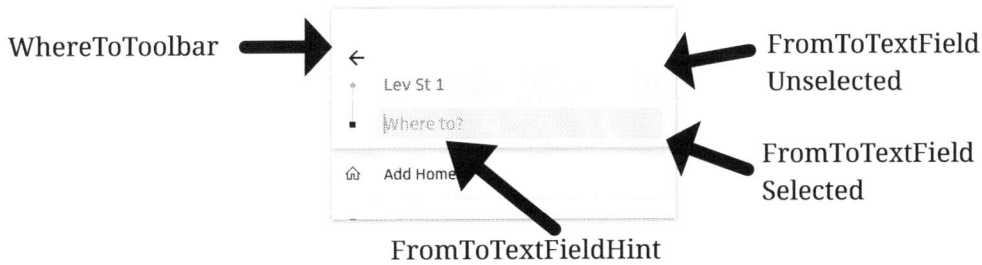

Figure 5. 5. The UIID's and pieces of the "Where to?" Toolbar

The WhereToToolbar style isn't used much since the background painter overrides the drawing aspects but the padding on the bottom leaves room for the drop shadow.

Listing 5. 13. WhereToToolbar Styling

```
Background Color: 0xffffff
Transparency: 0
Padding Left: 0
Padding Right: 0
Padding Top: 0
Padding Bottom: 5mm
Margin: 0
```

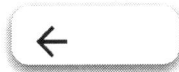

The `FromToTextField` has a slightly different styling from the default text field styling with a selected/unselected background color:

Listing 5. 14. FromToTextField Styling

Foreground Color: 0x000000
Background Color: 0xf9f9f9
Transparency: 255
Padding: 1mm
Margin: 1mm
Font: native:MainLight 2.8mm

Lev St 1

We do something slightly different in the selected style:

Listing 5. 15. FromToTextField Selected Styling

Background Color: 0xfededed
Derive: FromToTextField Unselected

The `FromToTextFieldHint` is needed, as the regular hint styling doesn't fit here.

Listing 5. 16. FromToTextFieldHint Styling

Foreground Color: 0xa4a4ac
Transparency: 0
Margin: 0
Derive: FromToTextField Unselected

Layers In Codename One

Codename One allows placing components one on top of the other and we commonly use layered layout to do that. The form class has a builtin `Container` that resides in a layer on top of the content pane of the form.

When you add an element to a form it implicitly goes into the content pane. However, you can use `getLayeredPane()` and add any `Component` there. Such a `Component` will appear above the content pane. Notice that this layer resides below the title area (on the Y axis) and won't draw on top of that.

When Codename One introduced the layered pane it was instantly useful. However, its popularity caused conflicts. Two separate pieces of code using the layered pane could easily collide with one another. Codename One solved it with `getLayeredPane(Class c, boolean top)`. This method allocates a layer for a specific class within the layered pane. This way if two different classes use this method instead of the `getLayeredPane()` method they won't collide. Each will get its own container in a layered layout within the layered pane seamlessly. The `top` flag indicates whether we want the layer to be the top most or bottom most layer within the layered pane (assuming it wasn't created already). This allows you to place a layer that can appear above or below the already installed layers.

We only make use of the layered pane in this book but there are two additional layers on top of it. The form layered pane is identical to the layered pane but spans the entire height of the `Form` (including the title area). As a result the form layered pane is slower as it needs to handle some special cases to support this functionality.

The glass pane is the top most layer, unlike the layered pane it's purely a graphical layer. You can only draw on the glass pane with a `Painter` instance and a `Graphics` object. You can't add components into that layer.

5

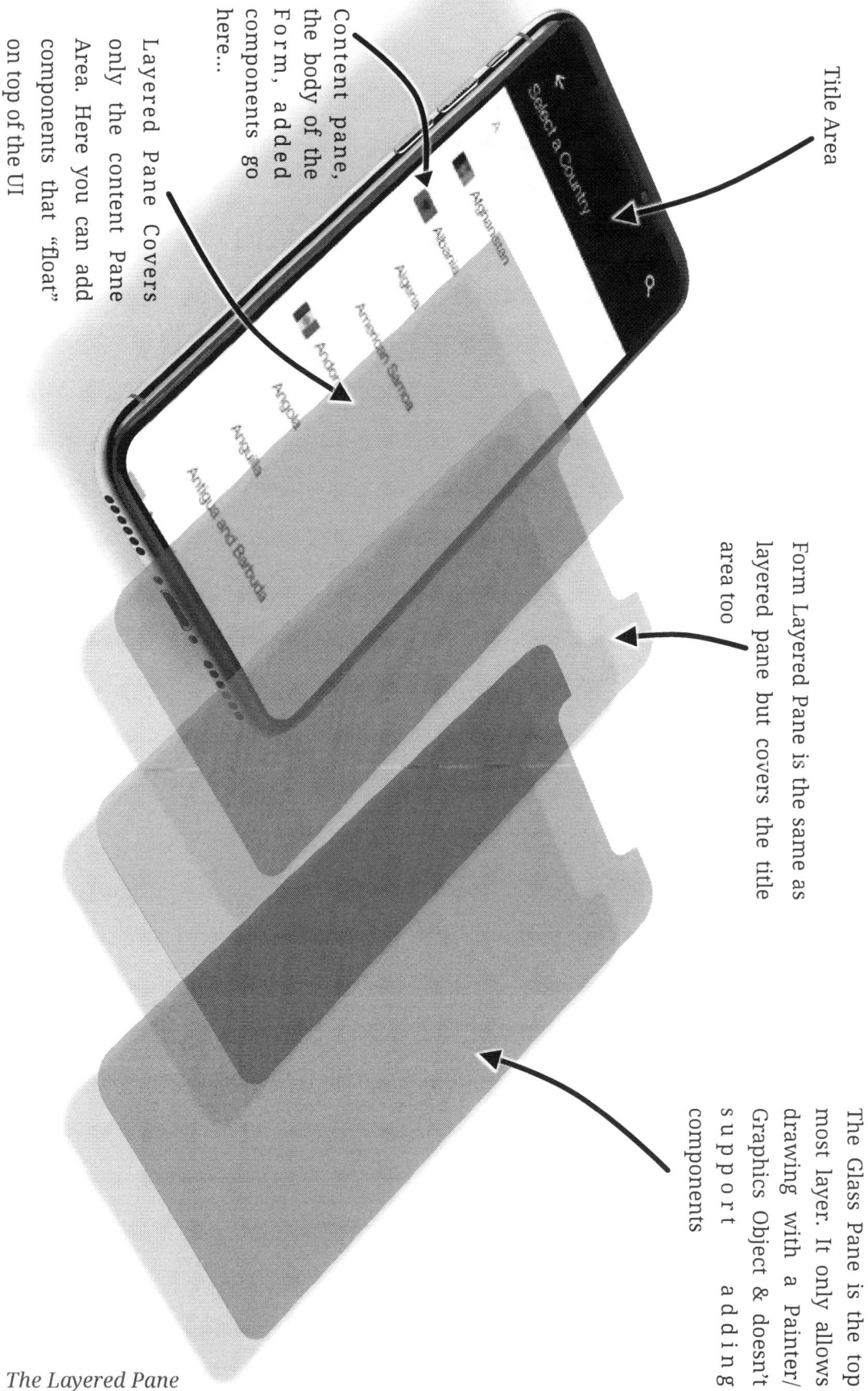

Content pane,
the body of the
Form, added
components go
here...

Layered Pane Covers
only the content Pane
Area. Here you can add
components that "float"
on top of the UI

Title Area

Form Layered Pane is the same as
layered pane but covers the title
area too

The Glass Pane is the top
most layer. It only allows
drawing with a Painter/
Graphics Object & doesn't
s u p p o r t   a d d i n g
components

Figure 5. 6. The Layered Pane

Navigation UI - Destination

The destination UI toggle is a huge part of the navigation UI. It's the bottom section of the form that contains the list of destinations. We can build it on top of the code we wrote for the navigation UI and place it in the center of the layer so it will play nicely with the rest of the UI.

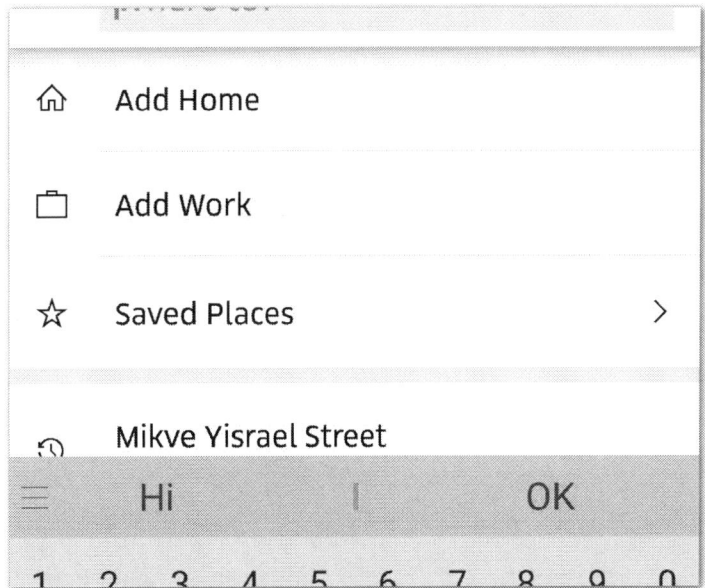

Figure 5. 7. Where to UI Destination Panel

ℹ️ The following code block relies on an import static com.codename1.ui.FontImage.*; statement to keep the code concise. This allows replacing code like FontImage.setMaterialIcon(addHome, FontImage.MATERIAL_HOME); with setMaterialIcon(addHome, MATERIAL_HOME);

Listing 5. 17. Where to UI

```
private void showToNavigationBar(Container parentLayer) {
    MultiButton addHome = new MultiButton("Add Home"); ←
    addHome.setUIID("Container");
    addHome.setUIIDLine1("WhereToButtonLine1");
    addHome.setIconUIID("WhereToButtonIcon");
    setMaterialIcon(addHome, MATERIAL_HOME);
    MultiButton addWork = new MultiButton("Add Work");
    addWork.setUIID("Container");
    addWork.setUIIDLine1("WhereToButtonLine1");
    addWork.setIconUIID("WhereToButtonIcon");
    setMaterialIcon(addWork, MATERIAL_WORK);
```

The top elements are relatively simple multi-buttons, we use Container as their UIID so they will be transparent with 0 padding/margin

```
MultiButton savedPlaces = new MultiButton("Saved Places");
savedPlaces.setUIID("Container");
savedPlaces.setUIIDLine1("WhereToButtonLineNoBorder");
savedPlaces.setEmblemUIID("WhereToButtonLineNoBorder");
savedPlaces.setIconUIID("WhereToButtonIcon");
savedPlaces.setEmblem(createMaterial(MATERIAL_NAVIGATE_NEXT,
        savedPlaces.getIconComponent().getUnselectedStyle()));
setMaterialIcon(savedPlaces, MATERIAL_STAR_BORDER);
Label whereSeparator = new Label("", "WhereSeparator");
whereSeparator.setShowEvenIfBlank(true);   <-----
MultiButton history1 = new MultiButton("Mikve Yisrael Str...");
history1.setUIID("Container");
history1.setUIIDLine1("WhereToButtonLine1");
history1.setIconUIID("WhereToButtonIcon");
setMaterialIcon(history1, MATERIAL_HISTORY);
Container result = BoxLayout.encloseY(addHome, addWork,
    savedPlaces, whereSeparator, history1);
result.setUIID("Form");   <-----
result.setScrollableY(true);
result.setScrollVisible(false); <-----
result.setY(getDisplayHeight());
result.setWidth(getDisplayWidth());
result.setHeight(result.getPreferredH());
parentLayer.add(CENTER, result);
parentLayer.animateLayout(200);   <-----
}
```

The separator is just a label with a specific style. Notice that blank labels/buttons etc. are hidden by default in Codename One and you should invoke setShowEvenIfBlank if you want such a label to still render

We can reuse the Form UIID here because that's effectively what we want. We want this UI to appear as if it's a Form

We need this to be scrollable but we don't want the scrollbar on the side as it might cause aesthetic issues

The showing of this element is animated from the bottom of the Form

5

While this UI is very simple it did define a few UIID's. Let's start with `WhereToButtonLine1` which represents the entries in the list of elements and also adds the underline. We put the underline here because the design placed the underline only under the text and didn't place it under the icon.

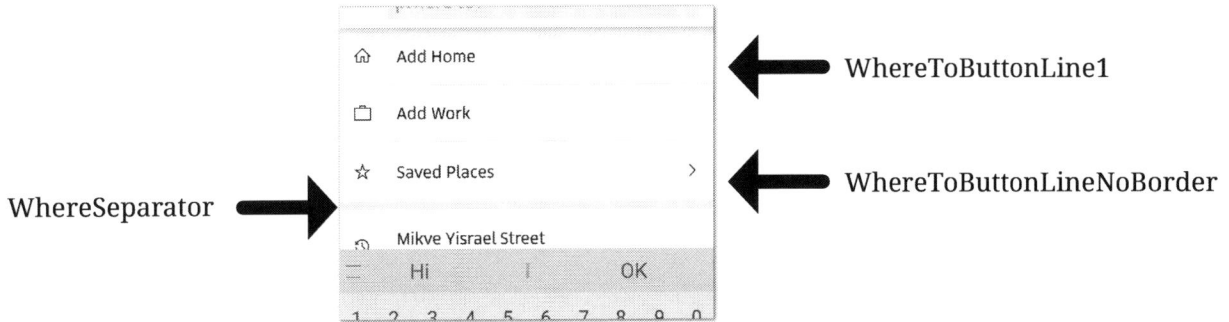

Figure 5. 8. Styles of the Destination UI

Listing 5. 18. WhereToButtonLine1 Styling

```
Foreground Color: 0x000000
Transparency: 0
Padding Left: 2mm
Padding Right: 4mm
Padding Top: 2.5mm
Padding Bottom: 2.5mm
Margin: 0
Border: Underline 2px 0xededed
Font: native:MainLight 2.8mm
```

The WhereToButtonIcon style tries to align with the WhereToButtonLine1 text while offering slightly different padding:

Listing 5. 19. WhereToButtonIcon Styling

```
Transparency: 0
Padding Left: 2mm
Padding Right: 2mm
Padding Top: 2.5mm
Padding Bottom: 2.5mm
Border: Empty
Derive: WhereToButtonLine1
```

Since we have a separator under the last line we need a special case: WhereToButtonLineNoBorder This removes the builtin underline, otherwise we'd see a separator followed by a separator:

Listing 5. 20. WhereToButtonLineNoBorder Styling

```
Border: Empty
Derive: WhereToButtonLine1
```

Saved Places

The WhereSeparator UIID is just the gray area separating the top entries from the bottom entries:

Listing 5. 21. WhereSeparator Styling

```
Background Color: 0xededed
Transparency: 255
Padding Left: 2mm
Padding Right: 2mm
Padding Top: 0
Padding Bottom: 2mm
Margin: 0
```

Now that we added this, we need to show this UI and hide it when the user toggles the focus in the text fields.

Listing 5. 22. Toggling the "Where to?" UI when focus changes

```
from.addFocusListener(new FocusListener() {
    public void focusGained(Component cmp) {
        fromSelected.setIcon(square);
        if(layer.getComponentCount() > 1) {
            Component c = layer.getComponentAt(1);
            c.setY(getDisplayHeight());
            layer.animateUnlayout(200, 150, () -> {
                c.remove();
                revalidate();
            });
        }
    }

    public void focusLost(Component cmp) {
        fromSelected.setIcon(circle);
    }
});
to.addFocusListener(new FocusListener() {
    public void focusGained(Component cmp) {
        fromSelected.setIcon(circle);
        toSelected.setIcon(square);
        showToNavigationBar(layer);
    }
    public void focusLost(Component cmp) {
        toSelected.setIcon(circle);
    }
});
```

When focus is lost/gained we toggle between the square and circle modes by setting the icon to the appropriate labels

We always have one container in the layer except for the case where the second component is the "Where To" container. It's always the second component because it's always added last

We set the position of this container below the forms

Animate "unlayout" moves the component outside of the screen to the position we asked for using a smooth animation

This callback is invoked when the unlayout completes. At this point we have an invalid UI that needs a layout but before we do that we remove the component that we animated out of the form

An animateLayout moves a Component from a place where it shouldn't be to a place where it should be based on the layout. animateUnlayout does the opposite. It lays out the components in the place where they should be based on the layout manager and then animates them back to the invalid position they had to begin with!

This is useful if we want to animate an operation that doesn't have a valid position. E.g. when deleting a button we might want to animate it floating out to the right side of the screen so we can do something like this:

Listing 5. 23. animateUnlayout Delete Button Sample

```
myButton.setX(getDisplayWidth());          This will position myButton in an illegal
                                           position outside the screen on the right side

parent.animateUnlayoutAndWait(200);        This will return the button to its original
                                           position over 200ms

myButton.remove();                         Even though the button is in an invalid place it's
                                           still physically there so we remove it

parent.animateLayout(150);                 After unlayout the UI is invalid and needs a
                                           revalidate to occupy the space left by the button
```

Now that the UI appears we also need to remove it when going back, so I'll update the back action listener from above to handle the "Where to?" UI as well.

Listing 5. 24. The back button should also remove the where to section

```
back.addActionListener(e -> {
    navigationToolbar.setY(-navigationToolbar.getHeight());
    if (layer.getComponentCount() > 1)
        layer.getComponentAt(1).setY(getDisplayHeight());      This is the exact same
    navigationToolbar.getParent().animateUnlayout(200,  120, () -> {      unlayout operation
            layer.removeAll();                                 we did before
            revalidate();
    });
});
```

We now need to make a subtle but important change to the background painter code from before:

Listing 5. 25. The drop shadow creates a gap between the pieces

```
// ... unchanged code ...
if (dropShadow != null) {
    if(layer.getComponentCount() > 1) {  ←───────────────
        g1.fillRect(rect.getX(), rect.getY(), rect.getWidth(),
            rect.getHeight());
    }
    g1.drawImage(dropShadow, rect.getX() - shadowHeight, rect.getY() +
        rect.getHeight() - dropShadow.getHeight() / 4 * 3);
    g1.fillRect (rect.getX(), rect.getY(), rect.getWidth(),
        rect.getY() + rect.getHeight() - shadowHeight);
} else {
    g1.fillRect(rect.getX(), rect.getY(), rect.getWidth(),
        rect.getHeight());
}
// ... unchanged code ...
```

Because of the drop shadow, a gap is formed between the top and bottom pieces so a special case here paints a white rectangle under the shadow to hide the gap. Without that the shadow would appear on top of the map and not on top of a white background.

Once this is done opening the "Where to?" UI and toggling the fields should work as expected.

The Side Menu

The last big missing piece is the side menu UI. I've moved that code into a separate hardcoded class for reuse in other forms. This UI isn't used in other forms at the moment but I think it's a good habit to separate the menu from the component code. We might want to show the menu in a different Form in the future.

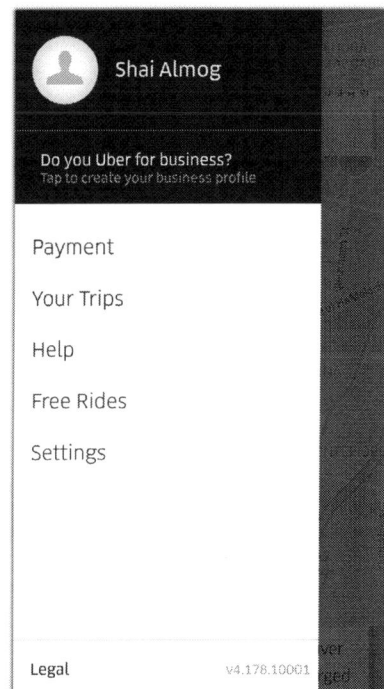

Figure 5. 9. The Side Menu UI can Open by Swiping or Clicking the Hamburger icon

147

Listing 5. 26. Side menu construction

```java
public static void constructSideMenu(Toolbar tb) {
    Label userAndAvatar = new Label("Shai Almog", getAvatar(),
        "AvatarBlock");
    userAndAvatar.setGap(convertToPixels(3));
    tb.addComponentToSideMenu(userAndAvatar);

    MultiButton uberForBusiness =
        new MultiButton("Do you Uber for business?");
    uberForBusiness.setTextLine2("Tap to create your business profile");
    uberForBusiness.setUIID("UberForBusinessBackground");
    uberForBusiness.setUIIDLine1("UberForBusinessLine1");
    uberForBusiness.setUIIDLine2("UberForBusinessLine2");
    tb.addComponentToSideMenu(uberForBusiness);

    tb.addCommandToSideMenu("Payment", null, e -> {});
    tb.addCommandToSideMenu("Your Trips", null, e -> {});
    tb.addCommandToSideMenu("Help", null, e -> {});
    tb.addCommandToSideMenu("Free Rides", null, e -> {});
    tb.addCommandToSideMenu("Settings", null, e -> {});

    Button legalButton = new Button("Legal", "Legal");
    Container legal = BorderLayout.centerCenterEastWest(null,
        new Label("v4.178.1001", "VersionNumber"), legalButton);
    legal.setLeadComponent(legalButton);
    legal.setUIID("SideNavigationPanel");
    tb.setComponentToSideMenuSouth(legal);
}
```

We'll discuss the getAvatar method soon, this code generates the avatar image at the top with the name next to it

The gap between the text and the icon in the avatar is larger than average

The "Legal" button is a "South" component. It's a special case in the on-top side menu that allows you to place an element below the menu itself. Its styling is separate and it slides in/out. So we need to give it the SideNavigationPanel styling too

148

The avatar is just an image of the user. When an image wasn't selected we use a placeholder image which is generated in the getAvatar method.

Listing 5. 27. Avatar factory method

```java
private static Image avatar;
public static Image getAvatar() {
    if(avatar == null) {
        int size = convertToPixels(10);
        Image temp = Image.createImage(size, size, 0xff000000);
        Graphics g = temp.getGraphics();
        g.setAntiAliased(true);
        g.setColor(0xffffff);
        g.fillArc(0, 0, size, size, 0, 360);
        Object mask = temp.createMask();
        Style s = new Style();
        s.setFgColor(0xc2c2c2);
        s.setBgTransparency(255);
        s.setBgColor(0xe9e9e9);
        FontImage x = FontImage.createMaterial(FontImage.MATERIAL_PERSON,
            s, size);
        avatar = x.fill(size, size);
        if(avatar instanceof FontImage) {
            avatar − ((FontImage)avatar).toImage();
        }
        avatar = avatar.applyMask(mask);
    }
    return avatar;
}
```

We create an opaque 10mm black image to use as a mask, masks allow us to crop out unwanted pieces of an image. In this case we want to make the image round

We fill the shape we want in white in this case an arc. Notice we activate anti-aliasing otherwise the resulting image will look jagged (which is also why we avoided shape clipping here)

The FontImage class can use the given color and opacity settings. We use the version of the class that accepts a Style object and size so we'll have fine grained control from code

We can't apply a mask to an image of a size that's different from the mask size. Masking doesn't work well with complex images such as font images so we convert it to a regular image first

5

Finally we also need two UIID's to get this to work...

The SideNavigationPanel is mostly black on white and relatively clean. We have an underline at the bottom to separate the panel from the component below (south component):

Listing 5. 28. SideNavigationPanel Styling

```
Background Color: 0xffffff
Transparency: 255
Padding Left: 0
Padding Right: 0
Padding Top: 0
Padding Bottom: 2px
Margin: 0
Border: Underline 2px 0xe0e0e0
```

The SideCommand reflects that as well. The padding of the side command prevents duplicate padding when commands are one on top of the other:

Listing 5. 29. SideCommand Styling

```
Foreground Color: 0x000000
Transparency: 0
Padding Left: 3mm
Padding Right: 3mm
Padding Top: 4mm
Padding Bottom: 1mm
Margin: 0
Font: native:MainLight 4mm
```

Settings

With that swiping in the side menu or clicking the hamburger icon should show the elegant side menu bar and the mockup is complete!

You can run the mockup and go through the stages of the signup wizard with fake data, this is a great starting point as it's easy to experiment with mockup code to get a feel for the application.

Summary

In this chapter, we learned:

- Since the simulator uses the JavaScript version of Google Maps it looks different to the native device rendering we get from a device build

- You can write your own Layout class and determine the explicit position of an object based on an abstract algorithm

- The background painter provides a lot of fine grained control over component rendering. We can literally draw anything as the background of any component without changing the code of that component...

- We can use image masking to change the shape of an image, this allows us to convert a square image to a circle, a rounded rectangle etc.

This included some challenges but overall it was still mostly mechanical. The next few days would be shorter in terms of content but might be harder in terms of concepts.

5

Day 2: The Server | 6

This chapter covers:

- Binding JPA business objects to the underlying database and setting up the abstraction through Spring Boot

- Creating WebSocket and WebService API's

- Mapping of the business logic to an abstract server implementation

Up until now we mocked the UI. It did give us a general sense of what we need to get started with the app. Today we'll try to build a simple server and a communication protocol. We won't do anything that's too fancy because the main goal of this book is mobile development.

We'll use WebSockets for the more verbose data as they are more efficient than web services.

To setup Spring Boot and MySQL check out Appendix B (page 393)

Unlike yesterdays work which was entirely visual today we will do everything purely in the backend. This might be a bit frustrating as there is very little visual feedback on success/failure. Don't despair! In the next day we will put it all together and tie the client/server together.

Server Features | 6.1

We don't need that much from the server as we will do a lot of the work on the client (e.g. SMS activation). In the real world the server should be far more elaborate and handle more but I don't want to spend too much time on it.

So the initial set of server tasks are:

- Add a new user

- User authorization

- Update user information

- Track cars

- Hail a car

- Pair car and user

- Log historic trip details

To proceed with these tasks we need to:

- Define a storage Schema

- Define a communication protocol

I won't discuss features such as server initiated push, billing or related complexities right now. We'll cover them later. I won't cover the rating process. It's relatively simple and won't teach anything new.

WebService invocations call the respective webservice class. DAO objects returned from the WebService arrive to the device as JSON

Layers are separate and classes only communicate with the next layer. DAO is the only exception as it transfers information between all tiers.

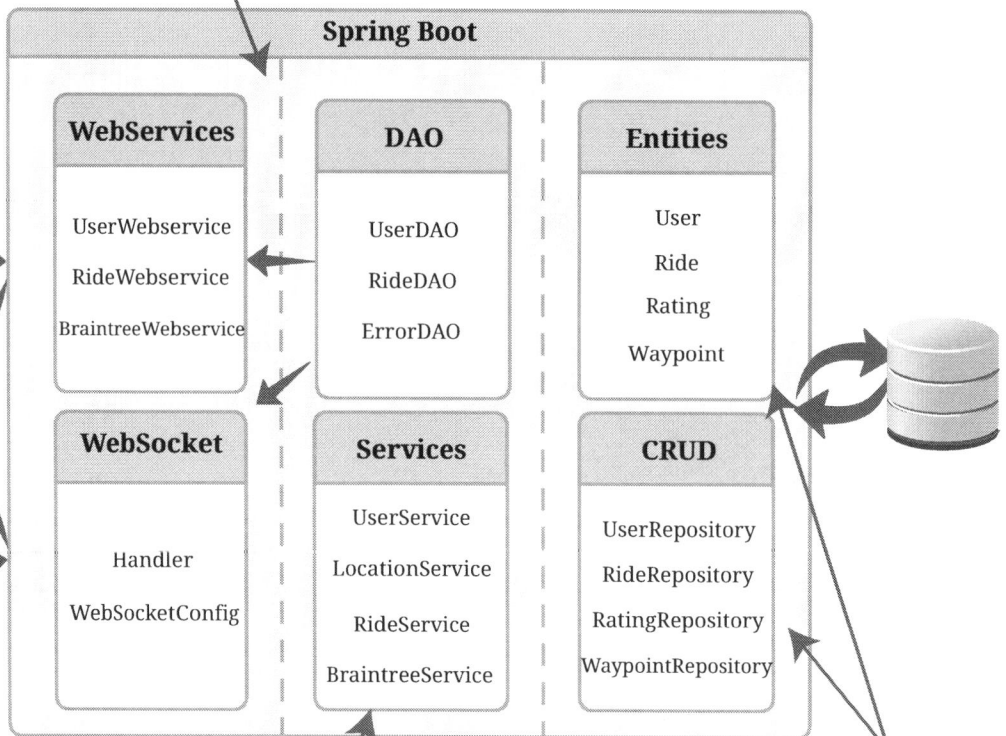

Spring Boot

WebServices	**DAO**	**Entities**
UserWebservice	UserDAO	User
RideWebservice	RideDAO	Ride
BraintreeWebservice	ErrorDAO	Rating
		Waypoint

WebSocket	**Services**	**CRUD**
Handler	UserService	UserRepository
WebSocketConfig	LocationService	RideRepository
	RideService	RatingRepository
	BraintreeService	WaypointRepository

All WebSocket communications go through this layer, data is passed in binary form

Services implement the generic application logic and hide the data-specific logic from the web tier; This promotes code reuse and easier testability

All access to the database is conducted purely by the entity layer which in turn is only accessed via the services layer

Figure 6. 1. The Tiers of the Server

It's OK if this diagram is unclear at this stage. It's meant as a broad map. As we build the code for the server during the day I suggest referencing this map to see where a specific class fits within it. The diagram give a bird's-eye view of the classes that make up the final server. You will notice that the server is divided into layers. Each layer can only communicate with the adjacent layers.

Storage Schema

I mentioned the necessary functionality first as it makes more sense to start there when I'm trying to explain a complex idea. However, I'm starting the code with the data model. This is an age-old developer adage that predated object oriented programming:

> git actually has a simple design, with stable and reasonably well-documented data structures. In fact, I'm a huge proponent of designing your code around the data, rather than the other way around, and I think it's one of the reasons git has been fairly successful [...] I will, in fact, claim that the difference between a bad programmer and a good one is whether he considers his code or his data structures more important.

— Linus Torvalds creator of Linux and Git

With that in mind I want to start coding by understanding what we want to store and what we want to know about the user:

- User - this will also include drivers
- History - historic trips taken by the user/driver
- Rating - a rating and review list for a specific driver

To keep things simple I use one element: User. I use it for drivers, hailing and end users.

Simple doesn't mean I'm taking a shortcut... Simple means I'm reusing the same ideas and will save code as a result. Saving code results in higher quality and more maintainable apps.

So we'll start by deciding on the data schema for the user object.

The User Object

The first thing we need in the server is the end user data model. We can turn to the UI to get a sense of what's necessary.

This is the basic information we need for an end user, notice this isn't "code", just the data that we need:

Listing 6. 1. Basic user information

```
String givenName;
String surname;
byte [] avatar;
String phone;
String email;
String password;
```

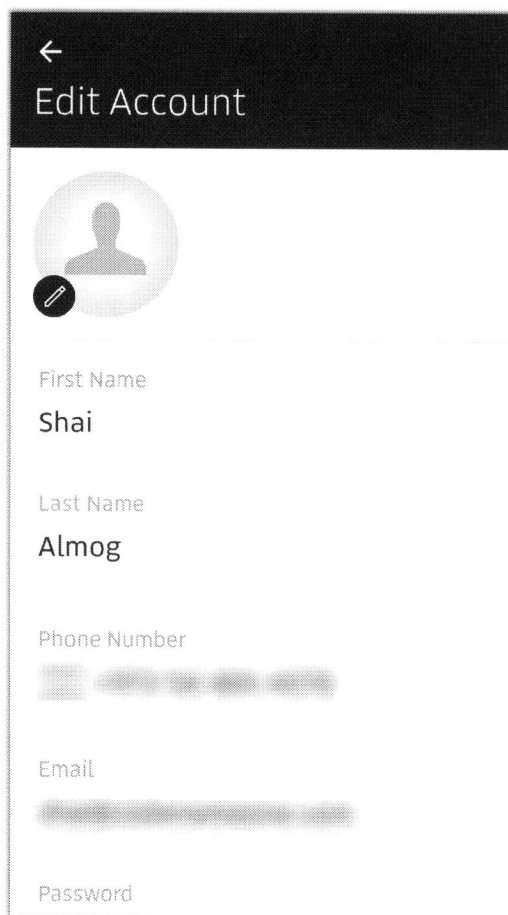
Figure 6. 2. Uber Settings UI

ℹ️ We Won't Store the Password

This would be a security risk, we'll store a salted hash of the password instead. We'll cover this in section 6.3 Salted Hashes vs. Encryption Sidebar (page 174)

There are a few other things I know we need from the UI we did earlier. E.g. we can login using Facebook or Google so we need the user ID's of those social services if they are applicable:

Listing 6. 2. Social login details

```
String facebookId;
String googleId;
```

We also need to know if this user is a driver and if so we need to know what car the user drives as Uber shows that information when hailing a taxi:

Listing 6. 3. Driver information

```
boolean driver;
String car;
```

Why No Driver Class?

Now you might be thinking: why not have a User subclass called Driver?

Wouldn't that be more object oriented?

Possibly. In these things right and wrong is often "flexible". While polymorphism can work for a Driver class and keep some of the common code generic the data storage logic can't. Ultimately we'd write more code to implement that with no significant benefit. Specifically:

- We'd need some duplicate boilerplate code for the CRUD interfaces
- The @Entity boilerplate in the Driver class would also grow the code
- We'd probably need a separate DAO object

The list goes on. I'm a big fan of doing the minimum amount of work to accomplish the goal at hand. In this case adding a couple of fields to the User class is far simpler than the inheritance option. Since we followed the object oriented principles of encapsulation it would be trivial to refactor this in the future if the need arises.

Moving on to hailing, we need to know where the car is right now; e.g. is it active/available? Also for a regular user we'd like to know if he's hailing a cab right now:

Listing 6. 4. Hailing and location information

```
Point location;
boolean hailing;
Long assignedUser;
```

With assignedUser we can mark the user that's assigned to a specific driver.

We also want to have the driver's rating. Normally we store it in the database with the information of each ride but querying the database every time a driver is viewed would be problematic. We cache the data within the user object to save on server processing power.

Listing 6. 5. Sharded rating data

```
float    currentRating;
```

An important piece of information we need is the location of every user/driver and the direction they are headed in. We can store this directly in the User object which is as good a place as any to store this data:

Listing 6. 6. Location meta-data

```
double latitude  ;
double longitude ;
float    direction  ;
```

Again Object-Oriented purists might "jump" at the use of these fields instead of a   Location object. I don't introduce an object unless there is a reason to introduce it. Let's examine this in a pro/con approach.

The pro for having a Location object would be:

• Better encapsulation

The cons would be:

• More code

• Slower queries requiring join statements

• Harder to write JPA queries across entities

• More classes to map to the client side

This would flip if we had a larger/more functional server. E.g. if we had landmarks which also had locations it might have made sense to have a common Location object/table that handles common code and delegate on.

I've been a consultant for a decade and one of the most common mistakes I've seen in the hundreds of projects I helped with was over-design. Developers spent months trying to solve potential future instead of solving the immediate problem correctly. If you design your code well and use abstraction you can always move things around and adapt to a more elaborate design, but once you have an elaborate design you can't go back to a simpler approach. You're stuck.

Notice that it's still crucial to use proper encapsulation. I'm not advocating a situation where you don't think about the future at all... In fact, the second worst problem is code stagnation. In that case developers treat the design as a fixed/permanent decision and are afraid to change large parts of the code.

JPA

The Java Persistence API (JPA) is an ORM (Object-Relational Mapper) that abstracts the underlying SQL database. An ORM seamlessly converts objects to SQL and SQL data into objects. I chose to use JPA to help us develop quickly without getting into database quirks. It lets me work with objects without relying on implementation details.

Why JPA?

This can be divided into two segments:

1. Why ORM and not SQL (or a lower level abstraction e.g. jOOQ).

2. Why JPA and not JDO?

ORM is a pretty divisive issue among programmers so I'll try to avoid the religious debate. I had several goals in picking ORM:

- I can get something working quickly
- I can avoid explaining complex issues like low level SQL/schemas, Object Oriented Databases etc.
- It's mostly easy to understand with the basic use cases we need

I'm a firm believer in build fast and fix as needed. If ORM becomes a hindrance we can replace it easily as all the code is abstracted in one place. The code is simple to understand even if you aren't a fan of ORM.

I specifically chose JPA as the ORM because it's well known, highly documented and deeply integrated into everything. JDO is a reasonably popular standardized approach as well but JPA seems to be more common for Spring Boot.

One of the cool things about JPA is the fact that it can automatically generate a database schema. This makes the setup and changes during development much easier.

> ℹ️ JPA is the name of the standard, the default implementation of that standard in Spring Boot is called Hibernate

I can put this all together as an Entity JPA object. Notice I redacted the getter/setters and constructors:

Listing 6. 7. The User Object

```java
@Entity
public class User {
    @Id
    @GeneratedValue(strategy = GenerationType.AUTO)
    private   Long id;   ←
    private   String givenName;
    private   String surname;
    private   String phone;
    private   String email;
    private   String password;
    private   String facebookId;
    private   String googleId;
    private   boolean driver;
    private   String car;
    private   boolean hailing;
    private   Long assignedUser;
    private   float currentRating;
    private   double latitude;
    private   double longitude;
    private   float direction;
    @Lob
    private   byte [] avatar;   ←
    // Getters, Setters and constructors
}
```

I didn't mention the auto-generated id value which allows us to keep the data unique. This is generally a good practice as the key is separate from business logic

I also had to add the @Lob annotation to the avatar image data so it will be stored properly in the database

The id value serves as the primary key to the table generated within the database. A primary key is always unique within the table and must have a value.

When we run this code within the Spring Boot application, the JPA implementation will automatically create a database table for us with the fields as names. It will implicitly map each field to a column in the table.

In theory we don't need to know SQL at all or understand what's going under the hood. In practice it's very useful to have an SQL table under the hood. Especially for a lean startup…
An SQL database lets you access the underlying data with 3rd party tools to produce reports/analysis and track issues. That's very convenient if you need to move quickly and understand the underlying data. The ability to launch an SQL browser utility and look through the tables/query easily is remarkably helpful when tracking issues. The ACID aspects of relational databases make them especially convenient workhorses.

ACID

The ACID acronym stands for Atomicity, Consistency, Isolation and Durability. The four principals of database reliability. These are remarkably hard to get right while maintaining high performance. These 4 principals effectively mean the database won't break in odd cases leading you down a rabbit hole of "weird bugs".

I made the mistake of working with Google's Data Store big table API which favors scale over reliability. The lack of even basic ACID support and the limits it places on queries made it difficult to work with. Surprisingly, most non-relational databases often perform worse when compared to modern SQL databases. Their performance advantage only kicks in for ridiculously large data loads.

Authorization

There's one big missing piece about the user and it's an important piece: "Authorization".

Listing 6. 8. Authorization Logic

```
@Column(unique=true)          This is the JPA syntax to indicate that this value must
private  String authToken;    be unique in the table. If we try to insert an authToken
                              with the same value the SQL database will stop us

public  User() {
     authToken = UUID.randomUUID().toString();
}

         We initialize the token in the default constructor, this
         works great for a new entity. When we load from the
         database JPA will replace that value
```

> ℹ️ The unique attribute is only applicable to the SQL table creation code, JPA doesn't enforce uniqueness so if you create the database manually this attribute has no impact

We use authorization keys to block hackers that reverse engineer the app/client side code or sniff the network traffic.

The UUID class generates a completely random 16 character long unique string. Let's elaborate a bit about those points. UUID stands for Universal Unique Identifier and it's used as a unique string we can rely on. E.g. it would look something like this: `123e4567-e89b-12d3-a456-556642440000`

How unique is it?

You have a 50% probability of coming up with the same UUID after going through 2.71 **quintillion** (10^{18}) iterations.

The next thing I mentioned is the initialization of `authToken` in the constructor. Before a User object is saved this value will be set to `authToken`. In subsequent runs as we load the User object with JPA it will override the new random value. That isn't ideal, that means that every time we load the object we'll also generate a UUID. However, I doubt something like this will ever be a performance bottleneck.

6

But let's explain what we are actually doing here. We are building a different path for authorization. Think of the authorization as a "key" to the server. We want to block a different user from sending a request that pretends to be our user. This is possible to do if a hacker sniffs our network traffic and tries to "pretend" he's our app. One approach would be sending the password to the server every time but that means storing and sending a password which holds risk.

In this case we generate a random and long key that's hard to guess with brute force. We send the key to the client and it stores that key. From that point on we have proof that this user is valid.

Token vs. Id

We have a numeric id for every user but we try not to use it for write operations. In fact if I was really concerned about security I'd use string tokens exclusively. String tokens are harder to guess/scan through in case of a hacker attack.

E.g. if I use numeric id's for a request a 3rd party attacking the service could scan through the numeric values and submit or query information. With a long string the number of options is an insurmountable block.

In this case we use the token for write operations. When a user logs in we provide the token so only the user can update his data. This means the password isn't stored on the device and a token can be updated/revoked. It's also long enough and random enough which isn't always the case for passwords.

Scanning sequential id's is a very common attack. In fact when I was a teenager our local phone company introduced paid phone numbers (similar to today's 1-900 numbers). We found out the each paid number mapped to a local phone number. But how do you guess that number? Each of those companies had advertised a "tech support" number as well. So we started scanning the local numbers close to the tech support number by dialing all numbers in the vicinity until we hit paydirt. That's a simple version of the numeric id scan hack which is still a very common attack vector.

5.2.2

Ride and Waypoint

Moving on we need to track the trips taken through the app and keep historic record of them.

We need to store 4 things about each ride:

- The passenger taking the ride
- The driver of the ride
- The cost of the ride
- The route taken

Most of these are pretty simple except for the route, how do we store that?

A route can be seen as a set of points at a given time e.g. this is a waypoint:

Listing 6. 9. The Waypoint class

```java
@Entity
public class Waypoint {
    @Id
    @GeneratedValue(strategy=GenerationType.AUTO)
    private  Long id;

    private  long  time;
    private  double latitude;
    private  double longitude;
    private  float   direction;

    // Getters, Setters and constructors
}
```

We use auto increment because it's convenient and simple

Notice that time is a regular system time that includes a date within, specifically it's the value of System.currentTimeMillis()

I use simple primitives to store the location instead of using a special object

6

GIS Extensions

MySQL and most modern databases have special datatypes for working with Geographic Information Systems (GIS). I chose not to use them because our use cases are simple by comparison. The mapping of these datatypes into Hibernate is done through a very complex API known as JTS.

ⓘ   For more coverage of this check out baeldung.com/hibernate-spatial

If you are interested in taking the location data further and have some complex computations then this complexity is worthwhile. I opted for simplicity and ignored that aspect.

With the Waypoint at hand we can now implement the Ride object:

Listing 6. 10. The Ride class

```java
public class Ride {
    @Id
    @GeneratedValue(strategy=GenerationType.AUTO)
    private Long id;

    @ManyToOne
    private User passenger;

    @ManyToOne
    private User driver;

    @OneToMany
    @OrderBy("time ASC")
    private Set<Waypoint> route;
    private BigDecimal cost;
    private String currency;

    // Getters, Setters and constructors
}
```

The passenger and driver are implicitly stored as relations within the database by JPA

The same is true for the waypoint set which will include our route as a set of points on the map with a time stamp for each point

JPA sorts the waypoint in ascending order for us so we can always rely on the routes order

I oversimplified payments as a currency and number pair but it should work for most cases

One of the cool things in SQL is relational integrity. That means a Ride references a User who was a passenger on that ride. So now we can't delete that user without impacting the Ride. If we change details about the user it will be reflected instantly. That's very valuable as we can rely on referencing the data instead of duplicating it.

Physically, this means the ride table generated by JPA will have two numeric columns called driver_id and passenger_id that reference the User primary key. This way for every Ride we can reference a different user which is a OneToMany relation. In JPA we have 4 basic relation types: OneToMany, ManyToOne, OneToOne and ManyToMany.

As you can see we have one ride entry that has multiple Waypoint objects associated with it. That's a One (Ride) to Many (Waypoint) relation. The many to one relation maps one of the many User objects to one Ride.

💡 If we had used a OneToOne relation a User would only be able to take one Ride

Rating

The last JPA object we'll cover is the rating class, again it's a simple implementation:

Listing 6. 11. The Rating class

```java
public class Rating {
    @Id
    @GeneratedValue(strategy=GenerationType. AUTO)
    private Long id;

    private long date;
    private float score;
    private String comment;

    @ManyToOne
    private User passenger;

    @ManyToOne
    private User driver;

    // Getters, Setters and constructors
}
```

This is pretty similar to the ride class so there isn't much to discuss

A rating might be date sensitive so we want to store that information

The optional comment collected from the specific user, this could be useful for a future visual display of ratings in the app interface

Currently I'm assuming a rating is from the passenger to the driver but this can easily be fixed by adding a flag to indicate the target of the rating

When a rating is submitted we can write this object to JPA storage to log every rating. Then a separate process can calculate the rating value.

CRUD Interfaces

One of the unique features of Springs JPA implementation is the CRUD interface. CRUD stands for "Create, Read, Update and Delete" all of which are the typical database operations. A typical implementation of the CRUD interface looks like this:

Listing 6. 12. Rating CRUD Interface

```
public interface RatingRepository extends CrudRepository<Rating , Long>{
}
```

This looks like nothing but it masks a lot of power. We can now inject the `RatingRepository` interface into our business logic and perform CRUD operations on that object.

That might seem "weird" if you haven't worked with Spring before. How can an interface provide functionality?
How can it provide that functionality without any methods?

That's the "magic" of Spring framework. Spring automatically implements the interface for us. We define our requirements based on a common convention and then use the `@Autowired` annotation to ask Spring to give us a working implementation. `CrudRepository` already has a few useful methods within that support a lot of what we need such as `findOne(id)` which finds an `Entity` by its primary key.

Securing CRUD Repositories

By default Spring Boot exposes CRUD repositories via a REST API and you can literally walk through URL's showing your entire database in the cloud. That's one of the few instances where I felt that Spring Boot was being stupid!

It's the equivalent of hardening security everywhere while leaving the door wide open.

The solution is to annotate every CRUD interface with @RepositoryRestResource(exported = false).

We can further enhance this CRUD interface with additional capabilities by using a common convention:

Listing 6. 13. User CRUD Interface

Spring automatically understands the method name and does the equivalent database select statement based on the naming convention. This method will query based on the authToken value in the User object

```java
public interface UserRepository extends CrudRepository<User, Long> {
    public List<User> findByAuthToken(
        String authToken);
    public List<User> findByPhone(String phone);
    public List<User> findByGoogleId(String googleId);
    public List<User> findByFacebookId(String facebookId);

    @Query("select b from User b where b.driver = true and b.latitude " +
        "between ?1 and ?2 and b.longitude between ?3 and ?4")
    public List<User> findByDriver(double minLat, double maxLat,
        double minLon, double maxLon);
```

There are limits to convention, here we define a custom JPA query where we try to find a driver within the given radius using the between keyword. We use this method when we display cars on the map, we want to show all cars even occupied cars

```java
    @Query("select b from User b where b.driver = true and " +
        "b.assignedUser is null and b.latitude between ?1 and ?2 " +
        "and b.longitude between ?3 and ?4")
    public List<User> findByAvailableDriver(double minLat, double maxLat,
        double minLon, double maxLon);
}
```

Here we do the same thing for an available driver. We use this when hailing a cab as we want to hail an available ride

6

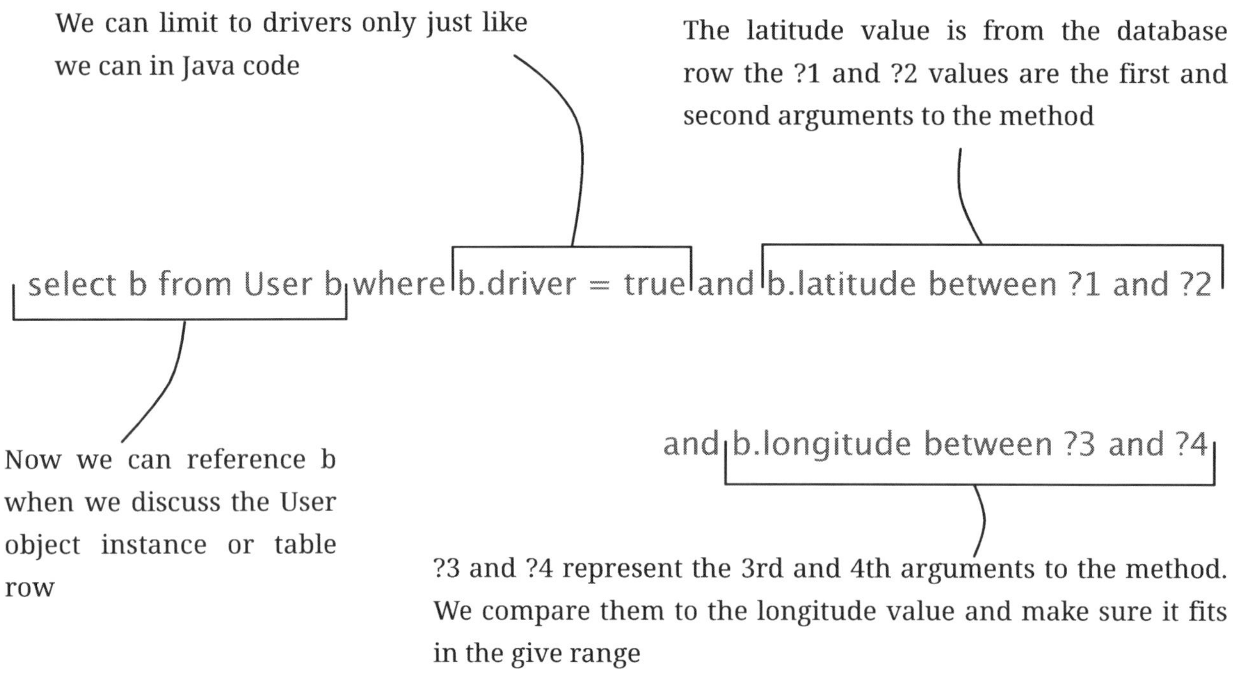

We can limit to drivers only just like we can in Java code

The latitude value is from the database row the ?1 and ?2 values are the first and second arguments to the method

select b from User b where b.driver = true and b.latitude between ?1 and ?2

Now we can reference b when we discuss the User object instance or table row

and b.longitude between ?3 and ?4

?3 and ?4 represent the 3rd and 4th arguments to the method. We compare them to the longitude value and make sure it fits in the give range

Figure 6. 3. findByAvailableDriver JPA Query Explained

6.2.5
Data Access Objects (DAO)

DAO stands for Data Access Object. This is a conceptual idea, there is no DAO API or requirement. You can skip it entirely!

However, it's a very common "best practice" when working with backend systems. E.g. in our application we have 3 layers:

- WebServices/WebSocket - the user facing code

- Service - the backend logic

- Entities/JPA - the database

The roles are clearly separate, that's important as it means we can replace or change one layer significantly without impacting the others. E.g. we can move everything to websockets replacing the WebServices layer or we can move to a NoSQL DB and throw away the entity layer.

So how do we transfer data between the layers while keeping them logically separate?

Enter the DAO objects, they aren't entities. Entities are too close to the data and are hard to modify. DAO's are in place to pass along the data. The cool part about DAO's is that Spring Boot can automatically convert them to JSON when sending a response from the webservice and automatically create a new instance from JSON when receiving a call. We could just pass the entity itself but that would break the separation of layers and might inadvertently expose private data to the client side (e.g. password hashes)!

DAO vs. DTO

I think of this layer as a DAO because it starts from the database. However, what we have here might be considered a DTO (Data Transfer Object) by some developers. In some cases I took objects that are clearly transfer objects (e.g. ErrorDAO) and kept the same naming convention to avoid confusion

There's another more subtle advantage. The User object includes a lot of information that might not make sense for every query. A good example is the avatar byte array which might be large. We don't want to pass it to the mobile device with every single query.

Keep the Protocol Secure

Even though we control the client side code, a hacker could gain control or sniff the network. It's crucial to maintain security in all tiers

Listing 6. 14. The UserDAO Object

```java
public class UserDAO implements Serializable {
    private Long id;
    private String givenName;
    private String surname;
    private String phone;
    private String email;
    private String facebookId;
    private String googleId;
    private boolean driver;
    private String car;
    private float currentRating;
    private double latitude;
    private double longitude;
    private float direction;
    private String authToken;   // You will notice I have the authToken and password
    private String password;    // values in the UserDAO despite the fact I explicitly said
    // Getters, Setters and constructors   // they shouldn't be there...
}
```

You will notice I have the authToken and password values in the UserDAO despite the fact I explicitly said they shouldn't be there...

We will never write to them in the server so they won't have a value and will always be null for the mobile app queries. However, when the mobile app needs to send a user object to us it will need to pass these values somewhere. That's where these two fields come in handy!

These are the methods of the User Entity that generates a UserDAO object:

Listing 6. 15. Generating DAO objects

```java
public  UserDAO getDao() {
    return  new  UserDAO(id, givenName, surname, phone, email, facebookId,
            googleId, driver, car, currentRating, latitude,
            longitude, direction);

public  UserDAO getPartialDao() {
    return  new UserDAO(id, givenName, surname, null,  null,  null,  null,
            driver, car, currentRating, latitude, longitude, direction);
}
```

You will notice that both the authToken and password are ignored in the code above since we never send them to the client side. However, when we create or update a user we can read the values submitted from the client for these fields. They are in effect, "write only" fields.

6.3
UserService

We need to define the business logic related to the user. We can do that within a service class that encapsulates the user related functionality. This is generally a good practice as we can access this code from a webservice/websocket etc. It will also make unit testing simpler in the future so you could easily test changes to the service or underlying data.

Since this listing is a bit long I'll split it into the class declaration and individual methods:

Listing 6. 16. The UserService class

```java
@Service
public class UserService {
    @Autowired
    private UserRepository users;

    @Autowired
    private PasswordEncoder encoder;

    // ...
}
```

This is the CRUD interface, Spring Boot implicitly generates the implementation of this interface! Notice I never give it a value in the class yet it's "magically" populated

We use this Spring Boot interface to hash and salt the passwords

6

PasswordEncoder uses salt and hashing to secure the underlying password. It means that even if the worse thing happens and hackers gain access to your database they still won't be able to figure out peoples passwords.

Listing 6. 17. The UserService User Methods

```java
public String addUser(UserDAO user) {
    User u = new User(user);
    u.setPassword(encoder.encode(
        user.getPassword()));
    users.save(u);
    return u.getAuthToken();
}
public void updateUser(UserDAO user) {
    User u = users.findByAuthToken(user.getAuthToken()).get(0);
    u.setCar(user.getCar());
    u.setEmail(user.getEmail());
    u.setFacebookId(user.getFacebookId());
    u.setGivenName(user.getGivenName());
    u.setSurname(user.getSurname());
    u.setGoogleId(user.getGoogleId());
    u.setLatitude(user.getLatitude());
    u.setLongitude(user.getLongitude());
    u.setPhone(user.getPhone());
    users.save(u);
}
```

Adding a user consists of creating a new User object with the DAO and invoking the builtin CRUD save method

Here we encode the password. This is pretty seamless in Spring but remarkably secure as it uses a salted hash

Notice that things such as password and token are special cases that we don't want to update using the same flow, as they are pretty sensitive

Salted Hashes vs. Encryption

Passwords aren't encrypted they are hashed and salted. Encryption is a bi-directional algorithm. You encode data and then decode it back. Hashing encodes the data in such a way that can't be reversed. To verify the password we need to rehash it and check the hashed strings.

Hashing alone isn't enough as it can be assaulted with various attacks. One of the tricks against hash attacks is salt. The salt is random data that's injected into the hash. An attacker can't distinguish between the salt and hash data which makes potential attacks much harder.

The password hashing algorithm of Spring Boot always produces a 60 character string which is hard to crack.

Listing 6. 18. The UserService Avatar Methods

```
public  byte[]  getAvatar(Long id) {
    User u = users.findOne(id);
    return  u.getAvatar();
}
```

Notice that getAvatar uses the id value. That leaves a small security weakness where a user can scan the id's for images of the drivers/users. I kept it in place for simplicity see the discussion in section 6.2 Token vs. Id Sidebar (page 164)

This is a method builtin to the CRUD interface

```
public  void  setAvatar(String token,  byte[] a) {
    User u = users.findByAuthToken(token).get(0);
    u.setAvatar(a);
    users.save(u);
}
```

When updating the avatar we needs a secure token

Finally we have the login and authentication methods. Since there are three ways to login to the service (Phone number, Facebook or Google we generalize the login code:

Listing 6. 19. The UserService login and authentication methods

```java
public UserDAO loginByPhone(String phone, String password)
        throws UserAuthenticationException {
    return loginImpl(users.findByPhone(phone), password);
}
public UserDAO loginByFacebook(String facebookId, String password)
        throws UserAuthenticationException {
    return loginImpl(users.findByFacebookId(facebookId), password);
}
public UserDAO loginByGoogle(String googleId, String password)
        throws UserAuthenticationException {
    return loginImpl(users.findByGoogleId(googleId), password);
}
private UserDAO loginImpl(List<User> us, String password)
        throws UserAuthenticationException {
    if (us == null || us.isEmpty()) {
        return null;
    }
    if (us.size() > 1) {
        throw new RuntimeException("Illegal state " + us.size() +
            " users with the same phone are listed!");
    }
    User u = us.get(0);
    if (!encoder.
        matches(password, u.getPassword())) {
        throw new UserAuthenticationException();
    }
    UserDAO d = u.getDao();
    d.setAuthToken(u.getAuthToken());
    return d;
}
public boolean existsByPhone(String phone) {
    List<User> us = users.findByPhone(phone);
    return !us.isEmpty();
}
```

The login methods delegate to the common loginImpl method as they have a lot in common

All login methods throw the UserAuthenticationException which is a simple subclass of Exception

This should never ever happen but it's important to test against such conditions as during a hack these "should never happen" conditions might occur

Since the passwords are hashed and salted we can't compare directly. Regenerating the hash and comparing that won't work either as the salt is random. The only way to test is to use the matches method see section 6.3 Salted Hashes vs. Encryption Sidebar (page 174)

When we login at first we need to check if the user with the given phone or social network exists. The UI flow for users that exist and don't exist is slightly different

With that, UserService is nearly done. For completeness this is the UserAuthenticationException class:

Listing 6. 20. The UserAuthenticationException class

```
public class UserAuthenticationException extends Exception {
}
```

We throw this exception when an error occurs. This is a good practice in Spring Boot as it allows us to represent errors in a clearer way when we generate the WebService implementation in Section 6.4 (page 178)

SecurityConfiguration

To get the code above to work we also need a special configuration class: SecurityConfiguration
This class essentially tunes various aspects of Spring Security to disable some default behaviors and
configure beans:

Listing 6. 21. The SecurityConfiguration class

```
@Configuration
public class SecurityConfiguration extends WebSecurityConfigurerAdapter {
    @Override
    protected void configure (HttpSecurity httpSecurity) throws Exception {
        httpSecurity.authorizeRequests().antMatchers("/").
            permitAll();
        httpSecurity.csrf().disable();
    }

    @Bean
    public PasswordEncoder passwordEncoder() {
        return new BCryptPasswordEncoder();
    }
}
```

By default Spring requires OAuth to access URL's
and also block csrf attacks. These attacks impact
web apps but don't impact native apps so we
don't need that protection or the OAuth support

The PasswordEncoder we
autowired in the UserSession
class is defined explicitly here so
the autowire code maps to this

ⓘ csrf stands for Cross Site Request Forgery. Since it doesn't apply to native apps I
won't cover it here

UserWebservice

So far so good but the UserService is a server only class. We'd like to expose this functionality to the client code... To do that we can add a JSON based WebService class by using the following code. Again I'll break this down to smaller pieces to make the code more readable:

Listing 6. 22. The UserWebservice class declaration

```
@Controller
@RequestMapping("/user")
public class UserWebservice {
    @Autowired
    private UserService users;

    @ExceptionHandler(
        UserAuthenticationException.class)
    @ResponseStatus(value = HttpStatus.FORBIDDEN)
    public @ResponseBody ErrorDAO handleException(
        UserAuthenticationException e) {
        return new ErrorDAO("Invalid Password",
            ErrorDAO.ERROR_INVALID_PASSWORD);
    }

    // ...
}
```

This maps the base URL, all HTTP requests to this class will be under the /user URL e.g. http://localhost:8080/user for development and http://mydomain.com/user for production

We inject the user service automatically using Spring Boot

In the UserService class we throw a UserAuthenticationException when login failed. This code automatically translates an exception of that type to an ErrorDAO object which returns a different error JSON

The JSON body will contain the error message of "Invalid Password"

When this exception type is thrown a user will receive a forbidden HTTP response

The ErrorDAO class which we return from that code looks like this:

Listing 6. 23. The ErrorDAO class

```java
public class ErrorDAO {
    private String error;          ←
    private int code;
    // Getters, Setters and constructors
}
```

A message and a numeric code which we can use in the client side

This is implicitly translated to JSON code by Spring Boot.

But the more interesting part of that code is this:

Listing 6. 24. Why Autowired and not new?

```java
@Autowired
private UserService users;
```

Why didn't we just do a `new UserService()`?

Spring Boot wraps all objects with a special proxy object. This object handles "under the hood" functionality such as transactional context. This means we can inject configuration dependencies into Spring without modifying classes. That's not a big deal when we have 5 classes but imagine a project with thousands of classes. In such a case we can control nuanced behavior globally. If we just used new the autowired elements within `UserService` might not work.

This is one of the core principals of Spring: IoC (Inversion of Control). IoC allows decoupling of the implementation pieces and thus allows testability and configurability. You can read more about the concepts behind Spring here:

docs.spring.io/spring/docs/current/spring-framework-reference/core.html

Listing 6. 25. The UserWebservice User Methods

The request method annotation indicates that an HTTP GET
method on the given /user/exists path will invoke this method

```
@RequestMapping(method=RequestMethod.GET, value = "/exists")
public @ResponseBody boolean exists(String phone){
    return users.existsByPhone(phone);
}
```

Maps the /user/exists?
phone=999 URL so it
will return the string
true or false based on
whether the user
actually exists

6

This maps the /user/login URL to the three login options: SMS,
Google and Facebook. The ResponseBody annotation indicates
that the response is returned in the HTTP response body as is

```
@RequestMapping(method=RequestMethod.GET, value = "/login" )
public @ResponseBody UserDAO login(
        @RequestParam(value="password", required=true)  String password,
        String phone, String googleId, String facebookId)
            throws UserAuthenticationException {
    if(phone != null) {
        return users.loginByPhone(phone, password);
    }
    if(facebookId != null) {
        return users.loginByFacebook(facebookId, password);
    }
    if(googleId != null) {
        return users.loginByGoogle(googleId, password);
    }
    return null;
}
@RequestMapping(method=RequestMethod.POST, value="/add")
public @ResponseBody String addEditUser(@RequestBody UserDAO ud)
    throws IOException {
    if(ud.getId() != null) {
        users.updateUser(ud);
        return ud.getId().toString();
    } else {
        return users.addUser(ud);
    }
}
```

The names of the
arguments to the HTTP
request are automatically
extracted from the
argument names. Notice we
can annotate arguments
too as we stated the
password is required!

We return a String which is written right into the body. If
we throw an IOException the client side will get a generic
HTTP access error in the 5xx range

We check whether an ID is set to determine if this is an add
or update operation. However, we don't use the ID value for
editing as the underlying API uses the token

The @ResponseBody annotation will return the data based on the request headers, if the client requests XML it will encode the objects as XML. In the client we add JSON request headers with the call `RequestBuilder.jsonContent()` so the objects will be encoded as JSON strings

It's really helpful to specify constraints at this level and throw exceptions immediately. That generally means the server won't enter a status we don't expect and is likely to be more robust/secure as a result.

Listing 6. 26. The UserWebservice Avatar Related Methods

Images just map to a URL for the given image id so the URL /user/avatar/userId will return the image e.g. for id==1 this will return the avatar /user/avatar/1

```java
@RequestMapping(value = "/avatar/{id:.+}" , method = RequestMethod.GET)
public ResponseEntity <byte []> getAvatar(
    @PathVariable("id") Long id) {
    byte [] av = users.getAvatar(id);
    if(av != null) {
        return ResponseEntity.ok().
            contentType(MediaType.IMAGE_JPEG).
            body(av);
    }
    return ResponseEntity.notFound().build();
}
```

We use the ResponseEntity to gain finer control over the returned data which, in this case, is literally the byte data of the user image

This lets us extract the value 1 from a request like /user/avatar/1 and it will pass that value to the id variable!

If the image isn't there we'll return an HTTP not-found error (404) which we can handle in the

We set the HTTP response to OK (HTTP 200) then set the response mime type to image/jpeg and return the content of the image

```java
@RequestMapping(method = RequestMethod.POST,
    value = "/updateAvatar/{auth:.+}")
public @ResponseBody String updateAvatar(
        @PathVariable ("auth") String auth,
        @RequestParam(name="img", required = true) MultipartFile img)
            throws IOException {
    users.setAvatar(auth, img.getBytes());
    return "OK";
}
```

This maps to the POST request on the URL /user/updateAvatar/authToken

This request is a mime multipart upload request. We need to use multipart to upload images or binary data

The path element representing the auth token is extracted into the auth argument

6

Multipart upload is a part of the HTTP specification. When you submit a form on the web with a file picker, multipart is used to perform the upload. Under the hood the binary data is encoded using Base64.

All of these details don't matter as much since both Spring Boot and Codename One handle those details with dedicated API's.

6

Location Updates Through WebSockets

WebSocket is a special type of socket that is created through HTTP/S requests. A webserver that supports websockets opens a regular HTTP/S connection and then uses the socket opened there to continue working as a regular socket. As a result the WebSocket setup is slower than a regular TCP socket but it provides the same level of flexibility as a regular socket after creation. The advantage over TCP sockets is compatibility and the ability to pass through potentially problematic firewalls who see a WebSocket as another HTTP connection.

Notice that all of these setup details don't really matter to us as the WebSocket API's, both in Spring Boot and Codename One, hide all of the gritty details. For us WebSockets appear like messages sent from/to a ws URL.

Up until now all our communications went through webservices which is convenient and scalable. The fact we can use tools like curl and the network monitor to see what is going on under the hood is very powerful. However, webservices suffer from the performance overhead and fixed structure issues of HTTP. For more interactive data websockets have clear advantages which is why we use them in ride tracking.

The WebSocket API includes two types of packets: Text and Binary. In this case I'll use the binary protocol because it's pretty easy to do this in Java.

Why not use WebSockets for Everything?

Some people do that and it might work for your use cases. A lot of developers use the text based websocket as a substitute to webservices altogether and in some cases that makes sense. However, as I mentioned before we have decades of experience with HTTP. It works well and has a huge infrastructure of tools behind it.

Websockets are a low level API. There are some higher level abstractions on top of them but these often go back to the problems of HTTP without giving much in return.

Spring Boot has decent support for WebSockets but you need to activate it first. We need to define a configuration class that sets up the WebSocket environment.

6.5.1. WebSocketConfig

You can configure Spring Boot with XML but I prefer working with classes and annotations where possible. The WebSocketConfig configures the websocket support:

Listing 6. 27. The WebSocketConfig Class

```
@Configuration                    The annotations at the top mark this class as a configuration class
@EnableWebSocket
public class WebSocketConfig implements WebSocketConfigurer {
    @Bean
    public  ServletServerContainerFactoryBean
            createWebSocketContainer () {
        ServletServerContainerFactoryBean container =
            new ServletServerContainerFactoryBean();
        container.setMaxTextMessageBufferSize(8192);
        container.setMaxBinaryMessageBufferSize(8192);
        return  container;
    }

    @Override
    public  void  registerWebSocketHandlers(
        WebSocketHandlerRegistry registry) {
        registry.addHandler(myHandler(), "/wsMsg");
    }

    @Bean
    public  WebSocketHandler  myHandler() {
        return  new  Handler();
    }
}
```

We set common configuration arguments for websocket messages. Notice this is similar to the PasswordEncoder Bean we mentioned earlier

This maps to packet sizes for communication. We won't need large packets for this

We bind the Handler class to the /wsMsg URL which will look like wss://myDomain.com/wsMsg (ws if we don't have an HTTPS certificate)

This is just a boilerplate class needed by Spring Boot.

Before we get into the WebSocket code we need a service class to abstract the location specific requests to the system.

LocationService

We'll encapsulate the location specific calls within the LocationService API:

Listing 6. 28. The LocationService class

```java
@Service
public class LocationService {
    @Autowired
    private   UserRepository users;   ←
                                         Most of the location API's map to the User class
                                         but it's logically separate from the UserService

    public  void  updateUserLocation(String token,  double  lat,
            double  lon,  float  dir) {←
        List<User> us = users.findByAuthToken(token);        We will periodically update the
        User u = us.get(0);                                  users location. Notice that
        u.setLatitude(lat);                                  location can only be updated
        u.setLongitude(lat);                                 by the user himself as the token
        u.setDirection(dir);                                 is required for that operation
        users.save(u);
    }

    public  List<UserDAO>  findAllDrivers(double  lat,       It's more intuitive to work
            double  lon,  double  radius) {                  with radius from the client but
        double  minLat = lat  – radius  *  0.009044;         the JPA query language makes
        double  minLon = lon  – radius  *  0.0089831;        it easier to work in absolute
        double  maxLat = lat  + radius  *  0.009044;         coordinates so I convert the
        double  maxLon= lon  + radius  *  0.0089831; ←       kilometer radius unit to
        return  toDaoList(                                   latitude/longitude values
            users.findByDriver(minLat, maxLat, minLon, maxLon));
    }
}
```

We have two versions of the query. One finds all of the drivers in the area so we can draw them on the map. The second searches for available drivers only for hailing purposes

```java
public  List<UserDAO>  findAvailableDrivers(double  lat,  double  lon,
        double  radius) {
    double  minLat  = lat  –  radius  *  0.009044;
    double  minLon = lon  –  radius  *  0.0089831;
    double  maxLat = lat  +  radius  *  0.009044;
    double  maxLon= lon + radius  *  0.0089831;
    return  toDaoList(users.findByAvailableDriver(minLat, maxLat,
        minLon, maxLon));
}

private  List<UserDAO>  toDaoList(List<User>  us) {
    ArrayList<UserDAO>  respone = new  ArrayList<>();
    for(User u : us) {
        respone.add(u.getPartialDao());
    }
    return  respone;
}
}
```

I use a version of the method that only returns a part of the user data as we normally don't need all of the data

Unfortunately this code is hard to generalize as we need four variables. I could have added another class and abstraction but I don't think it's worth it as it would take even more lines of code

6

186

WebSocket Handler

The Handler class handles all the communication messages from the client and our responses. Before we dig into this, let's design the format of the request/response...

First we want a packet type ID. This is useful if we want to change the protocol later on and also for supporting multiple types of requests. I don't think we need to support a big number of options so short should be enough. Size is hugely important in communication protocols even in this day and age.

> ℹ️ The following two listings are packet structures not source code. They are here to illustrate the structure of a packet passed through the network

Listing 6. 29. Packet structure for location update

```
short   messageType;         I picked message type 1 for location updates
                             from the user, we'll use other types later

short   tokenLength;         The length of the user token string followed by a byte array
byte [] token;               of the token length representing the string. Notice that I
double  latitude;            used bytes instead of chars. Since the token is 100% ASCII I
double  longitude;           can rely on that fact and reduce the packet size further
float   direction;
double  radius;              The location data and the radius/direction
byte  seeking;
```

A byte which is set to 1 when we are hailing a taxi in which case it will seek only the available drivers

Once this packet is processed the server returns the cars within the search radius by sending a packet back. In this case we don't need the token as this is a message from the server:

Listing 6. 30. Packet structure for server response

```
short  messageType;   ⟵        The response type can be 2 for driver position update
                               and 3 for available driver position update
int  responseSize;    ⟵        The number of drivers in the returned data
long  driverId;       ⟵
double  latitude;
double  longitude;
float  direction;
```

The rest of the lines repeat for every driver responseSize times and include the position data for every driver

Now that we understand the protocol, let's dig into the code that implements it:

Listing 6. 31. The Handler class

```
public  class  Handler extends BinaryWebSocketHandler {
    private  static  final  short  MESSAGE_TYPE_LOCATION_UPDATE = 1;
    private  static  final  short  MESSAGE_TYPE_DRIVER_POSITIONS =  2;
    private  static  final  short  MESSAGE_TYPE_AVAILBLE_DRIVER_POSITIONS = 3;
```

These are constants used in the binary protocol to communicate the type of request or response

```
    @Autowired
    private  LocationService loc;

    @Override
    protected  void  handleBinaryMessage(WebSocketSession session,
            BinaryMessage message)  throws  Exception {
```

Callback for a binary message from the client

```
ByteBuffer b = message.getPayload();
short  messageType = b.getShort();
short  stringLength = b.getShort();
StringBuilder bld = new StringBuilder();
for(int iter = 0 ; iter < stringLength ; iter++) {
    bld.append((char)b.get());
}
String token = bld.toString();
switch(messageType) {
    case MESSAGE_TYPE_LOCATION_UPDATE:
        double lat  = b.getDouble();
        double lon  = b.getDouble();
        float  dir  = b.getFloat();
        double radius = b.getDouble();
        boolean seeking = b.get() == 1;
        loc.updateUserLocation(
            token, lat, lon, dir);
        List<UserDAO> response;
        short  responseType;




        if ( seeking) {
            response = loc.findAvailableDrivers(lat, lon, radius);
            responseType = MESSAGE_TYPE_DRIVER_POSITIONS;
        } else {
            response = loc.findAllDrivers(lat, lon, radius);
            responseType = MESSAGE_TYPE_AVAILBLE_DRIVER_POSITIONS;
        }
        if(response != null && response.size() > 0) {
```

The API works with NIO's byte buffer which allows us to run through a request efficiently

We get the length of the user token string and the byte array. Again I used bytes instead of chars. Since the token is 100% ASCII we can rely on that

6

Assuming this is a location update we pull out the data and update the User object

We prepare to return a response based on the seeking flag. We also need to mark the response type correctly

```java
try (ByteArrayOutputStream
        bos = new ByteArrayOutputStream();
    DataOutputStream
        dos = new DataOutputStream(bos)) {
    dos.writeShort(responseType);
    dos.writeInt(response.size());
    for(UserDAO u : response) {
        dos.writeLong(u.getId());
        dos.writeDouble(u.getLatitude());
        dos.writeDouble(u.getLongitude());
        dos.writeFloat(u.getDirection());
    }
    dos.flush();
    BinaryMessage bin =
        new BinaryMessage(bos.toByteArray());
    session.sendMessage(bin);
    }
}
break;
    }
  }
}
```

I used a byte array output stream to construct the response. I use try with resources to close the streams automatically when I'm done. I just write out the response data to the steam

And finally we convert the byte array data from the stream to a byte array that's sent to the client

Summary

In this chapter, we learned:

- The Java Persistence API (JPA) is an ORM (Object-Relational Mapper) that abstracts the underlying SQL database

- Design your code around the data, rather than the other way around

- We use authorization keys to block hackers that reverse engineer the app/client side code or sniff the network traffic

- WebServices are convenient and scalable as we can use tools like `curl` and the network monitor to see what is going on under the hood. However, webservices suffer from the performance overhead and fixed structure issues of HTTP. For more interactive data websockets have an advantage

This wasn't as hard as day 1 at least not in volume of work. Server code is often simpler than client code and often smaller.

The difficult part with server development is the delayed gratification in testing it. I skipped a lot of the more important things such as unit tests and some of the more nuanced server complexities for scaling, security etc.

Again this isn't a big deal as the focus of the book is on client development...

6

Day 3: Connecting the Client/Server and SMS Activation

7

This chapter covers:

- Invoking server WebServices and connecting to WebSockets

- Binding server JSON responses to user objects using the properties API

- Abstraction of server glue code in the client side

- Finishing the SMS Activation Process and making it work with an actual phone number

In day 2 we created a Spring Boot server and now is the time to put this all together and get the basic process running. This means going through the login process and getting the networking/user setup working properly.

Before we Begin

7.1

Before we get started we need to add some things to the client project. First we need to add the Web Sockets cn1lib from the extension manager. This is pretty simple to do if you already added a cn1lib before. For more information about installing cn1libs check out Appendix D (page 413).

Next we need to signup to twilio.com/ as developers. Notice we don't need to install support for the Twilio lib since we already installed the SMS Activation cn1lib before. Twilio have a free trial account from which you will need the following values:

- Account SID
- Auth Token
- Phone Number

Pick US Based Phone

Make sure to pick a US phone number for the free account otherwise payment would be required

Click Here to show credentials

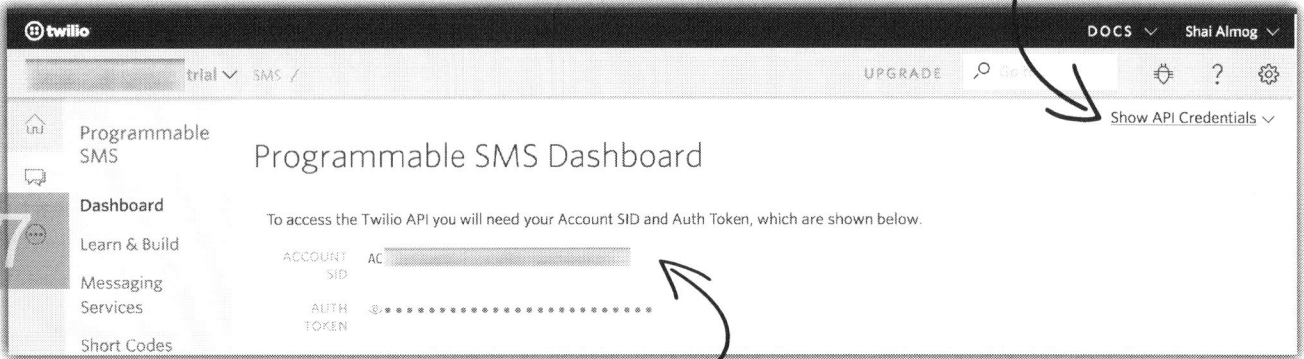

Credentials are shown here

Click Here for the phone number

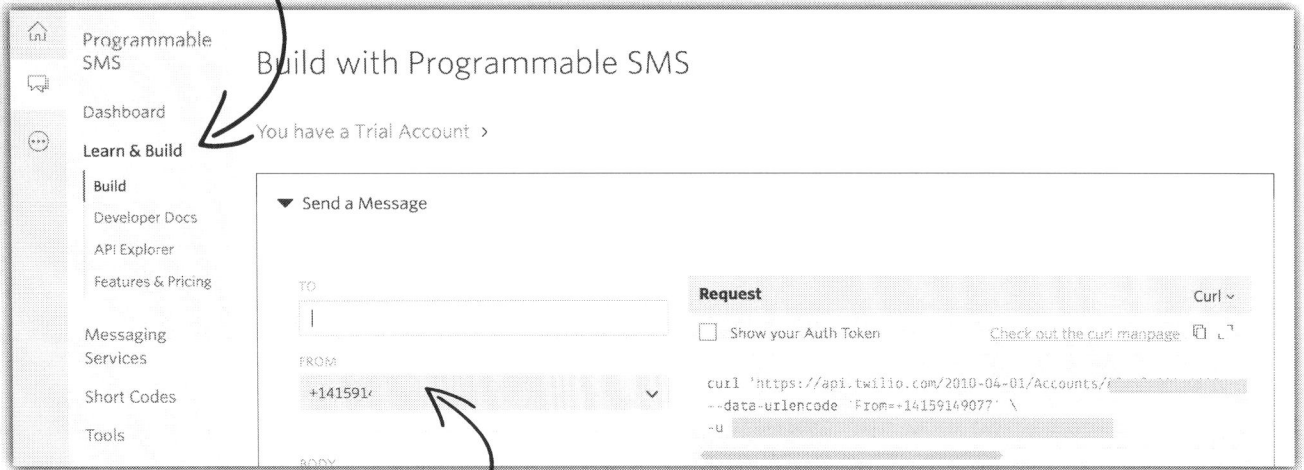

The phone number is here

Figure 7. 1. Getting the Information we Need from Twilio

Once you have those values we can create a new Globals class. I will concentrate all the global constants within this class including the keys from Twilio, server URL etc.

The main value of this class is in having everything we need in a single place during development. It contains no actual functionality only constants. We only need this class to save us from the hassle of looking through every source file later on and fixing keys/constants all over the place.

Listing 7. 1. The Globals class

Notice that you might want to replace localhost with your IP during development so you can test a device against a server running on your machine. Notice that the device needs to be connected to the same wifi

```java
public class Globals {
    public static final String SERVER_URL =
        "http://localhost:8080/";
    public static final String SERVER_SOCKET_URL =
        "ws://localhost:8080/wsMsg";
    public static final String TWILIO_ACCOUNT_SID =
        "AC....";
    public static final String TWILIO_AUTH_TOKEN = "1d....";
    public static final String TWILIO_FROM_PHONE = "+14.....";
}
```

The following values are the values we have from Twilio

For convenience I use static import for these constants within the code:

Listing 7. 2. Static import syntax

```java
import static com.codename1.apps.uberclone.server.Globals.*;
```

SMS Sending from Client

We are sending the SMS activation code from the client side. This is a bad practice. You should use the server Twilio API and send the SMS activation code from there.

I chose to use this approach because it's seamless and shows the usage of API's on the client which is what I'm trying to teach. However, keeping authentication code on the server is far more secure.

User and Properties

The next thing we need is information about the user of the application. We created a User object in the server both as a DAO and as an Entity. We need a similar abstraction in the client side to represent both the app user and the driver.

One of the cool things in Spring Boot is the ability to take a plain Java object representing the UserDAO and serialize it into JSON. We could have picked that UserDAO object "as is" and used it in the client. It would work but it wouldn't serialize from JSON so the benefit would be limited. Furthermore, the DAO makes sense for transferring information in the server but might not be ideal for the things we need in the client side.

Thankfully there is another option for working with simple objects that makes JSON parsing trivial: Properties.

Properties are an alternative to the get/set methods that are common in Java. The huge advantage is the ability to introspect such properties which allows us to automate processes such as database storage, parsing etc. Properties are a generic concept in programming but the implementation I'll discuss here is specific to Codename One.

I think this will be clearer once we look at the example. So if we have something like this in the server:

Listing 7. 3. Standard Java property

```java
private  String  name;
public  String  getName() {
    return  name;
}
public  void  setName(String name) {
    this . name = name;
}
```

The properties alternative is roughly:

Listing 7. 4. Codename One Property Objects

```java
public  final   Property<String, User> name = new  Property<>("name");
```

Notice that this is a public field but it's also final. This means that code like this won't compile:

Listing 7. 5. Properties Illegal Assignment

```
myUser.name = x;
```

To set or get the value we use this:

Listing 7. 6. Properties Legal Assignment

```
myUser.name.set("Name");
String n = myUser.name.get();
```

I won't go too much into introspection which is a huge subject but I will discuss observability which is a really cool feature of properties. Say I have an object with the name property above and I'd like to know when someone changes the name I can just do this:

Listing 7. 7. Observability

```
myUser.name.addChangeListener(p -> label.setText("Name: " +
    myUser.name.get()));
```

As you can see from the code I can instantly update the UI with details about the change. We actually have a ready made UI binding API for properties that does most of this stuff seamlessly. That binding API is based on this observability capability of properties. I will discuss this binding API later in the book.

With that in mind the client side version of the UserDAO class looks like this:

Listing 7. 8. The client side user property class

The PropertyBusinessObject interface
defines the getPropertyIndex() method

```java
public class  User implements PropertyBusinessObject  {
    public  final   LongProperty<User> id = new LongProperty<>("id" );
    public  final   Property<String, User> givenName =
        new Property<>("givenName");
    public  final   Property<String, User> surname = new Property<>("surname");
    public  final   Property<String, User> phone = new Property<>("phone");
    public  final   Property<String, User> email = new Property<>("email");
    public  final   Property<String, User> facebookId =
        new Property<>("facebookId");
    public  final   Property<String, User> googleId =
        new Property<>("googleId");
    public  final   BooleanProperty<User> driver =
        new BooleanProperty<>("driver");
    public  final   Property<String, User> car = new Property<>("car");
    public  final   FloatProperty<User> currentRating =
        new FloatProperty<>("currentRating");
    public  final   DoubleProperty<User> latitude =
        new DoubleProperty<>("latitude");
    public  final   DoubleProperty<User> longitude =
        new DoubleProperty<>("longitude");
    public  final   FloatProperty<User> direction =
        new FloatProperty<>("direction");
    public  final   Property<String, User> authToken =
        new Property<>("authToken");
    public  final   Property<String, User> password= new Property<>("password");
    private final   PropertyIndex  idx = new PropertyIndex (this,   "User",
            id, givenName, surname, phone, email, facebookId, googleId,
            driver, car, currentRating, latitude, longitude, direction,
            authToken, password);
    public  PropertyIndex  getPropertyIndex() {
        return   idx;
    }
}
```

Some properties use specific
types such as BooleanProperty,
LongProperty etc. This helps
with implicit parsing of values
into into type safe variables

The index object allows code to detect
the properties within a given object and
perform operations on the object such
as trasform it to/from JSON etc.

You will notice that we don't have a constructor and other common object features. We can create an object using this shorthand/fluent code:

Listing 7. 9. How to create a User object

```
User u = new User().
        id.set(3).
        givenName.set("Shai").
        surname.set("Almog");
```

If we want to send the User object as JSON to the server we can just do: u.getPropertyIndex().toJSON(). There are a lot of things we can do with property objects all the way up to implicitly creating a UI from the object.

Now that we have this in place we can connect to the server.

7

UserService

7.2.1

We need to define a connection layer that will abstract the server access code. This will allow us flexibility as we modify the server implementation and the client implementation. It will also make testing far easier by separating the different pieces into tiers. E.g. if we choose to migrate to WebSockets we can confine all our work to this one abstraction and ignore the rest of the code which should "just work".

The abstraction is similar to the one we have in the server. I chose to go with a mostly static class implementation for the user service as it's inherently a static web service. It makes no sense to have more than one UserService.

I'll split the class into smaller pieces to make it more readable:

Listing 7. 10. The UserService class on the client side

```java
public class UserService {
    private static User me;
    public static void loadUser() {
        me = new User();
        PreferencesObject.create(me).bind();
    }
    public static void logout() {
        Preferences.set("token", null);
    }
    public static boolean isLoggedIn() {
        return Preferences.get("token", null) != null;
    }
    // ... rest of code...
}
```

Once logged in we will cache the current user object here so we have all the data locally and don't need server communication for every query

We bind the user object to preferences so changes to the user object implicitly connect to the Preferences storage API and vice versa. Preferences allow us to store key/value pairs

Whether we are logged in or out is determined by the token value. We need the token to send updates to the server side

Next up we have the SMS activation code:

Listing 7. 11. UserService SMS Activation

```java
public static void sendSMSActivationCode(String phoneNumber) {
    TwilioSMS tw = TwilioSMS.create(TWILIO_ACCOUNT_SID,
        TWILIO_AUTH_TOKEN, TWILIO_FROM_PHONE);

    Random r = new Random();
    String val = "";
    for(int iter = 0 ; iter < 4 ; iter++) {
        val += r.nextInt(10);
    }
    Preferences.set("phoneVerification" , val);

    tw.sendSmsAsync(phoneNumber, val);
}
public static void resendSMSActivationCode(String phoneNumber) {
    TwilioSMS tw = TwilioSMS.create(TWILIO_ACCOUNT_SID,
        TWILIO_AUTH_TOKEN, TWILIO_FROM_PHONE);
    tw.sendSmsAsync(phoneNumber,
        Preferences.get("phoneVerification", null));
}
public static boolean validateSMSActivationCode(String code) {
    String val = Preferences.get(
        "phoneVerification", null);
    return code.indexOf(val) > -1 &&
        code.length() < 80;
}
```

I'm creating the 4 digit verification code and sending it via the Twilio SMS webservice API

I'm storing the value in Preferences so I can check against it when it's received even if the app dies for some reason

This method is invoked to validate the received SMS code

Notice I don't just use equals since the validation string might include the full SMS text. This can happen on Android where we can automatically validate

I still limit the length of the string to prevent an attack where a user can inject all the possible four code combinations into this method

On Android we intercept the SMS message and try to check it for the validation string. However, Twilio might add additional text into the SMS specifically in the free account. So we can't use equals we need to search within the string.

Now that we finished all of that we can get to the actual networking with the login/creation code. In the network layer we use the Rest API. The Rest API lets us construct HTTP REST requests with simple terse code and structure that is reminiscent of curl.

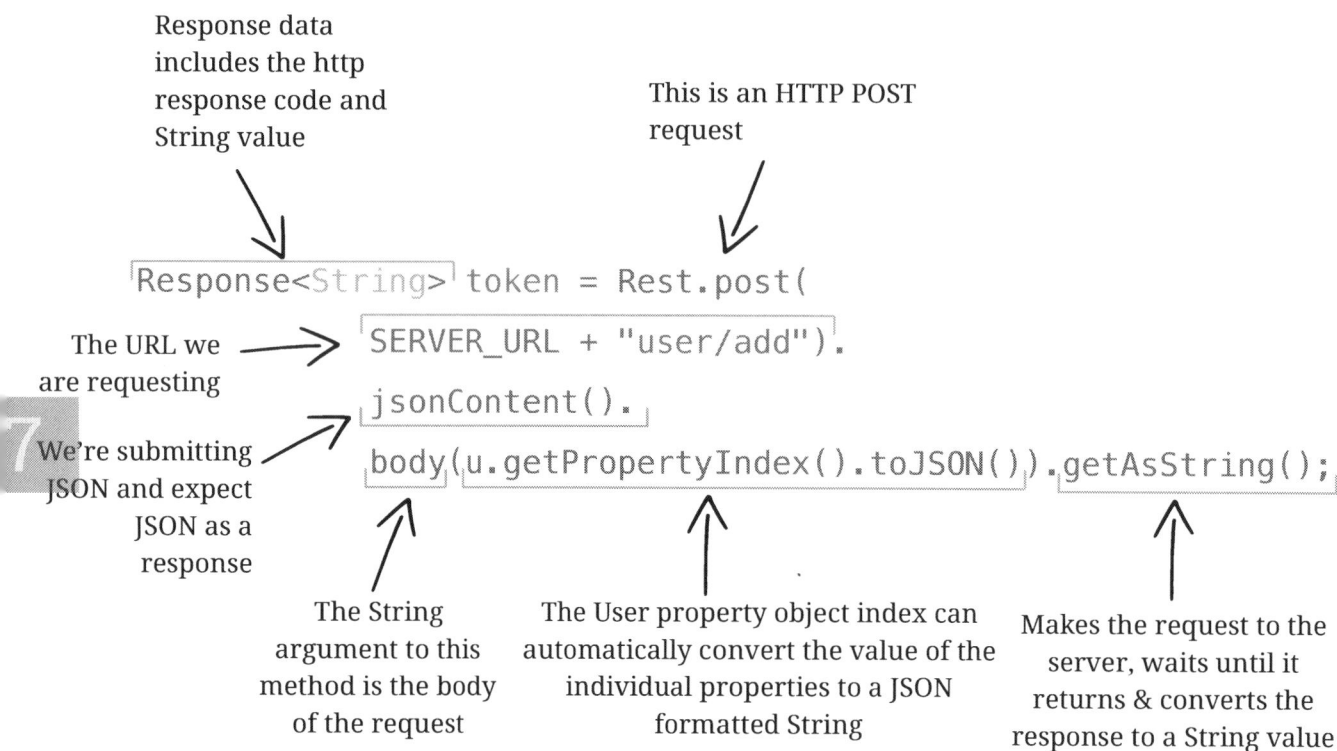

Response data includes the http response code and String value

This is an HTTP POST request

```
Response<String> token = Rest.post(
        SERVER_URL + "user/add").
        jsonContent().
        body(u.getPropertyIndex().toJSON()).getAsString();
```

The URL we are requesting

We're submitting JSON and expect JSON as a response

The String argument to this method is the body of the request

The User property object index can automatically convert the value of the individual properties to a JSON formatted String

Makes the request to the server, waits until it returns & converts the response to a String value

Figure 7. 2. Breaking down the Rest API Synchronous Call

The Rest API also contains an asynchronous variant that returns a Response object into a callback instead of returning it to the caller. I'll explain this more in the following code blocks. First lets map the user exists and add server calls:

Listing 7. 12. UserService userExists and addNewUser

```java
public static  boolean userExists(String phoneNumber) {
    Response<byte[]> b = Rest.get(
        SERVER_URL + "user/exists").
            acceptJson().
            queryParam("phone",  phoneNumber).getAsBytes();
    if(b.getResponseCode() == 200)
        return  b.getResponseData()[0] == (byte)'t';
    return  false ;
}


public static  boolean addNewUser(User u) {
    Response<String> token = Rest.post(
        SERVER_URL + "user/add").
            jsonContent().
            body(u.getPropertyIndex().toJSON()).getAsString();
    if(token.getResponseCode() != 200) return  false;
    Preferences.set("token", token.getResponseData());
    return  true;
}
```

We use the Rest API to make a single connection with the HTTP GET method

Maps to the user/exists method in the server which we use to determine add/login flows

In this case the response is the string true or the string false so we can just check against the letter t

When adding a user we use the Rest API's post method which maps to HTTP POST

Here we can set the body of the POST request to the value of the User object converted into a JSON String

The response is a String token representing the user which we can now store into Preferences

Preferences lets us store simple values as key/value pairs. This is very useful for keeping small details in persistent storage without the hassle.

Next lets review the loginWithPhone method which uses one of the callback versions of the Rest API. The Rest API has the ability to parse the returned JSON and return a Map object containing the data:

Listing 7. 13. UserService loginWithPhone

```
public  static   void  loginWithPhone(String phoneNumber,
        String password, final  SuccessCallback
        final   FailureCallback<Object> onError) {
    Rest.get(SERVER_URL + "user/login").
            acceptJson().
            queryParam("password",  password).
            queryParam("phone",   phoneNumber).
            getAsJsonMapAsync(new Callback<Response<Map>>() {
        public  void  onSucess(Response<Map> value) {
            me = new User();
            me.getPropertyIndex().populateFromMap(
                value.getResponseData());
            Preferences.set ("token",  me.authToken.get());
            PreferencesObject.create(me).bind();
            onSuccess.onSucess(me);
        }
        public  void  onError(Object sender, Throwable err,
             int errorCode, String errorMessage) {
            onError.onError(null, err, errorCode, errorMessage);
        }
    });
}
```

The login method accepts a phone and password and is invoked after we validated the phone

We use the callback variant of this API which accepts callbacks for error/success

In the case of a server error we need to communicate that to the caller of this API

If we get back a token that means the UserAuthenticationException wasn't thrown in the server and we can set it into the Preferences

Now that this is all in place we need to update the UI to make use of these API's.

first
the
on a
. It's
nted
the
rm

When you click the "Enter your mobile number" button you reach this Form the EnterMobileNumberForm

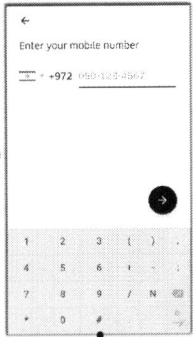

When the right arrow is pressed the 4 digit code form is shown the code is in the Form EnterSMSVerificationDigitsForm

If you already have an account you will be prompted for a password of that account in the EnterPassword Form

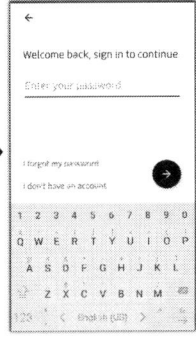

The MapForm is the first Form shown after the app was activated, this is the centeral part of the app

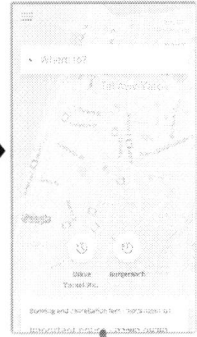

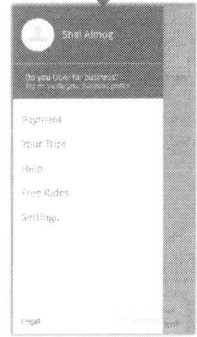

When we click "Where to?" We are presented with this search UI which is technically still a part of MapForm

We
do
bot
of
UI
Ma
dra
to
sea

When you enter a wrong SMS verification number you are presented with this error message

lets
via
or
The
code
in
Goog

The country picker UI opens from the enter mobile number Form. It's implemented in the CountryPickerForm class

When we press the menu button in the top left side of the MapForm or drag from the left side we can pull out this sidemenu implemented in the CommonCode class

We can reach this Form from the Settings entry in the side menu It's implemented in the SettingsForm class

Figure 7. 3. The SMS Activation Process Highlighted in the Screen Flow Diagram

The SMS activation process is practically done. All that remains is binding the whole thing to the user interface. The first step is in EnterMobileNumberForm where we need to change the event handling on the FloatingActionButton to:

Listing 7. 14. EnterMobileNumberForm Send SMS

This code might produce a Dialog. If we show it in the current form it might go back to this form instead of EnterSMSVerificationDigitsForm. By using this callback we can make sure the next Form is shown

```
fab.addActionListener(e -> {
    String number = phoneNumber.getText();
    if(number.startsWith("0")) {
        number = number.substring(1);
    }
    String phone = countryCodeButton.getText() + "-" + number;
    EnterSMSVerificationDigitsForm es =
        new EnterSMSVerificationDigitsForm(phone);
    es.show();
    es.addShowListener(ee -> {
```

Only Android supports intercepting SMS's so this code will only run on that platform. When running elsewhere we'll go directly to sendSMSActivationCode()

```
        if(SMSInterceptor.isSupported()) {
            SMSInterceptor.grabNextSMS(s -> {
                if(UserService.
                    validateSMSActivationCode(s)) {
                    new EnterPasswordForm(phone).show();
                    ToastBar.showMessage(
                        "Automatically Validated Phone Number!",
                        FontImage.MATERIAL_THUMB_UP);
                }
            });
        }
        UserService.sendSMSActivationCode(phone);
    });
});
```

In that case we automatically validate against the string we get from the next SMS if that works we automatically skip ahead to the password form

Regardless of the above we send an SMS message to the given phone number

Next we need to validate the input in a case where SMS isn't validated automatically or the user rejected the permission on Android. We can do this in the EnterSMSVerificationDigitsForm class by editing the isValid method:

Listing 7. 15. EnterSMSVerificationDigitsForm Validation Code

```
public final boolean isValid(String s) {
    return UserService.validateSMSActivationCode(s);
}
```

This pretty much does the SMS activation but we'd also want the countdown functionality to work. If you recall the UI there is a countdown label for resending the SMS. To implement that we need to first define two new member variables and define two helper methods:

Listing 7. 16. EnterSMSVerificationDigitsForm new Variables

```
private   int  resendTime = 120;          ← Countdown value in seconds
                                            for resending the SMS
private   UITimer timer; ←                The timer object which we
                                          need to cancel once it elapses
private   String formatSeconds(int time) {←
    return twoDigits(time / 60) + ":" + twoDigits(time % 60);
}                                                      Formats time in seconds
                                                       as two digits for minute
private   String twoDigits(int t) {                    and two digits for seconds
    if (t < 10) {
        return "0" + t;
    }
    return "" + t;
}
```

Next we need to make the following changes to the constructor code:

Listing 7. 17. EnterSMSVerificationDigitsForm Code Changes

```
Label  resend  = new Label("Resend code in " + formatSeconds(resendTime),
    "ResendCode");
add(SOUTH,resend);
timer = UITimer.timer(1000, true, this, () -> {
    if(resendTime > 0) {
        resendTime--;
        resend.setText("Resend code in " + formatSeconds(resendTime));
        return ;
    }
    timer.cancel();
    UserService.resendSMSActivationCode(phone);
});
```

We schedule the timer to repeat every second on the current Form

So we don't keep sending the SMS's over again

We update the text which redraws automatically. Notice that it's also a good practice to revalidate, but since the string size is roughly the same this shouldn't be necessary

Notice we don't cancel the timer in case of success... We don't need to. Since it's a UITimer it's bound to the Form and once we leave the current form it will no longer elapse.

> **UI Timers are on the EDT**
>
> UITimer executes on the event dispatch thread and thus requires no synchronization. It can modify the UI directly without callSerially

This sends us to the password entry form where we now have two versions of the UI:

Listing 7. 18. Password Form

```
InfiniteProgress ip = new InfiniteProgress();
Dialog dlg = ip.showInfiniteBlocking();
boolean exists = UserService.userExists(phone);
dlg.dispose();
getToolbar().setBackCommand("", Toolbar.BackCommandPolicy.AS_ARROW,
    e -> previous.showBack());
Container box = new Container(BoxLayout.y());
box.setScrollableY(true);
if (exists) {
    box.add(new SpanLabel("Welcome back, signin to continue",
        "FlagButton"));
} else {
    box.add(new SpanLabel("Please enter a new password", "FlagButton"));
}
```

We connect to the server to check if the user exists and show an infinite progress UI over the previous Form

If the user exists we show a welcome back prompt, otherwise we enter a new password

We also need to change the code that handles the FloatingActionButton event to actually add or load the user:

Listing 7. 19. Password Form Add/Load User

If the user exists we call the login
method and show the map on success

```java
fab.addActionListener(e -> {
    Dialog ipDlg = new InfiniteProgress().showInfiniteBlocking();
    if (exists){
        UserService.loginWithPhone(phone, password.getText(), (value) -> {
            password.stopEditing(() ->
                MapForm.get().show());
        }, (sender, err, errorCode, errorMessage) -> {
            ipDlg.dispose();
            error.setText("Login error");
            error.setVisible(true);
            revalidate();
        });
    } else {
        if (UserService.addNewUser(new User().
                phone.set (phone).
                password.set(password.getText()).
                driver.set(false))) {
            MapForm.get().show();
        } else {
            ipDlg.dispose();
            error.setText("Signup error");
            error.setVisible(true);
            revalidate();
        }
    }
});
```

The virtual keyboard is open as
we are currently editing the text
field. So I close the keyboard and
wait for it to close before going
to the MapForm otherwise the
transition might be "jumpy". This
is noticeable only on the device
especially on Android devices

If the server returned an error
on the login we dispose the
progress dialog and show the
error message label we prepared
before. We use revalidate() as the
error label size changed and will
occupy more space

If the user didn't exist before, we create a new User
object and add that user to the server. We then show the
map if the operation is successful. The error handling
code is pretty similar to the previous code

Location and WebSockets

Next on the agenda are the location specific API's which map to the websocket implementation on the server. We can get started with a LocationService class similar to the UserService class that abstracts the local location. Unlike the UserService class, the LocationService class should also deal with the physical location of the device by using the GPS.

As with previous large listings, I'm splitting this class up into smaller more digestible pieces:

Listing 7. 20. The LocationService Class

```java
public class LocationService {
    private static final short
        MESSAGE_TYPE_LOCATION_UPDATE = 1;
    private static final short MESSAGE_TYPE_DRIVER_POSITIONS = 2;
    private static final short MESSAGE_TYPE_AVAILBLE_DRIVER_POSITIONS = 3;
    private static final long
        MAX_UPDATE_FREQUENCY = 3000;



    private Location lastKnownLocation;


    private SocketConnection server;
    private CarAdded carCallback;



    private SuccessCallback<Location> locationCallback;
    private Map<Long, User> cars = new HashMap<>();
    public static interface CarAdded {
        void carAdded(User driver);
    }
    private LocationService() {}
    // ... rest of the code ...
}
```

We defined these constants in the server and need them here as well

When sending a location update to the server we don't want to exceed a fixed amount of updates so we won't burden the server or our network. This is currently limited to 3 seconds

Here we will store the location from the device's GPS

This class represents the WebSocket connection to the server

The UI binds itself as a listener using this callback interface. That way it can add a car to the UI as the server sends details about a driver in the area

When we first start the app we don't have a location and it might take seconds or more for the phone to zero in. Once that happens we can trigger this and the map will zoom into the right location

We cache all the cars on the map so we can update the right car object when there is a change. Since the cars are User objects they are observable (We'll discuss this in the map code later)

There is one class instance of this so we'll use the private constructor trick to block a user from allocating an instance inadvertently

This callback lets the MapForm know that a car was added in the server side so it can add it on the map

The next big thing is tracking GPS location.

> ### *Hybrid Location*
>
> Technically when I say "GPS" it's a bit misleading. Modern devices provide location update using a hybrid approach that combines data from multiple points such as network location and GPS to provide a more accurate location faster. Codename One implicitly uses these API's under the hood.

The bind method connects to the location update events so we can broadcast our location to the server using WebSockets:

Listing 7. 21. LocationService bind

The class has a private constructor so the only way to create the LocationService is via the bind method

```
public static void bind(CarAdded carCallback,
        SuccessCallback<Location> locationUpdate) {
    new LocationService().bindImpl(
        carCallback,
        locationUpdate);
}
```

We invoke bindImpl on the new instance and provide the two callbacks

This one is for adding a car which we use to bind a new car to the UI

This one is for location updates so we can position/zoom the map

```
private void bindImpl(CarAdded carCallback,
        SuccessCallback<Location> locationUpdate) {
    this.carCallback = carCallback;
    locationCallback = locationUpdate;
    LocationManager.getLocationManager().
```

The Location API maps to the Hybrid Location API (GPS)

```
setLocationListener(
    new LocationListener() {
```

Location updates notify the server about changes to the location and also invoke the callback once so we can position the map

```
    public void locationUpdated(Location location) {
        lastKnownLocation = location;
        if (location.getStatus() == LocationManager.AVAILABLE &&
                locationCallback != null) {
            SuccessCallback<Location> c = locationCallback;
            locationCallback = null;
            c.onSucess(location);
        }
        if (server != null) {
            server.sendLocationUpdate();
        }
    }
    public void providerStateChanged(int newState) {
    }
});
new SocketConnection().connect();
}
```

We invoke the callback with the location so the map can be shifted to our current position

Once the server socket is connected we start sending location updates there, the server variable is null until the connection is "ready"

We open the WebSocket connection using the connect() call

Notice that the server variable isn't initialized in the last line of code... That's because the server isn't ready to receive communication yet. This variable is initialized by the SocketConnection inner class.

This completed the LocationService class code however, we are still missing the inner class SocketConnection which implements the actual networking code. Since that inner class is still a bit big I'll break it down into smaller pieces too:

Listing 7. 22. The LocationService SocketConnection inner class

```java
class SocketConnection extends WebSocket {
    private double lat , lon;
    private float direction;
    private long lastUpdateTime;
    private EasyThread et;



    public SocketConnection() {
        super( Globals . SERVER_SOCKET_URL);
        et = EasyThread. start ("Websocket");
    }

    @Override
    protected void onOpen() {
        server = this;

        sendLocationUpdate();
    }

    // rest of code...
}
```

To implement a WebSocket connection we derive the WebSocket class and override the methods within

We cache the last set of location values so we don't send the same data to the server, we only want to send changes

We throttle update to the server so they don't happen to frequently. If a user or driver is moving we don't need an more than one update per 3 seconds

EasyThread lets us post "jobs" onto a dedicated thread so we don't have to block the main Event Dispatch Thread (EDT)

Until onOpen() is invoked the connection isn't ready. That's why the server member field is only initialized here when it's actually ready

If we already have a location we should send a user location update once we have the socket connection in place

Easy Thread

Working with threads is painful. This is such an error prone task that some platforms/languages took the route of avoiding threads entirely (looking at you JavaScript). Launching a new thread is easy. Communicating data between the current and new thread is hard. Synchronization is an error prone and painful process. It's possible but non-trivial.

When you want to synchronize a separate thread to the EDT you can use callSerially which is trivial to use. Why don't we have something that's as easy as that for a separate thread?

That's why we have EasyThread which takes some of the concepts of Codename One's threading and makes them more accessible to an arbitrary thread. This way you can move things like WebSocket into a separate thread and easily synchronize the data from the EDT as needed...

Once we create and start an EasyThread we can send "jobs" to run on that thread using code such as:

Listing 7. 23. Run on Easy Thread

```
et . run(() -> doThisOnEt());
```

The API supports versions of this method that return values and do other tasks that are normally very challenging with threads.

Another interesting feature is if(et.isThisIt()) which will be true if the current thread is the one represented by et. This is useful if we have generic code that invokes a specific method which we would always want on a specific EasyThread we can guard against it using code such as this:

Listing 7. 24. Easy Thread

```
private void  myThreadSafeMethod( final String  arg) {
    if (!myEasyThread.isThisIt ()) {          ← If this isn't the thread
        myEasyThread.run(e -> myThreadSafeMethod(arg));    then call the method
        return;   ←                            within the easy thread
    }
    // method body is here...        Then return as the code will
}                                    run on the easy thread
```

Unlike the other methods in SocketConnection, the sendLocationUpdate method isn't a callback. It sends a "message" (packet) to the server containing the binary data representing the current location. Since the following code implements a binary network protocol it's a bit obtuse but the core concept behind it is very simple:

Listing 7. 25. SocketConnection inner class sendLocationUpdate Method

The connection is single threaded. We use isThisIt() to determine if this is the WebSocket threads

```
public void sendLocationUpdate() {
    if (! et.isThisIt()) {
        et.run(() -> sendLocationUpdate());
        return;
    }
```

If the current thread isn't the one in et we invoke the method again within et and return from the current thread. This makes the entire method effectively thread safe

This can happen if we didn't get the location yet from the GPS

```
    if (lastKnownLocation != null) {
        double lt = lastKnownLocation.getLatitude();
        double ll = lastKnownLocation.getLongitude();
        float dir = lastKnownLocation.getDirection();
        if (ll ==lon && lt ==lat && dir ==direction) return;
        long time = System.currentTimeMillis();
        if (time - lastUpdateTime < MAX_UPDATE_FREQUENCY) return;
        lastUpdateTime = time;
        lon = ll;
        lat = lt;
        direction = dir;
```

If the location values didn't change since last update we do nothing

We don't update too much, there is a chance we'll miss an update here but it's probably not a deal breaker if a user didn't move much

216

```
try ( ByteArrayOutputStream  bos  = new ByteArrayOutputStream ();
     DataOutputStream dos = new DataOutputStream(bos))     {
     dos. writeShort ( MESSAGE_TYPE_LOCATION_UPDATE);
     String   token = Preferences.get ("token",  null);
     dos. writeShort ( token. length ());  ⟵
     for ( int   iter   = 0 ;   iter   < token. length ()  ;  iter ++)
          dos. writeByte (( byte) token. charAt ( iter ));
     dos. writeDouble ( lat );
     dos. writeDouble ( lon);
     dos. writeFloat  ( dir );
     dos. writeDouble (1);  ⟵
     dos. writeByte  (0);
     dos. flush ();
     send(bos. toByteArray ());
} catch ( IOException  err ) {
     Log. e( err );  ↑
}
}
}
```

We create a ByteArrayOutputStream into which we construct the message that we receive on the server with the header, location etc. see Listing 6.29 (page 222)

7

This one line sends the binary data, it's a similar process with text data but we save the parsing overhead. The IOException isn't likely as this is a RAM based stream

I currently hardcoded a 1 kilometer search radius and defined explicitly that we aren't in taxi hailing mode

If you understood the code in the server that parsed this data then that code is literally the mirror image. Now all that remains is the implementation of the callbacks. I'll start with the first batch of "simple" callbacks:

Listing 7. 26. The LocationService SocketConnection inner class Simple Callbacks

```
protected void onClose( int  i ,  String  string) {
    Log. p("Connection closed error!");
    UITimer. timer (5000,  false ,  ()  -> connect());
}
protected void onMessage( String  string )  {}
protected void onError ( Exception  e) {
    Log.e (e);
}
```

When a connection is closed due to connectivity issues or some other issues we can set a timer and try to reconnect. Remember cell phone networking is unreliable!

This is invoked for text messages. In this app we only use binary messages as they are slightly more efficient

This is really important. We need to handle errors properly in a WebSocket application otherwise a failure can leave us without a connection

Next we have the bigger callback method. The onMessage() method.
onMessage() handles incoming packets and translates them to car events:

Listing 7. 27. The LocationService SocketConnection inner class onMessage()

```java
protected void onMessage(byte[] bytes) {
    try {
        DataInputStream dis = new DataInputStream(
            new ByteArrayInputStream(bytes));

        short response = dis.readShort();
        int size = dis.readInt();
        for (int iter = 0; iter < size; iter++) {
            long id = dis.readLong();
            User car = cars.get(id);

            if (car == null) {
                car = new User().
                        id.set(id).
                        latitude.set(dis.readDouble()).
                        longitude.set(dis.readDouble()).
                        direction.set(dis.readFloat());
                cars.put(id, car);
                User finalCar = car;
                callSerially(() -> carCallback.carAdded(finalCar));
            } else {
                car.latitude.set(dis.readDouble()).
                    longitude.set(dis.readDouble()).
                    direction.set(dis.readFloat());
            }
        }
    } catch (IOException err) {
        Log.e(err);
    }
}
```

Binary messages from the server arrive at this callback method

DataInputStream is a powerful tool for when we want to break byte data into pieces

The specific messages sent from the server is the driver search results

We store User instances in a Map where the user ID is the key, this saves us from sending duplicate carAdded events and allows us to just mutate the User properties

Code in MapForm listens for changes on User object properties so when we set a value it updates the UI automatically

Notice that this code is running on the WebSocket thread so events need to go back into the EDT to prevent potential issues

This was a **big** class... It was mostly due to the communication protocol and the callbacks didn't help the verbosity. I also mixed two ideas into a single class (networking and location) which also ballooned it a bit. But this is all worthwhile now that we got to the map...

7

Updating the Map

Now that we have the communication infrastructure in place we can map it to the MapForm UI to plot out the location of drivers. Since this is a relatively large block of code I'll split it into three parts:

Listing 7. 28. MapForm Binding Location Service

```
Container  mapLayer = new Container();
mapLayer.setLayout(new MapLayout(mc, mapLayer));
Image carImage  = Resources. getGlobalResources().
    getImage("map-vehicle-icon-uberX.png" );



LocationService.bind(
    user  -> addDriver ( mapLayer, user,  carImage),



    loc  ->  mc.fitBounds (new BoundingBox(new Coord(loc . getLatitude(),
        loc . getLongitude ()),   0.009044, 0.0089831 )));
add(mapLayer);
```

New drivers are added to the map layer as the server sends their information to us

We draw the driver using this image, it must be a square image otherwise rotation will crop it

We bind to the LocationService where we get a callback every time a driver comes into play

This callback is invoked for every new driver, we'll review the implementation of this method next

fitBounds positions the map with the center pointing at the current coordinate and the given radius (1km)

This raises the question of addDriver which handles the actual addition of a Component representing a car :

Listing 7. 29. MapForm Positioning Cars on the Map

```
private   void  addDriver(Container mapLayer, User user, Image carImage) {
      Label  userCar  = new Label ();
      userCar. putClientProperty("angle" ,
         user. direction.get());


      userCar. setIcon(carImage.rotate((int)
         user.direction.getFloat()));
      userCar.getAllStyles().setOpacity(140);
      MapLayout.setHorizontalAlignment(userCar, MapLayout.HALIGN.CENTER);
      MapLayout.setVerticalAlignment(userCar, MapLayout.VALIGN.MIDDLE);
      mapLayer.add(new Coord(user. latitude. get(),  user.longitude.get()),
         userCar);
      mapLayer.revalidate();
      bindUserChange(user,  userCar,  carImage);   ⑥
}
```

A car is just a label with the right icon in place

We keep the angle in a client property so when there is a change event we can check if the angle actually changed

We set the icon with the angle of the car

We place the new car where the user is located thanks to the MapLayout

This code is invoked after the UI is shown. We need to revalidate so the car will be positioned correctly

This method binds property change listeners so we can update the UI based on changes to the User object

The location service only fires an event when a driver is added, not as the driver moves. When a car moves, the User object is updated with the change and we can observe these properties to update the UI. That's exactly what bindUserChange does:

Listing 7. 30. MapForm Positioning Cars on the Map

We can add a listener to a property that means that when the
location service changes a User object, we'll get the event callback

```
private   void  bindUserChange(User user, Label userCar, Image carImage) {
    user. direction.addChangeListener( p -> {
        Float   angle  = ( Float ) userCar. getClientProperty( "angle" );
        if (angle == null  ||
            angle. floatValue() != user. direction.getFloat()) {
            userCar.setIcon(carImage.rotate((int)
                user.direction.getFloat()));
            userCar. putClientProperty("angle", user.direction.get());
        }
    });



    user. latitude . addChangeListener( p -> {  .
        Coord crd = (Coord) mapLayer.getLayout ().
            getComponentConstraint(userCar);
        if (crd.getLatitude() != user.latitude.get()) {




            userCar.remove();
            mapLaycr.add(new Coord(user.latitude.get(),
                user.longitude.get()), userCar);
            mapLayer.animateLayout(100);
        }
    });
    user. longitude . addChangeListener( p -> {
        Coord crd = (Coord)
            mapLayer.getLayout().getComponentConstraint(userCar);
        if ( crd. getLongitude()!= user.longitude.get()) {
            userCar. remove();
            mapLayer.add(new Coord(user.latitude.get(),
                user. longitude.get()), userCar);
            mapLayer.animateLayout(100);
        }
    });
}
```

The change listener on the angle
property automatically rotates
the icon image in the right
direction but it does that only if
the angle changed to avoid a
performance penalty

We update latitude and longitude
separately but we need to guard
against duplicate changes so we
first test the existing value

We can't replace a constraint in
the layout so we remove the
component and add it back.
Animate layout still works in this
case and it will move the car
gracefully to its new position

> **!** **The Car Image MUST be Square**
>
> We use the rotate method on the car image which assumes a square image otherwise it will appear cropped. Notice that transparent pixels in the image are fine

7.4
Lets See it Working

We can now finally see everything running... To simulate the car position for testing we can insert a fake entry into the MySQL database using this SQL statement:

Listing 7. 31. Insert Fake Driver

```
insert  into  user ( driver,   password, phone, auth_token,  current_rating,
    hailing,   latitude,   longitude,  direction ) values ( true ,
    'dummyPassword', '999',  'fakeToken',  5,  false,   32.072449,
    34.778613, 0);
```

This will create a fake driver entry and allow you to see it when you login. Assuming you configured the values in Globals.java you should be able to run the server and client then activate the device using SMS and see the driver.

> **♡** **Place the Test Driver Next to You**
>
> Set the latitude and longitude values in the SQL above to your area

7.5
Summary

In this chapter, we learned:

- Properties are an alternative to the get/set methods that are common in Java. The huge advantage is the ability to introspect such properties which allows us to automate processes such as database storage, parsing etc.

- The Rest API lets us construct an HTTP REST requests with simple terse code and structure that is reminiscent of curl.

- UI Timers run on the EDT. They are very useful for manipulating the UI as we don't need callSerially when working with them

- Modern devices provide location update using a hybrid approach that combines data from multiple points such as network location and GPS to provide a more accurate location faster.

- EasyThread takes some of the concepts of Codename One's threading and makes them more accessible to an arbitrary thread

I'd say this was pretty easy, we're just filling in the blanks to get things working... The cool thing is that we now have a fully working app with a client server process and SMS based user activation. We place things on the map and control them via WebSockets.

All that is left now is the process of tacking on features and refinements. We did the "hard work".

7

7

Day 4: Search, Route and Hailing

This chapter covers:

- Using Google places Web Services for search and route, abstracting them and integrating them into the UI

- Search UI Autocomplete, this UI includes a complex mode with draggable portions

- Picking a location from the map by dragging it and locating the name under the marker position

After day 3 we finally have a client server application that works but we don't have any "real" functionality. With real I mean actually searching for a ride, seeing the route and hailing it. After all, that's the purpose of the application right?

Today we'll work on getting these top features working as expected. To do that we need to use some new webservices. I'll use some webservices from Google for location and route planning.

I chose to invoke the Google webservices from the device code instead of using our server to proxy the calls. This makes sense for a simple project and is arguably faster as I connect directly to Google.

However, if I was building a real world application I would have directed all requests to our server and invoked Google from there. This might have a performance penalty but it's worth it:

- My Google API keys would have been more secure in the server

- I can cache common queries in the server and reduce API costs to some degree

- I can monitor the calls sent out and identify trends

- I can instantly switch providers without shipping a new version of the app

8 8.1

SearchService

We'll start with the business logic of the underlying search API. Google provides some great webservices that we can leverage to implement almost all of the functionality in the Uber application:

- Reverse Geocoding - Provides the name of a given location. This is useful for pointing a pin on the map and naming the location

- Directions - Provides directions, trip time etc. We can get the points of the path and plot them out on the map

- Places Autocomplete - The places API allows searching for a place similar to the geocoding API. The autocomplete version lets us type into a text field and see "suggestions" appear

All of these will be very useful when we build the actual search and route features. I'll use the SearchService class to encapsulate this functionality for each of these services.

All of these API's require developer keys which you can obtain from their respective websites. I've edited the Globals class to include these new keys required by the 3 API's:

Listing 8. 1. Keys for Google WebServices

```
public  static  final  String  GOOGLE_DIRECTIONS_KEY = "----";
public  static  final  String  GOOGLE_GEOCODING_KEY = "----";
public  static  final  String  GOOGLE_PLACES_KEY = "----";
```

Make sure to replace ---- with the relevant key. You can get the keys by going to the following sites:

- Directions – developers.google.com/maps/documentation/directions/get-api-key

- Places – developers.google.com/places/web-service/get-api-key

- Geocoding – developers.google.com/maps/documentation/geocoding/get-api-key

> 💡 The keys look similar but it's a different key for every API and they can't be shared

Reverse Geocoding

We use the `/maps/api/geocode/json` URL for Reverse Geocoding. Google provides this example for usage of the API:

```
https://maps.googleapis.com/maps/api/geocode/json?
       latlng=40.714224,-73.961452&key=YOUR_API_KEY
```

It's just a latitude/longitude pair and your API key.

This produces the following JSON result:

Listing 8. 2. Reverse Geocoding Sample JSON result (trimmed)

```json
{
   "results" : [ ◄——
      {
         "address_components" : [
            {
               "long_name" : "277",
               "short_name" : "277",
               "types" : [ "street_number" ]
            },
            {
               "long_name" : "Bedford Avenue",
               "short_name" : "Bedford Ave",
               "types" : [ "route" ]
            },
            ... trimmed ...
         ],
         "formatted_address" :
            "277 Bedford, Brooklyn, NY 11211, USA", ◄——
         "geometry" : {
            "location" : {
               "lat" : 40.714232,
               "lng" : -73.9612889
            },
            ... trimmed ...
         },
         "place_id" : "ChIJd8BlQ2BZwokRAFUEcm_qrcA",
         "types" : [ "street_address" ]
      },
   ... Additional results ...
}
```

We need to get this result array from the response, we only care about the first element and will discard the rest

This is the only attribute we need at this time from this API

8

Now that we know what we are looking for lets look at the code that accomplishes this:

Listing 8. 3. SearchService Reverse Geocoding

```java
public class SearchService {
    private static ConnectionRequest lastLocationRequest;
    public static void nameMyCurrentLocation(Location l,
        SuccessCallback<String> name) {
        if (l == null ) {
            return ;
        }

        if (lastLocationRequest != null ) {
            lastLocationRequest.kill();
        }
        lastLocationRequest = Rest.get(
            "https://maps.googleapis.com/maps/api/geocode/json").
                queryParam("latIng", l.getLatitude() + "," +
                    l.getLongitude ()).
                queryParam("key" , GOOGLE_GEOCODING_KEY
                queryParam("language" , "en" ).
                queryParam("result_type",
                    "street_address|point_of_interest").

                getAsJsonMap(callbackMap -> {
                    Map data = callbackMap.getResponseData();
                    if(data != null) {

                        List results = (List)
                            data. get("results");
                        if (results != null && results.size() > 0) {
                            Map firstResult = (Map)results.get(0);
                            name.onSucess((String)firstResult.get(
                                "formatted_address"));
                        }
                    }
                });
    }
}
```

There is an edge case where location isn't ready yet when this method is invoked. Usually it's best to fail by throwing an exception but this is a valid situation to which we have a decent fallback option

If we send two such calls in rapid succession we only need the last one so we cancel the previous request

The reverse geocode API latIng argument determines the location for which we are looking

8

We get the parsed result as a Map containing a hierarchy of objects the callback is invoked asynchronously when the response arrives

This gets the results list from the JSON and extracts the first element from there. Check out the JSON sample from before to see how this maps to the data

We extract the one attribute we care about: formatted_address. We invoke the callback method with this result

Places Autocomplete

The places autocomplete API is a bit more challenging since this API is invoked as a user types the address. We'll need the ability to cancel a request just as we do with the geocoding calls. Caching is also crucial in this case, so we must cache as much as possible to avoid overuse of the API and performance issues.

Lets start by reviewing the API URL and responses:

```
https://maps.googleapis.com/maps/api/place/autocomplete/json?
      input=lev&location=32.072449,34.778613&radius=50000&key=API_KEY
```

The search is relevant to a specific location and radius. Otherwise it would suggest places from all over the world which probably doesn't make sense for an Uber style application. Notice the radius is specified in meters.

The input value is the string for which we need auto-complete suggestions.

This request produces this (trimmed) JSON result:

Listing 8. 4. Autocomplete Sample JSON result (trimmed)

```
{
  "predictions" : [          All predications are again within an array
    {                         but this time we'll need all of them
      "description" : "Levinsky, Tel Aviv–Yafo, Israel",
      "id" : "13fd8422602e10c4a7be775c88280b383a15f368",
      "matched_substrings" : [
        {
          "length" : 3,
          "offset" : 0
        }
      ],
      "structured_formatting" : {
        "main_text" : "Levinsky",          The UI requires the broken down
        "main_text_matched_substrings" : [  text so we need the main text
          {                                  property
            "length" : 3,
            "offset" : 0
          }
        ],
        "secondary_text" : "Tel Aviv–Yafo, Israel"   And we'll need the
      },                                              secondary text too
      "place_id" : "Eh9MZXZpbnNreSwgVGVywgSXNyYVs",
      "reference" : "-pQdrYHivUaFGV9GwZkfwp4xkjUL2Z2mpGNXJBv",
        ... trimmed ...
    },
    ...additional results ...
  ],
  "status" : "OK"            We'll also need the place_id and the reason for this is a **huge**
}                            omission in this API. Notice it has no location information... We
                             will need the place_id value to query again for the location
```

8

Before we move on to the code we'll need a way to send the results back. We can do that with a list of
SuggestionResult entries as such:

Listing 8. 5. SearchService SuggestionResult inner class

```
public static class SuggestionResult {
    private final String mainText;
    private final String secondaryText;
    private final String fullText;
    private final String placeId;

    public SuggestionResult(String mainText, String secondaryText,
            String fullText, String placeId) {
        this . mainText = mainText;
        this . secondaryText = secondaryText;
        this . fullText = fullText;
        this . placeId = placeId;
    }
    public String getPlaceId() {
        return placeId;
    }
    public String getMainText() {
        return mainText;
    }
    public String getSecondaryText() {
        return secondaryText;
    }
    public String getFullText() {
        return fullText;
    }
}
```

These fields map directly to the data we need from the JSON

We don't need a no argument constructor since this class is only created within the SearchService

We don't need setters which will just make this class more complicated

8

That was a pretty trivial class that doesn't require much explaining. But it still leaves the issue of getting the location for a specific entry open. We can accomplish that by adding this method to the SuggestionResult:

Listing 8. 6. SearchService SuggestionResult getLocation Method

```java
public  void  getLocation(SuccessCallback<Location> result) {
   Rest.get("https://maps.googleapis.com/maps/api/place/details/json").
        queryParam("placeid",    placeId).
        queryParam("key",   GOOGLE_PLACES_KEY).
        getAsJsonMap(callbackMap  -> {
            Map r = (Map)callbackMap.getResponseData().get("result");

            Map geomMap = (Map)r.get("geometry");
            Map locationMap = (Map)geomMap.get("location");
            double  lat  = Util.toDoubleValue( locationMap.get("lat" ));
            double  lon  = Util.toDoubleValue( locationMap.get("lng"));
            result.onSucess(new  Location (lat , lon));
       });
}
```

We do a HTTP GET request on the places API with placeId and key as arguments

The value is returned asynchronously in the callback as a parsed map of the JSON data

This maps directly to the geometry struct in the JSON response

We call the success callback directly once we have the values we need

8

Why Use queryParam *with a GET Request?*

In the previous example I did something similar to this:

Listing 8. 7. Why queryParam

```
Rest.get("https://maps.googleapis.com/maps/api/place/details/json").
    queryParam("placeid", placeId);
```

It would seem like this code is the equivalent of:

Listing 8. 8. Would this Be the Same as queryParam?

```
Rest. get("https://maps.googleapis.com/maps/api/place/details/json?" +
    "placeid=" + placeId);
```

The second listing has two basic drawbacks:

- It doesn't encode the argument so if placeId contained a character such as | or a space this wouldn't work

- It makes switching the code to POST harder

Using queryParam is more flexible and more robust than just appending to the URL.

There's one last thing we need before we go into the suggestion method itself. We need variables to cache the data and current request. Otherwise multiple incoming requests might collide and block the network:

Listing 8. 9. SearchService Additional Variables Needed for Autocomplete

```
private static ConnectionRequest         We need the lastSuggestionRequest
    lastSuggestionRequest; ←              so we can cancel it
private static String lastSuggestionValue;
```

The lastSuggestionRequest lets us distinguish duplicate values this can sometimes happen as an edit event might repeat a request that was already sent e.g. if a user types and deletes a character (this can happen since we will wait 500ms before sending characters. I will discuss this later on)

236

The locationCache reduces duplicate requests. Notice that this can grow to a level of a huge memory leak but realistically that would require a huge number of searches. If this becomes a problem the code can be ported to CacheMap which serializes extra data to storage

```java
private static final Map<String, List <SuggestionResult>>
    locationCache = new HashMap<>();   ←
```

Now we can go into the suggestion method itself:

Listing 8. 10. SearchService suggestLocations

```java
public static void suggestLocations(String input, Location l,
        SuccessCallback<List<SuggestionResult>> resultList) {
    if(lastSuggestionRequest != null) {   ←
        if (lastSuggestionValue.equals(input))  return;
        lastSuggestionRequest.kill();   ←
    }
```

If the last request is this request which can happen as a user types and deletes etc. then we don't want to do anything...

However, if it isn't then we want to kill the last request which might still be queued and blocking us from going forward

We check if an entry is already in the cache as users might type and revise a lot thus triggering significant webservice cost overhead

```java
    List<SuggestionResult> lr = locationCache.get( input );
    if ( lr != null ) {
        lastSuggestionValue = null;   ←
        lastSuggestionRequest = null;
        callSerially(() -> resultList.onSucess(lr));   ←
        return;
    }
    lastSuggestionValue = input;
    lastSuggestionRequest = Rest.get(   ←
        "https://maps.googleapis.com/maps/api/place/autocomplete/json").
            queryParam("input",  input).
            queryParam("location",  l.getLatitude() + "," + l.getLongitude()).
            queryParam("radius" , "50000").
            queryParam("key",  GOOGLE_PLACES_KEY).
            getAsJsonMap(callbackMap ->
                processSuggestionResponse( callbackMap. getResponseData(),
                        input ,  resultList));
}
```

We clean the variable values and then invoke the response

Notice I use callSerially in this case to defer the response to the next cycle

The REST request is a pretty standard GET asynchronous request

We delegate the logic to processSuggestionResponse so we can keep the method small

We use callSerially to defer responses from cache. If we call back immediately we might delay the input code which is currently in place. By shifting the callback to the next cycle of the EDT we guarantee that suggestLocations will behave in a similar way whether the data is cached locally or not the method will return immediately.

The final piece in the suggestLocations method is the processSuggestionResponse method.

Listing 8. 11. SearchService processSuggestionResponse

```java
private static void processSuggestionResponse(Map data, String input,
        SuccessCallback<List<SuggestionResult>> resultList) {
    if(data != null) {
        List<Map> results = (List<Map>)data.  get("predictions");
        if(results !=  null && results.size()>0) {
            ArrayList<SuggestionResult> resultSet = new ArrayList<>();
            for(Map r : results) {
                Map sf = (Map)r.get("structured_formatting");
                String mainText = (String)sf.get("main_text");
                String secondaryText = (String)sf.get("secondary_text");
                String description = (String)r.get("description");
                String placeId = (String)r.get("place_id");
                resultSet.add(new SuggestionResult(mainText,
                    secondaryText, description, placeId));
            }
            locationCache. put(input, resultSet);
            resultList.onSucess(resultSet);
        }
    }
}
```

The request extracts the predictions array so we can construct the result list

We iterate over the entries. Notice we discard the generic context which is legal in Java but might produce a warning

We extract the elements from the map and create the SuggestionResult entries. They are stored the location in cache

Finally we invoke the onSuccess callback. Notice that in this case we didn't need the callSerially since the response is already asynchronous

I discarded generic typing because it doesn't make sense for parsing JSON data. JSON data is essentially a data structure matching nested lists and maps in Java. The problem is we can't know at compile time the content of the JSON response and its depth. I could have used a generic such as: Map<String, Object> but once I would "dig deeper" into the nesting I'd need to cast again e.g.:

Listing 8. 12. Generics Don't Make this Readable

```
Map<String, Object> sf = (Map<String, Object>)r.get("structured_formatting");
```

Generics are useful when dealing with application data structures but they don't provide any value in this specific case.

With this the autocomplete logic is finished and we only need to bind it to the UI.

8

Directions

8.1.3

The final webservice API we will cover is the directions API which will allows us to set the path taken by the car on the map. The directions API is challenging. It returns encoded data in a problematic format. E.g. this is the sample query from Google:

```
https://maps.googleapis.com/maps/api/directions/json?
    origin=Toronto&destination—Montreal&key—API_KEY
```

💡 *We can use latitude and longitude*
Notice we can give the origin and destinations values as a longitude latitude pair which is what we'll actually do

The response is a bit large so I trimmed a lot of it to give you a sense of what we are looking for:

Listing 8. 13. Response for directions query

```
{
  "geocoded_waypoints" : [
     ... trimmed ...
  ],
  "routes" : [
    {
       ... trimmed ...
      "overview_polyline" : {
         "points" : "emiGhmocNilCeFmHaAmIgDpAmLeZqIcBeKLqIpIqEkF"
      },
      "summary" : "ON–401 E",
      "warnings" : [],
      "waypoint_order" : []
    }
  ],
  "status" : "OK"
}
```

This is the only thing that matters from this JSON response. We don't need anything else. Notice I trimmed this entry a lot so it can fit in print. The string was around 500 characters originally

The `overview_polyline` entry seems like a bunch of gibberish but it isn't. This is a special notation from Google that encodes the latitude/longitude values of the entire trip in a single string. This encoding is described by Google here:

developers.google.com/maps/documentation/utilities/polylinealgorithm

decodePolyline

Being lazy I found someone who already implemented the algorithm in Java and his code worked "as is": github.com/scoutant/polyline-decoder/blob/master/src/main/java/org/scoutant/polyline/PolylineDecoder.java

This is the block of code I needed, I won't go into it as it's not something I wrote. I'm listing it here for completeness:

Listing 8. 14. Polyline Decoder

```
private static List<Coord> decodePolyline(
    String str) {
  ArrayList<Coord> resultPath = new ArrayList<>();
  int index = 0;
  int lat = 0, lng = 0;
  while (index < str.length()) {
    int b, shift = 0, result = 0;
    do {
      b = str.charAt(index++) - 63;
      result |= (b & 0x1f) << shift;
      shift += 5;
    } while (b >= 0x20);
    int dlat = ((result & 1) != 0 ? ~(result >> 1) : (result >> 1));
    lat += dlat;
    shift = 0;
    result = 0;
    do {
      b = str.charAt(index++) - 63;
      result |= (b & 0x1f) << shift;
      shift += 5;
    } while (b >= 0x20);
    int dlng = ((result & 1) != 0 ? ~(result >> 1) : (result >> 1));
    lng += dlng;
    Coord p = new Coord((double) lat / 1E5, (double) lng / 1E5);
    resultPath.add(p);
  }
  return resultPath;
}
```

The method accepts an encoded String and returns latitude/longitude coordinates

I won't go into the code since it's mostly just bitwise shifting to satisfy the requirements from Google

8

With this method we can take the encoded String and return the path matching that string as a list of coordinates for the map.

DirectionResults

One last missing detail is the result of the direction call. I could have used something like SuccessCallback with the path but that would mean some pieces would be missing such as the duration value, distance etc.

I could have created another class for the result value like I did with the completion code. I could have also used multiple callbacks. But in this case I want to demonstrate a third approach to dealing with the same problem and that's a callback that accepts multiple arguments.

Listing 8. 15. DirectionResults Callback

```
public static interface DirectionResults {
    public void onDirectionResult(List<Coord> path, int duration, String distance);
}
```

8 💡 **A Dedicated class is more Flexible**

Using a dedicated class (e.g. SuggestionResult) instead of callback arguments is more flexible as we can add additional values to the argument class without changing the API signature

The Directions Method

Now that this is all out of the way the directions method is relatively simple:

Listing 8. 16. Directions Method

```
public static void directions(Location l, Location destination,
    DirectionResults response) {  ←
    Rest.get("https://maps.googleapis.com/maps/api/directions/json").
        queryParam("origin", l.getLatitude() + "," + l.getLongitude()).
        queryParam("destination", destination.getLatitude() + "," +
            destination.getLongitude()).
        queryParam("mode", "driving").  ←
        queryParam("key", GOOGLE_DIRECTIONS_KEY).
        getAsJsonMap(callbackMap -> {
            processDirections(callbackMap.getResponseData(), response);
        });
}
```

We accept source/ destination coordinates and return the result asynchronously via the callback

Again this is a standard REST GET request with a couple of argument location values

The main logic is in the processDirections method for simplicity

This leads us to processDirections which processes the parsed data again:

Listing 8. 17. processDirections

```
private static void processDirections(Map data,DirectionResults response) {
    if(data != null) {
        List results = (List)data.get("routes");
        if(results != null && results.size() > 0) {
            Map f = (Map)results.get(0);
            Map op = (Map)f.get("overview_polyline");
            List<Coord> polyline=decodePolyline((String)op.get("points"));
            List legs = (List)f.get("legs");
            Map firstLeg = (Map)legs.get(0);
            Map distance = (Map)firstLeg.get("distance");
            Map duration = (Map)firstLeg.get("duration");
            response.onDirectionResult(polyline,
                Util.toIntValue(duration.get("value")),
                (String)distance.get("text"));
        }
    }
}
```

We only need the first route as the Uber app doesn't suggest multiple routes (at least to passengers)

The overview_polyline from the first entry is what we came for

Finally we invoke the callback with the direction results

We also take the trip duration and distance so we can display them in the map UI over the path

8

This should give us the directions that we can soon integrate into the UI.

Search 8.2

Now that the basic "infrastructure" is out of the way we'll start wiring it into the UI, starting with search. The initial search UI I did in the mockup was very "naive". It just toggled the completion on and off.

The real Uber app allows us to swipe the search UI down and then pick a location in the map using a pin. This then updates the text field with the selected location. Alternatively, if you type into the text field locations are suggested to you as you type.

There is a great deal of nuanced behavior in this UI so I only focused on the "big ticket" features:

- Swipe
- Completion
- Map location picking

I didn't implement a lot of the relatively easy features such as bookmarked locations or history in the search UI. Those should be trivial to fill in.

In order to implement these I moved most of the UI logic into separate classes:

- AutoCompleteAddressInput is a TextField subclass representing the two text fields in the search UI
- CompletionContainer shows the search results for the AutoCompleteAddressInput

8.2.1

AutoCompleteAddressInput

A major feature of AutoCompleteAddressInput is its ability to fold/unfold the CompletionContainer. It accomplishes this by binding pointer listeners to the parent form and using them to implement the drag and drop behavior.

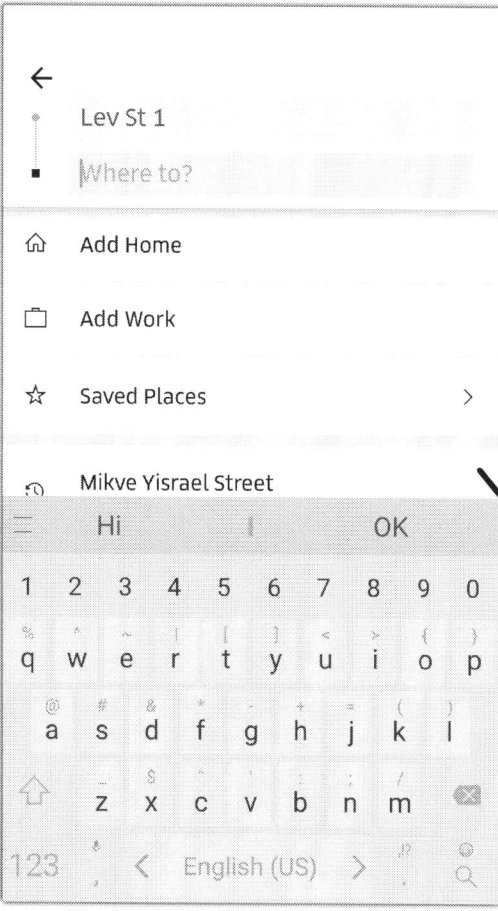

The completion and history area moves down

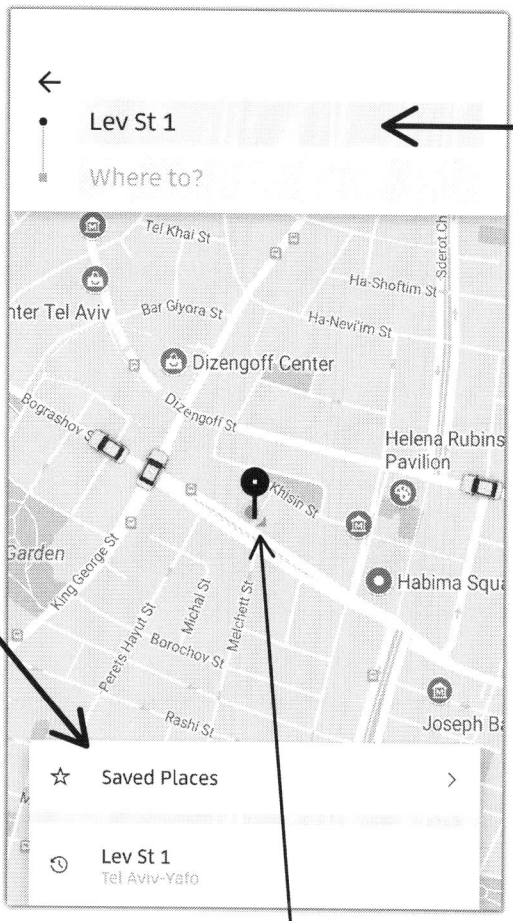

The map can be panned. Panning updates the value in the From field

Figure 8. 1. The Two Modes of the "Where to?" UI

Completion handling is still done in the MapForm itself where the business logic is still situated. Since there is a lot of code I'll break it down into smaller pieces starting with the class definition and constructor:

Listing 8. 18. The AutoCompleteAddressInput class

I chose to derive TextField rather than encapsulate it mostly due to convenience. Encapsulation would have worked just as well for this case

```
public class AutoCompleteAddressInput extends TextField {
    private final Container layers;
    private int firstX = -1, firstY = -1;
    private boolean dragStarted;
    private CompletionContainer completion;
    private ActionListener<ActionEvent> dragListener, releaseListener;
    private Location currentLocation;
    private boolean blockChangeEvent;
    public AutoCompleteAddressInput(String value, String hint,
            Container layers, CompletionContainer completion) {
        super(value, hint, 40, TextField.ANY);
        this.completion = completion;
        this.layers = layers;
        getHintLabel().setUIID("FromToTextFieldHint");
        setUIID("FromToTextField");
        addDataChangedListener((i, ii) -> {
            if(blockChangeEvent) return;
            if(!getText().equals(value)) {
                completion.updateCompletion(getText(), this);
            }
        });
    }
    public void setTextNoEvent(String text) {
        blockChangeEvent = true;
        setText(text);
        blockChangeEvent = false;
    }
    // rest of code here...
}
```

With the exception of these last two variables, every other variable here is in the service of the drag and drop logic, I'll discuss the variables as I use them in the code

We use the DataChangedListener to send events to the completion logic

DataChangedListener is invoked by setText which can cause an infinite recursion if setText is invoked from a DataChangedListener

The solution is a special version of setText that blocks this callback and reduces the noise in the completion code with the blockChangeEvent variable

I'll discuss updateCompletion soon when I cover CompletionContainer

Lets look at the smaller methods in `AutoCompleteAddressInput` before we dig into the big method:

Listing 8. 19. The AutoCompleteAddressInput Methods

```
protected void focusGained() {
    completion.initCompletionBar();
}
```

This is a callback from component that's invoked when the component receives focus

The last focused text field is the one that now handles the completion so if the user was in the to text field everything typed will now impact the completion for to and vice versa

deinitialize is invoked when we leave the current Form, we use it to cleanup. deinitialize is also invoked when a component is removed from the UI or its hierarchy is removed

```
protected void deinitialize() {
    if(dragListener != null) {
        Form f = getComponentForm();
        f.removePointerDraggedListener(dragListener);
        f.removePointerReleasedListener(dragListener);
    }
    super.deinitialize();
}
```

Pointer listeners on the Form allow us to detect pointer events everywhere. We bind them in the initComponent method and remove them in the deinitialize method

Removing these listeners prevents a memory leak and a situation where pointer processing code keeps running and taking up CPU.

```
public Location getCurrentLocation() {
    return currentLocation;
}
```

The location of a text field uses strings but what we really care about is coordinates on the map which is why I store them here

```
public void setCurrentLocation(Location currentLocation) {
    this.currentLocation = currentLocation;
}
```

This is used both by the map pin logic and by the search logic we will use later on

> initComponent is invoked when a component is "there". It will be invoked if a component is added to an already showing Form or if a parent Form is shown

```
protected void initComponent() {
    super.initComponent();
    if(dragListener == null) {
        dragListener = e -> processDragEvent(e);
        getComponentForm().addPointerDraggedListener(dragListener);
        releaseListener = e -> processReleaseEvent(e);
        getComponentForm().addPointerReleasedListener(releaseListener);
    }
}
```

I bind a drag listener and delegate the logic to processDragEvent

The release listener similarly delegates logic to the processReleaseEvent method

8

Notice that I used the shorthand lambda syntax for event handling but still kept a reference to the drag and release event objects so we can remove them in deinitialize().

> You can rely on initComponent and deinitialize working in tandem. They might be invoked multiple times in valid situations e.g. a Dialog shown on top of a Form triggers a deinitialize on the components of the Form followed by an initComponent when it's disposed

We are left with two final methods, the first handles the drag events that are used to swipe down/up the "Where to?" UI:

Listing 8. 20. The AutoCompleteAddressInput processDragEvent

```java
private void processDragEvent(ActionEvent e) {
    Component cmp = layers.getComponentAt(1);
    boolean dragUp = layers.getLayout().getComponentConstraint(cmp).
        equals(SOUTH);
    if(dragStarted) {
        e.consume();

        cmp.getUnselectedStyle().setMarginUnit(Style.UNIT_TYPE_PIXELS);
        if(dragUp) cmp.setPreferredSize(new Dimension(getDisplayWidth(),
            firstY - e.getY() + getDisplayHeight() / 8));

        else cmp.getUnselectedStyle().setMarginTop(Math.max(0,
                e.getY() - firstY));
        layers.revalidate();
    } else {
        Component draggedCmp = getComponentForm().
            getComponentAt(e.getX(), e.getY());
        if(!draggedCmp.isChildOf((Container)cmp)) return;
        if(firstX == -1) {
            firstX = e.getX();
            firstY = e.getY();
        }
        if((!dragUp && e.getY() - firstY > convertToPixels(2)) ||
                (dragUp && firstY - e.getY() > convertToPixels(2))) {
            e.consume();
            dragStarted = true;
        }
    }
}
```

The dragged element is always the second element (0 is the first). It can be dragged between the CENTER location and the SOUTH location

If this is indeed a drag operation we'd like to block the event from propagating onwards by consuming the event

When a component is in the SOUTH we set its preferred size to 1/8th of the display height so it won't peek up too much. When its dragged up we just increase that size during drag

Components in the CENTER ignore their preferred size and take up available space. So in this case we use margin to provide the drag effect

This prevents a drag event on a different region in the form from triggering this event. E.g. if a user drags the map

This implements the drag in both directions but it only represents the visual effects of drag. The drop effect happens when we release the finger from the screen and we process that in the processReleaseEvent method:

Listing 8. 21. The AutoCompleteAddressInput processReleaseEvent

```
private void processReleaseEvent(ActionEvent e) {
    if(dragStarted) {
        e.consume();
        Component cmp = layers.getComponentAt(1);
        boolean dragUp = layers.getLayout().getComponentConstraint(cmp).
            equals(SOUTH);
        cmp.remove();          ⟵  Dragging just displayed a motion. We now need to
                                   remove the component and place it where it should be

        cmp.setUIID(cmp.getUIID());  ⟵  We reset the UIID so styling changes (e.g. margin, unit
        boolean animateDown;            type etc.) will reset to the default

        if(dragUp) animateDown = !(firstY - e.getY() > convertToPixels(8));
        else animateDown = e.getY() - firstY > convertToPixels(8);
        if(animateDown) {
            layers.add(SOUTH, cmp);  ⟵  When we place the container in the SOUTH we
            cmp.setPreferredSize(        set the preferred size and margin to match
                new Dimension(getDisplayWidth(), getDisplayHeight() / 8));
            Style s = cmp.getUnselectedStyle();
            s.setMarginUnit(Style.UNIT_TYPE_DIPS);
            s.setMarginLeft(3);
            s.setMarginRight(3);      ⟵  When we place it in the CENTER we set the preferred
        } else {                         size to null which is a special case that resets previous
            layers.add(CENTER, cmp);  ⟵  manual settings and restores the default
            cmp.setPreferredSize(null);
        }
        layers.animateLayout(200);  ⟵  We finish by animating the layout into place which
        firstX = -1;                    implicitly validates the layout after completion
        firstY = -1;
        dragStarted = false;
    }
}
```

Moving on lets look at how this logic plays along with the CompletionContainer.

CompletionContainer

The CompletionContainer tries to coordinate the two instances of the AutoCompleteAddressInput class by providing a single class that handles the completion UI. Most of the code in this class should be very familiar as some of it's refactored code from the MapForm while other code relates to the suggestLocations API we implemented earlier...

Again as this is another large class I'll break this down into more digestible pieces:

Listing 8. 22. The CompletionContainer class

The name of the class is misleading. CompletionContainer is not a Container. Here, instead of deriving we encapsulate the UI logic and try to expose only the business logic

Event dispatchers allow us to broadcast events using the add/removeListener observer API. We use this to broadcast an event when a user presses a completion button

```
public class CompletionContainer {
    private Container result;
    private boolean completionUsed;

    private final EventDispatcher dispatcher=new EventDispatcher();
    void updateCompletion(String text,
        AutoCompleteAddressInput dest) {
        SearchService.suggestLocations(text,
            LocationService.getCurrentLocation(), resultList -> {
            if(resultList != null && resultList.size() > 0) {
                result.removeAll();
                completionUsed = true;
                for(SearchService.SuggestionResult r : resultList) {
                    MultiButton mb = createEntry(FontImage.MATERIAL_PLACE,
                        r.getMainText(), r.getSecondaryText());
```

Notice that the method is "package protected" as it's meant for use only by AutoCompleteAddressInput

This method is invoked when completion is in progress it invokes the WebService call to request completion suggestions for the given string

Listing 8. 22. The CompletionContainer class

We fill up the container with buttons

```
result.add(mb);
mb.addActionListener(e -> {
    dest.setTextNoEvent(r.getFullText());
    r.getLocation(l -> {
        dest.setCurrentLocation(l);
        dispatcher.fireActionEvent(e);
    });
});
}
result.animateLayout(150);
}
});
}
// .. rest of the code...
}
```

If one of the buttons is pressed we fetch the location from the webservice and fill it into the AutoCompleteAddressInput

We fire the event dispatcher to process the actual selection in the UI

This is the bulk of the CompletionContainer class. Everything that follows is mostly trivial stuff. I'll still spit it up a bit to reduce code clutter:

Listing 8. 23. The CompletionContainer Entries and Listener

```
private MultiButton createEntry(char icon,
        String title) {
    MultiButton b = new MultiButton(title);
    b.setUIID("Container");
    b.setUIIDLine1("WhereToButtonLine1");
    b.setIconUIID("WhereToButtonIcon");
    FontImage.setMaterialIcon(b, icon);
    return b;
}
```

We have two types of entries here, one with only one line of text and one with two lines of text

```
private MultiButton createEntry(char icon, String title,
    String subtitle) {
    MultiButton b = new MultiButton(title);
    b.setTextLine2(subtitle);
    b.setUIID("Container");
    b.setUIIDLine1("WhereToButtonLineNoBorder");
    b.setUIIDLine2("WhereToButtonLine2");
    b.setIconUIID("WhereToButtonIcon");
    FontImage.setMaterialIcon(b, icon);
    return b;
}
public void addCompletionListener(ActionListener<ActionEvent> a) {
    dispatcher.addListener(a);
}
public void removeCompletionListener(ActionListener<ActionEvent> a) {
    dispatcher.removeListener(a);
}
```

This one has the 2 lines of text. This separation is in place so we can fit the UIID's correctly with the right underline behavior

This lets us send an event into the UI code when a user clicks the completion button

Next we have the completion bar code, some of it's still hardcoded but it should be pretty trivial to generalize:

Listing 8. 24. The CompletionContainer initCompletionBar

```
public void initCompletionBar() {
    if(!completionUsed) return;
    completionUsed = false;
    result.removeAll();
    initCompletionBarImpl();
}
```

This method is invoked externally to clear up the content of the completion UI and show the "clean" set of initial options

```
private void initCompletionBarImpl() {
    MultiButton addHome =createEntry(FontImage.MATERIAL_HOME, "Add Home");
    MultiButton addWork =createEntry(FontImage.MATERIAL_WORK, "Add Work");
    MultiButton savedPlaces = createEntry(FontImage.MATERIAL_NAVIGATE_NEXT,
                        "Saved Places");
```

The buttons representing the various
options are currently hardcoded, these
should be easy to customize

```
    savedPlaces.setUIIDLine1("WhereToButtonLineNoBorder");
    savedPlaces.setEmblemUIID("WhereToButtonLineNoBorder");
    savedPlaces.setEmblem(
        FontImage.createMaterial(FontImage.MATERIAL_NAVIGATE_NEXT,
            savedPlaces.getIconComponent().getUnselectedStyle()));
    Label whereSeparator = new Label("", "WhereSeparator");
    whereSeparator.setShowEvenIfBlank(true);
    result.addAll(addHome, addWork, savedPlaces, whereSeparator);
    addHistoryToCompletionBar(); ⑤
}
```

This call adds the historic searches
entry which in itself is still hardcoded

This creates the > arrow next to the button
indicating more information

With that we reach the last two methods adding history and explicit showing of the completion bar:

Listing 8. 25. The addHistoryToCompletionBar and showCompletionBar

```
private void addHistoryToCompletionBar() {
    MultiButton history1 = createEntry(FontImage.MATERIAL_HISTORY,
        "Mikve Yisrael Str...");
    result.add(history1);
}
```

History is positioned here so we could
fill this with actual search history etc.

This method constructs and animates the completion UI into place

```
public void showCompletionBar(Container parentLayer) {
    result = new Container(BoxLayout.y());
    initCompletionBarImpl();
    result.setUIID("Form");
    result.setScrollableY(true);
    result.setScrollVisible(false);
    Container enclose = BorderLayout.center(result);
    enclose.setY(getDisplayHeight());
    enclose.setWidth(getDisplayWidth());
    enclose.setHeight(result.getPreferredH());
    parentLayer.add(CENTER, enclose);
    parentLayer.animateLayout(200);
}
```

We use the same common code as the initCompletionBar() method

Notice that we place the content in a Container which we wrap up in a BorderLayout. This allows us to manipulate the preferred size without breaking the scrolling behavior of the child Container

8

In order to accomplish the design for the buttons I had to add the WhereToButtonLine2 UIID. This just uses a slightly smaller font with gray foreground and an underline. I keep the top padding to 0 to keep the text together.

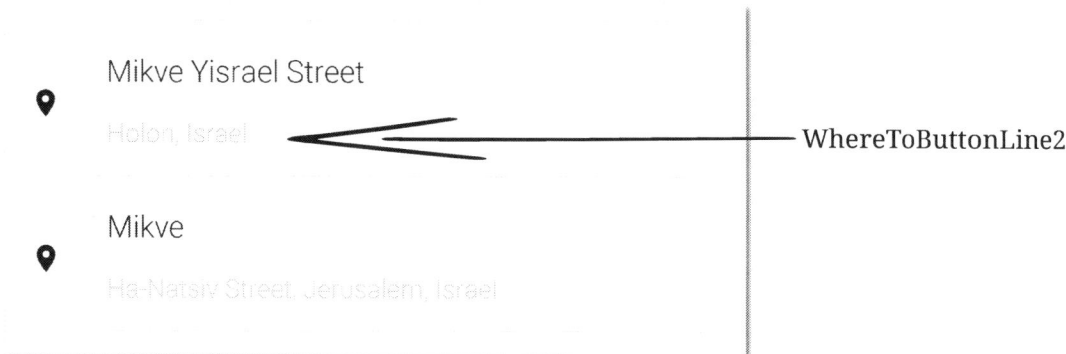

Mikve Yisrael Street
Holon, Israel ⟵ WhereToButtonLine2

Mikve
Ha-Natsiv Street, Jerusalem, Israel

Figure 8. 2. WhereToButtonLine2 Style

Listing 8. 26. WhereToButtonLine2 Styling

```
Foreground Color: 0xcccccc
Transparency: 0
Padding Left: 2mm
Padding Right: 4mm
Padding Top: 0
Padding Bottom: 2.5mm
Margin: 0
Border: Underline 2px 0xededed
Font: native:MainLight 2.4mm
```

8

8.2.3

MapForm

Lets combine these changes into the MapForm to incorporate search...

First we need to add a couple of members to the class:

Listing 8. 27. New members in MapForm

We use MapContainer to place a pin and position it. We can track map position events using this object

`private MapContainer mc;` ←

`private AutoCompleteAddressInput lastFocused;` ←

We need the lastFocused entry so we can set the text in the field when the user drags the map to point at a location

`private MapListener lastMapListener;` ←

The listener is important for cleanup to prevent multiple listener instances, that way we always have at most one

```
private UITimer lastTimer;
private Button whereTo;
private Container mapLayer;
private boolean inNavigationMode;
```

The timer instance allows us to cancel it. We use it to delay WebService requests so we don't send them too frequently

The "Where to?" Button. We need to hide it when the search UI is showing and show it again when it's done

Indicates whether we are in the navigation mode or in another mode such as map or browse mode. This is important as we can't enter navigation mode twice

We place a lot of elements in that layer on top of the map. It's pretty useful

8

Some of These Variables Already Exist

In the method body, I just moved them into the class level. I'm skipping that code since it's pretty trivial

Now that we have these variables in place lets look at the code. This method is very dense as it delegates large pieces of functionality to smaller methods. In the interest of readability I'll split the body of the method into two blocks of code:

Listing 8. 28. Updated showNavigationToolbar Text and Search

```
final Container layer = getLayeredPane(MapForm.class, true);
final Container pinLayer = createPinLayer(layer);
Button back = new Button("", "TitleCommand");
FontImage.setMaterialIcon(back, FontImage.MATERIAL_ARROW_BACK);
```

We create and place a layer for the pin image. This allows us to drag the CompletionContainer down and see the pin image on the map. That also means we can remove the layer easily once we exit the search UI

We refactored the text fields to use this new API and set the location to the current location by default. Normally a user wouldn't enter the origin address; only the destination so using the current location makes sense

```
CompletionContainer cc = new CompletionContainer();
AutoCompleteAddressInputfrom = new AutoCompleteAddressInput(
    "Current Location", "From", layer, cc);
AutoCompleteAddressInput to = new AutoCompleteAddressInput(
    "", "Where To?", layer, cc);
from.setCurrentLocation(LocationService.getCurrentLocation());
Image circle = createCircle();
Label fromSelected = new Label(circle);
Label toSelected = new Label(square);
SearchService.nameMyCurrentLocation(LocationService.getCurrentLocation(),
    name -> from.setTextNoEvent(name));
to.requestFocus();
lastFocused = to;
from.addFocusListener(createFromFocusListener(fromSelected, from, circle));
to.addFocusListener(createToFocusListener(fromSelected, circle, toSelected, to));
```

nameMyCurrentLocation method is used to fetch the name of the location of origin

The second block of code focuses on the map drag logic, event handling and animation:

Listing 8. 29. Updated showNavigationToolbar Listener and Animation

```
addMapListener((source, zoom, center) ->
    onMapChangeEvent(center));
Container navigationToolbar = BoxLayout.encloseY(back,
        BorderLayout.centerCenterEastWest(from, null, fromSelected),
        BorderLayout.centerCenterEastWest(to, null, toSelected));
```

The map listener is used for the point location on the map functionality

Listing 8. 29. Updated showNavigationToolbar Listener and Animation

```
navigationToolbar.setUIID("WhereToToolbar");
navigationToolbar.getUnselectedStyle().setBgPainter((g1, rect) ->
    paintWhereToToolbarBackground(g1, layer, rect, fromSelected,
        circle, toSelected));
cc.addCompletionListener(e ->
    onCompletionEvent(to, from, pinLayer, navigationToolbar, layer));
back.addActionListener(e ->
    onBackFromNavigation(pinLayer, navigationToolbar, layer));
layer.add(NORTH, navigationToolbar);
navigationToolbar.setWidth(getDisplayWidth());
navigationToolbar.setHeight(getPreferredH());
navigationToolbar.setY(-navigationToolbar.getHeight());
getAnimationManager().addAnimation(layer.createAnimateLayout(200),
        () -> cc.showCompletionBar(layer));
```

When a button is pressed in the search completion we get an event to begin navigation

We use the animation completion event to show the completion bar which also has an animation in place

8

That was dense but there is quite a bit more as I delegated a lot of functionality to other methods. Lets review them starting with onMapChangeEvent:

Listing 8. 30. Map Change Events

The map listener is used for the point location on the map functionality. It's invoked when the user pans or zooms the map

```
private void onMapChangeEvent(Coord center) {
    if(lastTimer != null) {
        lastTimer.cancel();
    }

    lastTimer = UITimer.timer(500, false, () -> {
        lastTimer = null;
        SearchService.nameMyCurrentLocation(
            new Location(center.getLatitude(), center.getLongitude()),
            name -> {
                lastFocused.setTextNoEvent(name);
                lastFocused.setCurrentLocation(
                    new Location(center.getLatitude(),
                        center.getLongitude()));
            });
    });
}
```

We cancel the timer if there is one that's already in the waiting stage

We wait 500ms before doing that so we don't send too many WebService requests

The nameMyCurrentLocation WebService is used to fetch the name for the given location so we can display it in the text field as the user pans the map

Most of the code in paintWhereToToolbarBackground is unchanged with one minor difference:

Listing 8. 31. paintWhereToToolbarBackground Changes for Search

```java
private void paintWhereToToolbarBackground(Graphics g1, Container layer,
        Rectangle rect, final Label fromSelected, Image circle, final
        Label toSelected) {
    // ... unchanged code ...        This used to be if(layer.getComponentCount() > 1)
                                     but that doesn't make sense anymore as the
                                     CompletionContainer is always there

    if(dropShadow != null) {
        if(((BorderLayout)layer.getLayout()).getCenter() != null) {
            g1.fillRect(rect.getX(), rect.getY(), rect.getWidth(),
                rect.getHeight());
        }
        g1.drawImage(dropShadow, rect.getX() – shadowHeight, rect.getY() +
            rect.getHeight() – dropShadow.getHeight() / 4 * 3);
        g1.fillRect(rect.getX(), rect.getY(), rect.getWidth(),
            rect.getY() + rect.getHeight() – shadowHeight);
    } else {
        g1.fillRect(rect.getX(), rect.getY(), rect.getWidth(),
            rect.getHeight());
    }
    // ... unchanged code ...
}
```

The CompletionContainer is only folded or expanded. So I check if the CompletionContainer is in the CENTER or SOUTH.

The onCompletionEvent method is invoked when a user presses a button in the CompletionContainer class:

Listing 8. 32. onCompletionEvent

When a button is pressed in the search completion we get an event to begin navigation at which point we ask for directions and enter navigation mode

```java
private void onCompletionEvent(AutoCompleteAddressInput to,
    AutoCompleteAddressInput from, final Container pinLayer,
    Container navigationToolbar, final Container layer) {
  if(to.getCurrentLocation() != null) {   ⟵
    SearchService.directions(from.getCurrentLocation(),
      to.getCurrentLocation(),   ⟵
        (path, duration, distance) -> {
          enterNavigationMode(pinLayer, navigationToolbar, layer,
            path, from.getText(), to.getText(), duration);
        });
    }
  }
```

We use the directions WebService to fetch the route and information about that route

I'll discuss the whole navigation mode in the route section.

The rest of the methods are mostly trivial, lets review them quickly:

Listing 8. 33. createPinLayer, onBackFromNavigation and createCircle

```java
private Container createPinLayer(Container layer) {
  layer.setLayout(new BorderLayout());   ⟵
  Container pinLayer =
    getLayeredPane(AutoCompleteAddressInput.class, false);
  pinLayer.setLayout(new BorderLayout(
    BorderLayout.CENTER_BEHAVIOR_CENTER_ABSOLUTE));
  Image pin = Resources.getGlobalResources().getImage("Pin.png");
  Label pinLabel = new Label(pin);
  MapLayout.setHorizontalAlignment(pinLabel, MapLayout.HALIGN.CENTER);
  MapLayout.setVerticalAlignment(pinLabel, MapLayout.VALIGN.BOTTOM);
  pinLayer.add(CENTER, pinLabel);
  return pinLayer;
}
```

The pin layer is a container we overlay in the hierarchy so a pin will appear on the map while we drag

Listing 8. 33. createPinLayer, onBackFromNavigation and createCircle

```java
private void onBackFromNavigation(final Container pinLayer,
    Container navigationToolbar, final Container layer) {
  pinLayer.removeAll();
  navigationToolbar.setY(-navigationToolbar.getHeight());
  layer.getComponentAt(1).setY(getDisplayHeight());
  navigationToolbar.getParent().animateUnlayout(200, 120, () -> {
    layer.removeAll();
    revalidate();
  });
}
private Image createCircle() {
  Image circle =
    Image.createImage(square.getWidth(), square.getHeight(), 0);
  Graphics g = circle.getGraphics();
  g.setColor(0xa4a4ac);
  g.setAntiAliased(true);
  g.fillArc(0, 0, circle.getWidth(), circle.getHeight(), 0, 360);
  return circle;
}
```

When we press the back arrow in the navigation mode we want to remove the UI related to search

We use the circle and square images when toggling between the to/from fields in the search to highlight the selection

We are almost done, we have two methods that create the focus listeners for the auto complete fields:

Listing 8. 34. Focus Events in showNavigationToolbar

```java
private FocusListener createToFocusListener(final Label fromSelected,
    Image circle, final Label toSelected, AutoCompleteAddressInput to) {
  return new FocusListener() {
    public void focusGained(Component cmp) {
      fromSelected.setIcon(circle);
      toSelected.setIcon(square);
      lastFocused = to;
    }
    public void focusLost(Component cmp) {
      toSelected.setIcon(circle);
    }
  };
}
private FocusListener createFromFocusListener(final Label fromSelected,
    AutoCompleteAddressInput from, Image circle) {
  return new FocusListener() {
    public void focusGained(Component cmp) {
      fromSelected.setIcon(square);
      lastFocused = from;
    }
    public void focusLost(Component cmp) {
      fromSelected.setIcon(circle);
    }
  };
}
```

The only reason these two methods exist is to toggle the circle and square icons between the text fields back and forth

One final thing to cover is the map listener which we bind using a new method:

Listing 8. 35. addMapListener

```
private void addMapListener(MapListener ml) {
    if(lastMapListener != null) {
        mc.removeMapListener(lastMapListener);
    }
    lastMapListener = ml;
    mc.addMapListener(ml);
}
```

We remove the last map listener if it was set

This prevents duplicate map listeners and allows us to easily clear the selection.

Summary

8.3   8

In this chapter, we learned:

- If I was building a real world application I would have directed all requests to our server and invoked Google from there

- Using queryParam is more flexible and more robust than just appending to the URL

- We can use callSerially to defer responses from cache. If we call back immediately we might delay the input code which is currently in place

- How to use low-level pointer events to implement complex drag gestures

We covered a lot but after two nights of rest I think we need to proceed to another night hack and finish the route logic!

8

Day 4: Search, Route and Hailing – Night Hack

This chapter covers:

- Picking a location from the map by dragging it and locating the name under the marker position
- Sending push notifications to the drivers
- The initial work required for the hailing process

Now that we have the WebServices in place all we need to do is wire this deep into the UI.

Route

Search should now work but we don't have any UI that displays the result?

For that we need to add additional features to the MapForm that address these capabilities. Before we go into that lets check out what that means:

The ride booking UI plots the path of the ride on the map and includes two tags: one pointing at your current location and one on the destination.

The first tag is divided into a "time indication" and name. The latter only contains the name.

Notice that the elements have a rounded rectangle shape with a pointy end on one side to point at the position within the path.

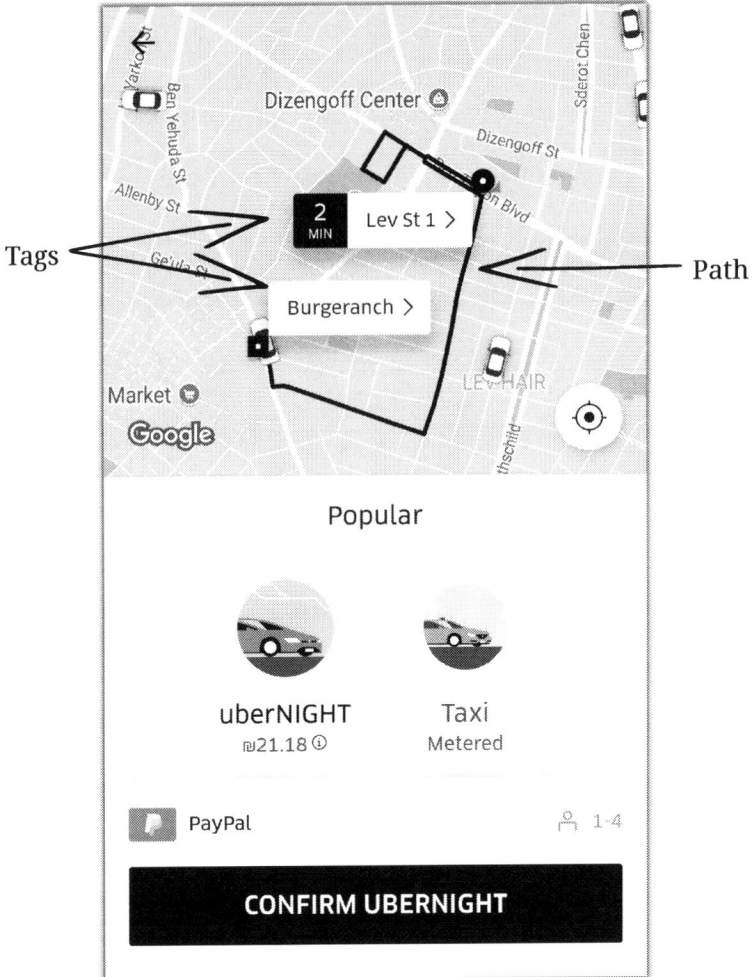

Figure 9. 1. Book Ride UI

9.1.1

Tags

Let's start with creating these tags. The tag code itself is trivial:

Listing 9. 1. MapForm createNavigationTag

We create a tag with an optional duration
that can be 0 to indicate no duration

```
private Component createNavigationTag(String location,
    int durationMinutes) {
  Label locationLabel = new Label(location, "NavigationLabel");
  if(durationMinutes > 0) {
    Label duration = new Label("" + durationMinutes,
      "NavigationMinuteLabel");
```

Assuming we have a duration we
create a label for that and place
everything in a BorderLayout

```
    Label min = new Label("MIN", "NavigationMinuteDescLabel");
    Container west = BoxLayout.encloseY(duration, min);
    Container result = BorderLayout.centerEastWest(locationLabel,
                        null, west);
    result.getUnselectedStyle().setBorder(BlackAndWhiteBorder.create().
      blackLinePosition(
        west.getPreferredW()));
    return result;
  }
  locationLabel.getUnselectedStyle().setBorder(
    BlackAndWhiteBorder.create());
  return locationLabel;
}
```

In order to
implement the
unique shape of
the tag we'll add a
new Border class

Notice we use the preferred
width of the west component to
determine the black section

9

269

I Would have Used a 9-piece Border

If this were a real application I would have just cut a 9-piece border and moved on. However, since the point is teaching I chose to do this the "hard way"...

A 9-piece border cuts an image into 9 pieces:

- Four corners
- Four sides
- Center

This is done so the border can be drawn in any resolution while maintaining its crisp undistorted appearance. The process of cutting a 9-piece border is supported both by the designer tool and by CSS.

Once cut the border can grow to any size. When it needs to grow vertically it tiles the sides and the center vertically. When it needs to grow horizontally it tiles the top, bottom and center horizontally. The corners are always fixed at the edges and never tile.

You can learn more about the 9-piece border here: www.codenameone.com/how-do-i---create-a-9-piece-image-border.html

Before we get into the BlackAndWhiteBorder there are a few UIID's we need to define.

Figure 9. 2. The UIID's Used for Tags

The NavigationLabel UIID is a the black on white label that appears in the tag. The only unique thing about it is the relatively small amount of padding:

Foreground Color: 0x000000
Transparency: 0
Padding: 1mm
Margin: 0
Font: native:MainLight 3mm

Lev St 1 >

The NavigationMinuteLabel UIID is the white on black minute value. It has 0 padding below to keep the text and number close together and has smaller font size. It is center aligned:

Foreground Color: 0xffffff
Transparency: 0
Alignment: Center
Padding Left: 1mm
Padding Right: 1mm
Padding Top: 1mm
Padding Bottom: 0
Margin: 0
Font: native:MainLight 2.5mm

2

9

The NavigationMinuteDescLabel UIID is used for the text below that (the word "MIN") and it just has an even smaller font:

Foreground Color: 0xffffff
Transparency: 0
Alignment: Center
Padding Left: 1mm
Padding Right: 1mm
Padding Top: 1mm
Padding Bottom: 0
Margin: 0
Font: native:MainLight 1.4mm

MIN

BlackAndWhiteBorder

Now that these are out of the way let's take a look at the border. Notice we can just subclass the Border class just like we can implement painters etc. This provides a similar path for customization but is sometimes more flexible. Most of the following code is based on the built-in RoundRectBorder class. As this is a large class, I'll break it down into smaller pieces:

Listing 9. 5. The BlackAndWhiteBorder class

We extend the Codename One Border class and enhance it

```java
public class BlackAndWhiteBorder extends Border {
    private static final String CACHE_KEY = "cn1$$-bwcache";

    private final float shadowBlur = 10;
    private final float shadowSpread;
    private final int shadowOpacity = 110;
    private final float cornerRadius = 1f;

    private int blackLinePosition = -1;

    BlackAndWhiteBorder() {
        shadowSpread = convertToPixels(0.2f);
    }
    public static BlackAndWhiteBorder create() {
        return new BlackAndWhiteBorder();
    }
    public BlackAndWhiteBorder blackLinePosition(
        int blackLinePosition) {
        this.blackLinePosition = blackLinePosition;
        return this;
    }
    // ... rest of code....
}
```

Drawing this type of border is pretty expensive so we draw onto an image and place that image in cache within the component using putClientProperty. This is just a random unique value to use as a key

The following variables are used as configuration properties for the border

This value determines the position of the black line in the tag that contains a duration. If this value is negative it means there is no separator

shadowSpread defaults to 0.2 millimeters. The constructor is package private as I expect a create() call

I can configure the black line position here, notice the return of this allows me to chain the create method and setters

9

The createTargetImage method is the workhorse of the border. We draw everything onto a mutable image so we can recycle the border efficiently:

Listing 9. 6. createTargetImage

Here we create the border image that we will cache for the given component. If the border has a shadow it can take some processing power, so we have two versions of the method: fast and slow

```java
private Image createTargetImage(Component c, int w, int h, boolean fast) {
    Image target = Image.createImage(w, h, 0);
    Graphics tg = target.getGraphics();
    tg.setAntiAliased(true);
    int shadowSpreadL =  convertToPixels(shadowSpread);
    int shapeW = w - shadowSpreadL;
    int shapeH = h - shadowSpreadL;
    int shapeX = Math.round(((float)shadowSpreadL) * 0.9);
    int shapeY = Math.round(((float)shadowSpreadL) * 0.9);
    for(int iter = shadowSpreadL - 1 ; iter >= 0 ; iter--) {
        tg.translate(iter, iter);
        fillShape(tg, 0, shadowOpacity / shadowSpreadL, w - (iter * 2),
            h - (iter * 2));
        tg.translate(-iter, -iter);
    }
    if(Display.getInstance().isGaussianBlurSupported() && !fast) {
        Image blured = Display.getInstance().
            gaussianBlurImage(target, shadowBlur/2);
        target = Image.createImage(w, h, 0);
        tg = target.getGraphics();
        tg.drawImage(blured, 0, 0);
        tg.setAntiAliased(true);
    }
    tg.translate(shapeX, shapeY);
    c.getStyle().setBorder(Border.createEmpty());
    GeneralPath gp = createShape(shapeW, shapeH);
    tg.setClip(gp);
    c.getStyle().getBgPainter().paint(tg, new Rectangle(0, 0, w, h));
    c.getStyle().setBorder(this);
    return target;
}
```

We create an image in RAM and draw onto that image using graphics primitives

The shadow effect is a blurred gradient with varying alpha degrees

Gaussian Blur is a very slow algorithm so we avoid it when we need speed

I delegated the shape creation code to the createShape method. I then clip and use the background painter to fill out everything based on the shape

9

We call the fast version of createTargetImage and invoke the slow version asynchronously to update the border later on. This is done in paintBorderBackground which we discuss next :

Listing 9. 7. paintBorderBackground

This is an overriden method of Border invoked to paint the border

```java
public void paintBorderBackground(Graphics g, final Component c) {
    final int w = c.getWidth();
    final int h = c.getHeight();
    int x = c.getX();
    int y = c.getY();
    if(w > 0 && h > 0) {
        Image background = (Image)c.getClientProperty(CACHE_KEY);
        if(background != null && background.getWidth() == w &&
           background.getHeight() == h) {
            g.drawImage(background, x, y);
            return;
        }
    } else return;
    Image target = createTargetImage(c, w, h, true);
    g.drawImage(target, x, y);
    c.putClientProperty(CACHE_KEY, target);
    callSeriallyOnIdle(() -> {
        if (w == c.getWidth() && h == c.getHeight()) {
            Image target1 = createTargetImage(c, w, h, false);
            c.putClientProperty(CACHE_KEY, target1);
            c.repaint();
        }
    });
}
```

If we have a cached version of the border image we will use that as the background of the component assuming the size of the component didn't change

Otherwise we create that image and update it later with the slower version that includes the gradient shadow effect

Once the slow version of the border is finished we repaint so the UI will update with the changes

Next we have `createShape` which we discussed before as well. There isn't much to discuss about this method. I'll talk more about shapes later on:

Listing 9. 8. createShape

```java
private GeneralPath createShape(int shapeW, int shapeH) {
    GeneralPath gp = new GeneralPath();
    float radius = convertToPixels(cornerRadius);
    float x = 0;
    float y = 0;
    float widthF = shapeW;
    float heightF = shapeH;
    gp.moveTo(x + radius, y);
    if(blackLinePosition > -1) {

        gp.lineTo(x + widthF, y);
    } else {
        gp.lineTo(x + widthF - radius, y);
        gp.quadTo(x + widthF, y, x + widthF, y + radius);
    }
    gp.lineTo(x + widthF, y + heightF - radius);
    gp.quadTo(x + widthF, y + heightF, x + widthF - radius, y + heightF);
    if(blackLinePosition > -1) {
        gp.lineTo(x + radius, y + heightF);
        gp.quadTo(x, y + heightF, x, y + heightF - radius);
    } else gp.lineTo(x, y + heightF);
    gp.lineTo(x, y + radius);
    gp.quadTo(x, y, x + radius, y);
    gp.closePath();
    return gp;
}
```

We create the shape of the component here

This moves a virtual pen to the starting location of drawing the shape

If it's the one with the black line we place the corner in the top right. Otherwise we place it in the bottom left

This draws a straight line from the current location of the virtual pen to the given coordinate

This performs a bezier curve to the given location from the location of the pen

Closing the path when done is generally good measure

Once we have a Shape object we can fill it, stroke it or even use it as a clipping shape.

ℹ Stroke draws a line around the shape

The fillShape method demonstrates the process of filling the shape with respect to the position of the black line:

Listing 9. 9. fillShape

```
private void fillShape(Graphics g, int color, int opacity,
    int width, int height) {
    g.setColor(0xffffff);          ←  We need to explicitly set
    g.setAlpha(255);                  colors as the behavior might
    GeneralPath gp = createShape(width, height);   be inconsistent otherwise


    if(blackLinePosition > -1) {   ←  We can now fill out the shape as
        int[] clip = g.getClip();     part of the image creation code if
        g.clipRect(blackLinePosition, 0, width, height);   we have a black line we do the
        g.fillShape(gp);              fill operation twice with different
        g.setClip(clip);              clip sizes to create that effect
        g.clipRect(0, 0, blackLinePosition, height);
        g.setColor(0);
        g.fillShape(gp);
        g.setClip(clip);
    } else {
        g.fillShape(gp);
    }
}
```

We need to override a few additional methods from the Border class

Listing 9. 10. The BlackAndWhiteBorder Boilerplate Methods

```
public int getMinimumHeight() {
    return convertToPixels(shadowSpread)+convertToPixels(cornerRadius) * 2;
}
public int getMinimumWidth() {
    return convertToPixels(shadowSpread)+convertToPixels(cornerRadius) * 2;
}
public boolean isBackgroundPainter() {
    return true;
}
```

Some borders define a minimum size so they don't look "weird", which is what I do here

Some borders paint after the background is drawn in which case this method returns false. Since we changed the background we need this

This was a bit difficult, highlighting my recommendation to use a 9-piece border.

If you have a complex border you should try using a 9-piece border first and only then go down the more complex road of building your own Border subclass

9

Navigation Mode

9.1.2

We've gone through quite a bit of code and it brought us to the point where the navigation UI should function as expected. This is implemented in the enterNavigationMode method which we mentioned before. As you might recall it's invoked when clicking an entry in the search results:

Listing 9. 11. enterNavigationMode

This method is invoked from a callback on navigation. We have the coordinates of the path to display on the map as the arguments to the method. As you may recall these coordinate are returned by the directions method

```
private void enterNavigationMode(final Container pinLayer,
      Container navigationToolbar, final Container layer,
      List<Coord> path, String from, String to, int duration) {
    pinLayer.removeAll();
    navigationToolbar.setY(-navigationToolbar.getHeight());
    layer.getComponentAt(1).setY(getDisplayHeight());
    navigationToolbar.getParent().animateUnlayout(200, 120, () -> {
        if(inNavigationMode) return;
        inNavigationMode = true;
        callSerially(() -> {
            layer.removeAll();
            insideNavigationMode(from, duration, to, path, layer, pinLayer);
        });
    });
}
```

The first thing we do is remove the existing search UI from the form and animate it out

Due to the way events are chained this method can be invoked more than once in some unique cases. This works around that behavior

To keep the method size under control we delegate the logic to the insideNavigationMode method

The insideNavigationMode contains more logic:

Listing 9. 12. MapForm insideNavigationMode

We convert the path to an array and add it to the map. This uses native path plotting for these coordinates

```java
private void insideNavigationMode(String from, int duration, String to,
    List<Coord> path, final Container layer, final Container pinLayer) {
  Coord[] pathCoords = new Coord[path.size()];
  path.toArray(pathCoords);
  MapContainer.MapObject pathObject = mc.addPath(pathCoords);
  BoundingBox bb = BoundingBox.create(pathCoords);
  mc.fitBounds(bb);
```

We move the camera to show the entire path within the Form

We use the trimmedString method to limit the string length. We'll cover that method soon

```java
  Component fromComponent=createNavigationTag(trimmedString(from),duration/60);
  Component toComponent=createNavigationTag(trimmedString(to),-1);
  MapLayout.setHorizontalAlignment(fromComponent, MapLayout.HALIGN.RIGHT);
  mapLayer.add(pathCoords[0], fromComponent);
  mapLayer.add(pathCoords[pathCoords.length - 1], toComponent);
  whereTo.setVisible(false);
  getToolbar().setVisible(false);
  Button back = new Button("", "TitleCommand");
  FontImage.setMaterialIcon(back, FontImage.MATERIAL_ARROW_BACK);
  layer.add(NORTH, back);
  back.addActionListener(e ->
    exitNavigationMode(layer, fromComponent, toComponent, pathObject));
  Resources gr = Resources.getGlobalResources();
  Label ride = new Label("Ride", "RideTitle");
  Label taxi = new Label("Taxi", gr.getImage("ride.png"), "RideTitle");
  taxi.setTextPosition(BOTTOM);
  Label separator = new Label("", "MarginSeparator");
  separator.setShowEvenIfBlank(true);
  Button blackButton = new Button("Confirm", "BlackButton");
  Container cnt = BoxLayout.encloseY(ride, taxi, separator, blackButton);
  cnt.setUIID("Form");
  layer.add(SOUTH, cnt);
  revalidate();
}
```

We create the two tags and add them to the UI. Notice that the from tag has a right alignment

This is the UI to approve the Taxi we are ordering. We use a white Container with the Form UIID on the SOUTH portion of the form as a layer

The back behavior is just a Button styled to look like a command it invokes the exitNavigationMode() method which we will get to shortly

This effectively shows the navigation UI!

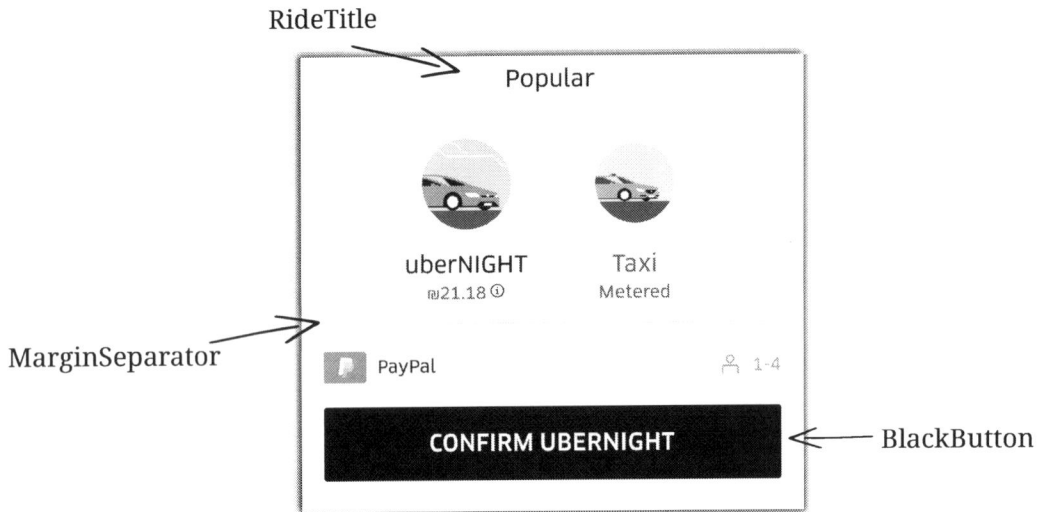

Figure 9. 3. UIID's Used in the Ride UI

We also have a few UIID's of note mentioned in the code. The first is RideTitle which is the title area for the ride UI. It's pretty much a Label that's centered:

Listing 9. 13. RideTitle Styling

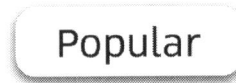

```
Foreground Color: 0x000000
Transparency: 0
Alignment: Center
Padding: 4mm
Margin: 0
Font: native:MainLight 3.2mm
```

MarginSeparator is a separator that has margins on the sides. It uses the underline border for the separator effect:

Listing 9. 14. MarginSeparator Styling

Transparency: 0
Padding Left: 0
Padding Right: 0
Padding Top: 0
Padding Bottom: 2px
Margin Left: 4mm
Margin Right: 4mm
Margin Top: 0
Margin Bottom: 0
Border: Underline 2px 0xededed

BlackButton is the button on the bottom of the UI. It's technically just a big black button:

Listing 9. 15. BlackButton Styling

Foreground Color: 0xffffff
Background Color: 0x000000
Transparency: 255
Alignment: Center
Padding Left: 2mm
Margin Left: 4mm
Margin Right: 4mm
Margin Top: 2mm
Margin Bottom: 2mm
Border: RoundRect 1mm
Font: native:MainRegular 3.5mm

9

Before I continue, I also used the trimmedString method in the code above to trim the tag components:

Listing 9. 16. trimmedString

```java
private String trimmedString(String str) {
    int p = str.indexOf(',');
    if(p > -1) {
        str = str.substring(0, p);
    }
    if(str.length() > 15) {
        str = str.substring(0, 15);
    }
    return str;
}
```

There isn't much to say about this method. We rely on the fact that addresses usually have a comma after them

If the string is missing that or is too long we have a special case for those. This guarantees a string of decent length for the tag elements

The one last missing piece is the exitNavigationMode call which just removes all elements and sets the invisible pieces back to visible. Again, it's pretty trivial:

Listing 9. 17. exitNavigationMode

```java
private void exitNavigationMode(final Container layer,
        Component fromComponent, Component toComponent,
        MapContainer.MapObject pathObject) {
    layer.removeAll();
    fromComponent.remove();
    toComponent.remove();
    mc.removeMapObject(pathObject);
    getToolbar().setVisible(true);
    whereTo.setVisible(true);
    revalidate();
    inNavigationMode = false;
}
```

We just remove all the elements

It's crucial to remove the native path object from the map

We restore the visibility of the Toolbar and the side menu

Now that all of this is done we can search for a Taxi. We can see the path and confirm it. Only one huge piece is left...

Hail a Car

The hailing process is relatively simple, we tint the UI show a beacon and during that time we ask the server for a car.

We can start by adding an event handler to the blackButton from the enterNavigationMode method:

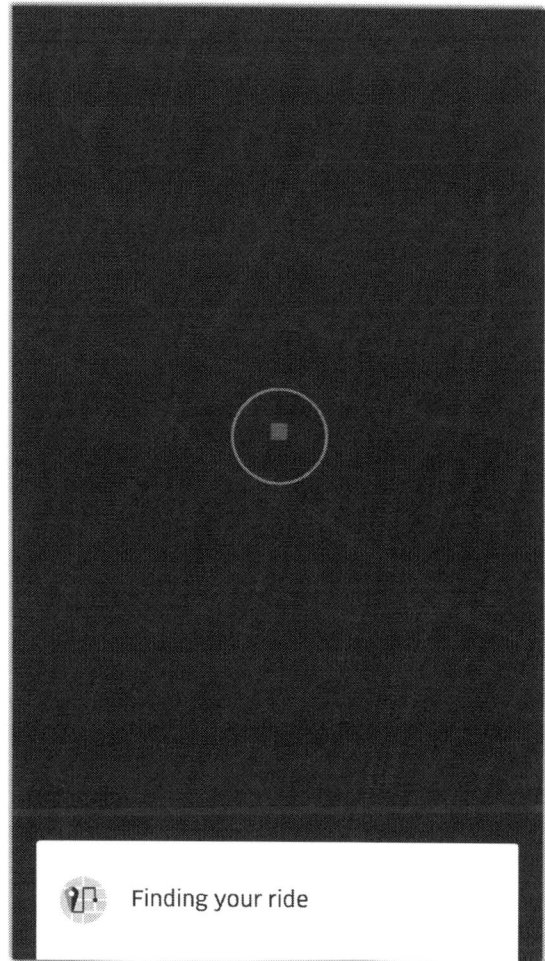

Figure 9. 4. Hailing UI

Listing 9. 18. UI for Hailing a Car

```
blackButton.addActionListener(e -> {
    exitNavigationMode(layer, fromComponent, toComponent, pathObject);
    Label searching = new Label("Finding your ride",
        Resources.getGlobalResources().getImage("searching-cab-icon.png"),
        "SearchingDialog");
    pinLayer.add(SOUTH, searching);
    pinLayer.getUnselectedStyle().setBgColor(0);
    pinLayer.getUnselectedStyle().setBgTransparency(120);
    pinLayer.add(CENTER, new BlinkDot());

    LocationService.hailRide(from, to, car -> {
        pinLayer.getUnselectedStyle().setBgTransparency(0);
        pinLayer.removeAll();
    });
});
```

We're effectively coloring the pin layer to create the tint effect

We added a new BlinkDot class to implement the pulsing blue dot effect

Another new API, the hailRide method in LocationService, allows us to hail a ride...

Notice we don't show anything when the ride is hailed, we'll add that workflow with the driver app in the next chapter

There is one UIID we need to cover here and it's the SearchingDialog UIID. It's mostly pretty standard except for the use of the special mode of the RoundRectBorder, the top only mode which allows only the top portion to be rounded. Technically this UI element isn't a Dialog it's a Label but it looks like a Dialog. We have some margin on the sides to space it out:

Listing 9. 19. SearchingDialog Styling

Foreground Color: 0x000000
Background Color: 0xffffff
Transparency: 255
Padding: 4mm
Margin Left: 3mm
Margin Right: 3mm
Margin Top: 0
Margin Bottom: 0
Border: RoundRect 2mm TopOnly Mode
Font: native:MainRegular 3.2mm

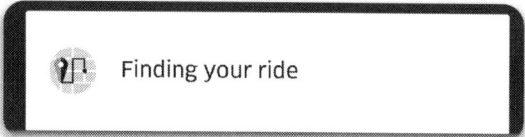
Finding your ride

BlinkDot

The BlinkDot class is pretty trivial. I could have used an animated gif but instead I just did this:

Listing 9. 20. The BlinkDot class

```
public class BlinkDot extends Component {
  private int value;
  private Motion growth;
  public BlinkDot() {
    setUIID("Label");
  }
  protected void initComponent() {
    super.initComponent();
    getComponentForm().registerAnimated(this);
  }
  protected void deinitialize() {
    getComponentForm().deregisterAnimated(this);
    super.deinitialize();
  }
  public boolean animate() {
    if(growth == null || growth.isFinished()) {
      growth = Motion.createEaseInOutMotion(3, getWidth() / 2, 1000);
      growth.start();
    }
```

Mostly for transparency we don't really use the UIID here

We use low level animations here so the best practice is to register/remove with initComponent/deinitialize

The motion class represents a timed motion between values which allows us to animate a value from point X to point Y

```
    int newValue = growth.getValue();
    if(newValue != value) {
        value = newValue;
        return true;
    }
    return false;
}
public void paint(Graphics g) {
    g.setAlpha(255);
    g.setColor(0x297aa7);
    int s = convertToPixels(2);
    g.setAntiAliased(true);
    g.fillArc(getX() + getWidth() / 2 - s / 2, getY() +
        getHeight() / 2 - s / 2, s, s, 0, 360);
    g.drawArc(getX() + getWidth() / 2 - value, getY() +
        getHeight() / 2 - value, value * 2, value * 2, 0, 360);
    g.drawArc(getX() + getWidth() / 2 - value - 1, getY() +
        getHeight() / 2 - value - 1, value * 2 + 1,
        value * 2 + 1, 0, 360);
}
protected Dimension calcPreferredSize() {
    return new Dimension(convertToPixels(15), convertToPixels(15));
}
protected void paintBackground(Graphics g) {}
}
```

The drawing logic is mostly hardcoded, I would have used the shape API to get a more refined effect but opted for simplicity instead

Motion is very useful for animations as it doesn't depend on framerate, only on time. But it's also very useful for business logic such as gradually expanding the hailing search radius. In this case I'm growing the circle using the value. Notice only the animate method mutates values as the paint method can be invoked more than once per cycle in theory.

LocationService

Up until now I kept hailing as a vague process. I think Uber probably has a far more elaborate system than the one I developed in an hour but this should work fine for most cases. The initial process of hailing includes the following phases:

1. We mark that we are interested in hailing in the location service WebSocket code

2. The server checks which drivers are available in the area and returns to us their push keys

3. We send push notifications to available drivers

4. As time moves on we expand the circle of search for drivers (in KM/radius)

I'll defer the more detailed explanation for tomorrow as this day is getting long if you want to follow up check out section 10.2.7 (page 327).

In order to do this I had to make some changes to the WebSocket protocol in the LocationService class. But first we need some additional variables in the Globals class. I'll go into more detail on those values in the next chapter but for now we need the variables only.

All of these API's require developer keys which you can obtain from their respective websites. I've edited the Globals class to include these new keys required by the 3 API's:

Listing 9. 21. Keys for Push

This is a key that allows us to send push messages using the Codename One push servers

This is a key from Google that lets us send a push using their servers

```
public static final String CODENAME_ONE_PUSH_KEY = "----";
public static final String GOOGLE_PUSH_AUTH_KEY = "----";
public static final String APNS_DEV_PUSH_CERT = "----";
public static final String APNS_PROD_PUSH_CERT = "----";
public static final String APNS_DEV_PUSH_PASS = "----";
public static final String APNS_PROD_PUSH_PASS = "----";
public static final boolean APNS_PRODUCTION = false;
```

To use the apple servers we need two separate certificates and the passwords for these certificates

Right now we will **leave these all blank and get to them in the next chapter**

Let's move to the LocationService class and the variables I had to add:

Listing 9. 22. LocationService new Members

When a driver accepts our hail, the server sends a
special message indicating that the hail was accepted

```
private static final short MESSAGE_TYPE_DRIVER_FOUND = 4;
private static final short HAILING_OFF = 0;
private static final short HAILING_ON = 1;
private static final short HAILING_TURN_OFF = 2;
```

Previously we had 2 modes
for polling the server for
searching and not searching.
I added a 3rd mode that
allows us to disable hailing

```
private static LocationService instance;
private int hailing;
```

I've made the LocationService
into a singleton

```
private Motion halingRadius;
```

These represent whether we are hailing and if
so to what radius? We use a Motion object to
get a growing radius that will stretch over
time to encapsulate a wider region for hailing

```
private String from;
private String to;
```

Our source and destination values
which we need to broadcast a hail

```
private List<String> notificationList;
```

When we send a push notification to a car we
need to make sure we didn't already notify it

```
private long driverId;
private CarAdded driverFound;
```

The unique id of the driver we've found

This is the callback we invoke
when a driver is found

Now that these are out of the way, let's look at the other things that need doing. We changed the way
we handle the communication protocol and we added some additional details.

Listing 9. 23. sendLocationUpdate Small Change

```
if(ll == lon && lt == lat && dir == direction && hailing == HAILING_OFF) {
    // no need to do an update
    return;
}
```

First we need to ignore location changes when doing hailing which we can do by adding that condition.

Next we need to change the protocol a little bit:

Listing 9. 24. sendLocationUpdate Bigger Changes

```
try(ByteArrayOutputStream bos = new ByteArrayOutputStream();
    DataOutputStream dos = new DataOutputStream(bos);) {
    dos.writeShort(MESSAGE_TYPE_LOCATION_UPDATE);
    String token = Preferences.get("token", null);
    dos.writeShort(token.length());
    for(int iter = 0 ; iter < token.length() ; iter++)
        dos.writeByte((byte)token.charAt(iter));
    dos.writeDouble(lat);
    dos.writeDouble(lon);
    dos.writeFloat(dir);
    if(hailing == HAILING_ON) {
        dos.writeDouble(((double)halingRadius.getValue()) / 1000.0);
        dos.writeByte(HAILING_ON);
        byte[] fromBytes = from.getBytes("UTF-8");
        byte[] toBytes = to.getBytes("UTF-8");
        dos.writeShort(fromBytes.length);
        dos.write(fromBytes);
        dos.writeShort(toBytes.length);
        dos.write(toBytes);
    } else {
        dos.writeDouble(1);
        dos.writeByte(hailing);
        if(hailing == HAILING_TURN_OFF) hailing = HAILING_OFF;
    }
    dos.flush();
    send(bos.toByteArray());
} catch(IOException err) {
    Log.e(err);
}
```

This was previously limited to 0 only and now we check if we are in hailing mode

During hailing mode the radius of search grows over time

We send the from/to values as UTF-8 encoded strings which allows us to communicate locale specific locations

When we turn off hailing in the server it's a "one time thing". After it's off we can go back to the regular mode

This isn't likely as this is a RAM based stream

We also need to handle message reception code, I broke that method down to smaller methods to increase readability:

Listing 9. 25. onMessage Changes

```
protected void onMessage(byte[] bytes) {
    try {
        DataInputStream dis = new DataInputStream(
            new ByteArrayInputStream(bytes));
        short response = dis.readShort();
        if(response == MESSAGE_TYPE_DRIVER_FOUND) {
            readFound(dis);
            return;
        }
        int size = dis.readInt();
        List<String> sendPush = null;
        for(int iter = 0 ; iter < size ; iter++) {
            long id = dis.readLong();
            User car = readCar(id, dis);
            if(hailing == HAILING_ON &&
                response == MESSAGE_TYPE_AVAILBLE_DRIVER_POSITIONS) {
                if(!notificationList.contains(car.pushToken.get())) {
                    notificationList.add(car.pushToken.get());
                    if(sendPush == null) sendPush = new ArrayList<>();
                    sendPush.add(car.pushToken.get());
                }
            }
        }
        if(sendPush != null) sendPush(sendPush);
    } catch(IOException err) {
        Log.e(err);
    }
}
```

This is a new special case that provides us with details on the driver that picked up the ride. We are provided with the driver id, car and name

This is a list of push keys of the drivers we should notify

If this is a hailing response we read the push token and add it to the list of push messages to send

If the car wasn't notified yet add it to the list of cars that we should notify

Send the push message to the applicable drivers

We introduced several new methods here so lets review them one by one. First we have readFound() which is invoked if the server found a suitable driver. This code happens when the servers message type is MESSAGE_TYPE_DRIVER_FOUND:

Listing 9. 26. readFound

```java
private void readFound(DataInputStream dis) throws IOException {
    driverId = dis.readLong();          ◄——————————————┤ That's the user id of the driver
    User u = cars.get(driverId);  ◄————————
    if(u == null) {                                    We check if the driver is cached. If it is
        u = new User().id.set(driverId);               we'll update the existing car instance
        cars.put(driverId, u);                         otherwise we'll create a new instance
    }
    u.car.set(dis.readUTF()).
        givenName.set(dis.readUTF()).
        surname.set(dis.readUTF()).               Notice we need the finalUser variable since car
        currentRating.set(dis.readFloat());       might change and a value that can change can't
    final User finalUser = u;  ◄————              be passed to an inner class or lambda in Java
    callSerially(() -> driverFound.carAdded(finalUser));
}
```

That's simple enough. Next we have the readCar method which is pretty similar to what we had before; only refactored into a new method:

Listing 9. 27. readCar

```
private User readCar(long id, DataInputStream dis) throws IOException {
    User car = cars.get(id);
    if(car == null) {
        car = new User().id.set(id).
                latitude.set(dis.readDouble()).
                longitude.set(dis.readDouble()).
                direction.set(dis.readFloat()).
                pushToken.set(dis.readUTF());
        cars.put(id, car);
        User finalCar = car;
        callSerially(() -> carCallback.carAdded(finalCar));
    } else {
        car.latitude.set(dis.readDouble()).
            longitude.set(dis.readDouble()).
            direction.set(dis.readFloat()).
            pushToken.set(dis.readUTF());
    }
    return car;
}
```

The only difference is a push token to the driver details so we can send a push message to a specific driver

The last piece of the onMessage related methods is the sendPush method which sends the actual push messages to the drivers:

Listing 9. 28. sendPush

```java
private void sendPush(List<String> sendPush) throws IOException {
    String[] devices = new String[sendPush.size()];      ←    We send the push message in a
    sendPush.toArray(devices);                                 batch to speed this up

    String apnsCert = APNS_DEV_PUSH_CERT;      ←    Production and development
    String apnsPass = APNS_DEV_PUSH_PASS;           certificates differ so we need to set
    if(APNS_PRODUCTION) {                           the right one based on the
        apnsCert = APNS_PROD_PUSH_CERT;             production flag
        apnsPass = APNS_PROD_PUSH_PASS;
    }
    new Push(CODENAME_ONE_PUSH_KEY,      ←    We send push type 3 which includes
            "#" + UserService.getUser().id.getLong() +    a data payload (the first section)
            ";Ride pending from: " + from + " to: " + to,  and a visual payload which you see
            devices).                                      after the semicolon
        pushType(3).
        apnsAuth(apnsCert, apnsPass, APNS_PRODUCTION).
        gcmAuth(GOOGLE_PUSH_AUTH_KEY).sendAsync();
}
```

9

With that the onMessage method is complete...

> **ℹ** ***Push Messages can only be Received on Devices***
>
> The simulator can send push messages but can't register for push or receive push
> notifications. We can only simulate push messages on the simulator

Before we can compile that, we need to add a pushToken attribute to User:

Listing 9. 29. pushToken in the User class

```
public final Property<String, User> pushToken =
    new Property<>("pushToken");

private final PropertyIndex idx = new PropertyIndex(this, "User", id,
        givenName, surname, phone, email, facebookId, googleId, driver,
        car, currentRating, latitude, longitude, direction, authToken,
        password, pushToken);
```

It's just a String attribute which we will get from the server for the drivers/cars

We also need to add it to the index

Finally we have the hailRide method which is relatively simple:

Listing 9. 30. hailRide

```
public static void hailRide(String from, String to, CarAdded callback) {
    instance.driverFound = callback;
    instance.from = from;
    instance.to = to;
    instance.notificationList = new ArrayList<>();
    instance.halingRadius = Motion.createLinearMotion(500, 2000, 30000);
    instance.halingRadius.start();
    instance.hailing = HAILING_ON;
    instance.server.sendLocationUpdate();
}
```

We initialize the variables with the right values

We start a Motion object for the expanding radius. A Motion object allows the search path to grow linearly over a fixed time period. In this case we start from 500 meters and grow to 2km over 30 seconds

Other than that we need a minor tweak for the bind method and we're good to go:

```
public static void bind(CarAdded carCallback,
    SuccessCallback<Location> locationUpdate) {
    instance = new LocationService();  ⟵
    instance.bindImpl(carCallback, locationUpdate);
}
```

We now save the instance object which was previously discarded. We need it for the hailRide method

Summary

9.3

In this chapter, we learned:

- If you have a complex border you should try using a 9-piece border before going down the more complex road of building your own Border subclass

- Motion is very useful for animations as it doesn't depend on framerate, only on time. But it's also very useful for business logic such as gradually expanding the hailing search radius

- The simulator can send push messages but can't register for push or receive push notifications. We can only simulate push messages on the simulator

This was a tough day with a lot of information and grit.

Today I broke the client/server protocol because I didn't want to cram too much work into a single day (and night). Tomorrow we'll fix the server protocol and proceed with push/the driver mode.

9

9

Day 5: Driver App and Push

This chapter covers:

- Hailing server business logic

- Creating two distinct apps from one project, the driver app is effectively the user app with some added features

- Receiving push notifications in the driver app

- Driver hailing experience. The client side hailing process as handled by the driver

When I started on this road I didn't want to create a "driver app" and wanted to focus only on the client app. Unfortunately a driver app is unavoidable as the main app is useless without it. Unlike the main Uber app I don't want to clone their driver app as this would throw the whole book out of focus. I decided to hack the existing app to implement driver specific features there and, as a result, reuse a whole lot of code. This is a very common approach especially with companies who sell custom software based on a common framework. They essentially repackage the same app with minor changes and re-sell it to multiple customers.

This means the driver app can reuse signup, map, networking code etc. This is important as code reuse breeds stability and maturity. Unfortunately it also means the app isn't as well made as the main app since it was designed for end users with driver mode tacked on top.

Server

Before we proceed into the actual driver app work and push notification we need to implement all the infrastructure in the server side. This means we need to add new properties to the User object to represent the ride and add new abstractions for ride/hailing. One of the cool things about picking JPA is that we can make all of these changes and the database schema will update automatically!

User

Lets start by looking at the User class. I had to add 3 new fields and modify/add some methods:

Listing 10. 1. New Fields in the User class

```
private String hailingFrom;        ←──┐  hailingFrom and hailingTo allow us to communicate
private String hailingTo;             │  our trip details with the driver community

private String pushToken;          ←──┐  We need the pushToken of a driver so we
                                      │  can hail him directly from the app

public RideDAO getRideDao() {      ←──────────────────────┐  We'll discuss the
    return new RideDAO(id, givenName, hailingFrom, hailingTo);  │  RideDAO class soon, it
}                                                          │  allows us to send details
                                                           │  about the trip to drivers
public UserDAO getDao() {
    return new UserDAO(id, givenName, surname, phone, email, facebookId,
        googleId, driver, car, currentRating, latitude, longitude,
        direction, pushToken);      ←──┐  Not much of a change but we added the
}                                      │  pushToken to the UserDAO factory methods

public UserDAO getPartialDao() {
    return new UserDAO(id, givenName, surname, null, null, null, null,
        driver, car, currentRating, latitude, longitude,
        direction, pushToken);
}
```

RideDAO

As you saw before we use the RideDAO class to transfer data about the current ride to the other tiers. We will make further use of it in the RideService class:

Listing 10. 2. The RideDAO class (trimmed)

```
public class RideDAO implements Serializable {
    private long userId;
    private String name;
    private String from;
    private String destination;

    public RideDAO() {
    }

    public RideDAO(long userId, String name, String from,
            String destination) {
        this.userId = userId;
        this.name = name;
        if(this.name == null) {
            this.name = "[Unnamed User]";
        }
        this.from = from;
        this.destination = destination;
    }

    // getters and setters trimmed out
}
```

A ride is associated with a specific passenger based on his id

We include the user name to save a back and forth with the server

Names can be null so we initialize a default here

10

The main usage for this class is in the new RideService which I will get to soon, but first we need to discuss the Ride class.

Ride, RideRepository and Waypoint

10.1.3

We need to store a lot more in the database both for scalability and for accountability. Specifically we need to track the rides so we can know the path the driver took. The server needs to track drivers and hailing so we can respond with a set of drivers when queried.

This is especially important for accountability where we need to verify that a ride actually happened. If we store paths in the database we can literally "see" the driver and passenger in the ride and know the details of the ride. In a case of a dispute we would have information we can evaluate.

Ride

Ride is a new `Entity` object. It isn't as simple as `RideDAO` despite their common name. Currently we don't use all of the information stored in `Ride` but the fact that it's logged will let you provide all of that information within the app or a management app easily.

A `Ride` entry connects the detail of a single ride (or trip) by including the passenger, driver, route and financial information.

The Ride class is a JPA `Entity` similar to the `User` class.

Listing 10. 3. The Ride class (trimmed)

```
@Entity
public class Ride {
    @Id
    @GeneratedValue(strategy=GenerationType.AUTO)
    private Long id;

    @ManyToOne
    private User passenger;

    @ManyToOne
    private User driver;

    @OneToMany
    @OrderBy("time ASC")
    private Set<Waypoint> route;

    private BigDecimal cost;
    private String currency;


    private boolean finished;
    private boolean started;
    // trimmed out constructors, getters and setters
}
```

We use an auto-increment value for the id instead of a random string. This keeps things simple but notice this can expose a security vulnerability of scanning for rides...

The passenger and driver are relational database references to their respective database objects

The route itself is a set of waypoints sorted by the time associated with the given waypoint

We'll discuss waypoints soon enough but technically it's just a set of coordinates

I really oversimplified the cost field. It should work for sum and currency but it's usually not as simple as that

We have two boolean flags, a ride is started once a passenger is picked up. It's finished once he is dropped off or if the ride was canceled

It's important to use something like BigDecimal and not double when dealing with financial values as double is built for scientific usage and has rounding errors

RideRepository

As usual every Entity has a CRUD object paired with it to perform database queries. This CRUD RideRepository is pretty standard with one exception:

Listing 10. 4. The RideRepository interface

```java
public interface RideRepository extends CrudRepository<Ride, Long> {
    @Query("select b from Ride b where b.finished = false " +
        "and b.driver.id = ?1")
    public List<Ride> findByNotFinishedUser(long id);
}
```

We added a special case finder that lets us locate the User that is currently hailing a car

Notice the syntax b.driver.id = ?1 which points through the relation to the driver object.

Waypoint

The Waypoint Entity represents a position on Earth and in time. Once we have a position and time we can use that to plot the path of a ride and extract further useful information from it.

Listing 10. 5. The Waypoint class (trimmed)

```java
@Entity
public class Waypoint {
    @Id
    @GeneratedValue(strategy=GenerationType.AUTO)
    private Long id;
    private long time;

    private double latitude;
    private double longitude;
    private float direction;

    // trimmed out constructors, getters and setters
}
```

As usual I use generated id's which is simpler in this case

Time is the value of System.currentTimeMillis() (milliseconds since EPOCH 1970) when this was added

Other than altitude which we don't need until we have the flying car Uber, the following 3 values point at our position on earth

The interesting part here is the time value which is the value of System.currentTimeMillis(). This allows us to build a path based on the time sequence. It will also allow us to reconstruct a trip and generate additional details such as speed/cost if we wish to do that in the future.

> **ⓘ** **There is also a** WaypointRepository **Interface**
> I'm skipping that class as it contains no actual code

RideService

The RideService class serves the same purpose as the UserService class, focusing on rides and driver related features. I could have just stuck all of this logic into one huge class but separating functionality to different service classes based on logic makes sense. This is still a non-trivial class so I'll split the code to smaller pieces for readability.

I'll start with the main class and more important method hailCar:

Listing 10. 6. The RideService class and hailCar

```
@Service
public class RideService {
    @Autowired
    private UserRepository users;
    @Autowired
    private RideRepository rides;
    @Transactional
    public UserDAO hailCar(String token, boolean h,
        String from, String to) {
      User u = users.findByAuthToken(token).get(0);
```

We manipulate both the rides and users CRUD objects from this class

Hailing is a transactional method, this means that all operations within the method will either succeed or fail depending on the outcome

```
                      This method can be invoked
                      to start and stop hailing
    if(h) {  ⟵
       if(u.getAssignedUser() != null) {
          long driverId = u.getAssignedUser();
          u.setAssignedUser(null);
          users.save(u);
          User driver = users.findOne(driverId);
          return driver.getPartialDao();  ⟵
       }                                        In this case we use the assigned user
    } else {                                    property to detect if a driver accepted
       u.setAssignedUser(null);                 the ride. If so we return the driver data
    }                                           to the client
    u.setHailing(h);
    u.setHailingFrom(from);
    u.setHailingTo(to);
    users.save(u);
    return null;
  }
  // rest of code
}
```

10

Transactional methods are important. They prevent an inconsistent state in the
database where one part is saved and another isn't

With that out of the way lets proceed to the rest of the code for accepting a ride and querying it:

Listing 10. 7. The RideService class Methods

```java
public RideDAO getRideData(long userId) {
    User u = users.findOne(userId);
    if(u == null) return null;
    return u.getRideDao();
}
@Transactional
public long acceptRide(String token,
        long userId) {
    User driver = users.findByAuthToken(token).get(0);
    User passenger = users.findOne(userId);
    if(!passenger.isHailing()) throw new RuntimeException("Not hailing");
    passenger.setHailing(false);
    passenger.setAssignedUser(driver.getId());
    driver.setAssignedUser(userId);
    users.save(driver);
    users.save(passenger);
    Ride r = new Ride();
    r.setDriver(driver);
    r.setPassenger(passenger);
    rides.save(r);
    return r.getId();
}
public void startRide(long rideId) {
    Ride current = rides.findOne(rideId);
    current.setStarted(true);
    rides.save(current);
}
public void finishRide(long rideId) {
    Ride current = rides.findOne(rideId);
    current.setFinished(true);
    rides.save(current);
}
```

When a driver gets a notification of a ride he invokes this method to get back the data about the ride

If the driver wishes to accept the ride he invokes this transactional method. The method accepts the token from the driver and the id of the user hailing the ride

We create a new Ride entity and return its ID. From this point on we need to refer to the Ride id and not the user id or token

Start ride and finish ride are invoked by the driver when he picks up the passenger and when he drops him off

Normally, finish ride should also handle elements like billing etc. but I won't go into that now

10

With that, the server API for hailing is in place. We just need to expose it to the client side. So the next step is bridging this to the user through a WebService…

RideWebservice

The RideWebservice class exposes the RideService calls almost verbatim to the client. It's mostly listed here for completeness but isn't really interesting:

Listing 10. 8. The RideWebservice class

```
@Controller
@RequestMapping("/ride")
public class RideWebservice {
    @Autowired
    private RideService rides;
    @RequestMapping(method=RequestMethod.GET,value = "/get")
    public @ResponseBody RideDAO getRideData(
        long id) {                            ⟵  The get call fetches the
        return rides.getRideData(id);              RideDAO for the given user id
    }
    @RequestMapping(method=RequestMethod.GET,value="/accept")
    public @ResponseBody String acceptRide(
            @RequestParam(name="token", required = true) String token,
            @RequestParam(name="userId", required = true)
        long userId) {                        ⟵  Normally I use POST for write methods
        long val = rides.acceptRide(token, userId);   but we can use GET just as well
        return "" + val;
    }
}
```

Listing 10. 8. The RideWebservice class

```
    @RequestMapping(method=RequestMethod.POST,value="/start")
    public @ResponseBody String startRide(
        @RequestParam(name="id", required = true)
        long rideId) {
      rides.startRide(rideId);
      return "OK";
    }
    @RequestMapping(method=RequestMethod.POST,value="/finish")
    public @ResponseBody String finishRide(
        @RequestParam(name="id", required = true) long rideId) {
      rides.finishRide(rideId);
      return "OK";
    }
}
```

Start and finish rides are again very simple with only one argument, which is the ride id

10

I used the HTTP GET method for acceptRide which isn't ideal for two reasons:

- It's confusing - people assume GET is a read operation

- It could trigger accidental double submission

The second issue isn't a problem. It would be a problem in a web environment where the user can accidentally reload and trigger a database change twice. So the problem is one of perception and habit both of which are important things that I don't want to discount...

Still I chose to use GET for the simple reason that passing arguments through a GET operation is easier and consistent. When we POST in this app we tend to pass JSON in the body of the request. I didn't want to create a JSON request specifically for one argument (the userId).

There was an option of making a POST with elements in the body using standard HTTP FORM POST semantics. I think this would have been confusing and inconsistent with the rest of the code both in the client and the server. So I chose to use GET.

UserService, LocationService and UserWebservice

We also have to add some minor changes to the UserService and LocationService classes. Lets start with the UserService class:

Listing 10. 9. Changes to the UserService class

```
public void updatePushToken(String token, String pushToken) {
    User u = users.findByAuthToken(token).get(0);
    u.setPushToken(pushToken);     ←──────┐ Drivers need a push token
    users.save(u);                        │ so we can hail them
}
```

The push token is always set outside of the user creation/update code for two reasons:

- When the user is created the push key isn't available yet (it arrives asynchronously)
- Push is re-registered in every launch and refreshed, there is no reason to update the entire object for that

Push keys can reach 4,104 bytes in length so it's crucial to store them in a database column that has enough space. This should work fine for our specific setup but if you use a different database or build your own schema you should take that into consideration

The UserWebservice class needs to mirror these changes obviously...

Listing 10. 10. Changes to the UserWebservice class

```java
@RequestMapping(method = RequestMethod.GET,value = "/setPushToken")
public @ResponseBody String updatePushToken(
        @RequestParam(name="token", required = true) String token,
        @RequestParam(name="pushToken", required = true)
          String pushToken) {
    users.updatePushToken(token, pushToken);
    return "OK";
}
```

We handle a GET request on the /setPushToken URL with a user token and push token

The LocationService needs a bit more work. We need to update the class so it will keep track of the drive and add new waypoints if we are in a ride:

Listing 10. 11. Changes to the LocationService class

```java
@Service
public class LocationService {
    @Autowired
    private UserRepository users;
    @Autowired
    private RideRepository rides;
    @Autowired
    private WaypointRepository waypoints;
    public void updateUserLocation(String token,
            double lat, double lon, float dir) {
        List<User> us = users.findByAuthToken(token);
        User u = us.get(0);
        u.setLatitude(lat);
        u.setLongitude(lat);
        u.setDirection(dir);
        users.save(u);
```

Every time we update a users location we check if he's a driver on a ride

```java
    if(u.isDriver() && u.getAssignedUser() != null) {
        List<Ride> r = rides.findByNotFinishedUser(u.getId());
        if(r != null && !r.isEmpty()) {
            Ride ride = r.get(0);
            if(ride.isStarted() && !ride.isFinished()) {
                Set<Waypoint> route = ride.getRoute();
                Waypoint newPosition = new Waypoint(
                    System.currentTimeMillis(), lat, lon, dir);
                waypoints.save(newPosition);
                route.add(newPosition);
                ride.setRoute(route);
                rides.save(ride);
            }
        }
    }
    // the rest is unchanged
}
```

Assuming we have a Ride object we check if this is currently an ongoing ride that wasn't finished

If so we add a waypoint to the ride and update it so we can later on inspect the path of the Ride

10

This pretty much tracks rides seamlessly. If we wanted to be really smart we could detect the driver and user position to detect them traveling together and automatically handle the ride. There are obviously problems with this as it means a user can't order a cab for someone else but it might be an interesting feature since we have two close data points...

Handler

Now that all of this is out of the way we can dive into the big changes in the Handler class in the WebSocket protocol.

Listing 10. 12. Added new Constants to Handler

I've added a new message type from the server to indicate that a driver was found

```
private static final short MESSAGE_TYPE_DRIVER_FOUND = 4;
private static final short HAILING_OFF = 0;
private static final short HAILING_ON = 1;
private static final short HAILING_TURN_OFF = 2;
@Autowired
private RideService rides;
```

Up until now we used the seeking/hailing flag as a boolean with 0 and 1 options. I've added another option of 2 which means hailing is turning off. To make this work consistently I switched to constants

The class updates the rides as well for drivers

Next lets look at the message interception code, since this code grew significantly I broke it down to smaller methods. Lets start with handleBinaryMessage itself. I didn't really change much there just moved stuff out:

Listing 10. 13. Handler Changes in handleBinaryMessage

```
protected void handleBinaryMessage(WebSocketSession session,
        BinaryMessage message) throws Exception {
    ByteBuffer b = message.getPayload();          ← All of this is
    short messageType = b.getShort();               practically identical
    short stringLength = b.getShort();
    StringBuilder bld = new StringBuilder();
    for(int iter = 0 ; iter < stringLength ; iter++)
        bld.append((char)b.get());
    String token = bld.toString();
    switch(messageType) {                           The handler code was moved
        case MESSAGE_TYPE_LOCATION_UPDATE:  ←       into a method of its own
            handleLocationUpdate(b, token, session);
            break;
    }
}
```

This leads us directly to handleLocationUpdate() which is where we handle the incoming message's binary data now:

Listing 10. 14. Handler handleLocationUpdate

```
private void handleLocationUpdate(ByteBuffer b, String token,
        WebSocketSession session) throws IOException {
    double lat = b.getDouble();     ←  This code is identical to the previous
    double lon = b.getDouble();        code we had in handleBinaryMessage
    float dir = b.getFloat();
    double radius = b.getDouble();
    int seeking = b.get();   ←
    loc.updateUserLocation(token, lat, lon, dir);   Seeking can accept more value
    List<UserDAO> response;                         types now specifically one of the
                                                    new hailing options. So it's no
                                                    longer a boolean value
```

311

```
UserDAO driver = null;
short responseType;
if(seeking == HAILING_ON) {
    response = loc.findAvailableDrivers(lat, lon, radius);
    responseType = MESSAGE_TYPE_DRIVER_POSITIONS;
    byte[] fromArray = new byte[b.getShort()];
    b.get(fromArray);
    byte[] toArray = new byte[b.getShort()];
    b.get(toArray);
    driver = rides.hailCar(token, true, new String(fromArray, "UTF-8"),
          new String(toArray, "UTF-8"));
} else {
    if(seeking == HAILING_TURN_OFF)
        rides.hailCar(token, false, null, null);
    response = loc.findAllDrivers(lat, lon, radius);
    responseType = MESSAGE_TYPE_AVAILBLE_DRIVER_POSITIONS;
}
sendDriverFoundMessage(driver, session);
sendResponse(response, responseType, session);
}
```

Hailing reads the "from" and "to" UTF-8 strings we sent from the client and passes them onwards so we can get the route

We use the new HAILING_OFF mode to force an explicit cancelation of hailing

These two methods handle the response messages. We'll discuss them next

That didn't change much but it would look a bit different due to the refactoring...

Next we have the sendDriverFoundMessage method. This method pushes the "driver found" event if a driver was found:

Listing 10. 15. Handler sendDriverFoundMessage

```java
private void sendDriverFoundMessage(UserDAO driver,
        WebSocketSession session) throws IOException {
    if(driver != null) {
        try(ByteArrayOutputStream bos = new ByteArrayOutputStream();
            DataOutputStream dos = new DataOutputStream(bos);) {
            dos.writeShort(MESSAGE_TYPE_DRIVER_FOUND);
            dos.writeLong(driver.getId());
            dos.writeUTF(notNull(driver.getCar()));
            dos.writeUTF(notNull(driver.getGivenName()));
            dos.writeUTF(notNull(driver.getSurname()));



            dos.writeFloat(driver.getCurrentRating());
            dos.writeLong(driver.getCurrentRide());
            dos.flush();
            BinaryMessage bin = new BinaryMessage(bos.toByteArray());
            session.sendMessage(bin);
        }
    }
}
```

It's possible a driver wasn't found. In that case we do nothing

If we have a driver, we construct a message to send to the client indicating that a driver was found

Notice we use the notNull method which I will get to shortly. We need those methods since writeUTF doesn't handle null values correctly and we don't have a UI to enter the drivers name yet

This sends the WebSocket message to the user

10

One of the reviewers for the book commented on notNull asking if Java 8's Optional would be a better fit. I could have reworked the UserDAO object to use Optional as some developers enthusiastically do. It would have made the entries blank instead of null. I'm not sure if it would have been better. I think Optional has its place when we use functional features in Java (e.g. Streams) but in this case I'm not sure if there is an advantage.

Next we have the sendResponse method which updates us with the current position of all the cars. It's the same code as before only refactored to a new method:

Listing 10. 16. Handler sendResponse

```java
private void sendResponse(List<UserDAO> response, short responseType,
        WebSocketSession session) throws IOException {
    if(response != null && response.size() > 0) {
        try(ByteArrayOutputStream bos = new ByteArrayOutputStream();
            DataOutputStream dos = new DataOutputStream(bos);) {
            dos.writeShort(responseType);
            dos.writeInt(response.size());
            for(UserDAO u : response) {
                dos.writeLong(u.getId());
                dos.writeDouble(u.getLatitude());
                dos.writeDouble(u.getLongitude());
                dos.writeFloat(u.getDirection());
                dos.writeUTF(notNull(u.getPushToken(), ""));
            }
            dos.flush();


            BinaryMessage bin = new BinaryMessage(bos.toByteArray());
            session.sendMessage(bin);
        }
    }
}
```

> Again this code is nearly identical to the previous code we had in handleBinaryMessage

> The one change is the push token added to the standard driver responses so we can notify the driver

10

That's it. Since we made the matching changes in the client side this should allow us to receive the push tokens of the drivers and ping them directly.

This is the notNull method I mentioned before it should be self explanatory:

Listing 10. 17. notNull Helper Methods

```
private static String notNull(String val, String defaultVal) {
   if(val == null) {
      return defaultVal;       ←   If it's null we return
   }                               the default value...
   return val;
}
private static String notNull(String val) {
   return notNull(val, "[unknown]");
}
```

This sums up the changes to the server and we can now move along to the driver app.

The Driver App   10.2

10

We often build one app and sell it to multiple customers. After all, most customers ask for similar things with minor changes. E.g. if I build a restaurant app and then sell it to one establishment I can then resell it to another with almost no change at all...

Another common use case is the demo or free version of a paid app, you want to reuse as much of the work as possible without maintaining two code bases.

Another case which is relevant to what I'm building today is two target audiences of roughly the same functionality. E.g. in this case the driver app has many common elements with the passenger app so why not build the same app with minor modifications?

How does the Appstore Identify the App?   10.2.1

The first thing we need to understand is how the appstore identifies your application.

Pretty much all apps use a unique identifier string that is similar to package names, which we map to the main application package name.

> 💡 **Don't use Underscores in Package Names**
> Apple doesn't allow underscores in these names, Java doesn't allow the minus character – so avoid both

So the trick is to add a new package for the new app. In this case our main app is com.codename1.apps.uberclone.UberClone so the driver app can be com.codename1.apps.uberclone.driverapp and the main class there can be DriverApp.

The basic "Hello Driver" is:

Listing 10. 18. Initial implementation of DriverApp

```
public class DriverApp extends UberClone {        ← I just derive the
    @Override                                         original main class
    public void init(Object context) {
        Log.p("Loaded Driver App");
        super.init(context);
    }
    @Override
    public void start() {
        super.start();        ←                 I override and call super
    }                                            mostly for clarity
    @Override
    public void stop() {
        super.stop();
    }
    @Override
    public void destroy() {
        super.destroy();
    }
}
```

Notice that this would have worked too:

Listing 10. 19. Initial implementation of DriverApp

```
public  class  DriverApp  extends  UberClone {      ←   We don't need to override
}                                                       any of the methods
```

But I prefer overriding the lifecycle methods for clarity in this case.

This isn't enough though. The codenameone_settings.properties file contains all of the internal configuration details about the project. I copied it aside and renamed it to: codenameone_settings_user.properties.

I then edited the file to use the driver details and copied that into: codenameone_settings_driver.properties.

Listing 10. 20. codenameone_settings.properties file

It's important to update the app id to use your apple developer account prefix and package name. This is automatically generated when you run the signing wizard to create iOS developer certificates

```
codename1.ios.appid=Q5GHSKAL2F.com.codename1.apps.uberclone.driverapp
codename1.ios.release.provision=
# ... trimmed ...
```

The certificates should be the same between the driver and user app but provisioning profiles should be regenerated for both when you build an iOS version of your app

```
codename1.mainName=DriverApp
```

Update codename1.mainName to match the class name

```
codename1.ios.release.certificatePassword=
codename1.packageName=com.codename1.apps.uberclone.driverapp
```

Update codename1.packageName to match the main package name

10

Other than certificates there are many nuances you need to customize in this file such as the app name and the icon. Once this is all done you have a separate app that does the exact same thing...

Customizing the Driver App   10.2.2

It's really easy for us to detect the driver app and write custom code for it. First lets change the UberClone class to add driver detection:

Listing 10. 21. Driver Detection in UberClone (trimmed)

```java
public class UberClone {
   private static boolean driverMode;
   private Form current;
   private Resources theme;

   protected boolean driverMode() {
      return false;
   }

   public static boolean isDriverMode() {
      return driverMode;
   }

   public void init(Object context) {
      driverMode = driverMode();
      NetworkManager.getInstance().updateThreadCount(2);
      theme = UIManager.initFirstTheme("/theme");
      Toolbar.setGlobalToolbar(true);
      Log.bindCrashProtection(true);
      Display.getInstance().lockOrientation(true);
   }

   // rest of the code is unchanged...
}
```

We introduce a public isDriverMode() method into the UberClone class

It always returns false unless we make one tiny addition to DriverApp:

Listing 10. 22. Driver Detection in DriverApp (trimmed)

```java
@Override
protected boolean driverMode() {
   return true;
}
```

Now we can start writing the custom code for the driver app.

Push Notification

A huge part of the driver app is the push notification process, that's how we notify a driver that there is a ride pending.

I'm assuming that you know about push and understand how to use it if this isn't the case please check out Appendix E (page 417).

Before we Begin with Push

We need the values from Google and Apple to fill the Globals class constants. We need the iOS credentials/certificates and the Google API key.

Push Registration and Interception

Once this is out of the way we can start handling the push messages. To do that we need to implement the PushCallback interface in the DriverApp.

> **This MUST be in the Main Class**
>
> The PushCallback interface must be defined in the main class, otherwise it won't work

Listing 10. 23. DriverApp with Push

```java
public class DriverApp extends UberClone implements PushCallback {
   private long lastId;
   protected boolean driverMode() {
      return true;
   }
   public void init(Object context) {
      super.init(context);
   }
   public void start() {
      super.start();
      callSerially(() -> {
         if(UserService.isLoggedIn()) registerPush();
      });
   }
   public void push(String value) {
      Log.p("Received push callback: " + value);
      if(value.startsWith("#")) {

         lastId = Long.parseLong(value.substring(1));
      } else {
         ToastBar.showMessage(value, FontImage.MATERIAL_INFO, 6000, e->{
            MapForm map = MapForm.get();
            if(map != getCurrentForm()) map.show();
            map.showRide(lastId);
         });
      }
   }
   public void registeredForPush(String deviceId) {
      Log.p("Registered for push device key: " + Push.getPushKey());
      UserService.registerPushToken(Push.getPushKey());
   }
   public void pushRegistrationError(String error, int errorCode) {
      Log.p("Error registering for push: " + error);
   }
}
```

We need to register for push every time the app loads. The logic is that the push key might change so we need to keep it up to date

We send a type 3 push which will invoke this method twice

The first time around we'll receive a # symbol followed by a numeric id. That's the hidden part of the messages

The second time we'll receive the display value which will reach the else statement

When we receive the display value we can show a notification to the driver and, if he clicks this notification, we can show him the details of the ride

When register succeeds this method is invoked. The main use case is sending the push key to the server so it can trigger push messages

We send the push key every time, even if the value didn't change. It's not a "big deal" in terms of overhead. Notice that deviceId != Push.getPushKey() . **deviceId is the historic native device key and shouldn't be used**

Ideally we would also have a Rides menu item in the side menu but I want to keep the code concise.

DriverService and Ride

Before we go into the big UI changes lets go over some of the networking level changes in the code. In order to encapsulate the new Ride JSON object from the server I added an equivalent properties object locally:

Listing 10. 24. Ride Client Side class

```
public class Ride implements PropertyBusinessObject {
    public final LongProperty<Ride> userId = new LongProperty<>("userId");
    public final Property<String, Ride> name = new Property<>("name");
    public final Property<String, Ride> from = new Property<>("from");
    public final Property<String, Ride> destination=new Property<>("destination");
    private final PropertyIndex idx = new PropertyIndex(this, "Ride",
        userId, name, from, destination);
    public PropertyIndex getPropertyIndex() {
        return idx;
    }
}
```

The properties match the RideDAO properties exactly but in this case I didn't have to trim the class as it's already small

10

It's a pretty standard properties object, mostly here to encapsulate the JSON we get from the server. Let's move on to the DriverService class.

The DriverService class is a static representation of the driver-specific server API's:

Listing 10. 25. The DriverService class

```java
public class DriverService {
    private static String currentRide;
    public static void fetchRideDetails(long id,
            SuccessCallback<Ride> rideDetails) {
        Rest.get(SERVER_URL + "ride/get").
            acceptJson().queryParam("id", "" + id).
            getAsJsonMap(response -> {
                Map data = response.getResponseData();
                if(data != null) {
                    Ride r = new Ride();
                    r.getPropertyIndex().populateFromMap(data);
                    rideDetails.onSucess(r);
                }
            });
    }
    public static boolean acceptRide(long id) {
        Response<String> response = Rest.get(SERVER_URL + "ride/accept").
            acceptJson().
            queryParam("token", UserService.getToken()).
            queryParam("userId", "" + id).getAsString();
        if(response.getResponseCode() == 200) {
            currentRide = response.getResponseData();
            return true;
        }
        return false;
    }
    public static void startRide() {
        Rest.post(SERVER_URL + "ride/start"). acceptJson().
            queryParam("id", currentRide).getAsString();
    }
    public static void finishRide() {
        Rest.post(SERVER_URL + "ride/finish").acceptJson().
            queryParam("id", currentRide).getAsString();
    }
}
```

This field represents the id of the current ride from this driver

Here we have the standard GET method I mentioned earlier to retrieve the ride details and return them via a callback

We use accept to indicate that a driver is accepting a users hailing. If he doesn't we don't care... Once accepted he gets a reference to the id of the newly created Ride object in the server. Notice that failure is indeed a possibility. E.g. if the user canceled the ride or a different driver accepted first

When we invoke startRide and finishRide we use the currentRide id, unlike the userId, which we used to create the ride

SearchService Changes

In SearchService we had to add support for geocoding. Before this, we only had the reverse geocoding which we use to locate the from/to points on the map. We need this API since the driver only gets the to/from location names and we want to plot them on the map:

Listing 10. 26. findLocation in SearchService

```
public static void findLocation(String name,
    SuccessCallback<Coord> location) {
    Rest.get("https://maps.googleapis.com/maps/api/geocode/json").
        queryParam("address", name).
        queryParam("key", Globals.GOOGLE_GEOCODING_KEY).
        getAsJsonMap(callbackMap -> {
            Map data = callbackMap.getResponseData();
            if(data != null) {
                List results = (List)data.get("results");
                if(results != null && results.size() > 0) {
                    Map firstResult = (Map)results.get(0);
                    Map geometryMap = (Map)firstResult.get("geometry");
                    Map locationMap = (Map)geometryMap.get("location");
                    double lat = Util.toDoubleValue(
                        locationMap.get("lat"));
                    double lon = Util.toDoubleValue(
                        locationMap.get("lng"));
                    location.onSucess(new Coord(lat, lon));
                }
            }
        });
}
```

We make a standard GET request to the geocode API with the given address

The geometry value in the first result points at the location we want

10

There isn't all that much to say about this method. It just searches the Google geocode API for a location with the given name and returns the coordinate of that location.

UserService Changes

There were many small changes in the UserService class. Most of them relate to the way identity is managed in the app.

One of the big problems in having two applications with one project is that both projects share the same data in the simulator. So if I want to launch the project twice – once to run the user version and once for the driver version – I will have a problem. Both will inspect the same storage information and use the same user identity. They might collide...

> **This is Purely a Simulator Problem**
>
> The simulator doesn't currently isolate separate applications. Ideally this is something to improve in the simulator and might not be an issue in the future

The solution is simple though. We can just save the data to different "locations" or "keys" if we are in the driver app. Since most of the class remained the same I'll just list the code blocks that changed:

Listing 10. 27. Changes to UserService getToken

```
public static String getToken() {
   if(UberClone.isDriverMode()) {
      return Preferences.get("driver-token", null);
   } else {
      return Preferences.get("token", null);
   }
}
```

We use a different token to determine if the user is logged in for the case of a driver

Notice we replaced the invocations of Preferences.get("token", null) that were all over the code with this method

In this case I chose to do a simple if statement to support both types of apps built from a single source code. What if I wanted to build 10 apps from one source?

In that case I would probably create a dedicated class to handle each app and use polymorphism to handle the differences instead of a simple if statement. Since we have just two apps in this case I chose the easy/simple approach.

Next I needed to make a similar change to the loadUser() code to add a prefix for the driver app:

Listing 10. 28. Changes to UserService loadUser

```
public static void loadUser() {
    me = new User();
    if(UberClone.isDriverMode()) {
        PreferencesObject.create(me).setPrefix("driver").bind();  ←
    } else {
        PreferencesObject.create(me).bind();
    }
    if(Display.getInstance().isSimulator()) {
        Log.p("User details: " + me.getPropertyIndex().toString());
    }
}
```

The PreferencesObject bind API lets us set a different prefix for the driver object that will be prepended to the properties in the Preferences

10

The addNewUser method needs to use a similar strategy to save the driver instance in the right preferences location:

Listing 10. 29. Changes to UserService addNewUser

```
public static boolean addNewUser(User u) {
    Response<String> token = Rest.post(SERVER_URL + "user/add").
        jsonContent().
        body(u.getPropertyIndex().toJSON()).getAsString();
    if(token.getResponseCode() != 200) {
        return false;
    }
    if(UberClone.isDriverMode()) {
        Preferences.set("driver-token", token.getResponseData());
        registerPush();          ⟵          After the first activation
    } else {                                of the driver app we
        Preferences.set("token", token.getResponseData());     need to register for push
    }
    return true;
}
```

10

Notice I'm using the version of registerPush() from the CN class with static import but the callback will go as expected into the DriverApp class

Finally we need the registerPushToken method which I mentioned in the main class. It sends the push key to the server so we can notify drivers of a ride. We don't need to test for a driver here as this method is only invoked for drivers.

Listing 10. 30. Changes to UserService registerPushToken

```
public static void registerPushToken(String pushToken) {
    Rest.get(SERVER_URL + "user/setPushToken").
        queryParam("token", getToken()).
        queryParam("pushToken", pushToken).
        getAsStringAsync(new Callback<Response<String>>() {

        public void onSucess(Response<String> value) {
        } ②
        public void onError(Object sender, Throwable err,
            int errorCode, String errorMessage) {
        }
    });
}
```

Sends the push token to the server. This is invoked on registration success and allows the server to send driver push keys to the client

Right now we don't need to do anything in the event callback

With that, the connection layer should work correctly for the driver app. It should register for push and receive notifications.

10

MapForm Changes

10.2.7

With the MapForm we are finally implementing the visual aspects of the driver app. Ideally we'd hide the search button and do a lot of refinement work on the UI but I don't have the space to address all of that...

Before we dive into the code lets look at the flow from a birds eye view:

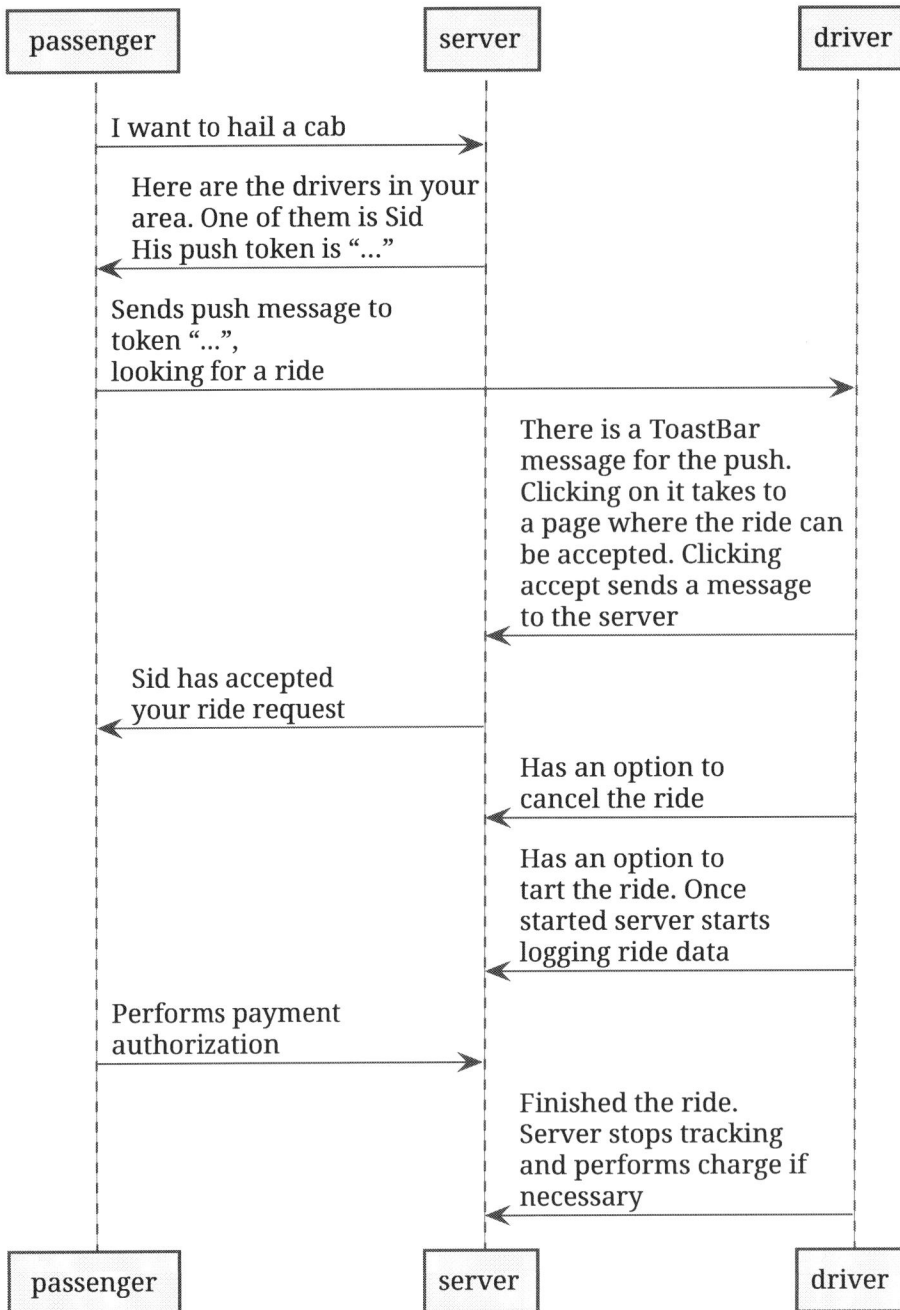

Figure 10. 1. The Hailing Process

These are the stages for hailing covered in the diagram:

1. A user confirms hailing and sends the details to the server

2. The server answers with a list of drivers in the area and their push tokens

3. The user starts sending push messages to the drivers in the region

4. The driver app receives a push message

5. Driver app shows a ToastBar message which the driver can click

6. If the driver clicks the ToastBar message. He is presented with details of a potential ride – specifically the route

7. If the driver accepts the route the server is notified

8. The user is sent a WebSocket message that a driver accepted the ride

9. The user sees a notice with the name of the driver, rating etc.

10. The driver is shown a dialog that allows him to cancel the ride or mark that he picked up the passenger

11. Once the driver clicks that he picked up the passenger, the ride starts

12. During the ride the location of the driver is used to gather the route to the destination

13. The driver is shown a Dialog that allows him to finish the ride

This is a gross oversimplification of the Uber user flow. The actual app has a lot of nuances within this flow that include many edge cases. I didn't even go into the complexities of billing, ride splitting etc.

But those are mostly low level details that might not be applicable in your real world use case so using this simplified model should be sufficient.

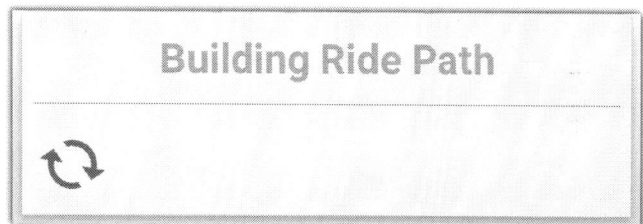

Figure 10. 2. Interaction Dialog with progress indicator as shown by the showRide method

Let's see how this all comes together in the changes made to MapForm. The first method we saw in the callback from the push notification is the showRide method.

Listing 10. 31. The showRide Method of MapForm

We use an InteractionDialog for simplicity, I show it in the bottom of the form. The arguments for position indicate the distance from each to edge so it touches all the edges other than the top edge. As a side note, notice that the regular Dialog doesn't work well on top of maps

```java
public void showRide(long userId) {
    InteractionDialog id = new InteractionDialog(new BorderLayout());
    id.setTitle("Loading Ride Details");
    id.add(CENTER, new InfiniteProgress());
    id.show(getHeight()-id.getPreferredH(), 0, 0, 0); ←
    DriverService.fetchRideDetails(userId, ride -> {
        id.setTitle("Building Ride Path");
        final Coord[] locations = new Coord[2];
        if(ride.from.get() == null) { ←
            id.dispose();
            ToastBar.showErrorMessage("Ride no longer available...");
            return;
        }
        SearchService.findLocation(ride.from.get(),
                fromLocation -> { ←
            locations[0] = fromLocation;
            onShowRideResponse(id, ride, locations);
        });
        SearchService.findLocation(ride.destination.get(), toLocation -> {
            locations[1] = toLocation;
            onShowRideResponse(id, ride, locations);
        });
    });
}
```

By the time the callback is returned from fetchRideDetails the ride might no longer be available so we can just dispose the UI and continue as usual

We need to find the coordinates on the map of the source and destination

10

I could have just transferred the map coordinates in the ride data (but I didn't)... If findLocation was synchronous I could just invoke find on from then on destination and everything would work but it would be slow as it would require that we make the first WebService call and then the second one. In this way both calls might happen concurrently. The first one to complete will have one location in the locations array and the second one will have both. The onShowRideResponse doesn't do anything unless both locations are set. A race condition won't be possible here since the callbacks are invoked on the EDT so they will always happen in sequence

Dialogs, Peer Components and Maps

The Map component is a native peer component. Most Codename One components are drawn by Codename One itself which is why they are so portable and flexible. However, most 3rd party components are implemented using the native OS API's e.g. the Google Maps implementation is implemented using Android/iOS native widgets. Codename One refers to such components as peer components.

There are some nuances to working with peer components. E.g. they handle their own scrolling and events so a few of the things we can do with a regular Codename One component just won't work.

Dialogs are subclasses of the Form class. They appear to float on top of the parent Form but that's an illusion. They are a Form that shows the previous Form behind them to create that effect. This in itself is perfectly fine. It's also one of the reasons dialogs can block the UI easily, there is nothing going on behind them.

InteractionDialog appears like a regular Dialog but that's just styling. Under the hood it's a Container placed into the layered pane. That means you can show an interaction dialog and still interact with the UI behind it. That's very useful for some cases.

The problem with Dialog and peer components is this. We have a peer which is rendered by the native OS. A Dialog shows a separate Form and then tries to grab a screenshot of the previous Form to show behind it... This sometimes fails due to the complex nature of some native components so artifacts might appear. Since an InteractionDialog is just a Container under the hood, the current Form stays in place and we won't see any odd flickering issues.

The obvious next step is the onShowRideResponse method.

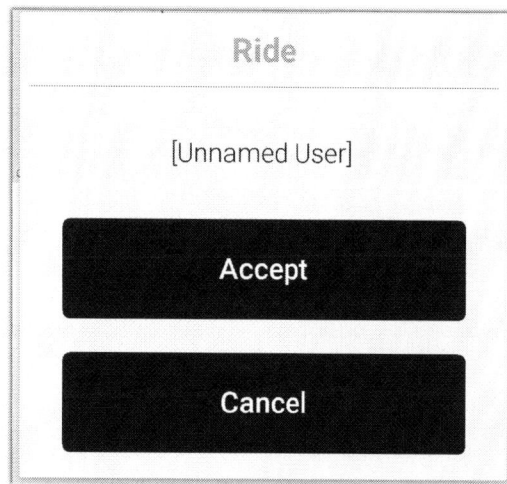

Figure 10. 3. The Accept/Cancel InteractionDialog shown by onShowRideResponse

Listing 10. 32. The onShowRideResponse Method of MapForm

As we mentioned before the from/destination values are fetched concurrently so this method will be invoked twice. Only the second time is valid

```
void onShowRideResponse(InteractionDialog dlg,Ride ride,Coord[] locations) {
    if(locations[0] == null || locations[1] == null) return;
    SearchService.directions(toLocation(locations[0]),
        toLocation(locations[1]), (path, duration, distance) -> {
    dlg.dispose();
    String from = ride.from.get();
    String to = ride.destination.get();
```

Coord is used at some points and Location at others. The reason for both objects is mostly historic where the map API works with one and the GPS API's work with another, so the toLocation method translates Coord to the Location object type

```
    Component fromComponent =
        createNavigationTag(trimmedString(from), duration / 60);
    Component toComponent = createNavigationTag(trimmedString(to), -1);
    MapContainer.MapObject pathObject = addPath(path, fromComponent,
        toComponent, duration);
```

This creates a map path similar to the one the user sees on his phone so the driver and user have a similar view of the trip properties and duration. We'll discuss the addPath method later. This is refactored code from the enterNavigationMode method

```
    InteractionDialog id=new InteractionDialog("Ride",BoxLayout.y());
    id.add(new Label(ride.name.get(), "RideTitle"));
    Button acceptButton = new Button("Accept", "BlackButton");
    Button cancelButton = new Button("Cancel", "BlackButton");
    id.setAnimateShow(false);
    id.add(acceptButton);
    id.add(cancelButton);
```

We create a new InteractionDialog to prompt the driver whether he is interested in accepting this ride or not

```
cancelButton.addActionListener(e -> {
    fromComponent.remove();
    toComponent.remove();
    mc.removeMapObject(pathObject);
    id.dispose();
});
acceptButton.addActionListener(e ->
    onAccept(ride, id, pathObject, fromComponent, toComponent));
id.show(getHeight() - id.getPreferredH(), 0, 0, 0);
    });
}
```

In the case he doesn't want to accept the ride the work is pretty easy. We just remove everything we added

In the action listener, I invoked the onAccept method to keep the code size smaller. This is the implementation of that method:

Listing 10. 33. The onAccept Method of MapForm

```
private void onAccept(Ride ride, InteractionDialog id, MapObject pathObject,
        Component fromComponent, Component toComponent) {
    boolean accept=DriverService.acceptRide(ride.userId.getLong());

    callSerially(() -> {
        if(accept) {
            id.dispose();
            pickUpPassenger(pathObject, ride, fromComponent,
                toComponent);
```

If the driver accepts the ride, we trigger the accept method. Notice that the accept call is a blocking call so, just to be safe, we use callSerially afterwards to flush any EDT related animation before showing the next UI

This shows the pickup UI and passes all the components/objects we'll need to eventually "clean up" such as the path and the components on the map

```
    } else {
        id.dispose();   ←──────────────────┐
        fromComponent.remove();             │  This is essentially identical to the code
        toComponent.remove();               │  we have for canceling the ride
        mc.removeMapObject(pathObject);
        getAnimationManager().flushAnimation(() ->
            ToastBar.showErrorMessage("Failed to grab ride"));
    }
});
}
```

For completeness the toLocation method is:

Listing 10. 34. The toLocation Method of MapForm

```
private Location toLocation(Coord crd) {
    return new Location(crd.getLatitude(), crd.getLongitude());
}
```

Now we can proceed to the pickUpPassenger method where we handle the rest of the ride:

Listing 10. 35. The pickUpPassenger Method of MapForm

```java
public void pickUpPassenger(MapContainer.MapObject pathObject,
        Ride ride, Component fromComponent, Component toComponent) {
    InteractionDialog id = new InteractionDialog("Pick Up",BoxLayout.y());
    id.add(new Label(ride.name.get(), "RideTitle"));
    Button acceptButton = new Button("Picked Up", "BlackButton");
    Button cancelButton = new Button("Cancel", "BlackButton");
    id.add(acceptButton);
    id.add(cancelButton);
    acceptButton.addActionListener(e -> {
        DriverService.startRide();
        id.dispose();
        InteractionDialog dlg=new InteractionDialog("Driving...",BoxLayout.y());
        dlg.add(new Label(ride.name.get(), "RideTitle"));
        Button finishButton = new Button("Finished Ride", "BlackButton");
        dlg.add(finishButton);
        finishButton.addActionListener(ee -> {
            DriverService.finishRide();
            fromComponent.remove();
            toComponent.remove();
            mc.removeMapObject(pathObject);
            dlg.dispose();
        });
        dlg.show(getHeight() - dlg.getPreferredH(), 0, 0, 0);
    }),
    cancelButton.addActionListener(e -> {
        fromComponent.remove();
        toComponent.remove();
        mc.removeMapObject(pathObject);
        id.dispose();
    });
    id.show(getHeight() - id.getPreferredH(), 0, 0, 0);
}
```

This is again a pretty standard approach. By now we're creating another dialog

The Accept button leads us to the last step, which is the Finish button

Once we picked up a passenger we can only finish the ride, not cancel it. Since we didn't integrate any billing yet this makes sense. With billing we'll obviously need a way to pay and refund a ride

10

I'll skip the last two screenshots since they look pretty much the same (with "Picked Up" and "Finish" for the buttons). Lets move to the end user experience and changes...

I used the addPath method in the onShowRideResponse so I'm showing it here for completeness:

Listing 10. 36. The addPath Method of MapForm

```
private MapContainer.MapObject addPath(List<Coord> path,
    Component fromComponent, Component toComponent, int duration) {
  Coord[] pathCoords = new Coord[path.size()];
  path.toArray(pathCoords); ←
  MapContainer.MapObject pathObject = mc.addPath(pathCoords);
  BoundingBox bb = BoundingBox.create(pathCoords).
    extend(new BoundingBox(pathCoords[0],0.01,0.01)).
    extend(new BoundingBox(pathCoords[pathCoords.length-1],0.01,0.01));
  mc.fitBounds(bb);
  MapLayout.setHorizontalAlignment(fromComponent,MapLayout.HALIGN.RIGHT);
  mapLayer.add(pathCoords[0], fromComponent);
  mapLayer.add(pathCoords[pathCoords.length - 1], toComponent);
  return pathObject;
}
```

This code should be familiar as we covered it in enterNavigationMode before

The addPath method generalizes some of the common code for adding a path and zooming into the map.

In the enterNavigationMode method I changed the hailRide call to:

Listing 10. 37. Minor Change to enterNavigationMode Method of MapForm

```
LocationService.hailRide(from, to, car -> {
  hailRideImpl(car, pinLayer);
});
```

The hailRideImpl method implements the UI for ride hail response to the user.

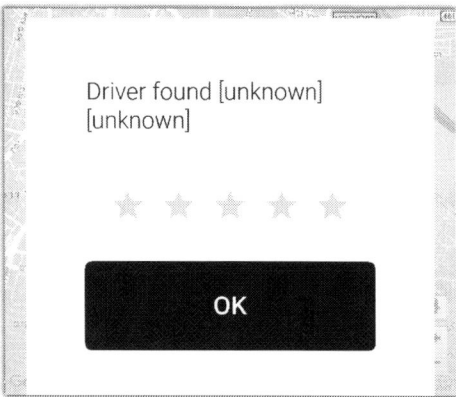

Figure 10. 4. Ride Hailed Successfully Driver Details

Listing 10. 38. The hailRideImpl Method of MapForm

```java
private void hailRideImpl(User car, final Container pinLayer) {
    pinLayer.getUnselectedStyle().setBgTransparency(0);
    pinLayer.removeAll();
    String driverName = car.givenName.get();
    String carBrand = car.car.get();
    SpanLabel driver=new SpanLabel("Driver found "+driverName+"\n"+carBrand);
    Container stars = new Container(new FlowLayout(CENTER));
    for(int iter = 0 ; iter < 5 ; iter++) {
        if(iter + 1 >= car.currentRating.getFloat()) {
            Label fullStar = new Label("", "Star");
            FontImage.setMaterialIcon(fullStar, FontImage.MATERIAL_STAR);
            stars.add(fullStar);
        } else {
            if(iter + 1 >= Math.round(car.currentRating.getFloat())) {
                Label halfStar = new Label("", "Star");
                FontImage.setMaterialIcon(halfStar,
                    FontImage.MATERIAL_STAR_HALF);
                stars.add(halfStar);
            } else break;
        }
    }
}
```

Both fields include no actual data currently since we don't have the UI to fill in the driver or user names

We build the text and add stars based on the level of ranking, this is essentially a set of star labels in a container based on the value of the rank field

Listing 10. 38. The hailRideImpl Method of MapForm

```
Button ok = new Button("OK", "BlackButton");
Container dialog = BoxLayout.encloseY(driver, stars, ok);
dialog.setUIID("SearchingDialog");
pinLayer.add(SOUTH, dialog);
revalidate();
ok.addActionListener(ee -> {
    dialog.remove();
    revalidate();
});
}
```

We call this a "dialog" but it's really just a
Container with a special style like before

10

In order to produce these stars I needed a Star UIID which is just a yellow, low-padding label. I needed low padding so they will be close enough to one another:

Listing 10. 39. Star Styling

```
Foreground Color: 0xffff00
Transparency: 0
Padding Left: 1mm
Padding Right: 1mm
Padding Top: 3mm
Padding Bottom: 3mm
Margin: 0
Font: native:MainLight 3mm
```

Summary

In this chapter, we learned:

- How to create two or more apps from a single application code base and reuse the common parts
- How to define a process of negotiation between two app instances through a common server
- The process of receiving and processing incoming push notifications

The main challenge of this day is the ride sharing logic. There are two difficult things you will run into with any mobile application and the difficulty is usually evenly spread:

- Getting the UI right
- Getting the business logic right

I skimmed on both in the driver app. This isn't a book about business logic as that varies too much. As a result there are functional compromises and difficulties and I don't want to "overcomplicate" the design of the app.

With the current set of changes the app should work and should allow simple cases for rides. It won't handle all the error edge cases or even simple cases like user cancelation etc. But those should be easy enough to implement based on this starting point.

10

Day 6: Billing and Social Activation 11

This chapter covers:

- How billing works through Braintree. Simplified integration of Braintree both in client and server

- Concepts of social network login and registration

- Native Facebook and Google login processes through the API

The last two "big ticket items" are billing and social login. I won't implement them with adherence to the way they were implemented by Uber. I want to keep both of these features simple as they are both very volatile. Features and requirements within both of these API's can change literally overnight.

Billing 11.1

I will implement billing as a request before the ride starts. I'll use Braintree to do this, mostly because it's already implemented in Codename One. The original implementation in Uber checks whether a billing method already exists. This is possible to do in Braintree but it requires some extra work.

To keep billing simple I'll just charge $1 per minute and do the charge in the server side.

In-App Purchase vs. Credit Cards

In-app purchase is one of the big ticket features in mobile apps. Codename One supports this rather well but we can't use in-app purchase for this case.

In-app purchase was devised as a tool to buy "virtual goods" inside an application. This reduces friction as no credit card is needed (Google/Apple already have it) and makes purchases more fluid. The definition of "virtual goods" has some gray areas but generally the idea is that a good or service sold is something that has no immediate physical cost.

Good examples for virtual goods are: in-game item, upgrade of software functionality, app subscription etc.

However, physical items and services are explicitly prohibited from using in-app purchase. This isn't a bad thing. In-app purchase takes a hefty commission of 30% which isn't viable for most physical goods sold.

11.1.1

Braintree

Braintree is a part of PayPal and provides an easy-to-integrate mobile payment SDK for selling physical goods and services. In theory we could just collect a credit card and call it a day but that's naive. Securing online transactions is a nuanced. Task by using a trusted 3rd party, a great deal of the risk and liability is transferred to them.

One of the core concepts when working with Braintree is opacity. The developer doesn't get access to the credit card or billing information. Instead a nonce and token are passed between the client and server. Even if a security flaw exists in the app a hacker wouldn't gain access to any valuable information as the values expire.

> 💡 A nonce is an arbitrary number that can be used just once. In this context it means you get a "single use" key to bill the user

The following diagram and explanation cover the process of purchasing via Braintree.

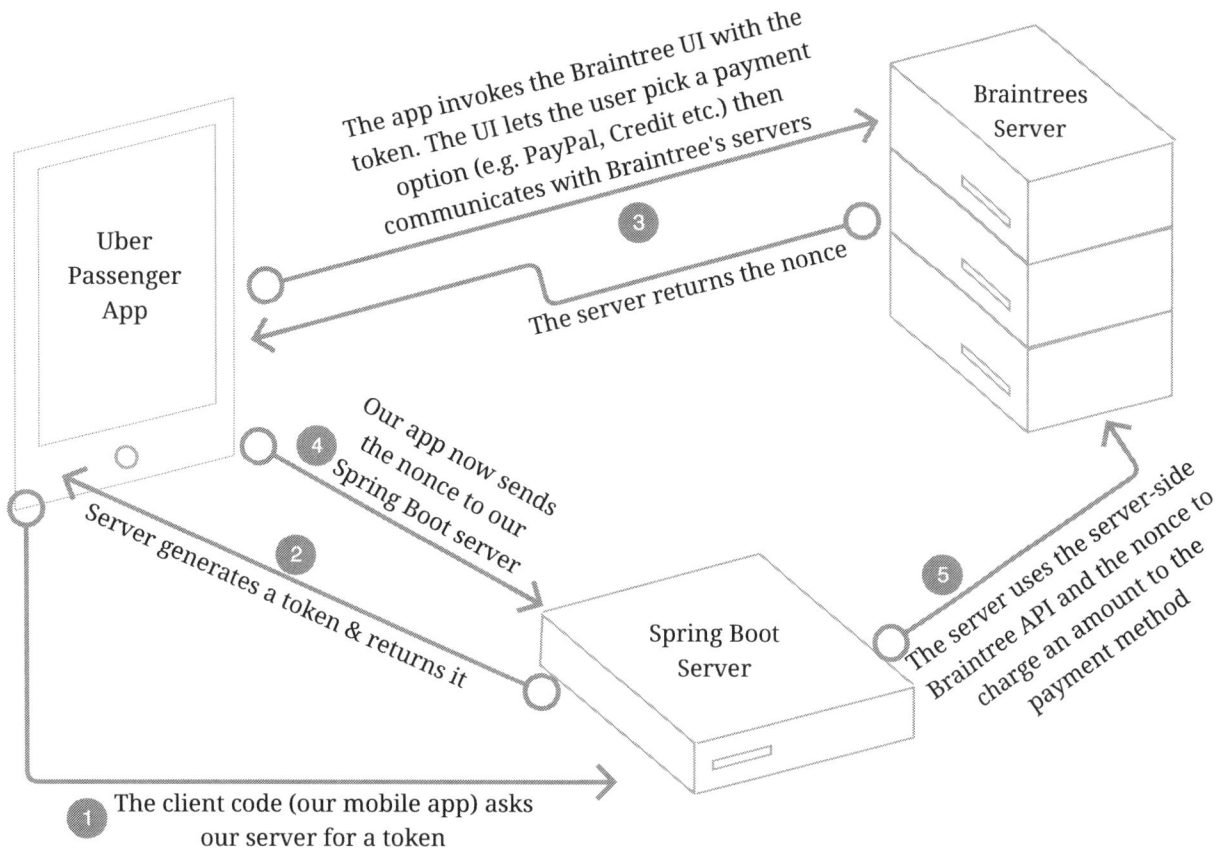

Figure 11. 1. The Flow of a Purchase in Braintree

1. The client code (our mobile app) asks our server for a token

2. The server generates a token with the Braintree server code and returns it. A client token is a signed data blob that includes configuration and authorization information needed by Braintree to associate the transaction correctly. It can't be reused and should be hard to spoof in an attack

3. The mobile app invokes the Braintree UI with the token. That UI lets the user pick a credit card or other payment option (e.g. PayPal, Android Pay, Apple Pay etc.) then communicates with Braintree's servers. The result of all this is a nonce which is a unique key that allows you to charge this payment method

4. Our app now sends the nonce our Spring Boot server

5. The server uses the server side Braintree API and the nonce to charge an amount to the payment method. Notice that the amount charged is completely up to the server and isn't a part of the client-side UI!

Server Side

11.1.2

The Braintree SDK for Java is pretty easy to use. We already have it in Maven but just in case you skipped those lines:

Listing 11. 1. Maven dependency for Braintree

```xml
<dependency>
  <groupId>com.braintreepayments.gateway</groupId>
  <artifactId>braintree-java</artifactId>
  <version>2.71.0</version>
</dependency>
```

BraintreeService

Next we add a BraintreeService class which is remarkably simple:

Listing 11. 2. The BraintreeService class

```java
@Service
public class BraintreeService {
    private final static BraintreeGateway gateway = new BraintreeGateway(
        Environment.SANDBOX,
        "your_merchant_id",
        "your_public_key",
        "your_private_key"
    );
    @Autowired
    private RideRepository rides;
    public String getClientToken() {
        return gateway.clientToken().generate();
    }
    public void saveNonce(long rideId, String nonce) {
        Ride r = rides.findOne(rideId);
        r.setNonce(nonce);
        rides.save(r);
    }
    public void pay(BigDecimal amount, String nonce) {
        new TransactionRequest().amount(amount).paymentMethodNonce(nonce)
            .options().submitForSettlement(true).done();
    }
}
```

These values should be updated from Braintree and SANDBOX should be updated to production once everything is working

This is the client token that we use to identify the transaction. Notice we generate a new one for every request

We save the nonce into the Ride object. This assumes payment authorization happens before the ride is completed. Once the ride is finished the nonce is instantly available to perform the charge

Payment is pretty standard, we can also check the results of the transaction but I skipped that here. The main values required are the amount and the nonce

Before we proceed further the obvious next step is the webservice to match:

Listing 11. 3. BraintreeWebservice

```java
@Controller
@RequestMapping("/pay")
public class BraintreeWebservice {
   @Autowired
   private BraintreeService payment;

   @RequestMapping(method=RequestMethod.GET,value = "/token")
   public @ResponseBody String getClientToken(long id) {
      return payment.getClientToken();        ← This maps /pay/token to return the
   }                                            client token needed to start the process

   @RequestMapping(method=RequestMethod.GET,value="/nonce")
   public @ResponseBody String nonce(
       @RequestParam(name="ride", required = true) long rideId,
       @RequestParam(name="nonce", required = true) String nonce) {
      payment.saveNonce(rideId, nonce);       ← This maps /pay/nonce so it will be saved
      return "OK";                             in the server once the client generates it
   }
}
```

It's mostly trivial but I'd like to point out a small nuance. pay isn't mapped. We invoke pay in the server so we don't need to expose it to the client side.

The nonce

The code above required some unexpected changes which I will get to shortly. The first change was pretty predictable though:

Listing 11. 4. Added nonce field to the Ride Server object

```java
private String nonce;
public String getNonce() {
    return nonce;
}
public void setNonce(String nonce) {
    this.nonce = nonce;
}
```

Here's the part I didn't expect. I need to add the ride id to the User object:

Listing 11. 5. Added Ride id to User

```java
private Long currentRide;
public Long getCurrentRide() {
    return currentRide;
}
public void setCurrentRide(Long currentRide) {
    this.currentRide = currentRide;
}
```

A driver has a reference to the Ride object which is why we didn't need this up until now. However, when the user tries to pay he can't set this anywhere else...

Unfortunately there is no other place where the nonce fits. Since it's transient we can't add it to the User as, we'd want some logging. TheRide object is the "right place" for the nonce.

To get this to work I had to make a few changes to the acceptRide method:

Listing 11. 6. acceptRide Changes to Support Braintree

```java
public long acceptRide(String token, long userId) {
    User driver = users.findByAuthToken(token).get(0);
    User passenger = users.findOne(userId);
    if(!passenger.isHailing()) {
        throw new RuntimeException("Not hailing");
    }
    passenger.setHailing(false);
    passenger.setAssignedUser(driver.getId());
    driver.setAssignedUser(userId);
    Ride r = new Ride();
    r.setDriver(driver);
    r.setPassenger(passenger);
    rides.save(r);
    driver.setCurrentRide(r.getId());
    passenger.setCurrentRide(r.getId());
    users.save(driver);
    users.save(passenger);
    return r.getId();
}
```

I added the ride reference to both the driver and passenger for future reference

I moved these lines downward because the ride ID will only be available after the rides.save() call

In retrospect I think I should have made the driver and passenger bi-directional relations in the database instead of using the ride id as a value. I was thinking about what I need and I didn't need the object reference so I didn't map it as bi-directional.

The Actual Payment

Since payment is handled on the server side we can go directly to it, even before we do the client side... I've decided to do this in the finishRide method:

Listing 11. 7. finishRide changes for billing

```java
public void finishRide(long rideId) {
    Ride current = rides.findOne(rideId);
    current.setFinished(true);
    if(current.isStarted() && current.getNonce() != null) {
        Set<Waypoint> s = current.getRoute();
        Iterator<Waypoint> i = s.iterator();
        if(i.hasNext()) {
            long startTime = i.next().getTime();
            long endTime = -1;
            while(i.hasNext()) endTime = i.next().getTime();

            if(endTime > -1) {
                BigDecimal cost = BigDecimal.valueOf(endTime - startTime).
                    divide(BigDecimal.valueOf(60000));
                current.setCost(cost);
                payments.pay(current.getCost(),
                    current.getNonce());
            }
        }
    }
    rides.save(current);
}
```

A ride that was finished before it was started is effectively canceled. A ride without a nonce can't be charged

I use the route which is ordered based on time to find the start time of the ride

I then go to the last element and find the end time of the ride

Assuming the ride has more than one Waypoint (otherwise endTime would be -1) we can just charge 1USD per 60 seconds

The nonce is the key sent to us by the client providing us with a single use authorization to bill his account

And payment is effectively done on the server. Again, I oversimplified a lot and ignored basic complexities, like the driver forgetting to press "Finish".

Client Side

Before we begin we need to download the Braintree cn1lib from the extension manager. Right-click the project and select Refresh Libs.

🛈   See Appendix D (page 413) for cn1lib installation instructions

We'll start the client side with the PaymentService class which encapsulates the WebService aspects:

Listing 11. 8. The PaymentService class

> PaymentService has a private constructor so it can't be instantiated by other classes. We use the instance of this class to get callback events from the client-side purchase API using the Purchase.Callback interface. Notice that we need a rideId in the object instance so we can communicate purchase results to the server correctly

```
public class PaymentService implements Purchase.Callback {
   private String rideId;
   private PaymentService(String rideId) {
      this.rideId = rideId;
   }
   public static void sendPaymentAuthorization(String rideId) {
      Purchase.startOrder(new PaymentService(rideId));
   }
```

This is literally the entire purchase API process. We just invoke the native purchase UI and provide the callback instance for the native code

```
   public void onPurchaseSuccess(String nonce) {
      Rest.get(SERVER_URL + "pay/token").acceptJson().
         queryParam("ride", rideId).queryParam("nonce", nonce).
         getAsStringAsync(new Callback<Response<String>>() {
```

onPurchaseSuccess is the first callback from the callback interface. It occurs when a purchase succeeded and produced a nonce. We can then send the nonce to the server with the ride id

349

```
        public void onSucess(Response<String> value) {}
        public void onError(Object sender, Throwable err,
              int errorCode, String errorMessage) {
        }
    });
}
public void onPurchaseFail(String a) {
    ToastBar.showErrorMessage("Error processing payment: " + a);
}



public void onPurchaseCancel() {
}
public String fetchToken() {
    return Rest.get(SERVER_URL + "pay/token").
          acceptJson().getAsString().getResponseData();
}
}
```

Here we'll need to handle success/failure messaging to the user in a production app

onPurchaseFail or cancel aren't very interesting in this use case. I chose to ignore them but you might need them to know whether the charge UI should be shown again. Notice the only way to verify purchase success is on the server

fetchToken is a callback method in the callback interface. It's invoked internally by the purchase process to fetch the server token value that initializes the purchase process

11

This is pretty much everything. The only remaining piece is binding this into the UI:

Listing 11. 9. Adding purchase into hailRideImpl (snipped)

```
private void hailRideImpl(User car, final Container pinLayer) {
    // snipped the top as the code is unchanged
    Button ok = new Button("Pay With Cash",
        "BlackButton");
    Button pay = new Button("Pay With Credit", "BlackButton");
    Container dialog = BoxLayout.encloseY(driver, stars, ok, pay);
    dialog.setUIID("SearchingDialog");
    pinLayer.add(SOUTH, dialog);
    revalidate();
    ok.addActionListener(ee -> {
        dialog.remove();
        revalidate();
    });
    pay.addActionListener(ee -> {
        dialog.remove();
        revalidate();
        PaymentService.sendPaymentAuthorization("" +
            car.currentRide.getLong());
    });
}
```

I've changed the OK button to pay with cash and added an option to pay with credit which essentially maps to Braintree

This implements the full payment process integration including credit card verification and everything involved...

11

With that the process of billing should work for the passenger on the devices. Notice that the braintree SDK doesn't work on the simulator so you would need to test it on the actual devices.

Social Login

11.2

We already prepared a lot of the groundwork for social login on the server but didn't finish all the pieces so, before I step into the client side changes needed for social login, let's discuss some of the required server-side work.

Listing 11. 10. Changes for Social Login in UserService

```java
public boolean existsByFacebook(String fb) {
    List<User> us = users.findByFacebookId(fb);
    return !us.isEmpty();
}

public boolean existsByGoogle(String google) {
    List<User> us = users.findByGoogleId(google);
    return !us.isEmpty();
}
```

We need to include support for the exists functionality that works based on a social token

I also had to include a similar call in the UserWebservice class:

Listing 11. 11. Changes for Social Login in UserWebservice

```java
@RequestMapping(method=RequestMethod.GET,value = "/exists")
public @ResponseBody boolean exists(String v) {
    return users.existsByPhone(v);
}

@RequestMapping(method=RequestMethod.GET,value = "/existsFacebook")
public @ResponseBody boolean existsFacebook(String v) {
    return users.existsByFacebook(v);
}

@RequestMapping(method=RequestMethod.GET,value = "/existsGoogle")
public @ResponseBody boolean existsGoogle(String v) {
    return users.existsByGoogle(v);
}
```

We have a small, subtle change to the regular exists method. The argument name was phone and is now v

v is used in all 3 methods which means we can invoke all 3 WebServices with very similar code on the client side

That's it. Pretty much everything else was already done.

Client Side

Social login lets us authenticate a user without getting into the username/password complexity. This is usually almost seamless on devices, where the preinstalled social app is invoked explicitly and the user just needs to "approve the permissions".

This is defined as a "low friction" approach to authenticate the user and is often superior to phone number activation. In Codename One this is pretty trivial to accomplish, especially for Google and Facebook login both of which are built into Codename One and Android/iOS respectively.

Connection to social networks in Codename One has several common concepts:

- If the device has native support, or the social app installed, this native integration will perform a login

- If it doesn't but we are on the device, the native SDK will show a web-based login

- If we are on the simulator we will fallback to an OAuth based login

This leads to a situation where login might work on one device but fail on the simulator, or fail on a different device type. It also makes the configuration process a bit more tedious. To be fair the native configuration is **much** harder and involves more code.

Troubleshooting Social Login

Push and Social login are some of the pain points of mobile development in general since they include multiple moving parts that are outside of your control. There are often cases of misconfiguration or missing pieces that sometimes break.

Both Google and Facebook constantly change the underlying UI/implementation in a way that breaks working code. The best thing to do is seek help online which you can do by asking a question in:

- StackOverflow: stackoverflow.com/tags/codenameone

- Discussion Forum: www.codenameone.com/discussion-forum.html

If you miss one small detail, this day can stretch into a week. Google and Facebook are unforgiving of even the tiniest mistake in this process, and getting this working the first time around can be challenging. My best advice is to go over things again and try to isolate where the issue happens. Then seek help if you can't get through.

Driver and User Apps

You will need to go through this process twice: Once for the driver app and once for the user app. You will then need to implement both copies of the properties file appropriately with the respective values.

Facebook Login

A core concept of the login process in Facebook is the "app", which is a Facebook internal term unrelated to your actual app. Facebook's view of an app is anything that uses the Facebook graph API and authentication. In this case we need to create a new app and should name it like we do our actual app so the user will be able to identify it.

The steps are pretty easy. We navigate to developers.facebook.com/apps/ and press the + Add a new app button.

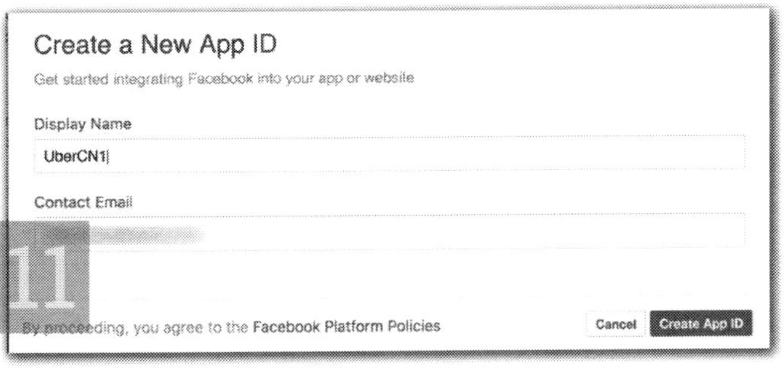

Figure 11. 2. Create a new Facebook App

Next we need to select the product we are trying to use and select Facebook login. Once there we are presented with a wizard containing multiple steps to set up your app.

You need to run through the wizard twice. Once for iOS and once for Android.

iOS Wizard

The content of the wizard changes but the gist is the same. We don't really need much information can skip almost everything...

These are the current steps for iOS:

1. Download and Install the Facebook SDK for iOS - this is obviously unnecessary for us so we can just press Next

2. Add Login Kit to your Xcode Project - Again there is no need to do anything click Next

3. Add your Bundle Identifier – We need to enter the project package name here and press Save then Next

4. Enable Single Sign On for Your App. This is up to you. I left it off and pressed Next

All the rest doesn't require any action, so you can skip it!

Android Wizard

The Android wizard has one task that is a bit challenging but other than that it should be trivial.

Before we begin we need to generate key hashes for facebook, which need to be done on your development machine. To do that you will need a command-line with the JDK's bin directory in your path. You will also need the path to the Android keystore you use for signing. You can find this file in the Android signing section in Codename One Settings. If there is no certificate file there, make sure to generate it as explained in the signing section in the first chapter.

Once all of this is in place you can use the following command for Linux/Mac:

Listing 11. 12. Linux/Mac Command to generate hash value

```
keytool –exportcert –alias YOUR_RELEASE_KEY_ALIAS –keystore YOUR_RELEASE_KEY_PATH |
     openssl sha1 –binary | openssl base64
```

Or for Windows:

Listing 11. 13. Windows Command to generate hash value

```
keytool –exportcert –alias androiddebugkey –keystore
     "C:\Users\USERNAME\.android\debug.keystore" | "PATH_TO_OPENSSL_LIBRARY\bin\openssl"
     sha1 –binary | "PATH_TO_OPENSSL_LIBRARY\bin\openssl" base64
```

These are the current steps on Android:

1. Download the Facebook SDK for Android - this is obviously unnecessary for us so we can just press Next

2. Import the Facebook SDK - Again there is no need to do anything Next

3. Tell Us about Your Android Project - We need to specify the package name for the application which, in our case, is com.codename1.apps.uberclone. We also need to specify the main class which is com.codename1.apps.uberclone.UberCN1Stub. The main class is effectively the main class name with the word "Stub" (case sensitive) appended at the end. Then press Next

4. Add Your Development and Release Key Hashes - you need to add the hash you got before and press Next

The rest isn't important.

integration

We need a few more values from the dashboard. You should see something like this:

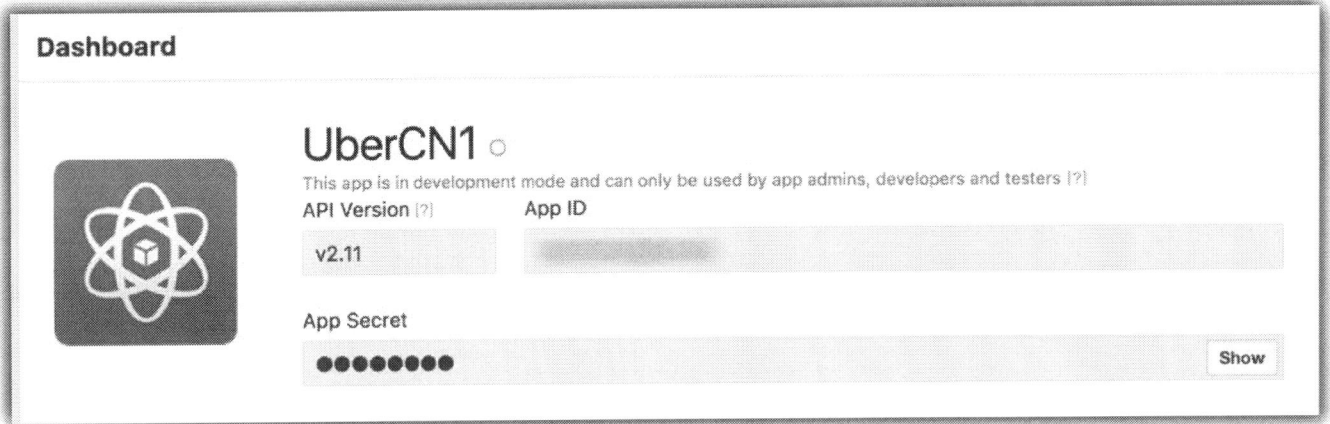

Dashboard

UberCN1 ○

This app is in development mode and can only be used by app admins, developers and testers [?]

API Version [?]   App ID

v2.11

App Secret

●●●●●●●●   Show

Figure 11. 3. The Details Needed for the Facebook App

To get the native login working we only need one step: Add the build hint facebook.appId=AppId.

ℹ Build hints can be customized via Codename One Settings as explained in Appendix D (page 413)

Where AppId is the id from the dashboard above. This will make Facebook work on the devices.

11❗ *You need to set 2 values*
One value in the User properties and one in the Driver properties file

To get login working on the simulator we'll need a bit more. We'll also need to write code that supports the login process within the FacebookOrGoogleLoginForm class.

Listing 11. 14. Changes Required for Facebook Login in FacebookOrGoogleLoginForm

FacebookConnect is a subclass of the Login class that lets us login into facebook and request publish permissions if necessary

```
facebook.addActionListener(e -> {
    final Login fb = FacebookConnect.getInstance();
    if(UberClone.isDriverMode()) {
        fb.setClientId("value for driver app");
        fb.setClientSecret("value for driver app");
    } else {
        fb.setClientId("value for user app");
        fb.setClientSecret("value for user app");
    }
    fb.setRedirectURI("https://www.codenameone.com/");
    fb.setCallback(new LoginCallback() {
        public void loginFailed(String errorMessage) {
            ToastBar.showErrorMessage("Login failed: " + errorMessage);
        }
```

The client id and secret aren't used on devices. These are here strictly for the simulator! If you don't need to test on the simulator these lines are redundant... We have two versions of these values for the User app and driver app

The callback is invoked upon login. If a login is successful we get the token from facebook which is an "authorization token". This allows us to access information within the Facebook graph API to query facts about the user. Notice we have a new constructor for EnterPasswordForm which I will discuss later

```
        public void loginSuccessful() {
            String token = fb.getAccessToken().getToken();
            Response<Map> resp = Rest.get(
                "https://graph.facebook.com/v2.12/me").
                queryParam("access_token", token).
                acceptJson().getAsJsonMap();
            String userId = (String)resp.getResponseData().get("id");
            new EnterPasswordForm(null, token, null).show();
        }
    });
    fb.doLogin();
});
```

Facebooks tokens can change and can be revoked, we need to fetch the user ID which is permanent and we can do that with the with the me REST request

This triggers the actual login but the method is asynchronous and login will only actually succeed or fail when the callback is reached

Full Integration

Before we go to the Google login support lets look at the additional changes we need to get both Facebook and Google working. I already discussed the changes to `EnterPasswordForm` so lets start there:

Listing 11. 15. Changes to EnterPasswordForm for Social login (snipped)

The constructor accepts one of the 3 options the other two should be null in this case

```
public EnterPasswordForm(String phoneNumber,String facebookId,String googleId) {
    super(new BorderLayout());
    Form previous = getCurrentForm();
    InfiniteProgress ip = new InfiniteProgress();
    Dialog dlg = ip.showInfiniteBlocking();
    boolean exists=UserService.userExists(phoneNumber,facebookId,googleId);
    // ... same code as before snipped ...
    fab.addActionListener(e -> {
        Dialog ipDlg = new InfiniteProgress().showInfiniteBlocking();
        if(exists) {
            UserService.login(phoneNumber, facebookId, googleId,
                password.getText(), (value) -> {
                MapForm.get().show();
            }, (sender, err, errorCode, errorMessage) -> {
                ipDlg.dispose();
                error.setText("Login error");
                error.setVisible(true);
                revalidate();
            });
        } else {
```

We also update the UserService method accordingly, we'll get into that shortly

The login method now accepts the Google/Facebook credentials as an optional argument

```
if(UserService.addNewUser(new User().phone.set(phoneNumber).
    facebookId.set(facebookId).googleId.set(googleId).
    password.set(password.getText()).
    driver.set(UberClone.isDriverMode())))) {
   MapForm.get().show();
} else {
   ipDlg.dispose();
   error.setText("Signup error");
   error.setVisible(true);
   revalidate();
}
}
});
}
```

Two of the three values for identification will be null so we can set all of them and only one will have a value

Next lets see the changes to the `UserService` class:

Listing 11. 16. Changes to the UserService class for Social Login

This is the main method we use which
we broke up for the other types

```java
public static boolean userExists(String phoneNumber, String facebookId,
        String googleId) {
    if(phoneNumber != null) return userExistsPhone(phoneNumber);
    if(facebookId != null) return userExistsFacebook(facebookId);
    return userExistsGoogle(googleId);
}
public static boolean userExistsPhone(String phoneNumber) {
    return userExistsImpl("user/exists", phoneNumber);
}
public static boolean userExistsFacebook(String phoneNumber) {
    return userExistsImpl("user/existsFacebook", phoneNumber);
}
public static boolean userExistsGoogle(String phoneNumber) {
    return userExistsImpl("user/existsGoogle", phoneNumber);
}
private static boolean userExistsImpl(String url, String val) {
    Response<byte[]> b = Rest.get(SERVER_URL + url).
            acceptJson().
            queryParam("v", val).getAsBytes();
    if(b.getResponseCode() == 200) return b.getResponseData()[0]==(byte)'t';
    return false;
}
```

This generic implementation
demonstrates why we
changed the argument name
from phone to v so it can now
suite all the permutations of
this method

This is the t from the word true

11

Listing 11. 16. Changes to the UserService class for Social Login

```java
public static void login(String phoneNumber, String facebookId,
        String googleId, String password, SuccessCallback<User> onSuccess,
        final FailureCallback<Object> onError) {
    Rest.get(SERVER_URL + "user/login").
        acceptJson().
        queryParam("password", password).
        queryParam("phone", phoneNumber).
        queryParam("facebookId", facebookId).
        queryParam("googleId", googleId).
        getAsJsonMapAsync(new Callback<Response<Map>>() {
            // ... this code was unchanged ...
    });
}
```

Login is almost identical to the original code. I added the new values to the mix. If they are null the arguments won't be sent and everything will work as expected

Once this is done Facebook login should work on the device and simulator.

11

Google Login

The process for Google is pretty similar:

- First we need to access the Google Developer Portal at developers.google.com/mobile/add and follow the steps to create an app for "Google Sign-In". Notice we need to run through the process 4 times: once for Android, once for iOS, and again for the driver app

- For both Android and iOS you will receive a file at the end of the process. For iOS you will receive a file named GoogleService-Info.plist and for Android you will receive a file named google-services.json

- Notice that in the Android version you need the SHA1 value similarly to the Facebook process

- Save GoogleService-Info.plist into the native/ios directory in your project hierarchy

- Save google-services.json into the native/android directory in your project hierarchy

That will enable native login. To get the values used in the client code you should login to the Google Cloud Platform console console.cloud.google.com/apis. There you will need to follow these steps:

- In the top portion of the browser make sure the correct app name is selected (e.g. UberCN1)

- Select the Credentials menu

- Find the Web Client entry and click it. You should see the Client ID and Client Secret values there

- In the "Authorized redirect URIs" section, you will need to enter the URL to the page that the user will be sent to after a successful login. This page will only appear in the simulator for a split second, as Codename One's BrowserComponent will intercept this request to obtain the access token upon successful login. You can use any URL you like here, but it must match the value you give to GoogleConnect.setRedirectURL() in the code

Once all of this is in place we can add the code to handle the Google login process:

Listing 11. 17. Changes Required for Google Login in FacebookOrGoogleLoginForm

```
google.addActionListener(e -> {
   Login gc = GoogleConnect.getInstance();
   if(UberClone.isDriverMode()) {
      gc.setClientId("value for driver app");
      gc.setClientSecret("value for driver app");
   } else {
      gc.setClientId("-------.apps.googleusercontent.com");
      gc.setClientSecret("------");
   }
   gc.setRedirectURI("https://www.codenameone.com/login");
   GoogleConnect.getInstance().setCallback(new LoginCallback() {
      public void loginFailed(String errorMessage) {
         ToastBar.showErrorMessage("Login failed: " + errorMessage);
      }
      public void loginSuccessful() {
         String token = GoogleConnect.getInstance().
            getAccessToken().getToken();
         Response<Map> resp = Rest.
            get("https://www.googleapis.com/plus/v1/people/me").
            header("Authorization", "Bearer " + token).
            acceptJson().getAsJsonMap();
         String userId = (String)resp.getResponseData().get("id");
         new EnterPasswordForm(null, null, userId).show();
      }
   });
   GoogleConnect.getInstance().doLogin();
});
```

We could have made this generic as both Google and Facebook login derive the Login class

We get the user id to match the given token from the google WebService

11

You'll notice that the code is almost identical to the Facebook login code. In fact both GoogleConnect and FacebookConnect derive the Login class which means we can write very generic login code, at least in theory.

Summary

In this chapter, we learned:

- In-app purchase is one of the big ticket features in mobile apps. Codename One supports this rather well but we can't use in-app purchase for this case

- One of the core concepts when working with Braintree is opacity. The developer doesn't get access to the credit card or billing information. Instead a nonce and token are passed between the client and server

- If the device has native support or the social app installed, this native integration will perform a login

This day focused on external tools and integrations which are a crucial piece of every project. I could have spent more time discussing the graph API or extracting user data from Facebook to fill in user details within the app but most of that is just more REST calls with the token we got from Facebook/Google respectively.
I think we covered enough of that so there isn't as much of a need.

As a whole, the day wasn't hard on the technical front but if you actually go through the process and try to get it to work you will understand why I allocated a full day for this... It's hard due to configuration hell.

11

Day 7: Transitions and Refinement

This chapter covers:

- Rendering the pattern in the LoginForm with repeating Shape objects
- Animating the LoginForm with background rotation
- Using the Morph and Cover Transitions. Preventing Cover from colliding with other transitions
- Saving user settings and managing them through the UI
- Photo capture and upload for the user avatar image

The app has been pretty functional for the last couple of days and there isn't much left to do. In this final day I will focus on a few additional symbolic refinements so the app will feel a bit more complete. These refinements can be divided into two parts:

- Functionality - we will add some forms that let the user configure application settings
- Animations - transitions and animations create a more fluid UI that forms an emotional bond with the user

Animations are often seen as fluff but in reality they serve a crucial role of continuity within the UI. E.g. when a user navigates to a new form the old form slides away to the left. But when we go back it slides back in from the left to the right. Subtle hints like that help users form a connection with the UI and a deeper understanding of the actions they take.

Login Form Rotation Animation

The Android version doesn't include the rotation animation of the LoginForm for reasons that are just unclear to me. I think it might collide with some of the material design transitions or some other problem. It works nicely on all OS's with the way I implemented it.

I could just rotate the tiles and call it a day, the effect would look decent and perform well. However, I want better control and in order to get that I need shapes...

Shapes allow us to draw arbitrary vectors/curves in a performant way. Since this is effectively a vector API, rotation and scaling don't distort the result. In order to use this API I need to use the low level graphics API and the background painter.

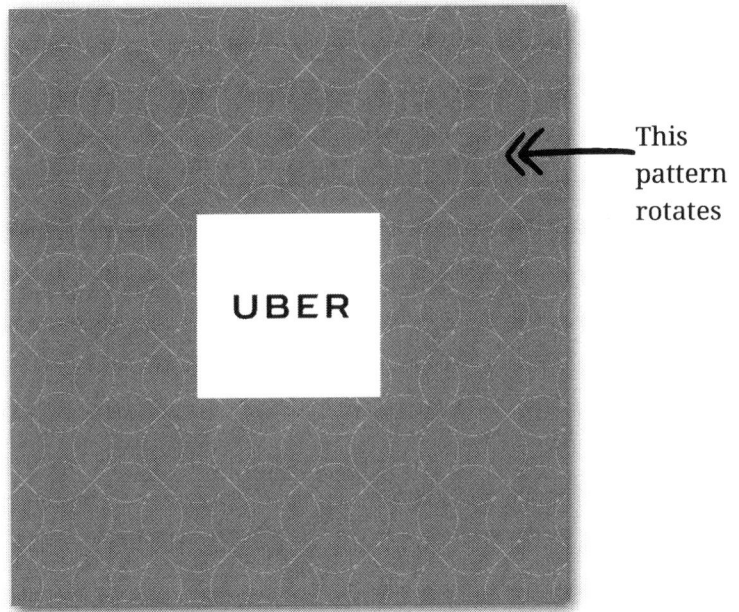

Figure 12. 1. The Pattern that Rotates

Background Painters

Styling can only go so far. If you want to customize the background of a component in a completely custom way you can use the Painter API to define the actual rendering of the background. This overrides all style rendering and provides you with a Graphics object you can use for drawing.

Notice that the Graphics API is a low level API and might have platform specific behaviors that aren't as refined as the component/style API's. It's harder to optimize low level graphics code so use it with caution.

We can set the painter for the logo object using:

Listing 12. 1. LoginForm Setting the painter

```
logo.getUnselectedStyle().setBgPainter(new LoginFormPainter(logo));
```

Notice that normally we don't need a reference to the parent component (logo) but in this case we need it for the animation. Next we'll go into the LoginFormPainter inner class. Since it's a relatively big class, I'll split it into smaller pieces:

Listing 12. 2. LoginForm The Painter Inner Class and Constructor

The rotation angle in degrees. We increment this as part of the animation logic. I set this to -1 by default so the first iteration of paint will draw the content

```java
class LoginFormPainter implements Painter, Animation {
    private double angle = -1;
    private final GeneralPath gp = new GeneralPath();
    private final Component parentCmp;
    private int counter;

    public LoginFormPainter(Component parentCmp) {
        this.parentCmp = parentCmp;
        int x;
        int y;
        int w = Display.getInstance().convertToPixels(10);
        int h = w;
        int x0 = getX() - getWidth();
        int xn = getX() + 2 * getWidth();
        int y0 = getY() - getHeight();
        int yn = getY() + 2 * getHeight();
        for (int offset : new int[]{0, w/2}) {
            x = x0 +offset;
            y = y0 + offset;
            while (x < xn) {
                while (y < yn) {
                    drawShape(gp, x, y, w, h);
                    y += h;
                }
                x += w;
                y = y0 + offset;
            }
        }
        registerAnimated(this);
    }
    // rest of code...
}
```

The shape object representing the background pattern. We draw it (or stroke it) like a rubber stamp

The constructor and drawShape create the pattern shape that we stroke later. This code happens once to generate the "lines" and we can then color them later on

The registerAnimated method of Form is needed for low level animations. It triggers invocations of the animate() method with every EDT tick so we can update the animation state, e.g. change the rotation angle

Listing 12. 3. LoginForm The Painter drawShape

```
private void drawShape(GeneralPath gp, float x, float y, float w,
              float h) {
    float e = w/6;
    float ex1 = x + (w-e)/2;
    float ex2 = x + (w+e)/2;
    float ey1 = y + (h-e)/2;
    float ey2 = y + (h+e)/2;
    gp.moveTo(ex1, y);
    gp.lineTo(ex2, y);
    gp.quadTo(x+w, y, x+w, ey1);
    gp.lineTo(x+w, ey2);
    gp.quadTo(x+w, y+h, ex2, y+h);
    gp.lineTo(ex1, y+h);
    gp.quadTo(x, y+h, x, ey2);
    gp.lineTo(x, ey1);
    gp.quadTo(x, y, ex1, y);
}
```

The drawShape method adds logical lines and quads to the given path. You can see three methods used on the path element

moveTo moves the virtual pen in the air without drawing anything to a starting point

lineTo draws a line from the last position of the pen to the given position

quadTo draws a quadratic curve (bezier curve) to the given position through the given curve position

Next we have the actual paint method which is a part of the Painter interface:

Listing 12. 4. LoginForm The Painter Paint Method

12

```
public void paint(Graphics g, Rectangle rect) {
    g.setAlpha(255);
    g.setColor(0x128f96);
    g.fillRect(rect.getX(), rect.getY(), rect.getWidth(),
        rect.getHeight());
    g.setColor(0xffffff);
    g.setAlpha(72);
    g.setAntiAliased(true);
    g.rotate((float)(Math.PI/4f + Math.toRadians(angle % 360)),
        getX() + getWidth()/2, getY() + getHeight()/2);
    g.drawShape(gp, new Stroke(1.5f, Stroke.CAP_SQUARE,
        Stroke.JOIN_BEVEL, 1f));
    g.resetAffine();
    g.setAlpha(255);
}
```

The paint method is the callback from the painter

We fill the background, rotate the graphics context, and draw the shapes

Notice we just invoke drawShape and it is drawn with the current alpha and color in place

With that, drawing should work as it did with the tiled image. We can stop here and have behavior that's pretty similar to the original code. To animate the code we need to override the animate() method which handles the low level logic:

Listing 12. 5. LoginForm The Painter Animation Code

```
public boolean animate() {
    counter++;
    if(counter % 2 == 0) {
        angle += 0.1;
        parentCmp.repaint();
    }
    return false;
}

public void paint(Graphics g) {
}
```

The low level animation code invokes animate() at fixed intervals based on EDT "heart beats"

Notice that I only change the angle and move every other frame to conserve CPU

Also notice I rotate by 0.1 degrees which creates a very smooth, slow and subtle rotation

Normally we return true to trigger a repaint but here I only want to repaint a specific component

This paint method belongs to the Animation interface. We don't need it as we always return false

Once all of this is done the login UI rotates in the background slowly and smoothly.

Cover and Material Transition

I kept most of the default transitions and did a few animations along the way but I didn't spend too much time on either one of those.

By default Codename One uses the slide or slide+fade transitions. These should look decent for the most part but I want to demonstrate and discuss some of the nuanced transitions in the Uber app.

12.2.1

Morph Transitions

In the native Uber app transitions look a bit different between iOS and Android. I didn't go there because I don't think this was done on purpose. In Android's material design, a common transition pattern is one where we move an element from one view to the next; and, indeed this is what we have between the LoginForm and the EnterMobileNumberForm.

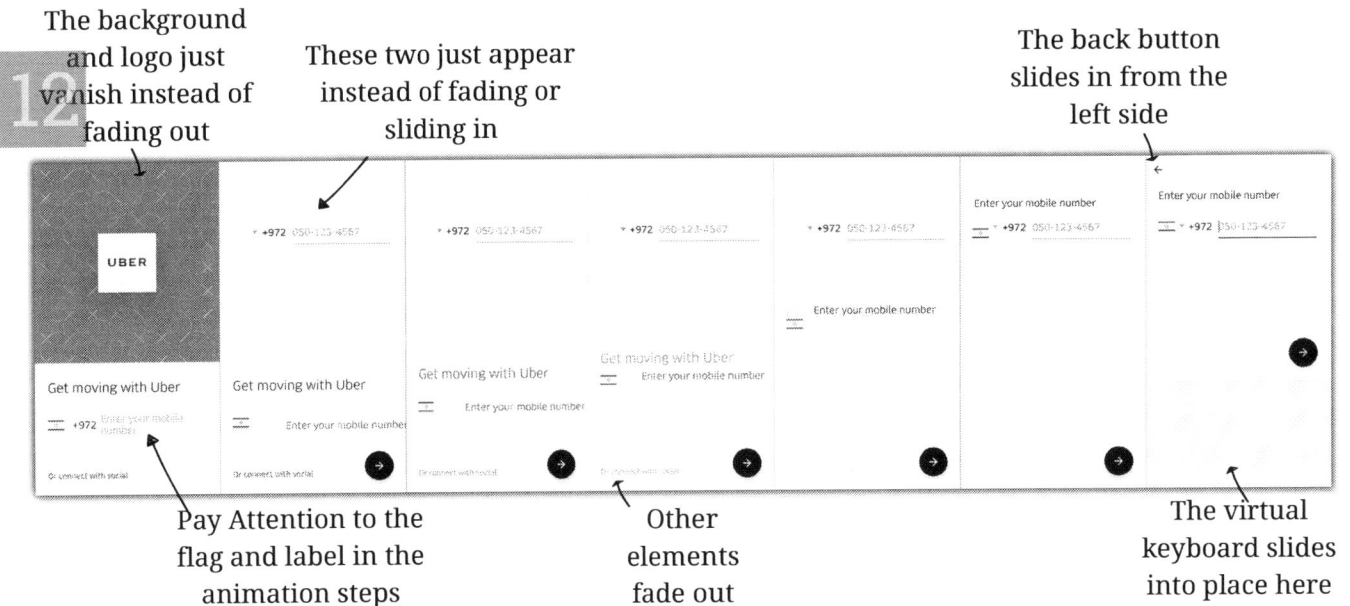

The background and logo just vanish instead of fading out

These two just appear instead of fading or sliding in

The back button slides in from the left side

Pay Attention to the flag and label in the animation steps

Other elements fade out

The virtual keyboard slides into place here

Figure 12. 2. Uber's native Android app transition

As you can see, the Enter your mobile number and flag elements animate to the place in the next form while other elements fade out/in respectively. This transition repeats itself in reverse when we press back. There are a couple of things that might not be immediately obvious when you look at this:

- The background pattern instantly disappears instead of fading - this might be on purpose but it doesn't look good

- This is a bit hard to see as it happens relatively quickly but the back arrow slides in from the left

Codename One has a MorphTransition which doesn't include the slide in/out option for some elements. It does allow components from one Form to "slide" into the next Form but doesn't support a brand new component sliding in. It only supports the fade in/out of these elements so we'll pass on that aspect. I chose to fade the background pattern in/out as it looks much better, I'm not sure why Uber chose not to do that.

Transitions are decoupled from the forms or components that they transition. This allows us to define a transition regardless of the contents of a Form. In order to use the MorphTransition we need to communicate to it the components we'd like to animate but they might not be instantiated at this time yet... So we need to use component names. If the components on both forms have the same name we can make the code even shorter.

So we can perform the transition using this code in LoginForm:

Listing 12. 6. MorphTransition in LoginForm

```
phoneNumber.setName("EnterMobileNumber");
countryCodeButton.setName("CountryCodeButton");
MorphTransition morph = MorphTransition.create(400).
    morph(phoneNumber.getName()).
    morph(countryCodeButton.getName());
setTransitionOutAnimator(morph);
```

We need to set the component names so morph will find the components

We can use getName() to avoid typing the name twice

We will obviously need the corresponding code in the EnterMobileNumberForm:

Listing 12. 7. EnterMobileNumberForm Morph In Code

```
Label mobileNumber = newLabel("Enter your mobile number", "FlagButton");
mobileNumber.setName("EnterMobileNumber");  ←————  Notice we set the names
add(mobileNumber);                                  to the identical values

CountryCodePicker countryCodeButton = new CountryCodePicker();
countryCodeButton.setName("CountryCodeButton");
```

We could have used different names and then just specified those different names in the morph method.

We also want morph to run in reverse when going back so the obvious thing to do is define a morph transition in the back command. But there is a nuance with the virtual keyboard:

Listing 12. 8. EnterMobileNumberForm Morph In Code

```
TextField phoneNumber = newTextField("", "050-123-4567", 40,
    TextField.PHONENUMBER);
getToolbar().setBackCommand("", Toolbar.BackCommandPolicy.AS_ARROW, e -> {
    MorphTransition morph = MorphTransition.create(400).
        morph("EnterMobileNumber").
        morph("CountryCodeButton");  ←———  Notice I used strings instead of getName
    setTransitionOutAnimator(morph);           as the back command is defined before
    if(phoneNumber.isEditing()) {              the components in the full code listing
        phoneNumber.stopEditing(() ->
        previous.showBack());
    } else {
        previous.showBack();
    }
});
```

This is one of those things that you only see on the device. The virtual keyboard opens when we enter the mobile number Form, so when we go back it looks a bit "weird" on Android

To stop the "weirdness" with the virtual keyboard and the animation we need to stop the editing.

Unfortunately just stopping isn't enough as this happens asynchronously. So we need to stop editing and use the callback to detect when the keyboard actually finished closing. Otherwise the transition will run before the form has had time to adjust.

The problem is that if you run this code it will fail badly... The background animation tries to repaint() while the transition is in progress...

The solution for that is a small, simple change to LoginFormPainter:

Listing 12. 9. Make LoginFormPainter more robust

```
@Override
public boolean animate() {
    if(!Display.getInstance().isInTransition()) {
        counter++;
        if(counter % 2 == 0) {
            angle += 0.3;
            parentCmp.repaint();
        }
    }
    return false;
}
```

I'm effectively blocking the rotation animation of the background during transitions which also makes the transition smoother as a result

Cover Transition

This code broke another thing, it broke the FacebookOrGoogleLoginForm which looks awful going in now because morph is generally designed for a specific Form...

I want to use the vertical cover effect which is common on iOS and looks pretty decent on Android too. Cover slides the Form on top of the existing Form from the bottom. It's usually combined with uncover which slides the Form out in the reverse way.

Because of this unique semantic the cover transition uses both the in and out transition flags. However, this can pose a problem with the default out transition of the Form that we are leaving. In this case you see the out animation of the login form (morph) followed by the incoming cover animation.

Listing 12. 10. Cover Transitions in FacebookOrGoogleLoginForm

Notice the first transition is cover and the second is uncover.
Also notice the direction is reversed (the boolean flag)

```
setTransitionInAnimator(CommonTransitions.
   createCover(CommonTransitions.SLIDE_VERTICAL, false, 300));
setTransitionOutAnimator(CommonTransitions.
   createUncover(CommonTransitions.SLIDE_VERTICAL, true, 300));
CommonCode.removeTransitionsTemporarily(previous);
```

I disable the other transition until the next Form is shown

The solution is to remove the out animation from the outgoing Form and restore it to the original value when we get back. We do that within the removeTransitionsTemporarily method:

Listing 12. 11. removeTransitionsTemporarily

```
public static void removeTransitionsTemporarily(final Form f) {
   final Transition originalOut = f.getTransitionOutAnimator();
   final Transition originalIn =
      f.getTransitionInAnimator();
   f.setTransitionOutAnimator(CommonTransitions.createEmpty());
   f.setTransitionInAnimator(CommonTransitions.createEmpty());
   f.addShowListener(new ActionListener() {
      @Override
      public void actionPerformed(ActionEvent evt) {
         f.setTransitionOutAnimator(originalOut);
         f.setTransitionInAnimator(originalIn);
         f.removeShowListener(this);
      }
   });
}
```

We need to remove both the in and out transitions as we might show a cover transition on top of another cover transition Form

When we return to the original Form we restore its transitions to their original values

We remove the show listener to prevent a memory leak and multiple restore calls when going back and forth

374

We also need to add a small nuance to initBlackTitleForm in CommonCode. We need to add a call to removeTransitionsTemporarily as that code also uses cover transition:

Listing 12. 12. initBlackTitleForm Cover Transition

```
public static Button initBlackTitleForm(Form f, String title,
        SuccessCallback<String> searchResults) {
    Form backTo = getCurrentForm();
    f.getContentPane().setScrollVisible(false);
    Button back = new Button("", "TitleCommand");
    removeTransitionsTemporarily(backTo);   ⟵   Removes the previous transition to
                                                 make this UI work for all cases

    // the rest is the same
}
```

Now that this is in place, the cover transition should work seamlessly regardless of the transitions used by the calling Form.

Circle Animated FloatingActionButton   12.3

Animations often evolve in close proximity to the final application. I didn't want to spend too much time building up things that are overly specific to Uber's design as you have to throw them away anyway. One Uber specific animation that I liked a lot is a blue highlight circle around the FloatingActionButton. This is Android specific for Uber. On iOS they have a circle but it's inside the FloatingActionButton, I'm guessing this has more to do with the implementation than a deliberate design choice.

This is pretty easy to implement. The round border allows us to stroke the border with any color and to any angle. Thanks to this feature the implementation of this animation is trivial. It's still a bit large for a single listing so I've split this to two listings:

Listing 12. 13. The FabProgress Class and Constructor

```java
public class FabProgress {
    private UITimer timer;
    private Motion angle;
    private String originalUiid;
    private Stroke stroke;
    private FabProgress(FloatingActionButton fab) {
        originalUiid = fab.getUIID();
```

The class has a private constructor associated with the FloatingActionButton. We create instances of this class by using the bind method

We need the existing UIID of the FloatingActionButton which might be different from the default. We change the Style object directly and use the UIID to restore the default

The animation stroke and speed are hardcoded to 0.5mm stroke and 1.5 second per progress rotation. This can be manipulated to create a more deterministic progress indicator

```java
        stroke = new Stroke(convertToPixels(0.5f), Stroke.CAP_SQUARE
            Stroke.JOIN_MITER, 1);
        angle = Motion.createEaseInMotion(0,360,1500);
        angle.start();
        timer = UITimer.timer(30, true, fab.getComponentForm(), () -> {
            int ang = angle.getValue();
            if(angle.isFinished()) {
                angle = Motion.createEaseInMotion(0, 360, 1500);
                angle.start();
            }
            updateFabStyle(fab.getUnselectedStyle(), ang);
            updateFabStyle(fab.getSelectedStyle(), ang);
        }); updateFabStyle(fab.getPressedStyle(), ang);
            fab.repaint();

    }
    // ... rest of the methods ...
}
```

We use a timer every 30 milliseconds to update the UI. Notice that if a timer runs too fast it will be throttled and invoked much later

Lets review the rest of the methods in the class:

Listing 12. 14. FabProgress Methods

```java
private void updateFabStyle(Style s, int angle) {
    RoundBorder rb = (RoundBorder)s.getBorder();
    s.setBorder(rb.stroke(stroke).
        strokeColor(0x297aa7).
        strokeOpacity(255).
        strokeAngle(angle));
}

public static void bind(FloatingActionButton fab) {
    FabProgress ff = new FabProgress(fab);
    fab.putClientProperty("$internFabProgress", ff);
}
public static void stop(FloatingActionButton fab){
    FabProgress fp = (FabProgress)fab.
        getClientProperty("$internFabProgress");
    if(fp != null) {
        fp.timer.cancel();
        fab.setUIID(fp.originalUiid);
        fab.repaint();
    }
}
```

We update all 3 styles individually instead of using getAllStyles. The main reason is preserving the uniqueness of each style

bind starts the timer and sets the animation on. We store the instance of this class in a client property so we can stop the animation later

When stopping the animation we also set the UIID again to reset all the changes that were made to the Style objects

12

Unlike the other animations we've had, I took the radically different approach of using the UITimer and the style. If a timer is throttled it won't make much of a difference since we use Motion to determine the actual speed of progress. Every time the Motion finishes a cycle we start again from scratch to give the feel of an infinite progress.

UITimer Runs on the EDT

I used UITimer instead of Timer as it makes sure to run the callbacks directly on the event dispatch thread so there is no need for callSerially

I've added this to the code in EnterPasswordForm so the progress indication appears there. I essentially replaced all of the code that referred to InfiniteProgress with FabProgress.

Listing 12. 15. EnterPasswordForm FabProgress integration

```
fab.addActionListener(e -> {                          This used to be an InfiniteProgress
  FabProgress.bind(fab);  <─────────────             and I just dropped this in
  if(exists) {
    UserService.login(phoneNumber, facebookId, googleId,
         password.getText(), (value) -> {
      MapForm.get().show();
    }, (sender, err, errorCode, errorMessage) -> {
      FabProgress.stop(fab);  <─────────            I can stop instead of disposing
      error.setText("Login error");                 the InfiniteProgress
      error.setVisible(true);
      revalidate();
    });
  } else {
    if(UserService.addNewUser(new User().
         phone.set(phoneNumber).
         facebookId.set(facebookId).
         googleId.set(googleId).
         password.set(password.getText()).
         driver.set(UberClone.isDriverMode()))) {
      MapForm.get().show();
    } else {
      FabProgress.stop(fab);
      error.setText("Signup error");
      error.setVisible(true);
      revalidate();
    }
  }
});
```

Once we make these changes we'll see the blue progress bar around the FloatingActionButton instead of the default InfiniteProgress I used before.

User Information

Up until now the app focused on a very narrow use case and the side menu was just for show. I won't fill up the entire app, as the full Uber app is very wide and nuanced, but I want to add a few essential UI elements to show just how easy it is and how much work we already did in the server to prepare ourselves for this...

The Uber signup process prompts the user for details, which is a nuance we skipped early on. I won't rectify it but I will map the menu item for Settings to show the SettingsForm; and I'll map a click on the user's avatar to the EditAccountForm:

Listing 12. 16. constructSideMenu Changes for Settings and Account

```
public static void constructSideMenu(Toolbar tb) {
    Button userAndAvatar = new Button("Shai Almog", "AvatarBlock");
    userAndAvatar.setIcon(getAvatar(i -> userAndAvatar.setIcon(i)));
    userAndAvatar.setGap(convertToPixels(3));
    userAndAvatar.addActionListener(e ->
        new EditAccountForm().show());          ← A new EditAccountForm
    tb.addComponentToSideMenu(userAndAvatar);      to show user settings

    // this code didn't change

    tb.addCommandToSideMenu("Settings", null, e ->
        new SettingsForm().show());      ← Added a new SettingsForm for more
                                            generic app information
    // this code didn't change either

}
```

This means we need to add two new forms: SettingsForm and EditAccountForm.

Settings Form

I didn't take the full UI of the SettingsForm and didn't implement everything. However, the basic design is there and it should provide a good framework for additional forms in this application.

This is encapsulated in the following code:

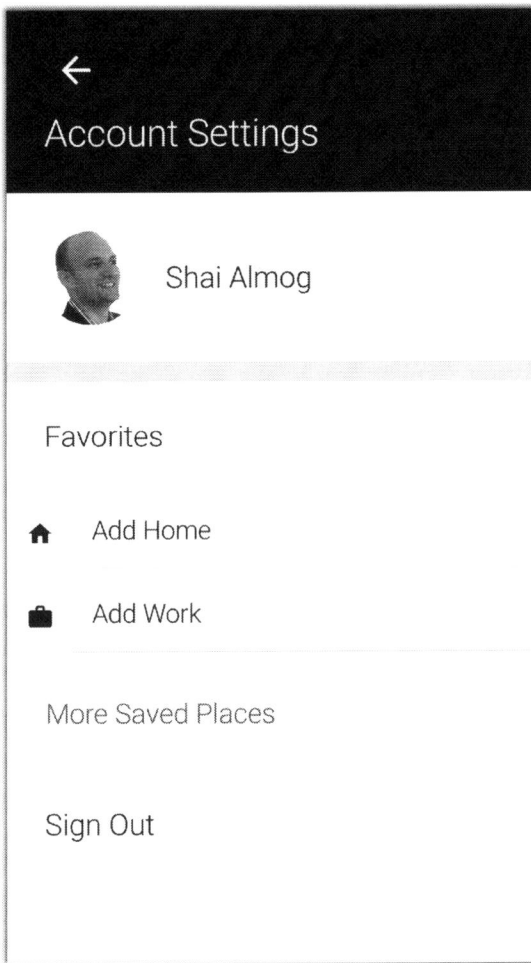

Figure 12. 3. The SettingsForm UI

12

Listing 12. 17. SettingsForm

This is the standard header for forms with the black title. It initializes the UI and adds the scroll down collapse effect. We defined this method before and it hasn't changed

```
public class SettingsForm extends Form {
    public SettingsForm() {
        super(BoxLayout.y());
        CommonCode.initBlackTitleForm(this, "Account Settings",null); ①
        Button userAndAvatar = new Button("Shai Almog", "Label");
```

We changed getAvatar to return an Image as a callback. This can happen if the image wasn't downloaded yet from the server

```java
userAndAvatar.setIcon(CommonCode.getAvatar(i->userAndAvatar.setIcon(i)));
userAndAvatar.setGap(convertToPixels(3));
userAndAvatar.addActionListener(e -> new EditAccountForm().show());
MultiButton addHome=CommonCode.createEntry(MATERIAL_HOME,"Add Home");
MultiButton addWork=CommonCode.createEntry(MATERIAL_WORK,"Add Work");
Button moreSavedPlaces =
    new Button("More Saved Places", "ConnectWithSocialButton");
Button signOut = new Button("Sign Out", "Label");
signOut.addActionListener(e -> {
    if(Dialog.show("Sign Out","Are you sure?","Sign Out","Cancel")){
        UserService.logout();
        new LoginForm().show();
    }
});
```

The rest of the code is mostly UI mockup meant to replicate some of the UI elements in the Uber app. Most of these things aren't challenging. Notice that I have new createEntry methods in CommonCode. I refactored them from the CompletionContainer as is

```java
    addAll(userAndAvatar, CommonCode.createSeparator(),
        new Label("Favorites"),addHome,addWork,moreSavedPlaces,signOut);
    }
    protected void initGlobalToolbar() {
        super.initGlobalToolbar();
        getToolbar().setUIID("BlackToolbar");
    }
}
```

12

We added a relatively trivial createSeparator method which we'll reuse later in EditAccountForm as well

For completeness this is the createSeparator method from CommonCode

Listing 12. 18. createSeparator

```java
public static Label createSeparator() {
    Label sep = new Label("", "WhereSeparator");
    sep.setShowEvenIfBlank(true);
    return sep;   ←——————┐  It's just a Label with the
}                         │  WhereSeparator UIID
```

There isn't much to discuss about that method so lets move on to the next step.

The next step is a review of the changes to the getAvatar method:

Listing 12. 19. The getAvatar Method

```java
private static Image avatar;
public static Image getAvatar(SuccessCallback<Image> avatarChanged) {
    if(avatar == null) {
        int size = convertToPixels(10);
        Image temp = Image.createImage(size, size, 0xff000000);
        Graphics g = temp.getGraphics();
        g.setAntiAliased(true);
        g.setColor(0xffffff);
        g.fillArc(0, 0, size, size, 0, 360);   ←——
        Object mask = temp.createMask();
        UserService.fetchAvatar(i -> {   ←——
            avatar = i.fill(size, size).applyMask(mask);
            avatarChanged.onSucess(avatar);
        });
```

Most of the code is the same as it was before. We still need the mask object, regardless of the outcome, as we will need to mask an image avatar from the server too

The fetchAvatar method might fetch the avatar image from local storage or download it from the internet. When it's done it will invoke the callback method with the image object

Listing 12. 19. The getAvatar Method

If the image was fetched from local storage the avatar might already be there so we don't need to do anything else. Otherwise we can continue with the same code we had before in the getAvatar method

```
    if(avatar != null) return avatar;
    Style s = new Style();
    s.setFgColor(0xc2c2c2);
    s.setBgTransparency(255);
    s.setBgColor(0xe9e9e9);
    FontImage x=FontImage.createMaterial(MATERIAL_PERSON, s, size);
    avatar = x.fill(size, size);
    if(avatar instanceof FontImage) avatar=((FontImage)avatar).toImage();
    avatar = avatar.applyMask(mask);
  }
  return avatar;
}
```

The reason we need to mask the image in the client is that only the client knows the size of the image it needs. This will also give the server flexibility in the future to increase image resolution/size. At this time the server is oblivious to our device type but the client can size the image in millimeters so it will have dimensions that fit.

Now lets look at the fetchAvatar method in UserService which we used in that code:

Listing 12. 20. fetchAvatar in UserService

```
public static void fetchAvatar(
    SuccessCallback<Image> callback) {
    fetchAvatar(me.id.getLong(), callback);
}
```

We have two variants of the method, one accepts the ID of the user whose avatar we are fetching and the other one uses our ID

In this case it fetches the avatar of the current user

This method is more generic in purpose and can fetch the avatar of any user

```
public static void fetchAvatar(long id, SuccessCallback<Image> callback) {
    ConnectionRequest cr = new ConnectionRequest(
        SERVER_URL + "user/avatar/" + id, false);
```

This is a WebService I already mapped in the server code a while back. The image is returned for the user with the given id in the path

```
    cr.setFailSilently(true);
```

A new user won't have an avatar and we will get a 404 response which is 100% valid for this case. Without this line we get a default error prompt which we don't want

```
    cr.downloadImageToStorage("avatarImage-" + id, callback);
}
```

This method automatically downloads/caches the image

12

downloadImageToStorage from ConnectionRequest checks if an image already exists in storage under the given name and, if so, invokes the callback with that image object. Otherwise it:

1. Adds the download request to the queue

2. Downloads the image to the storage file name

3. Loads it and invokes callback with that image object

Right now I only use the fetchAvatar method that doesn't take the ID. However, it should be trivial to show the image of the driver scheduled to pick us up next to his name.
All of this leads us to the one last piece missing from the SettingsForm: the EditAccountForm...

EditAccountForm

The native Uber app is a bit weird when it comes to account editing. When you want to edit any entry within the account you click on it and it sends you to a different Form where you can edit/save. I'm assuming there is some logic in that flow as it makes it harder to edit details by mistake. But it's not exactly intuitive.

I chose to just use text fields and map them automatically to the User object with the binding API. This makes everything really simple.

One caveat is that I didn't want to send user details for every minor change and only wanted to send that detail when going out of the Form to save on bandwidth noise. So I bound the actual save to the back button in a creative way.

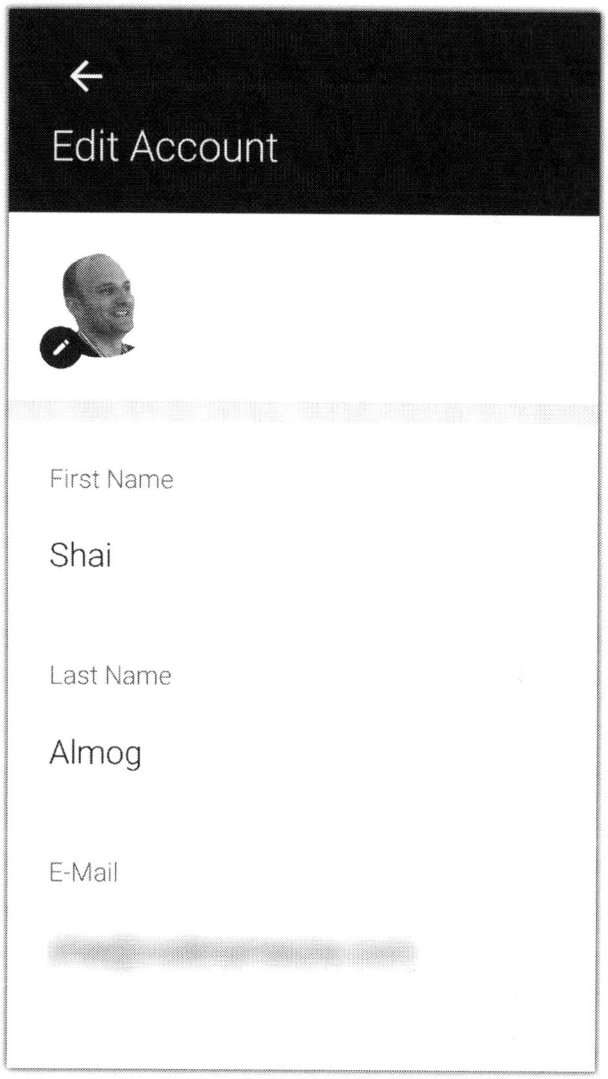

Figure 12. 4. The EditAccountForm UI

I need some additional changes to the networking layer for this functionality, but lets start with the EditAccountForm itself first. The class isn't very big but it's still easier to read when it's broken down to smaller pieces so I'll split it to three pieces:

Listing 12. 21. The EditAccountForm Class Body

Since the constructor is the largest block of code in this class, I separated it to the third listing

```java
public class EditAccountForm extends Form {
    private TextField createTextField(UiBinding uib, PropertyBase p,
            int constraint) {
        TextField t = new TextField("", "", 80, constraint);

        uib.bind(p, t);
        t.setUIID("Label");
        return t;
    }

    protected void initGlobalToolbar() {
        super.initGlobalToolbar();
        getToolbar().setUIID("BlackToolbar");
    }
    // ... rest of methods ...
}
```

This is a helper method for creating a text field and binding it

UiBinding automatically maps changes, back and forth, from a TextField to a property and vice versa

Text fields look like labels in the UI design

We override the Toolbar with the black styled variant

12

There are two additional methods in that class before we get to the constructor code:

Listing 12. 22. The EditAccountForm Remaining Methods

When we click on the avatar button in this Form we can open the camera to capture a new picture and set that as our avatar

```java
private Button createAvatarButton() {
    Button avatar = new Button("", "Label");
    avatar.setIcon(CommonCode.getAvatar(i -> avatar.setIcon(i)));
    avatar.addActionListener(e -> {
        String file = Capture.capturePhoto(512, -1);
        if(file != null) {
            avatar.setIcon(CommonCode.setAvatar(file));
            UserService.setAvatar(file);
        }
    });
    return avatar;
}
```

Notice that we set the image to be 512 pixels wide. The -1 argument indicates we want to maintain aspect ratio for the height

There are two setAvatar methods. We'll explain why when covering the methods themselves

```java
private Label createEditLabel() {
    Label edit = new Label("", "Container");
    Style s = edit.getUnselectedStyle();
    s.setMarginUnit(Style.UNIT_TYPE_DIPS);
    s.setPaddingUnit(Style.UNIT_TYPE_DIPS);
    s.setMargin(3, 3, 3, 3);
    s.setPadding(1, 1, 1, 1);
    s.setFgColor(0xffffff);
    s.setBgTransparency(0);
    FontImage.setMaterialIcon(edit, FontImage.MATERIAL_EDIT, 2f);
    s.setBorder(RoundBorder.create().color(0).opacity(255).
        rectangle(false).shadowOpacity(0));
    return edit;
}
```

This is the small circle on top of the avatar image indicating that it can be clicked. We used a label, and style it in code

The padding makes the circle bigger and the margin positions it on top of the image

12

We need to limit picture width to 512 pixels since the server limits the sizes of files it can receive. We can customize that in Spring Boot settings but it's not a good idea to overdo the size as it could be an attack vector (denial of service by submitting large files).

I use the UiBinding code to bind the User object to the text fields. This will automatically update the Preferences whenever the user types in a text field, as the properties of the User object will change. Notice that the text fields get their values automatically from the User object too as the binding works both ways.

Now lets look at the body of the constructor:

Listing 12. 23. The EditAccountForm Constructor Body

```
public EditAccountForm() {
    super(BoxLayout.y());
    CommonCodeinitBlackTitleForm(this, "Edit Account", null);
    Button avatar = createAvatarButton();
    Label edit = createEditLabel();
    Container avatarContainer = LayeredLayout.encloseIn(avatar,
        FlowLayout.encloseBottom(edit));
    User user = UserService.getUser();
    UiBinding uib = new UiBinding();



    String userString = user.getPropertyIndex().toString();
    TextField firstName =createTextField(uib,user.givenName,TextField.ANY);
    TextField surname = createTextField(uib, user.surname, TextField.ANY);
    TextField email =createTextField(uib, user.email, TextField.EMAILADDR);
    addAll(avatarContainer, CommonCode.createSeparator(),
        new Label("First Name","GrayLabel"), firstName,
        new Label("Last Name","GrayLabel"), surname,
        new Label("E-Mail","GrayLabel"), email
    );
    final Form previous = getCurrentForm();
```

We position the edit circle on top of the avatar using the LayeredLayout where we place the image below and enclose the edit label in a FlowLayout to push it down

We only want to save a user if the data within the user changed. We'll use the toString value of the User object later to compare it to the current value. If the values differ then the User object was changed. Notice that toString() is overridden in the User class

Data is saved when the user leaves this Form. There is only one way out: back. We can detect the return to the previous form and save the data to the server there

```
previous.addShowListener(new ActionListener() {
    public void actionPerformed(ActionEvent evt) {
        previous.removeShowListener(this);
```

This statement is why we couldn't use the lambda shorthand syntax. Had we used the shorter syntax this would have mapped to EditAccountForm

```
        UiBinding.unbind(user);
        String newUserString = user.getPropertyIndex().toString();
        if(!newUserString.equals(userString)) UserService.editUser(user);
    }
});
}
```

Here we check that the User was modified as we explained before and send the data to the server asynchronously

It's important to unbind the object since the me object is a global object and if we keep the binding it can cause a memory leak

Without the unbind() call we'd get a memory leak. The User object will reference the binding, which references the text fields. The text fields include the entire Form hierarchy indirectly etc.

Lets start with the easiest missing piece: editUser from UserService.

Listing 12. 24. editUser from UserService

```
public static void editUser(User u) {
    Rest.post(SERVER_URL + "user/add").
        jsonContent().
        body(u.getPropertyIndex().toJSON()).
        getAsStringAsync(new Callback<Response<String>>() {
    public void onSucess(Response<String> value) {
    }
    public void onError(Object sender, Throwable err,
        int errorCode, String errorMessage) {
    }
});
}
```

It's a standard JSON post request

On the server we have a single method for add/edit user: addEditUser. It's mapped to /user/add but it does edit too. We already have an addNewUser method in the client but that method is synchronous and we don't want a blocking call. That's why we need this version that works asynchronously.

Avatar

We have two separate methods for saving the avatar, the first one is in CommonCode it saves the avatar image to the local storage:

Listing 12. 25. setAvatar in CommonCode

```
public static Image setAvatar(String imageFile) {
    int size = convertToPixels(10);
    Image temp = Image.createImage(size, size, 0xff000000);
    Graphics g = temp.getGraphics();
    g.setAntiAliased(true);
    g.setColor(0xffffff);
    g.fillArc(0, 0, size, size, 0, 360);
    Object mask = temp.createMask();
    try {
        Image img = Image.createImage(imageFile);
        avatar = img.fill(size, size).applyMask(mask);
    } catch(IOException err) {
        Log.e(err);
    }
    return avatar;
}
```

This is the exact masking code we have in getAvatar. it might have made sense to extract it to a common method but the gist of it is simple. We need to mask the image

We mask and set the image to the variable instance that is used later by getAvatar

This is unlikely as we just grabbed the image...

We return this value so it can be updated into the UI instantly

12

Notice that this is all entirely local to my phone so we need to update the user account in the Spring Boot server. Again this relies on a method that we added a while back to the Spring Boot Server:

Listing 12. 26. setAvatar in UserService

MultipartRequest is a standard for file upload and it's used when you submit an html form tag over http with a file. It takes care of base64 encoding and related complexities almost seamlessly

```
public static void setAvatar(String imageFile) {
    try {
        MultipartRequest mp = new MultipartRequest();
        mp.setUrl(SERVER_URL + "user/updateAvatar/" + getToken());
        mp.addData("img", imageFile, "image/jpeg");
        addToQueue(mp);
```

Since Capture returned a file name, passing it is literally the simplest approach at this point

We need the token to write data. Notice we encode it in the URL instead of as an argument. Adding arguments to MultipartRequest is a bit challenging in Spring Boot and this was easier

```
    } catch(IOException err) {
        Log.e(err);
        ToastBar.showErrorMessage("Error uploading avatar file: " + err);
    }
}
```

And that's it. Avatar upload and download should now work!

Summary

12.5 12

In this chapter, we learned:

- Styling can only go so far. If you want to customize the background of a component in a completely custom way you can use the Painter API to define the actual rendering of the background

- Transitions are decoupled from the forms or components that they transition. This allows us to define a transition regardless of the contents of a Form

- Use UITimer instead of Timer as it makes sure to run the callbacks directly on the Event Dispatch Thread so there is no need for callSerially

- The reason we need to mask the image in the client is that only the client knows the size of the image it needs. This will also give the server flexibility in the future to increase image resolution/size

In this final day I focused on loose ends that are important not on their own but rather in terms of completeness. There is still a lot more I could have covered but most of the additional things would have been "more of the same".

In the next chapter I want to discuss the application as a whole and how you can move this forward.

12

Day 5: Summary and Moving Forward 13

Congratulations 13.1

We went through a lot of material in this book. If you followed through everything you should have the skill set to build a mobile startup MVP.

> MVP (Minimal Viable Product) is a common term from lean startup methodology commonly used in the process of proving the viability of a startup

We went through a long process of building a client/server application that communicates using webservices and websockets. This application stores the data in a highly scalable SQL database and uses a high-end enterprise-grade backend server.

On the client we built a UI that is very similar to one of the most popular applications ever made. In this application we implemented some of the most complicated features from authentication to map based tracking.

In total we built 4 apps:

- Hello World

- A Todo App

- The User Uber Clone

- The Driver App

I'm confident you can build a hundreds more...

Key Takeaways and Lessons Learned

I didn't expect to learn much when I started on this endeavor, I was wrong. A few things really surprised me. One such thing was the heavy usage of material design on iOS in the native Uber app.

Historically I always thought native widgets promoted engagement through familiarity. In fact, Chen (Fishbein co-founder of Codename One) and I used to argue about this constantly. I pushed towards a more "native widget feel" approach while Chen pushed towards a single UI for all platforms.

I always thought mobile apps should look very different in iOS and Android. We invested a lot of effort in making apps feel native and "different". This made a lot of sense to us in the days of Android 2.3 vs. iOS 4. Those two OS's made remarkably different design choices. However, things changed and Android has a back button on the top left part of the screen. A heresy during the days of Android 2.x. Convergence in the UI design seems to have shifted the paradigm.

It seems Uber sided with Chen. Uber has one UI design that is almost identical in iOS and Android. Using one design makes sense, as it enables them to reuse the design. E.g. they only need one screenshot to support both OS's in their training materials. As long as the app looks decent and everything is still in place, this is still intuitive.

To me, the biggest takeaway from the Uber app itself is that I think Uber follows function over form. The app looks good. But it's explicitly very minimal. The core functionality of the app is key.

One of the first big apps built with Codename One had a "flaky" UI (I'm not naming it here, I don't want to "app shame" anyone). It's a bit odd and performance isn't great because the engineer that wrote it did so before Codename One had any documentation or best practices. Despite that it has millions of installs and a 4.2 rating. It has amazing functionality and at the end of the day that's the most important thing.

Rapid Prototyping

I think the key for success in mobile apps, and in anything you do, is to move fast. Not because of some theoretical "first mover advantage"...

If you don't move fast you end up nitpicking over things that don't matter and never finish the important things. This is very much in line with the "lean startup" MVP philosophy. I've cut a lot of corners getting this app working, but it works. Frankly, I could have cut a lot of other corners to make it even better (rotation of background, tag border etc.).

Releasing often is crucial in the mobile world which revolves around appstores. Besides the obvious advantages of responsiveness to your users there is a huge additional benefit. When you release an update it gets featured in the "What's New" section in the store. Users who already have the app installed are reminded of it when the app is updated which helps boost active user count. Releasing often is one of the best forms of advertising.

Different Approaches and Next Steps 13.3

With any book there comes a point where we need to stop; otherwise it won't end. We covered a lot of ground. As a result there were things I avoided to keep the book readable and manageable.

Here are a few things I think you should look at as you journey past the subjects covered in the book.

TDD (Test Driven Development) 13.3.1

Codename One supports test recording and automation. It also supports continuous integration which lets you build native apps automatically with every commit to git then run the tests on physical devices in the cloud. That's very useful in preventing app regressions.

TDD is even more important when dealing with the backend server, we can make use of the separate tiers to test each tier in isolation. This helps us avoid regressions as we develop new features. Developing test cases while developing your code will save you time in the long run. However, when we only had a week for the app building any meaningful set of tests would have made this book much longer. It would have also made this book a bit tedious to read...

I decided to avoid this subject as there are great sources for TDD in Spring and I don't want to go too deep into that.

GUI Builder 13.3.2

I chose to hand code the application. Using the GUI builder to build the UI of the application might be a superior approach for some developers. The new GUI builder is a very powerful tool that leverages a sophisticated layout philosophy and makes things such as the login screen trivial.

It also includes sophisticated styling capabilities baked into the tool which would make a lot of the low level UIID and getAllStyles code redundant.

So why didn't I use the GUI builder?

It's hard to teach visual tools in book form. It would have made this book into a picture book. By understanding the underlying code, moving to the GUI builder would be easier. The inverse of picking up handcoding after learning the GUI builder UI is **much** harder.

I plan to cover the GUI builder more in depth in the online course at the Codename One Academy here: codenameone.teachable.com/

13.3.3
CSS

I dedicated an appendix to CSS based theming. I think it's a very interesting approach to theming Codename One applications. I was conflicted about using CSS or the designer tool and eventually chose the latter.

In retrospect I regretted that decision to some degree as CSS is easier to document, I could have just written the CSS code in the book. In the followup online course covering the Facebook Clone I used CSS. If this makes it to book form as well it will be covered there.

13.3.4
WebSockets Everywhere

I talked about using WebSockets for everything in Day 2. I think it's a direction worth exploring for a real world application. This would allow developers to lower the communication overhead and make it far more efficient.

13.3.5
Kotlin

I'm considering a version of this book in Kotlin. Spring Boot already supports Kotlin and produces base code that works with it. Codename One supports it too.

Having worked with Kotlin I see a lot to like especially with the fact that we can easily mix it with Java.

13.4
Summary

Thanks for reading this far, I hope you enjoyed this book!

If you did or didn't please let me know. You can reach out to me on stackoverflow and the Codename One forum.

You can also write an email, but I process hundreds of emails per day, so please accept my apology if I somehow miss your email shai@codenameone.com

Appendix A: Setup Codename One

This section is divided into the three separate IDE's supported by Codename One: IntelliJ/IDEA, NetBeans and Eclipse.

Before you begin make sure to install JDK 8. We recommend the version from Oracle. If you install OpenJDK make sure to install JavaFX support as well.

> **As of this writing JDK 9 isn't supported yet!**
> Support for newer JDK's is planned for Codename One 5.0 so this might change by the time you read this. Check out www.codenameone.com/download.html for the current status

Since the IDE runs on top of a JDK instance we recommend running the IDE itself on JDK 8 to avoid problems.

> The screenshots are from Mac OS but the process should work exactly the same on Windows and Linux

A.1. IntelliJ/IDEA

Codename One recommends IntelliJ/IDEA 2016 or newer.

> Codename One **doesn't support** Android Studio! You can use IntelliJ/IDEA community edition instead

1 Launch IntelliJ, Click Configure and Select "Plugins"

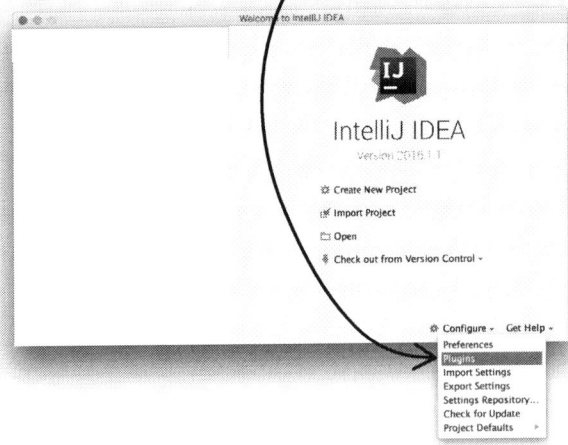

2 Click "Browse repositories..."

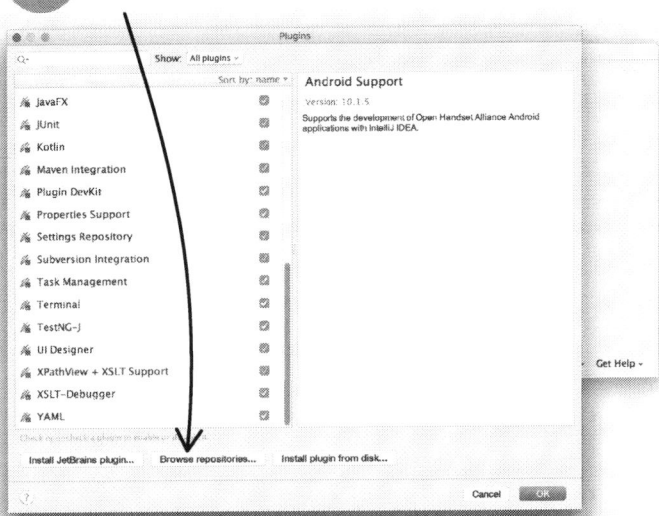

3 Type in "Codename" in the search field select the result and click "Install"

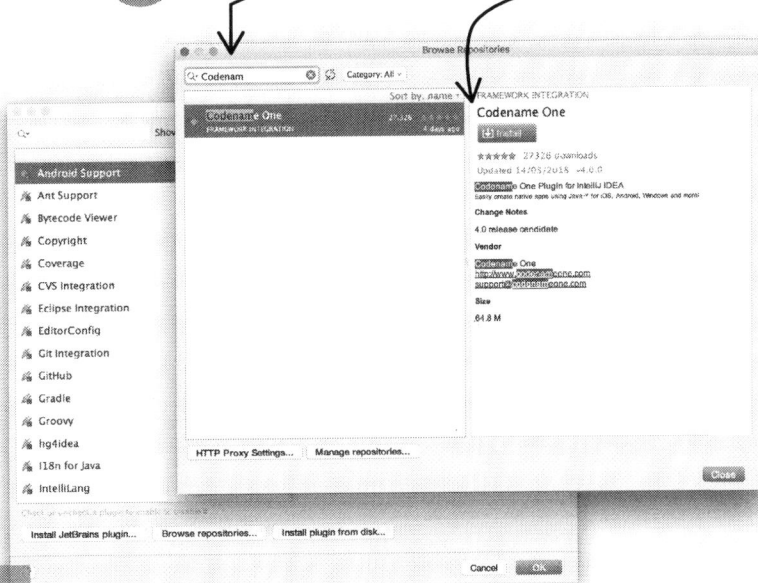

Figure 14. 1. IntelliJ Installation Instructions

A.2

NetBeans

NetBeans install is pretty simple although the default "plugin center" for NetBeans is notoriously unreliable. That's why we recommend using the Codename One plugin center:

www.codenameone.com/files/netbeans/updates.xml

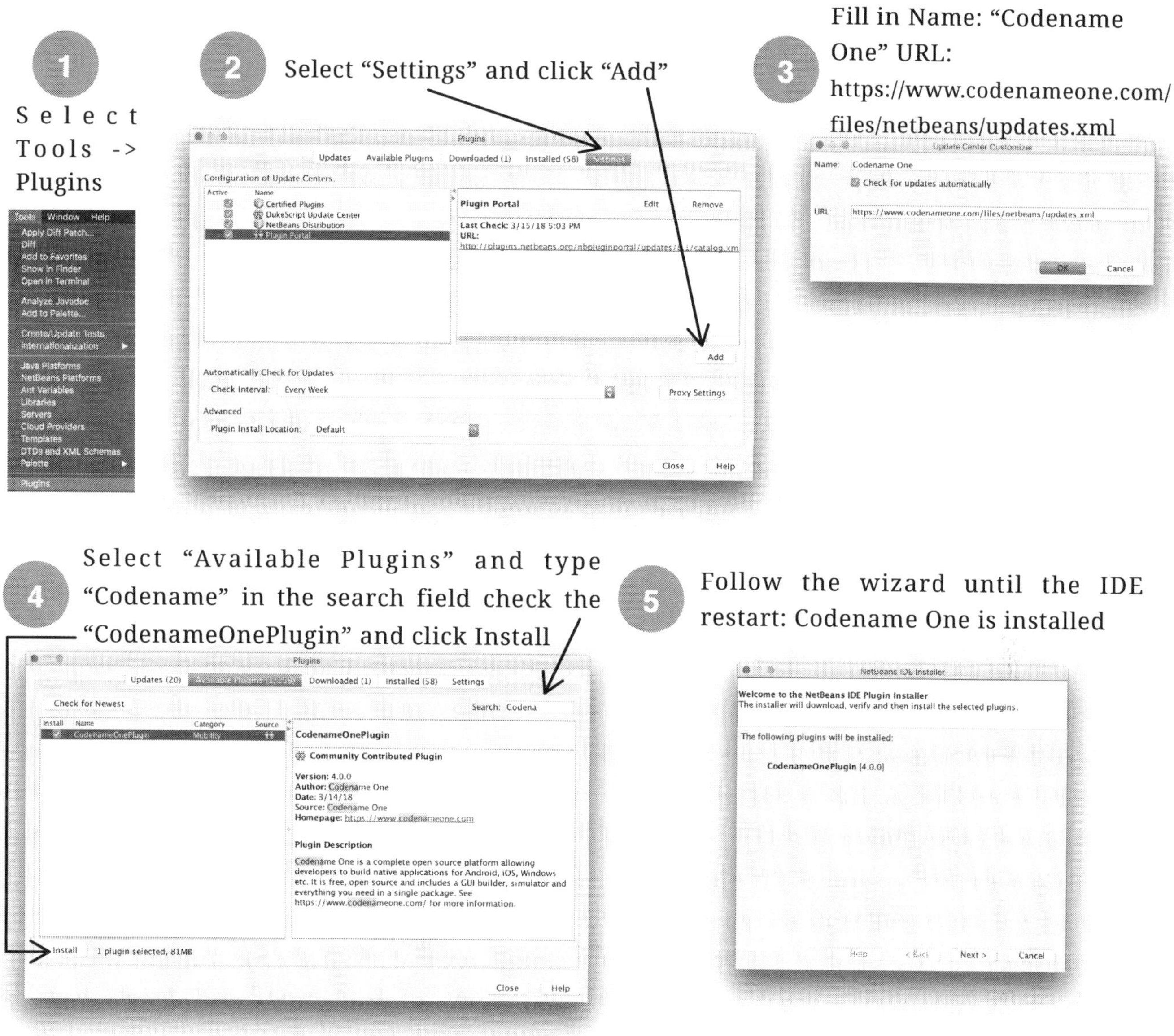

Figure 14. 2. NetBeans Installation Instructions

Make sure you are using a NetBeans version that includes Java support, don't download a version for Ruby/PHP or J2ME and make sure the IDE runs on top of JDK 8

Eclipse

Codename One supports Eclipse Neon 2 or newer. There are a few pitfalls that can happen with an Eclipse install specifically when other JVM versions are installed on your machine.

⚠ If you are new to Java, Eclipse might be intimidating. It's a very powerful IDE but its configuration is rough

Make sure your JAVA_HOME environment variable points at JDK 8 and that the path to the JDK 8 bin directory is first in the PATH statement. If all else fails edit the eclipse.ini file to force Eclipse to use your JDK 8 install. See this site for help with editing the eclipse.ini file: wiki.eclipse.org/Eclipse.ini

1 Click "Help" -> "Eclipse Marketplace..."

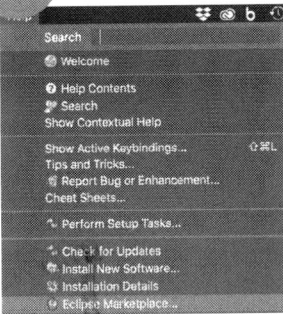

2 Type "Codename" into the find field then click "Install"

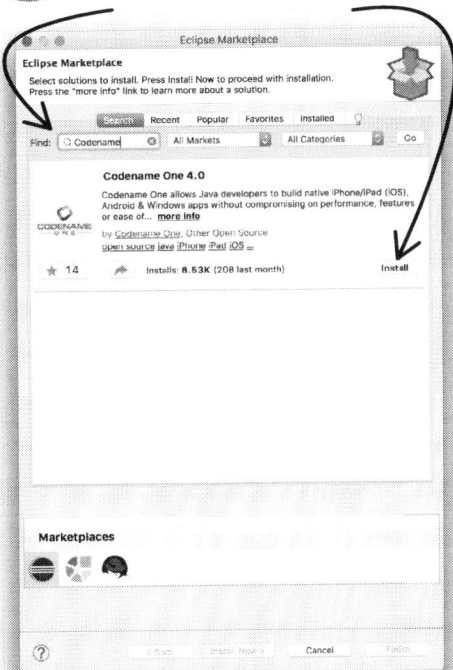

3 Accept the license agreement and follow through the install process

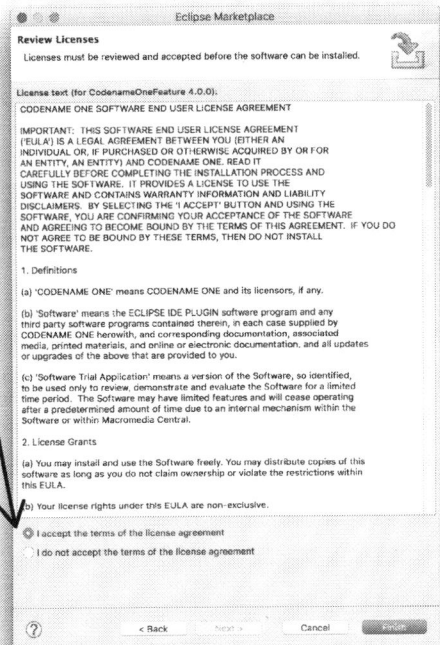

Figure 14. 3. Eclipse Installation Instructions

❗ In order to run the app in Eclipse make sure to select the .launch file in Eclipse

Appendix B: Setup Spring Boot and MySQL

B

This chapter covers:

- How to setup MySQL/MariaDB and map it to Spring Boot

- How to setup a Spring Boot with the Maven build process

We use Spring Boot for the server and use Maven to build it. When I developed the code for the book 1.5.7 was the latest stable version of Spring Boot so I stuck to that. However, the followup Facebook clone application worked with 2.0 without a problem and only required minor adjustments so this should be reasonably easy to migrate if you choose to do so.

All 3 major Java IDE's have Maven plugins or builtin support, so working with Maven should be simple.

MySQL Setup

B.1

We begin by installing MySQL or MariaDB on the development machine. I use MySQL during development since it has an easy to use Mac OS installer. However, in production of apps on Linux I tend to prefer MariaDB which is compatible with MySQL. Both should be practically interchangeable as MariaDB is a fork of MySQL.

Installation of both databases is trivial, Oracle provides a free community edition of MySQL here: dev.mysql.com/downloads/mysql/

You can download MariaDB from: downloads.mariadb.org/

Both sites include detailed setup instructions that you should follow.

Once installed you can launch the MySQL command prompt:

Listing 15. 1. Launch MySQL Unix/Linux

```
/usr/local/mysql/bin/mysql -h localhost -u root -p
```

The syntax is identical on Windows except for the path to the MySQL executable.

You need to provide the password given to you during the install process when the app prompts you. At this point you should have a MySQL prompt.

> **A Simpler Way**
>
> You can use a visual tool such as NetBeans or Toad to connect to the MySQL database and manage it

In the prompt create the new Uber database:

Listing 15. 2. Create Database

```
CREATE DATABASE uberapp;
```

It's possible the database will make you set the password the first time around. You can do it with this code:

Listing 15. 3. Set new Password

```
Password=PASSWORD('your_new_password') WHERE User='root';
```

B.2

Setup Spring Boot Project

One of the best ways to start with Spring Boot is through one of the IDE plugins that offer instant setup wizards. At the time of this writing I found these IDE plugins but check your IDE for updated developments:

- NetBeans - plugins.netbeans.org/plugin/67888/nb-springboot
- IntelliJ - www.jetbrains.com/help/idea/2016.3/creating-spring-boot-projects.html
- Eclipse - spring.io/tools/sts/all

You can use the Spring Boot Initializer to generate a project with the following options:

- Cloud Security

- Web Services

- Websocket

- JPA

- MySQL

- Jersey

Alternatively you can just use this maven project which does the same thing and automatically fetches the dependencies:

Listing 15. 4. Maven Spring Boot pom.xml build file

```xml
<?xml version="1.0" encoding="UTF-8"?>
<project xmlns="http://maven.apache.org/POM/4.0.0"
   xmlns:xsi="http://www.w3.org/2001/XMLSchema-instance"
   xsi:schemaLocation="http://maven.apache.org/POM/4.0.0
              http://maven.apache.org/xsd/maven-4.0.0.xsd">
   <modelVersion>4.0.0</modelVersion>
   <groupId>com.codename1.uberclone</groupId>
   <artifactId>UberClone</artifactId>
   <version>0.0.1-SNAPSHOT</version>
   <packaging>jar</packaging>
   <name>UberClone</name>
   <description>Uber style application</description>
   <parent>
      <groupId>org.springframework.boot</groupId>
      <artifactId>spring-boot-starter-parent</artifactId>
      <version>1.5.7.RELEASE</version>
      <relativePath/>
      <!-- lookup parent from repository -->
   </parent>
   <properties>
      <project.build.sourceEncoding>UTF-8</project.build.sourceEncoding>
      <project.reporting.outputEncoding>UTF-8
      </project.reporting.outputEncoding>
      <java.version>1.8</java.version>
   </properties>
   <dependencies>
```

This is standard Maven boilerplate project header with no real data

The following couple of lines include descriptive strings about the app. Since this is internal to the server they don't really matter

B

```xml
    <dependency>
      <groupId>org.springframework.boot</groupId>
      <artifactId>spring-boot-starter-data-jpa</artifactId>
    </dependency>
    <dependency>
      <groupId>org.springframework.boot</groupId>
      <artifactId>spring-boot-starter-jersey</artifactId>
    </dependency>
    <dependency>
      <groupId>org.springframework.boot</groupId>
      <artifactId>spring-boot-starter-web</artifactId>
    </dependency>
    <dependency>
      <groupId>org.springframework.boot</groupId>
      <artifactId>spring-boot-starter-websocket</artifactId>
    </dependency>
    <dependency>
      <groupId>org.springframework.boot</groupId>
      <artifactId>spring-boot-starter-security</artifactId>
    </dependency>
    <dependency>
      <groupId>mysql</groupId>
      <artifactId>mysql-connector-java</artifactId>
      <scope>runtime</scope>
    </dependency>
    <dependency>
      <groupId>org.springframework.boot</groupId>
      <artifactId>spring-boot-starter-test</artifactId>
      <scope>test</scope>
    </dependency>
    <dependency>
      <groupId>com.braintreepayments.gateway</groupId>
      <artifactId>braintree-java</artifactId>
      <version>2.71.0</version>
    </dependency>
  </dependencies>
  <build>
    <plugins>
      <plugin>
        <groupId>org.springframework.boot</groupId>
```

These are the modules we need for this book

B

```
          <artifactId>spring-boot-maven-plugin</artifactId>
          <configuration>
            <fork>true</fork>
            <executable>true</executable>
          </configuration>
        </plugin>
      </plugins>
    </build>
</project>
```

This packages Spring Boot as an executable JAR we can run on the server very easily

The basic main class for a Spring Boot application is trivial. If you used the Spring Boot initializer then the main class is created for you. If not you can use this code:

Listing 15. 5. Main Source file for Spring Boot app

```java
@SpringBootApplication
public class UberCloneApplication {
    public static void main(String[] args) {
        SpringApplication.run(UberCloneApplication.class, args);
    }
}
```

You will notice there isn't much here. Everything else is automatically wired

We do need to configure the properties file for Spring specifically:

B

Listing 15. 6. application.properties file

```
spring.datasource.url=jdbc:mysql://localhost/uberapp
spring.datasource.username=root
spring.datasource.password=DatabasePassword
```

This is the URL for the database. Here it's hosted on the same machine but you can point at a different machine. You can provide a different database name as well

```
spring.jpa.hibernate.ddl-auto=update
spring.jpa.generate-ddl=true
```

These 2 lines indicate that we want the database created and updated automatically based on our Java JPA objects

```
spring.jpa.database-platform=org.hibernate.dialect.MySQL5InnoDBDialect
spring.datasource.driver-class-name=com.mysql.jdbc.Driver
```

This driver and following syntax declaration work for MariaDB too

```
spring.http.multipart.max-file-size=800KB
spring.http.multipart.max-request-size=2048KB
```

We define the maximum file size for file upload to the server. Limits are important to prevent an attacker from uploading huge files and crashing our servers

Once we do this we should have Spring Boot and it should map seamlessly to our locally installed SQL databases.

B

Appendix C: Styling Codename One with CSS

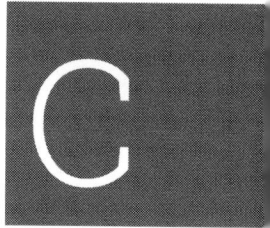

C

To enable CSS support in Codename One you need to flip a switch in Codename One Settings.

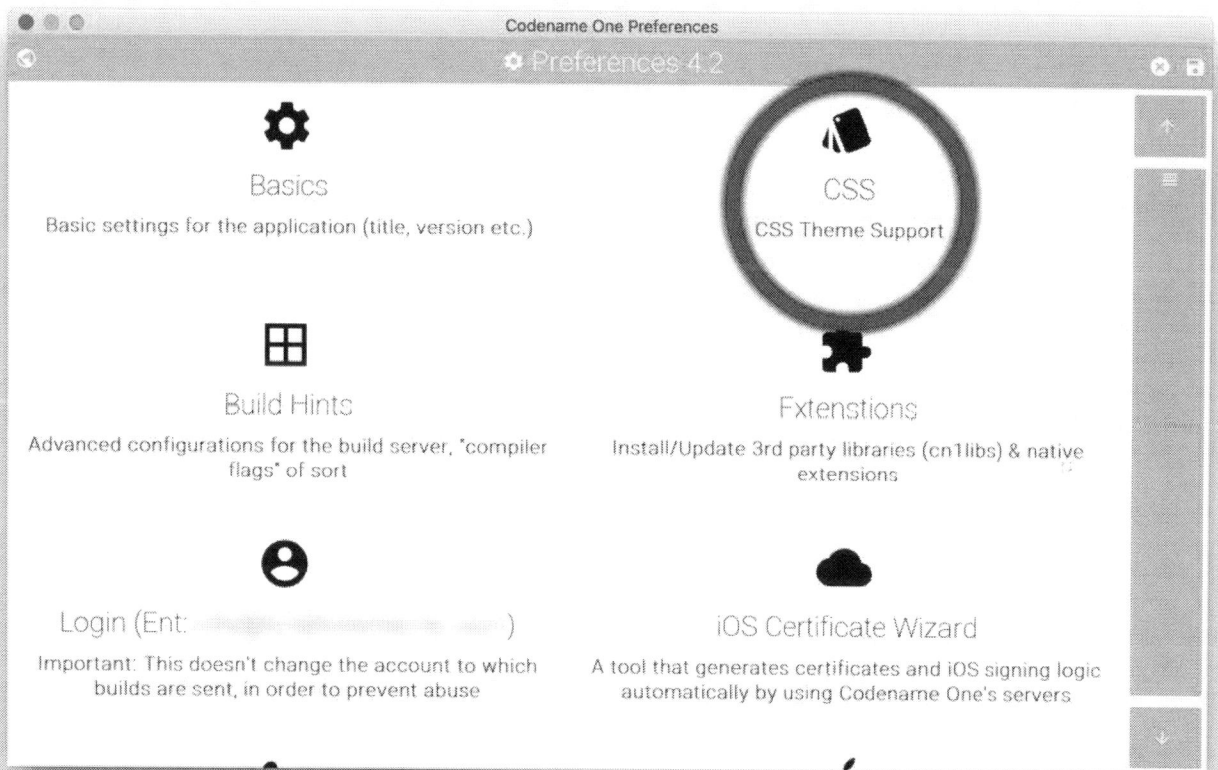

Figure 16. 1. The CSS Option in Codename One Settings Part I

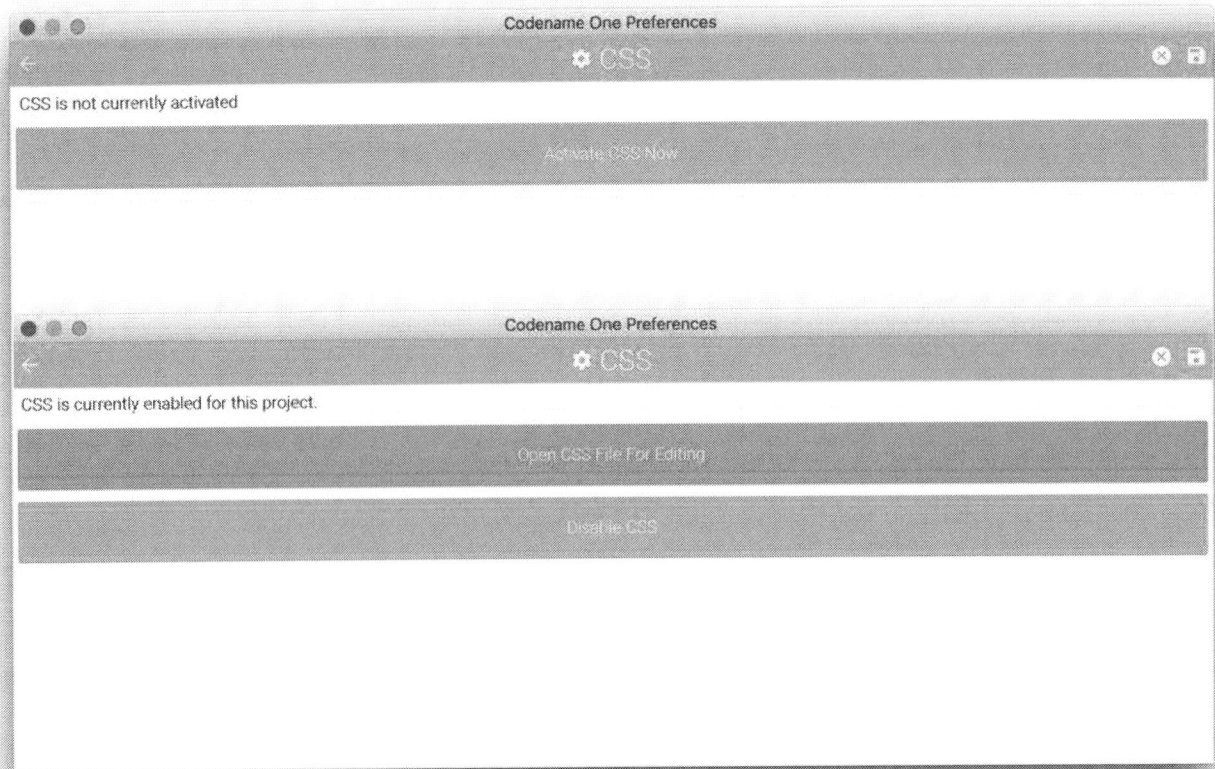

Figure 16. 2. The CSS Option in Codename One Settings Part II

Once enabled your theme.res file will regenerate from a CSS file that resides under the css directory. Changes you make to the CSS file will instantly update the simulator as you save. However, there are some limits to this live update so in some cases a simulator restart would be necessary.

ⓘ This appendix assumes you are familiar with CSS and typical CSS terms such as selectors

C.1

Getting Started with CSS

We can now add css files into the css directory. If we add the file css/theme.css when we compile the project, it will generate the src/theme.res file. So changes you make to the resource file in the designer tool will get overwritten!

A most basic hello CSS file would look like this:

Listing 16. 1. Hello CSS

```
#Constants {          ← Theme constants can be defined
   includeNativeBool: true;   in this special selector
}                     ← This is a crucial constant. Otherwise
                         the native theme won't load
Label {               ← The selector matches the UIID so this is
   color: blue;          the same as defining the Label UIID
}
```

Standard CSS attributes should work as expected, color matches foreground and the typical constants work (e.g. blue)

Selectors

All CSS selectors are effectively UIID's. There is no support for most of the complex selectors e.g. you can't do something like this:

Listing 16. 2. Nesting Doesn't Work

```
ContentPane Button {
   /* ... */
}
```

Since CSS is statically compiled it can't support features that don't exist in Codename One and complex selectors aren't supported.

You can however override a specific state of the selector using the suffixes: .pressed, .selected, .unselected or .disabled.

Listing 16. 3. Set the Button Pressed Styling

C

```
Button.pressed {
   /* ... */
}
```

You can also select multiple targets at once:

Listing 16. 4. Applying Styling to Multiple Types

```
Button.selected, TextField, MyComponent {
    /* ... */
}
```

There are a few extra features I didn't mention which you can read about here: github.com/shannah/cn1-css/wiki/Supported-CSS-Selectors

C.1.2

Properties

The following table lists the main supported properties and notes related to them. For a full list and more details check out github.com/shannah/cn1-css/wiki/Supported-Properties

Table 16. 3. Main Supported Properties

Property	Notes
padding	
margin	
border	Supports the border property and most of its variants (e.g. border-width, border-style, and border-color. It will try to use native CN1 styles for generating borders if possible. If the border definition is too complex, it will fall-back to generating a 9-piece image border at compile-time.
border-radius	
background	
background-color	
background-repeat	
background-image	
font	For more about fonts check out github.com/shannah/cn1-css/wiki/Fonts
font-family	font-family: "native:MainLight";

Property	Notes
font-style	
font-size	font-size: 3mm;
color	Foreground color
text-align	
text-decoration	One of: underline , overline , line-through , none cn1-3d cn1-3d-lowered cn1-3d-shadow-north
opacity	

Most of the entries include their respective variants e.g. both margin-top: and margin: 1px 1px 1px 1px; would work.

Images

To add images to the resource file you can place them in the css folder commonly under the images folder within.

Listing 16. 5. Simple Image Usage in CSS

```
SomeStyle {
    background-image: url(images/my-image.png);
    cn1-source-dpi: 480;    ←————————————————  This special property defines
}                                               the source DPI of the image
```

This effectively creates a Multi Image in the resource file and automatically scales the image to all the various resolutions. 480 is effectively an HD DPI image.

We can also generate 9-patch borders using images e.g.:

Listing 16. 6. Cutting a 9-patch Border in CSS

```
MyStyle {
    background-image: url(myimage.png);          The distance for
    cn1-9patch: 5px 8px 4px 10px;    ←————————  cutting from the edge
}
```

Summary

I just barely scratched the surface of the CSS functionality in Codename One. We plan to include thorough coverage of CSS in the Codename One Developer guide version 5.0.

Appendix D: Installing cn1libs D

Installing a cn1lib is a relatively easy, as illustrated here:

1 Right click the project and select "Codename One" -> "Codename One Settings"

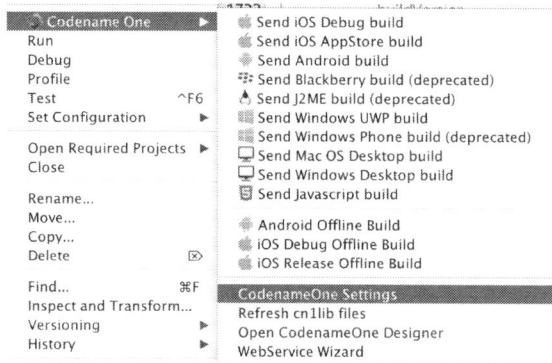

2 Click "Extensions"

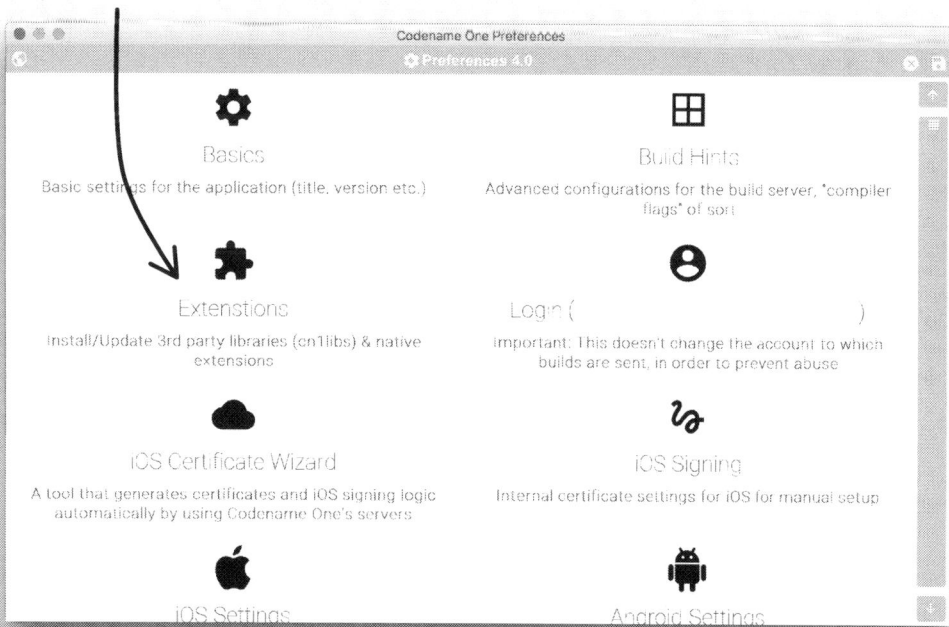

Figure D. 1. Overview of the cn1lib Install Process 1 & 2

Type the name of the extension you are looking for in the search field and click the Download Button

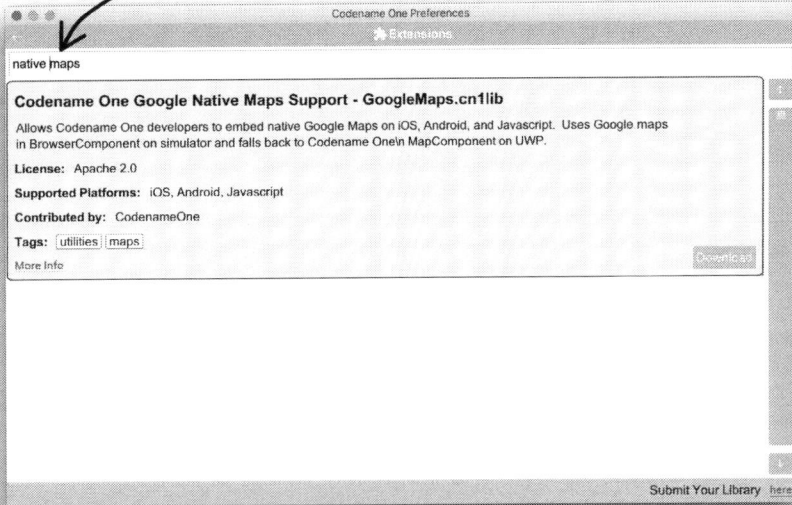

Close Settings. Right-click the project and select "Codename One" -> "Refresh cn1lib files"

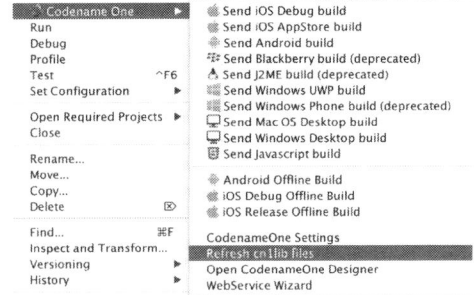

Figure D. 2. Overview of the cn1lib Install Process 3 & 4

You might be done already. If your cn1lib needs custom build hints (e.g. Google Maps) relaunch Codename One Settings and click "Build Hints"

You can edit the values in the build hints. Specifically, the google maps requires adding entries like android.xapplication which you can add by pressing the "Add Hint" button below

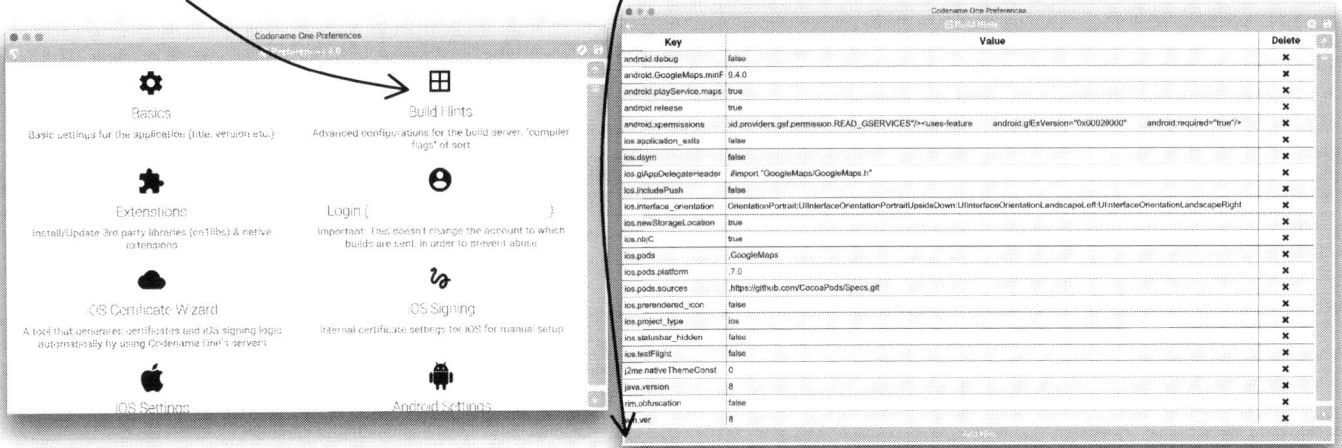

Figure D. 3. Overview of the cn1lib Install Process 5 & 6

Installing a cn1lib is usually seamless:

D

- Launch Codename One Settings
- Click Extensions
- Select the extension which is downloaded for you (you can type in the search box)
- Select Refresh Cn1Libs in the right click menu

There are a few cn1libs that require additional configuration and the native Google Maps is one of those cn1libs as it requires several build hints that can't be picked in runtime. Specifically the build hints are:

```
javascript.googlemaps.key=YOUR_JAVASCRIPT_API_KEY android.xapplication=<meta-data
    android:name="com.google.android.maps.v2.API_KEY"
    android:value="YOUR_ANDROID_API_KEY"/> ios.afterFinishLaunching=[GMSServices
    provideAPIKey:@"YOUR_IOS_API_KEY"];
```

The reason these are needed is due to the key values that must be present during build time. The key values are values you need to retrieve from the Google Cloud Console as explained here: github.com/codenameone/codenameone-google-maps/

D

D

Appendix E: Push Notification

A huge part of the driver app is the push notification process, that's how we notify a driver that there is a ride pending. But what is push and why should we use it in this case?

Push notification allows us to send a notification to a device while the application might be in the background. This is important both as a marketing tool and as a basic communications device. In this case the driver might be in a different app but we still want him to notice that we are looking for a ride...

Why Push and Not Polling/WebSocket?

Polling the server (periodically asking the server for an update) seem like sensible time proven strategy. However, there are many complexities related to that approach in mobile phones.

The biggest problem is that a polling application will be killed by the OS as it is sent to the background to conserve OS resources. While this might work in some OS's and some cases this isn't something you can rely on. E.g. Android 6+ tightened the background process behavior significantly.

The other issue is battery life, new OS's expose battery wasting applications and as a result might trigger uninstalls. This makes even foreground polling less appealing.

What Is Push?   E.1

If you are new to mobile development then you might have heard a lot of buzzwords and very little substance. The problem is that iOS and Android have very different ideas of what push is and should be. For Android, push is a communication system that the server can initiate. E.g. the cloud can send any packet of data, and the device can process it in rather elaborate ways.

For iOS push is mostly a visual notification triggered by the server to draw attention to new information inside an app. These don't sound very different until you realize that in Android you can receive/process a push without the awareness of the end user. In iOS a push notification is displayed to the user, but the app might be unaware of it!

> **Background Push in iOS is Different**
>
> iOS will only deliver the push notification to the app, if it is running or if the user clicked the push notification popup!

Codename One tried to make both OS's "feel" similar so background push calls act the same in iOS and Android as a result.

> **Push isn't 100% Reliable**
>
> You shouldn't push important data. Push is lossy and shouldn't include a payload that **MUST** arrive!
>
> Instead, use push as a flag to indicate that the server has additional data for the app to fetch

For this case we use push to let the drivers know, but pass the actual important information within the socket connection.

E.2

Various Types of Push Messages

In the driver app we send a push type 3 message which might have been a bit unclear. Before we proceed I think it's a good time to discuss the various types of push messages.

- 0, 1 – The default push types. They work everywhere and present the string as the push alert to the user

- 2 – hidden, non-visual push. This won't show any visual indicator on any OS!
  In Android this will trigger the push(String) call with the message body. In iOS this will only happen if the application is in the foreground otherwise the push will be lost

- 3 – allows combining a visual push with a non-visual portion. Expects a message in the form: This is what the user won't see;This is something he will see. E.g. you can bundle a special ID or even a JSON string in the hidden part while including a friendly message in the visual part. When active this will trigger the push(String) method twice, once with the visual and once with the hidden data.

- 4 – Allows splitting a visual push request based on the format title;body to provide better visual representation in some OS's.

- 5 – Sends a regular push message but doesn't play a sound when the push arrives

- 100 – Applicable only to iOS. Allows setting the numeric badge on the icon to the given number. The body of the message must be a number e.g. unread count.

- 101 – identical to 100 with an added message payload separated with a space. E.g. 30 You have 30 unread messages will set the badge to "30" and present the push notification text of "You have 30 unread messages".

Push Details   E.3

When sending a push message we need some details in order to send a push message to the right device. These details provide us with the authorization required for push. Otherwise, anyone could send a push notification to any device...

Google and Apple have very different approaches to push. In the following sections I describe how to get the values you need from them. In the Uber Clone app we set these values in the Globals class constants.

Google   E.3.1

Android Push goes thru Google servers, and to do that, we need to register with Google to get keys for server usage.

We need one important value: GOOGLE_PUSH_AUTH_KEY (for the Globals class). To generate this value follow these steps:

- Login to console.cloud.google.com/

- Select APIs & Services

- Select Library

- Select Developer Tools

- Select Google Cloud Messaging

- Click Enable and follow the instructions

- The value we need is the API key, which you can see under the credentials entry

Apple   E.3.2

You will need to re-run the certificate wizard for the driver project. If you generated certificates before say no to the step that asks you to revoke them and copy your existing credentials (certificate P12 file and password) to the new project. Make sure to check the Include Push flag in the wizard so the generated provisioning includes push data.

Once this is done you should receive an email that includes the certificate details. This will include URL's for the push certificates we generated for you and the passwords for those certificates.

Apple has two push servers:

- Sandbox - use this during development
- Production - this will only work for shipping apps

You need to toggle the APNS_PRODUCTION flag (in the Globals class) when building a release version of the app.

E.4. Push Registration and Interception

Once this is out of the way we can start handling the push messages. To do that we need to implement the PushCallback interface in the main class of our app.

> **This MUST be in the Main Class**
> The PushCallback interface must be defined in the main class. Otherwise it won't work correctly

A simple push listener works similarly to this code. Notice I trimmed the boilerplate so the push code stands out:

Listing 18. 1. DriverApp with Push

```java
public class MyApp implements PushCallback {
   public void init(Object context) {
      // trimmed init code
   }
   public void start() {
      // trimmed start code
      callSerially(() -> {
         registerPush();
      });
   }
   public void stop() {
      // trimmed stop code
   }
   public void destroy() {
      // trimmed destroy code
   }
   public void push(String value) {
      Log.p("Received push callback: " + value);
   }
   public void registeredForPush(String deviceId) {
      Log.p("Registered for push device key: " +
         Push.getPushKey());
   }


   public void pushRegistrationError(String error,
         int errorCode) {
      Log.p("Error registering for push: " + error);
   }
}
```

We need to implement the PushCallback interface in the main class

registerPush should be invoked every time. Notice I use callSerially to defer the permission prompt so it appears after the Form is shown

The push callback is invoked when push is received from the server

When registration succeeds this method is invoked. Notice the deviceId isn't the push key! It's the native OS key, it's here for compatibility only

The push key is what we use to identify this device and send push messages to it. This method usually sends that key to the server so we can receive push messages here

If there was an error in registration this method is invoked

E

E

Appendix F: How Does Codename One Work?

Codename One uses a SaaS based approach so the information in this appendix might (and probably will) change in the future to accommodate improved architectures. I included this information for reference only, you don't need to understand this in order to follow the content of the book...

Since Android is already based on Java, Codename One is already native to Android and "just works" with the Android VM (ART/Dalvik).

On iOS, Codename One built and open sourced ParparVM, which is a very conservative VM. ParparVM features a concurrent (non-blocking) GC and it's written entirely in Java/C. ParparVM generates C source code matching the given Java bytecode. This effectively means that an xcode project is generated and compiled on the build servers. It's as if you handcoded a native app and is thus "future proof" for changes that Apple might introduce. E.g. Apple migrated to 64bit and later introduced bitcode support to iOS. ParparVM needed no modifications to comply with those changes.

> ℹ️ Codename One translates the bytecode to C which is faster than Swift/Objective-C. The port code that invokes iOS API's is hand coded in Objective-C

For Windows 10 desktop and Mobile support, Codename One uses iKVM to target UWP (Universal Windows Platform) and has open sourced the changes to the original iKVM code.

JavaScript build targets use TeaVM to do the translation statically. TeaVM provides support for threading using JavaScript by breaking the app down in a rather elaborate way. To support the complex UI Codename One uses the HTML5 Canvas API which allows absolute flexibility for building applications.

For desktop builds Codename One uses javafxpackager, since both Macs and Windows machines are available in the cloud the platform specific nature of javafxpackager is not a problem.

Lightweight Architecture

What makes Codename One stand out is the approach it takes to UI: "lightweight architecture".

Lightweight architecture is the "not so secret sauce" to Codename One's portability. Essentially it means all the components/widgets in Codename One are written in Java. Thus their behavior is consistent across all platforms and they are fully customizable from the developer code as they don't rely on OS internal semantics. This allows developers to preview the application accurately in the simulators and GUI builders.

One of the big accomplishments in Codename One is its unique ability to embed "heavyweight" widgets into place among the "lightweights". This is crucial for apps such as Uber where the cars and widgets on top are implemented as Codename One components yet below them we have the native map component.

Codename One achieves fast performance by drawing using the native gaming API's of most platforms e.g. OpenGL ES on iOS. The core technologies behind Codename One are all open source including most of the stuff developed by Codename One itself, e.g. ParparVM but also the full library, platform ports, designer tool, device skins etc.

Index I

36899449R00241

Printed in Great Britain
by Amazon